T0398130

THE KINGFISHER
ILLUSTRATED POCKET
DICTIONARY

THE KINGFISHER
ILLUSTRATED POCKET
DICTIONARY

KINGFISHER

BOSTON

KINGFISHER

a Houghton Mifflin Company imprint
222 Berkeley Street
Boston, Massachusetts 02116
www.houghtonmifflinbooks.com

This revised edition published in 2007
2 4 6 8 10 9 7 5 3
2TR/0907/PROSP/PICA(PICA)/115MA/C

First published by Chambers in hardback in 1996
First published in paperback by Kingfisher Publications Plc in 1997

Text updates by Susan Harvey
Editor: Marcus Hardy
Coordinating editor: Caitlin Doyle
Designer: Tony Cutting
Production controller: Teresa Wood
Artwork research: Cee Weston-Baker
DTP operator: Claire Cessford
Proofreader: Kate Lawn

LIBRARY OF CONGRESS CATALOGING-IN-PUBLICATION DATA
has been applied for.

ISBN 978-0-7534-6116-7

Printed in China

MAKING THE MOST OF YOUR DICTIONARY

Definitions explain what a word means.

Example sentences show how to use a word.

Alternative forms of a word. Look at the next page for more information on these.

Words with the **same spelling** have small numbers after them.

Usage labels show if a word is old-fashioned, literary, or informal, for example.

winch *n.* a machine for lifting things, worked by winding a rope around a revolving cylinder. **winch** *v.*

wind¹ *(rhymes with* kind) *v.* (winding, wound) **1** to wrap something around and around another thing. **2** to turn a key or handle around to make something work. *Wind up the clock.* **3** to twist and turn. *The river winds through a valley.* **wind down** *(informal)* to dimish slowly.

wind² *(rhymes with* grinned) *n.* moving air. **windy** *adj.*

Different meanings of a word are numbered.

Pronunciation guides for difficult words. The syllable that is stressed is shown in bold print: (*fluh-rish*), for example.

Related words and **phrases** are listed at the end of the entry.

Part of speech labels show how words act in a sentence. To find out more about each part of speech, look it up in the main part of the dictionary.

adj.	adjective
adv.	adverb
conj.	conjunction
n.	noun
prep.	preposition
pron.	pronoun
v.	verb

flow *v.* to move along smoothly, as water does in a river. **flow** *n.*
flower¹ *n.* the colored part of a plant that produces seeds.
flower² *v.* to produce flowers.
flown *past participle of* fly.
flu *n.* (*short for* influenza) an illness that

o
p
q
r
s
t
u
v
w
x
y
z

flower

stigma (receives pollen grains)
anther (stores pollen)
style
petal
ovule
stamen (male part)
stem
sepal (protects flower bud)
ovary (female part)

gives you a high temperature, headache, and aching muscles.
fluctuate *v.* to change all the time. *Her mood fluctuates between delight and despair.* **fluctuation** *n.*

Pictures help you understand the meanings of words, and there are often **labels** that give you extra vocabulary.

HELP WITH SPELLING

The dictionary lists words in their main form, but you will often want to know how the spelling of a word changes to make it plural or past tense, for example. The information below will help you get more from your dictionary and figure out how to spell these alternative forms.

Adjectives

Using adjectives for comparing:
*Amy got a **small** present, Billy's was **smaller**, and Hassan's was the **smallest**.*

With most adjectives of one syllable you add **-er** and **-est** to make these comparing forms. If the adjective ends in **-e**, you just add **-r** and **-st**:

small......small**er**......small**est**
rare......rar**er**......rar**est**

With most adjectives of two or more syllables, you use **more** and **most**:

more beautiful
the **most** beautiful

However, some adjectives act differently, and these spellings are shown in the dictionary.

big *adj.* (bigger, biggest)
bad *adj.* (worse, worst

Nouns

You form the plural of most nouns by adding an **-s** to the singular:

rag......rag**s**
house......house**s**

If the singular form of the noun ends in **-s**, **-ss**, **-x**, **-sh**, or **-tch**, add **-es**:

bus......bus**es**
boss......boss**es**
fox......fox**es**
watch......watch**es**

For many nouns that end in **-y**, lose the **-y** and add **-ies** to make the plural:

fairy......fair**ies**

Plurals that do not follow these rules are shown in the dictionary.

potato *n.* (*pl.* potatoes)
child *n.* (*pl.* children

Adverbs

You form most adverbs by adding **-ly** to the adjective:

quick......quick**ly**
Exceptions are shown in the dictionary.

Verbs

You can add **-ing** and **-ed** to many verbs without changing the spelling of the first part of the verb:

clean......clean**ing**......clean**ed**

If a verb ends in **-e**, you take off the **-e** before adding **-ing** and **-ed**:

stare...star**ing**...star**ed**

Verb forms that do not follow these rules are given in the dictionary.

stop *v.* (stops, stopping, stopped)
cry *v.* (cries, crying, cried)

Some common verbs change their spelling when you use them in different ways. These alternative forms are shown in the dictionary.

wear *v.* (wearing, wore, worn)
*Ben is **wearing** his blue shirt today.*
*Ben **wore** his blue shirt yesterday.*
*Ben has **worn** his blue shirt all week.*

aardvark *n.* an African mammal with a long, sticky tongue that feeds on insects.

aardvark

abacus *n.* a frame with rows of sliding beads, used for counting.

abandon *v.* **1** to leave a thing, place, or person forever or for a long time. *She had to abandon her car in the snow.* **2** to stop doing something before it is finished. *We abandoned the game of football when it started to rain.*

abbey *n.* a group of buildings where monks or nuns live and work.

abbot *n.* the man in charge of the monks in an abbey.

abbreviation *n.* a short way of writing a word or group of words. *CD is an abbreviation of compact disk.*

abdicate *v.* to give up the position of king or queen. **abdication** *n.*

abdomen *n.* the part of the body that contains the stomach.

abduct *v.* to take somebody away using force. **abduction** *n.*

abhor *v.* (abhorring, abhorred) to hate something very much.

abhorrent *adj.* horrible; disgusting.

abide *v.* **cannot abide** cannot bear something. *I can't abide her!*

ability *n.* the power, skill, or knowledge to do something.

able *adj.* having the power, skill, or time to do something. *I will be able to come to your party.*

abnormal *adj.* strange; not normal. **abnormality** *n.,* **abnormally** *adv.*

aboard *adv., prep.* on or in a ship, an aircraft, or a train. *They went aboard the ship.*

abolish *v.* to put an end to something. *When was slavery abolished?* **abolition** *n.*

abominable *adj.* very bad or unpleasant.

Aborigines

Aborigine *(ab-o-rij-in-ee) n.* (*pl.* Aborigines) the first people to live in a country, especially the first Australians. **aboriginal** *adj.*

abort *v.* to stop a task or mission before it is completed because of a problem. *Scientists aborted the space mission and brought the rocket back to Earth.*

abortion *n.* the removal of a fetus from its mother's womb in order to end a pregnancy.

about *prep., adv.* **1** concerning. *a story about cats.* **2** nearly; approximately. *about two o'clock.* **about to** going to. *The school bell is about to ring.*

above *prep.* **1** higher than. **2** more or greater than. *temperatures above freezing.* **above** *adv.*

abrasive *adj.* **1** rough and able to wear something away by repeated rubbing or scratching. *Sandpaper is abrasive.* **2** rude and unpleasant. *Jack was abrasive.*

abreast *adv.* side by side. *We stood abreast*

abridged *adj.* shortened. *an abridged novel.*

abroad *adv.* in or to another country.

abrupt *adj.* **1** sudden and unexpected. **2** rude or sharp in the way you speak.

abscess *(ab-sess) n.* a painful swelling on the body containing pus.

A

absent *adj.* not there; away. *Sarah is absent from school today.* **absence** *n.*

absolute *adj.* complete. *What absolute garbage!* **absolutely** *adv.*

absorb *v.* to soak up liquid. *A sponge absorbs water.* **absorbent** *adj.*

abstain *v.* **1** to choose not to do something, especially when it is something that you would like to do. **2** to choose not to vote. **abstention** *n.*

abstract *adj.* based on ideas, not real things. *abstract paintings. Anger and happiness are abstract nouns.*

absurd *adj.* ridiculous or extremely silly. **absurdity** *n.*

abundant *adj.* available in large quantities. *an abundant supply of food.* **abundance** *n.*

abuse[1] *(ab-yooz) v.* **1** to say rude or unkind things to somebody. **2** to treat somebody in a cruel or violent way. **3** to use something incorrectly or badly. **abusive** *adj.*

abuse[2] *(ab-yooss) n.* **1** the incorrect or bad use of something. *the abuse of power.* **2** insults. **3** cruel treatment.

abysmal *(a-biz-mul) adj.* very bad.

abyss *(a-biss) n.* a very deep hole.

academic *adj.* having to do with study, education, or teaching.

academy *n.* a school or college.

accelerate *v.* to go faster; to speed up. **acceleration** *n.*

accelerator *n.* the pedal in a motor vehicle that you press with your foot to make the vehicle go faster.

accent *n.* **1** the way that somebody pronounces a language. *He speaks English with an Australian accent.* **2** a mark written over a letter that shows you how to pronounce it, as in *fiancé.*

accept *v.* **1** to take something that is offered. **2** to agree to something that is proposed. **acceptance** *n.*

acceptable *adj.* satisfactory.

access[1] *n.* a way to enter somewhere or reach something. *They gained access to the house through a window.*

access[2] *v.* to get information stored in a computer.

accessible *adj.* easy to reach or get.

accessory *n.* **1** an extra part that can be attached to something. *bike accessories.* **2.** something, such as a belt or a bag, that goes with your clothes.

accident *n.* an event that happens by chance, often one in which somebody gets hurt. **accidental** *adj.,* **accidentally** *adv.*

accommodate *v.* to provide a place for somebody to stay or live.

accommodation *n.* a place to stay, live, or work in.

accompany *v.* (accompanies, accompanying, accompanied) **1** to go with somebody. **2** to happen at the same time as something else. *The lightning was accompanied by a clap of thunder.* **3** to play a musical instrument along with another instrument or a voice. *Jane sang, and Lucy accompanied her on the guitar.* **accompaniment** *n.*

accomplice *n.* a person who helps another person commit a crime.

accomplish *v.* to complete something successfully. **accomplishment** *n.*

accomplished *adj.* skilled. *an accomplished musician.*

accord *n.* agreement. **of your own accord** because you want to; freely.

according to *prep.* as said or told by somebody. *According to Henry, you should do this.*

accordion *n.* a musical instrument like a box, played by pressing keys while squeezing the two sides together.

account *n.* **1** a description or report of an event. **2** an arrangement to keep your money in a bank. **3** a record of money that is owed, received, or paid.

accountant *n.* a person whose job is to look after monetary accounts.

accumulate *v.* to collect together; to pile up. **accumulation** *n.*

accurate *adj.* exact; correct. **accuracy** *n.*

accuse *v.* to say that someone has done something wrong; to blame somebody. **accusation** *n.*

accustomed *adj.* used to something. *She's not accustomed to waiting.*

ace *n.* **1** the "one" in playing cards. *the ace of clubs.* **2** a person who is extremely good at something. *an ace pilot.* **3** a successful unreturned serve in tennis.

ache *(rhymes with bake) n.* a dull, steady pain such as a stomachache or an earache. **ache** *v.*

achieve *v.* to do something successfully. **achievement** *n.*

acid[1] *n.* a chemical substance that can dissolve metal and that may burn your skin. **acidic** *adj.*

acid[2] *adj.* sharp or sour in taste.

acid rain *n.* rain that has been polluted by harmful chemicals absorbed from the surrounding air and that destroys plants.

acknowledge *v.* **1** to admit that something is true. **2** to say that you have received something. **acknowledgment** *n.*

acne *(ak-nee) n.* pimples on the face and body, common in teenagers.

acorn *n.* the nut of the oak tree.

acoustic guitar *n.* a guitar that does not need an amplifier.

acoustics *n. pl.* the qualities of a room that make it easy or difficult to hear sounds in it.

acquaintance *n.* a person who you don't know very well.

acquire *v.* to obtain something.

acquit *v.* (acquitting, acquitted) to state in

acorn

court that a person is not guilty. **acquittal** *n.*

acre *n.* an area of land, equal to around 43,560 sq. ft. (4,047 m²).

acrobat *n.* a person who can perform a variety of difficult balancing acts or somersaults. **acrobatics** *n. pl.*

acronym *n.* a word that is made up of the initial letters of other words such as NATO, which stands for North Atlantic Treaty Organization.

across *prep., adv.* from one side to the other.

act[1] *v.* **1** to do something. *The doctor acted quickly to save his life.* **2** to perform in a play or movie. **3** to behave in a certain way. *She's acting very strangely.*

act[2] *n.* **1** an action; something you do. *a kind act.* **2** a pretense. *She's not happy really—she's just putting on an act.* **3** a part of a play. **4** a law passed by the government.

action *n.* **1** something that you do. *a foolish action.* **2** fighting in a war.

active *adj.* busy; lively.

activity *n.* **1** liveliness. **2** something that you do as a sport or hobby.

actor *n.* a man or woman who acts in a play, a movie, or on television.

actress *n.* a female actor.

actual *adj.* real. **actually** *adv.*

acupuncture *(ak-yoo-punk-cher) n.* a way of treating illness or pain by sticking thin needles just beneath the skin of the patient's body.

acute *adj.* very severe or great. *an acute shortage of teachers.*

acute accent *n.* a mark (´) used over some letters to change their sound such as in the word *fiancé.*

acute angle *n.* an angle of less than 90°. See **triangle**.

ad *n.* (*informal, short for* advertisement) a notice in a newspaper, magazine, or on a poster or a short movie on television telling people about something that you want to sell.

A.D. *short for* Anno Domini (Latin for "in the year of our Lord"), used with dates to show the number of years after the birth of Jesus Christ.

adapt *v.* to change to suit a new situation. **adaptable** *adj.*, **adaptation** *n.*

adaptor *n.* a device for connecting two or more pieces of electrical equipment.

add *v.* to put things together to make more. **addition** *n.*, **additional** *adj.* extra.

adder *n.* a small, poisonous snake.

addict *n.* a person who is unable to stop doing or wanting something, especially harmful drugs.

adder

addicted *adj.* unable to stop doing or wanting something. *addicted to drugs.* **addiction** *n.*, **addictive** *adj.*

address¹ *n.* **1** the number of the house and name of the street and town where somebody lives. **2** a formal speech.

address² *v.* **1** to write the name and address of a person on an envelope. **2** *(formal)* to speak to. **3** to deal with a matter or problem.

adenoids *n. pl.* small lumps in the back of your nose that help prevent an infection.

adequate *adj.* just enough; sufficient.

adhesive¹ *n.* a substance used to stick things together; glue.

adhesive² *adj.* sticky.

adjacent *adj.* next to; by the side of.

adjective *n.* a word that describes something. In *a big blue car,* the words *big* and *blue* are adjectives.

adjourn *v.* to stop a meeting or trial until a later time. **adjournment** *n.*

adjust *v.* to change something slightly to make it work or fit better. **adjustment** *n.*

administration *n.* the process of controlling and managing something such as a country or a company.

admiral *n.* a very senior officer in the navy.

admire *v.* to like or respect somebody or something very much. *I admire her honesty.* **admirable** *adj.*, **admiration** *n.*

admission *n.* **1** acceptance or owning up that something is true. *an admission of guilt.* **2** the price of entering a place.

admit *v.* (admits, admitting, admitted) **1** to agree that something is true. *Jo admitted that she was wrong.* **2** to allow somebody to enter. *This ticket admits one person to the museum.* **admittedly** *adv.*

ado *n.* unnecessary fuss.

adolescence *n.* the time of life when you change from being a child to being an adult. **adolescent** *adj., n.*

adopt *v.* to take somebody else's child into your home and treat the child as your own. **adoption** *n.*

adore *v.* to feel great love for somebody or something. *She adored her grandmother.* **adoration** *n.*, **adorable** *adj.*

adorn *v.* to decorate something.

adult *n.* a fully grown person or animal. **adult** *adj.*, **adulthood** *n.*

advance¹ *v.* to move forward.

advance² *n.* **1** movement forward; progress. **2** a loan of money. **in advance** before; earlier.

advanced *adj.* **1** difficult; at a high level. *advanced computer studies.* **2** highly developed. *advanced technology.*

advantage *n.* **1** something that puts you in a better position than other people. **2** in tennis the point scored after deuce.

advent *n.* **1** the coming or arrival of something. *the advent of computers.* **2 Advent** in the Christian church, the four weeks before Christmas.

adventure *n.* an exciting and often dangerous experience.

adverb *n.* a word used to describe a verb or adjective. *carefully, quickly,* and *very* are adverbs.

adversary *n.* an enemy or opponent.

adverse *adj.* unfavorable. *adverse weather conditions.*

advertise *v.* to tell people about something that you want to sell.

advice *n.* helpful recommendations.

advise *v.* to tell somebody what you think that he or she should do. *The doctor advised him to stay in bed.* **advisable** *adj.*

aerobics *n. pl.* physical exercises that increase the supply of oxygen to the heart. **aerobic** *adj.*

aerodynamic *adj.* designed to move through the air quickly and easily.

aeronautics *n. pl.* the study of the design and flight of aircraft.

aerosol *n.* a small container in which a liquid, such as paint, is kept under pressure. You press a button to release the liquid as a fine spray.

airplane

A B C D E F G H I J K L M N O P Q R S T U V W X Y Z

affair *n.* **1** an event or situation. **2** business. *That's none of your affair. financial affairs.*

affect *v.* to influence or make a change

spray

gas under pressure (forces liquid up the tube)

liquid

aerosol

in something. *What you eat affects your health.*

affection *n.* a feeling of love or strong liking for somebody. **affectionate** *adj.*

affirm *v.* to state that something is definitely true.

affix *v.* to attach one thing to another. *Affix a stamp to the envelope.*

afflict *v.* to cause somebody pain or trouble. *Some illnesses afflict men more than women.* **affliction** *n.*

affluent *adj.* wealthy. **affluence** *n.*

afford *v.* to have enough money to buy something. *They can't really afford a vacation this year.*

afloat *adj.* floating.

afraid *adj.* frightened. **I'm afraid** I am sorry. *I'm afraid I can't help.*

aft *adv.* toward the back of a ship or an aircraft.

after *prep.* **1** later than. **2** behind, following. *He ran after me.* **after** *conj.*

aftermath *n.* the period following a disaster. *the aftermath of war.*

afternoon *n.* the part of the day between morning and evening.

afterward, afterwards *adv.* later.

again *adv.* **1** once more. **2** as before.

against *prep.* **1** next to; resting on. *Lean the ladder against the wall.* **2** in opposition to; versus. *Which team are we playing against?*

age¹ *n.* **1** the length of time that a living thing has been alive or that something has existed. **2** a period in history. *the Stone Age, the Bronze Age.* **3 ages** a long time. *I've been waiting ages.*

age² *v.* to get older.

aged *adj.* **1** (*rhymes with* caged) at the age of. *a child aged five, middle-aged.* **2** (**ay**-*jid*) very old. *an aged woman.*

agency *n.* the work or office of somebody who provides a service to others. *an advertising agency.*

agenda *n.* a list of subjects to be discussed at a meeting.

agent *n.* **1** a person who does business or arranges things for other people. *an actor's agent, a travel agent.* **2** a spy. *a secret agent.*

aggravate *v.* **1** to make something worse. **2** (*informal*) to annoy somebody. **aggravation** *n.*

aggressive *adj.* always wanting to attack or argue with other people. **aggression** *n.*, **aggressor** *n.*

agile *adj.* able to move quickly and easily. **agility** *n.*

agitate *v.* to make somebody excited and worried. **agitation** *n.*

agnostic *n.* a person who believes that it is not possible to know whether or not God exists. **agnostic** *adj.*

ago *adv.* before now; in the past.

agony *n.* great pain and suffering.

agree *v.* (agreeing, agreed) **1** to say yes to something. **2** to have the same ideas as somebody else. **agreement** *n.*

agreeable *adj.* **1** pleasant. **2** willing or happy to do something.

agriculture *n.* farming. **agricultural** *adj.*

aground *adv.* stranded on the bottom of the ocean or river, in shallow water. *The ship ran aground.*

ahead *adv.* **1** in front. *We saw a light ahead.* **2** in the future. *Think ahead.*

aid¹ *n.* **1** help. **2** something that gives help or makes something easier. *a hearing aid.* **3** money, food, or equipment sent to people in need.

aid² *v.* to help somebody.

AIDS *n.* (*short for* acquired immunodeficiency syndrome) a serious illness that destroys the body's ability to protect itself against infections.

ailment *n.* a minor illness.

aim¹ *v.* **1** to point a weapon at something. **2** to plan to do something.

aim² *n.* a plan or purpose.

air¹ *n.* **1** the mixture of gases that we breathe. **2** an appearance. *The house has an air of neglect.*

A
B
C
D
E
F
G
H
I
J
K
L
M
N
O
P
Q
R
S
T
U
V
W
X
Y
Z

air² *v.* **1** to expose a room to fresh air. **2** to put something in a warm place to dry. **3** to make something known. *to air your views.* **4** to broadcast on radio or TV.

air conditioning *n.* a way of keeping the air in a building fresh and at a cool temperature. **air-conditioned** *adj.*

aircraft *n.* (*pl.* aircraft) a vehicle that can fly such as a plane or a helicopter.

air force *n.* the fleet of aircraft that a country uses for fighting in the air and the people who fly them.

airline *n.* a company that owns and flies a fleet of aircraft.

airliner *n.* a large plane that is used for carrying passengers.

airplane *n.* a vehicle that can fly, with wings and one or more engines.

airport *n.* a place where aircraft take off and land and where people are able to get on and off.

airship *n.* a large balloon with an engine.

airtight *adj.* so tightly shut that air cannot get in or out.

aisle (*rhymes with* smile) *n.* a long, narrow passage where people can walk between rows of seats, for example in a church or a theater.

ajar *adj.* partly open. *The door is ajar.*

alarm¹ *n.* **1** sudden fear. **2** a device that warns you of danger. *a car alarm.*

alarm² *v.* to frighten or disturb somebody.

alarm clock *n.* a clock that makes a noise to wake you up.

albino *n.* (*pl.* albinos) a person or animal that has no natural coloring in their skin, hair. or eyes.

album *n.* **1** a book for keeping stamps or photographs in. **2** a collection of songs on a CD, record, or tape.

alcohol *n.* a clear liquid that is found in drinks such as whiskey and beer and that can make people drunk.

alcoholic¹ *adj.* containing alcohol.

alcoholic² *n.* a person who cannot stop drinking alcohol. **alcoholism** *n.*

alcove *n.* a part of a room that is set back into a wall.

ale *n.* a type of beer.

alert¹ *adj.* paying full attention; watchful. **On the alert** watchful.

alert² *v.* to warn of danger. **alert** *n.*

algae (*al-jee*) *n. pl.* a group of simple plants that includes seaweed.

algebra *n.* a type of math that uses letters and signs for numbers.

alias (*ay-lee-us*) *n.* a false name. *The criminal had several aliases.*

alibi (*al-i-bye*) *n.* (*pl.* alibis) proof that a person was somewhere else when a crime was committed.

alien¹ *adj.* **1** foreign. **2** strange.

alien² *n.* **1** a creature from outer space. **2** a foreigner.

alight *adj.* on fire; burning.

alike *adj., adv.* almost the same. *My sister and I look alike.*

alive *adj.* living; not dead.

alkali (*al-ka-lie*) *n.* (*pl.* alkalis) a substance that reacts with acids to form chemical salts. **alkaline** *adj.*

all *adj., adv., pron.* every one, or the whole of something.

Allah *n.* God in the Islamic religion.

allege (*a-lej*) *v.* to say that something is true without being able to prove it. **allegation** (*a-le-gay-shun*) *n.*

allegiance (*a-leej-uns*) *n.* loyalty.

allergy *n.* an illness that affects you when you eat, drink, breathe, or touch something that does not normally make people sick. **allergic** *adj.*

alley *n.* (*pl.* alleys) a narrow path or street.

alliance *n.* an agreement between countries or groups.

alligator *n.* an animal similar to a crocodile, found mostly in the U.S. and China.

allocate *v.* to give a share to each person or thing. *How will the money be allocated?* **allocation** *n.*

allotment *n.* a share of something.

allow *v.* to let somebody do something. *My parents allow me to stay up late on weekends.*

allowance *n.* an amount of money that is paid regularly to somebody, especially the money that a child gets from its parents.

alloy *n.* (*pl.* alloys) a mixture of metals.

all right *adj., adv.* **1** fine or well. **2** used as a way of saying yes.

allude *v.* to refer to something in an indirect way. **allusion** *n.*

ally *n.* a person or country that helps another, especially in a war.

almighty *adj.* having great power.

almond *n.* a type of nut.

almost *adv.* nearly; not quite.

alone *adj., adv.* without anybody else.

along[1] *prep.* from one end to the other.

along[2] *adv.* **1** forward; onward. *to drive along.* **2** accompanying somebody. *We're going out—why don't you come along with us?*

alongside *adv., prep.* next to.

aloud *adv.* in a voice that can be heard.

alphabet *n.* all of the letters of a language arranged in order. **alphabetical** *adj.*

alpine *adj.* having to do with mountains.

already *adv.* before now.

also *adv.* as well; too.

altar *n.* a table in a church or temple, used in religious ceremonies.

alter *v.* to change. *She altered the dress to make it fit.* **alteration** *n.*

alternate *(all-ter-nit)* *adj.* first one and then the other; in turns. *alternate stripes of red and green.* **alternate** *(all-ter-nate)* *v.*

alternative *n.* a choice between two or more things. **alternative** *adj.*, **alternatively** *adv.*

although *conj.* in spite of; even though.

altitude *n.* the height above sea level.

altogether *adv.* **1** in total. **2** completely; entirely.

aluminum *n.* a light, silver-colored metal.

always *adv.* at all times; all the time.

am *form of* be.

A.M. *short for* ante meridiem (Latin for "before noon"). *9 A.M. is nine o'clock in the morning.*

amalgamate *v.* to join together. **amalgamation** *n.*

amateur *n.* a person who does something, such as a sport, for enjoyment. **amateur** *adj.*

amaze *v.* to surprise somebody very much; to astonish. **amazement** *n.*, **amazing** *adj.*

ambassador *n.* an important official who represents his or her own country abroad.

amber *n.* **1** a hard, golden-yellow, see-through substance, used for making jewelry. **2** a golden-yellow color.

ambidextrous *adj.* able to use both hands equally well.

ambiguous *adj.* having more than one possible meaning; not clear. **ambiguity** *n.*

ambition *n.* **1** the strong desire to succeed. **2** something that a person wants to do more than anything else. *It's her ambition to become a vet.* **ambitious** *adj.*

amble *v.* to walk without hurrying.

ambulance *n.* a vehicle for carrying sick or injured people.

ambush *v.* to hide and wait for somebody and then make a surprise attack on the person. **ambush** *n.*

amend *v.* to correct something; to change something to make it better.

amenity *n.* something that makes living in a place more pleasant or convenient. *The town has a community center, a library, and many other amenities.*

amid *prep.* (*formal*) in the middle of.

ammonia *n.* a sharp-smelling liquid or gas that is often used for making cleaning substances.

ammunition *n.* bullets and other things that are fired from guns.

amnesia *(am-neez-ya)* *n.* loss of memory.

amnesty *n.* an official pardon, especially of prisoners.

amoeba *(a-mee-ba)* *n.* a one-celled organism that is able to change its shape.

among *prep.* **1** in the middle of; surrounded by. *a house among the trees.* **2** between; in shares. *He divided the money among his four children.*

amoeba

amount[1] *n.* how much of something there is.

amount[2] *v.* **amount to** to add up to. *The bill amounted to $30.*

amphibian *n.* an animal that can live both on land and in the water. *Frogs are amphibians.* **amphibious** *adj.*

amphitheater *n.* an open area surrounded by rows of seats sloping upward, used for sporting events and performing plays, especially in Roman times.

amphitheater

ample *adj.* enough; plenty.

amplifier *n.* a piece of electrical equipment that makes sounds louder.

amplify *v.* (amplifies, amplifying, amplified) to make louder. **amplification** *n.*

A

amputate *v.* to cut off part of the body, often for medical reasons. **amputation** *n.*

amuse *v.* to make somebody smile or laugh or to keep somebody happy for a short time. **amusing** *adj.*

amusement *n.* **1** the feeling you get when someone makes you smile. **2** a way of passing the time pleasantly. **3** a fun place or activity at a fairground such as a merry-go-round.

anachronism *n.* something shown or mentioned in a historical period in which it did not exist.

anagram *n.* a word or phrase made from the letters of another word or phrase, but spelled in another order. *"Alps" is an anagram of "slap."*

analogue *adj.* (of a clock) showing the time with hands on a dial (*can also be spelled* analog).

analogy *n.* the comparison made between similar things.

analyze *v.* to examine something closely so that you can see what it is made of. **analysis** *n.*, **analyst** *n.*

anarchy *n.* a situation where nobody pays attention to any rules or laws. **anarchic** *adj.*, **anarchist** *n.*

anatomy *n.* the study of the structure of the body. **anatomical** *adj.*

ancestor *n.* any person in your family who lived before you and from whom you are descended. **ancestral** *adj.*, **ancestry** *n.*

anchor *n.* a heavy, metal, hooked object on a long chain that is thrown into the water to stop a boat moving. **anchor** *v.*

anchovy *n.* a small fish of the herring family, with a strong, salty taste.

ancient *adj.* very old; from a time long ago.

anecdote *n.* a short, interesting, and sometimes amusing story about something that happened.

anemia *(a-nee-mee-ya) n.* an illness that makes you tired and pale because your body does not have enough red blood cells. **anemic** *adj.*

anemone *(a-nem-uh-nee) n.* a garden or woodland flower.

anesthetic *(an-is-thet-ik) n.* a substance used by doctors to prevent people from feeling pain during an operation.

angel *n.* a messenger from God. **angelic** *adj.*

anger *n.* the strong feeling that you have when you think that something is unfair or wrong.

angle *n.* the space between two straight lines or surfaces that meet.

angler *n.* a person who goes angling.

angling *n.* fishing with a rod.

angry *adj.* (angrier, angriest) filled with anger. **angrily** *adv.*

anguish *n.* very strong suffering.

animal *n.* **1** any living thing that is not a plant. **2** any mammal other than a human being.

animation *n.* **1** liveliness. **2** the making of movies in which puppets and drawings appear to move.

animosity *n.* a feeling of strong dislike.

ankle *n.* the joint connecting the foot to the leg.

annex *n.* a building added to another building to make it bigger.

anniversary *n.* the day each year when a particular event is remembered. *a wedding anniversary.*

announce *v.* to make something known to a lot of people. *John and Liz announced their engagement.* **announcement** *n.*, **announcer** *n.*

annoy *v.* to behave in a way that makes somebody irritated. **annoyance** *n.*

annual[1] *adj.* happening every year. **annually** *adv.*

annual[2] *n.* **1** a book or magazine published once a year. **2** a plant that lives for one year only.

anonymous *(a-non-i-mus) adj.* without the name of the author being known. *an anonymous poem.* **anonymity** *(a-non-nim-it-ee) n.*

anorak *n.* a warm, waterproof jacket, usually with a hood; parka.

anorexia *n.* an illness that makes sufferers refuse to eat food, because they think that eating it will make them fat. **anorexic** *adj.*

another *adj., pron.* **1** one more. **2** a different thing or person.

answer[1] *v.* to say or write something when somebody has asked you a question or spoken or written to you.

answer[2] *n.* **1** something that you say or write to answer somebody. **2** a solution to a problem.

ant *n.* a small,

ants

crawling insect that lives in large groups called colonies.

antagonize *v.* to do or say something that makes another person feel angry toward you. **antagonism** *n.*,

Antarctic

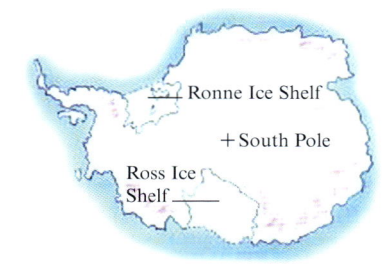
Ronne Ice Shelf
+ South Pole
Ross Ice Shelf

antagonistic *adj.*

Antarctic *n.* the region of Earth located around the South Pole. **Antarctic** *adj.*

ante- *prefix* before. *antedote.*

anteater *n.* a South American mammal that feeds on insects using its long snout.

antelope *n.* a graceful animal that is like a deer and that can run very fast.

antenna *n.* (*pl.* antennae) **1** one of a pair of feelers on an insect's head. See **insect.** **2** (*pl.* antennas) a device made of wire that sends out or receives television or radio signals.

anthem *n.* a song or hymn written for a special occasion.

anther *n.* the part of a flower that contains its pollen. See **flower.**

anthology *n.* a collection of poems or other writings in one book.

anti- *prefix* against; opposite. *antiterrorism.*

antibiotic *n.* a medical drug that helps destroy harmful bacteria.

anticipate *v.* to expect or look forward to something. **anticipation** *n.*

anticlimax *n.* something that disappoints you because it is not as exciting as you expected it to be.

antics *n. pl.* odd or funny behavior. *The children laughed at the monkey's antics.*

antidote *n.* something that stops a poison from working.

antiperspirant *n.* a substance applied to your skin to reduce sweating.

antique *n.* an old and valuable object.

antiseptic *n.* a substance that kills germs.

antler *n.* the branched horn of a deer.

anxiety *(ang-zye-uh-tee) n.* a feeling of worry. **anxious** *adj.*

anybody *pron.* any person.

anyhow *adv.* **1** anyway. **2** in a careless or untidy way.

anyone *pron.* any person.

anything *pron.* any thing.

anyway *adv.* whatever happens; in any case.

anywhere *adv.* in or to any place.

apart *adv.* **1** away from each other. *The two houses are one mile apart.* **2** into pieces. *She took apart the clock so that she could fix it.*

apartment *n.* a set of rooms.

apathy *n.* a lack of interest and enthusiasm. **apathetic** *adj.*

ape *n.* an animal like a monkey but without a tail. *Chimpanzees and gorillas are apes.*

apex *n.* (*pl.* apexes *or* apices) the highest point of something.

apologize *v.* to say you are sorry for something. **apologetic** *adj.,* **apology** *n.*

apostle *n.* one of the 12 men chosen by Jesus Christ to spread his teaching.

apostrophe *(a-pos-tro-fee) n.* a mark (') used in writing. It shows that letters are left out of a word (*I'm* for *I am*), or it shows ownership (*David's cat*).

appal *v.* (appals, appalling, appalled) to shock greatly; to horrify. **appalling** *adj.*

apparatus *n.* the equipment used to do a particular job.

apparent *adj.* **1** clear and obvious. **2** seeming to be true. **apparently** *adv.*

apparition *n.* a ghost.

appeal *v.* **1** to ask in a serious way for something. *Police appealed for witnesses to the attack.* **2** to be attractive. *The idea appeals to me.* **3** to take a legal case that you have lost to a higher court to ask the judge for a new decision. **appeal** *n.*

appear *v.* **1** to come into sight. *The Sun appeared from behind a cloud.* **2** to seem to be. *A microscope makes things appear to be bigger than they really are.*

appearance *n.* **1** the appearing of somebody or something. **2** what somebody or something looks like.

appease *v.* to do what somebody wants in order to stop the person from being angry.

a b c d e f g h i j k l m n o p q r s t u v w x y z

A
B
C
D
E
F
G
H
I
J
K
L
M
N
O
P
Q
R
S
T
U
V
W
X
Y
Z

appendicitis *(a-pen-dis-eye-tis) n.* a painful infection of the appendix.

appendix *n.* (*pl.* appendixes *or* appendices) **1** a part of the body that is attached to the intestine. **2** extra information in a book.

appetite *n.* the desire to eat; hunger.

applaud *v.* to clap in order to show that you like something. **applause** *n.*

apple *n.* a crunchy, round red, green, or yellow fruit.

appliance *n.* a machine or device that does a particular job in the home such as a vacuum cleaner or a washing machine.

applicant *n.* a person who applies for something, often a job.

apply *v.* (applies, applying, applied) **1** to ask officially for something. *apply for a job.* **2** to be relevant. *The rule applies to children under ten.* **3** to put a substance onto something. *Apply glue to the surface.* **application** *n.*

appoint *v.* to choose somebody to do a specific job.

appointment *n.* a time that has been agreed for a meeting.

appreciate *v.* to know the value of something; to be grateful for something. *I really appreciate what you have done to help me.* **appreciation** *n.*, **appreciative** *adj.*

apprehensive *adj.* a little afraid.

apprentice *n.* a person who works with an experienced worker in order to learn a skill. **apprenticeship** *n.*

approach[1] *v.* **1** to come closer. **2** to deal with something. *We need to approach the problem in a different way.*

approach[2] *n.* **1** a way leading toward something. *The approach to the house was through a forest.* **2** a way of dealing with something.

appropriate *adj.* suitable.

approve *v.* to be in favor of something. **approval** *n.*

approximate *adj.* almost correct, but not exact. *the approximate cost.*

apricot *n.* a small, soft fruit with orange-yellow flesh and a pit inside.

April *n.* the fourth month of the year.

apron *n.* a piece of clothing that is worn over the front of your clothes to keep them clean, especially while cooking.

apt *adj.* suitable. *an apt description.*

aptitude *n.* a natural ability to do something well.

aqua- *prefix* water. *aquarobics.*

Aqua-Lung *n.* breathing apparatus that is worn underwater by divers.

aquarium *n.* (*pl.* aquaria) **1** a glass tank to keep fish in. **2** a building, especially in a zoo, where fish and other underwater animals are kept.

aquatic *adj.* having to do with water. *aquatic plants.*

aqueduct *n.* a long bridge that carries water across a valley.

arable *adj.* suitable for growing crops. *arable land.*

Roman aqueduct

arc *n.* a curved line; part of a circle.

arcade *n.* **1** a covered passage where there are small stores. **2** an amusement center with coin-operated games.

arch *n.* a curved structure, for example as part of a bridge or a door.

arch- *prefix* chief; main. *archenemy.*

archaeology *(ar-kee-ol-o-jee) n.* the study of history by looking at the things that people have made and built. (*can also be spelled* archeology.) **archaeological** *adj.*, **archaeologist** *n.*

archaic *(ar-kay-ik) adj.* very old or old-fashioned.

archbishop *n.* a head bishop.

archery *n.* the sport of shooting with a bow and arrow. **archer** *n.*

archipelago *(ar-kee-pel-a-go) n.* (*pl.* archipelagos) a group of small islands.

architect *n.* a designer of buildings.

architecture *n.* the style of buildings. *The architecture of Bath, England, is Georgian in style.* **architectural** *adj.*

archives *n. pl.* a collection of historical documents and records.

Arctic *n.* the region of Earth around the North Pole. **Arctic** *adj.*

ardent *adj.* very enthusiastic.

arduous *adj.* difficult and tiring.

Canada
Russia
North Pole
Greenland
Arctic

are *form of* be.

area *n.* **1** the size of a surface, measured in square feet, yards, or miles. *If a room is four yards long and three yards wide, it has an area of 12 square yards.* **2** a part of a town, of a country, or of the world.

arena *n.* a place where sports and other events take place.

aren't *contr.* are not.

argue *v.* **1** to talk angrily with somebody who you do not agree with. **2** to discuss; to give reasons for something. **argument** *n.*

argumentative *adj.* always arguing.

arid *adj.* so dry that few plants can grow there. *arid desert.*

arise *v.* (arising, arose, arisen) to begin to exist. *A problem has arisen.*

aristocracy *n.* the highest of all the social classes; the nobility.

aristocrat *n.* a member of the aristocracy. **aristocratic** *adj.*

arithmetic *n.* the science of numbers.

ark *n.* in the Bible, the vessel in which Noah escaped from the Flood.

arm¹ *n.* the part of the body from the shoulder to the hand.

arm² *v.* to give weapons to somebody.

armada *n.* a fleet of warships.

armadillo *n.* (*pl.* armadillos) a southern U.S. and Central and South American mammal with a shell made up of bony scales.

armchair *n.* a comfortable chair with parts to support your arms.

armed forces *n. pl.* the army, navy, marines, and air force of a country.

armistice *(ar-miss-tiss)* *n.* an agreement between enemies to stop fighting.

armor *n.* **1** *(historical)* a covering, usually of metal, to protect the body during battle. **2** protective clothing or other covering. *The police wear body armor in dangerous situations.*

arms *n. pl.* weapons.

army *n.* a large group of people who are armed and trained to fight.

aroma *n.* a pleasant smell. **aromatic** *adj.*

arose *past of* **arise**.

around *prep., adv.* **1** on all sides. *We sat around the table.* **2** in different directions. *They walked around the town all morning.* **3** about; approximately. *The meeting should finish at around three o'clock.*

arouse *v.* **1** to stir up a feeling. **2** to wake somebody up. **arousal** *n.*

arrange *v.* **1** to put things in a certain place or order. *I arranged the flowers in a vase.* **2** to plan or organize something. *We are arranging a party.* **arrangement** *n.*

array *n.* (*pl.* arrays) a large range of or display of things.

arrest *v.* to take somebody as a prisoner. *The police have arrested a man who they believe is the robber.* **arrest** *n.*

arrive *v.* **1** to reach a place or a decision. **2** to come. **arrival** *n.*

arrogant *adj.* considering yourself to be more important than others. **arrogance** *n.*

arrow *n.* **1** a pointed stick that is shot from a bow. **2** a shape like an arrow on a sign showing direction.

arsenal *n.* a place where weapons or ammunition are stored or made.

armor

helmet
visor
breastplate
besagew
gauntlet
cuisse
greave
sabaton

A
B
C
D
E
F
G
H
I
J
K
L
M
N
O
P
Q
R
S
T
U
V
W
X
Y
Z

arsenic *n.* a very strong poison.

arson *n.* the crime of deliberately setting fire to property.

art *n.* **1** the creation of drawings, paintings, sculpture, music, literature, and other beautiful or interesting things. **2** a skill. *the art of conversation.*

artery *n.* one of the tubes that carry blood from your heart to the rest of your body.

arthritis *n.* a medical condition in which the joints of the body are swollen and painful. **arthritic** *adj.*

artichoke *n.* **1** a round, green vegetable that looks like a thistle. **2** (*short for* Jerusalem artichoke) a whitish vegetable that grows underground.

article *n.* **1** any object. **2** a piece of writing in a newspaper or magazine. **3** the word *an* or *a* (indefinite articles) or the word *the* (definite article).

articulate *adj.* being able to express yourself clearly.

artificial *adj.* made by people; not found in nature. **artificially** *adv.*

artillery *n.* large, powerful guns used by an army.

artist *n.* a person who draws, paints, or makes other works of art. **artistic** *adj.*, **artistically** *adv.*

ascend *(a-send) v.* to go up. **ascent** *n.*

ash *n.* **1** the powder that is left after something has burned. **2** a tall tree with gray bark.

ashamed *adj.* feeling guilty or bad about something that you have done. *He was ashamed of his bad behavior.*

ashore *adv.* onto the land from the sea.

aside *adv.* **1** to or on one side. *She stepped aside to let me pass by.* **2** besides. *Do you write anything else aside from poetry?*

ask *v.* **1** to put a question to somebody because you want to know something. *I asked her what time it was.* **2** to say that you want something. *I asked for a drink of water.* **3** to invite. *Matt asked me out to the movies.*

asleep *adj., adv.* sleeping; not awake.

aspect *n.* **1** one part of a subject or problem. *Which aspect of the matter should we discuss first?* **2** the look or appearance of something.

aspirin *n.* a drug that is commonly used to reduce pain and fever.

asses

ass *n.* a donkey.

assassinate *v.* to kill an important person such as a ruler or politician. **assassin** *n.*, **assassination** *n.*

assault *v.* to attack somebody violently. **assault** *n.*

assemble *v.* **1** to put the parts of something together. **2** to come together in one place. **3** to bring people together in one place.

assembly *n.* **1** a gathering of people, especially for a meeting. *The principal called the students together for an assembly.* **2** putting something together.

assent *n.* agreement.

assert *v.* to state something clearly and firmly. **assertion** *n.*

assess *v.* to decide the value or cost of something. **assessment** *n.*

asset *n.* useful and valuable thing or skill.

assets *n. pl.* valuable things that a company or person owns.

assign *v.* to give somebody something to do or to use.

assignment *n.* a job that somebody is given to do.

assist *v.* to help. **assistance** *n.*, **assistant** *n.*

associate *v.* to connect something in your mind with something else. *Most people associate dentists with teeth.*

association *n.* a group of people working together for a specific purpose.

assortment *n.* a mixture of different things. **assorted** *adj.*

assume *v.* **1** to accept that something is true, even though it may not be. **2** to take on power or responsibility for a thing or situation. **assumption** *n.*

assure *v.* to tell somebody something definitely. *I can assure you that the dog won't bite you!* **assurance** *n.*

asterisk *n.* a star-shaped mark (*) used in printing.

asteroid *n.* a very small planet that moves around the Sun.

asthma *(az-ma) n.* an illness that makes breathing difficult. **asthmatic** *adj.*

asteroids

astonish *v.* to surprise somebody greatly. **astonishment** *n.*

astound *v.* to astonish somebody.

astray *adv.* away from the right direction; lost.

astrology *n.* the study of the movements of the planets and stars and how these are supposed to influence our lives. **astrologer** *n.*, **astrological** *adj.*

astronaut *n.* a traveler in space.

astronomy *n.* the study of the Moon, Sun, stars, and planets. **astronomer** *n.*

asylum *n.* **1** a place to shelter; protection. *She was granted political asylum in France.* **2** *(historical)* a hospital for mentally ill people.

ate *past of* eat.

atheist *n.* a person who does not believe that there is a God. **atheism** *n.*

athlete *n.* a person who is good at sports. **athletic** *adj.*

athletics *n. pl.* the sports of running, jumping, and throwing.

atlas *n.* a book of maps.

atmosphere *n.* **1** the air around Earth. **2** the feeling in a place. *This café has a friendly atmosphere.*

atom *n.* the smallest part of a chemical

atom

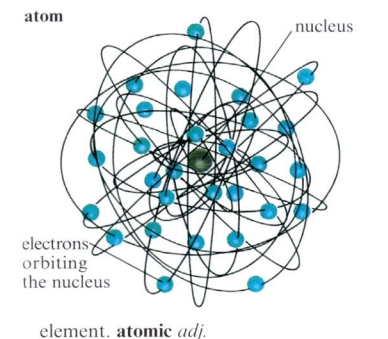

nucleus

electrons orbiting the nucleus

element. **atomic** *adj.*

atrocious *adj.* very bad or very cruel.

atrocity *n.* a cruel, evil act.

attach *v.* to join or fasten one thing to another. **attachment** *n.*

attack *v.* to suddenly try to hurt or damage somebody or something. **attack** *n.*

attain *v.* to gain or achieve something. **attainment** *n.*

attempt *v.* to try to do something. **attempt** *n.*

attend *v.* to be present. **attend to** to deal with something. *She has business to attend to.* **attendance** *n.*

attendant *n.* someone whose specific job it is to help visitors or customers.

attention *n.* looking, listening, or thinking carefully. *Please pay attention to what you are doing.*

attentive *adj.* listening carefully.

attic *n.* a room in the roof of a house.

attire *n.* *(formal)* clothing.

attitude *n.* a way of thinking or behaving.

attract *v.* **1** to make somebody like or be interested in somebody or something. **2** to pull something toward something else. *Magnets attract iron objects.* **attraction** *n.*

attractive *adj.* pleasant to look at.

auburn *adj.* (of hair) reddish-brown.

auction *n.* a public sale in which each item is sold to the person who will pay the most money for it. **auction** *v.*, **auctioneer** *n.*

audible *adj.* loud enough to be heard.

audience *n.* **1** a group of people watching or listening to something. **2** a formal interview. *The president had an audience with the Pope.*

audition *n.* a short performance to test the ability of an actor or musician.

auditorium *n.* (*pl.* auditoriums *or* auditoria) the part of a concert hall or theater where the audience sits.

August *n.* the eighth month of the year.

aunt *n.* the sister of your mother or father or your uncle's wife.

au pair *n.* a young person, often from another country, who lives with a family, helping with the housework and taking care of the children.

authentic *adj.* genuine; real.

author *n.* a person who writes a book, article, play, or other work.

authority *n.* **1** the power to tell somebody what to do. **2** a person or group that tells other people what to do. **3** an expert. **authorize** *v.*

autism *n.* a disability, found in some children, which affects their ability to relate to and communicate with other people. **autistic** *adj.*

A

autobiography *n.* the story of a person's life written by that person. **autobiographical** *adj.*

autograph *n.* a famous person's name, written in his or her own handwriting.

automatic *adj.* working on its own without being taken care of. *an automatic washing machine.* **automatically** *adv.*

automation *n.* the use of machines to do work in factories.

automobile *n.* a car.

available *adj.* able or ready to be used or bought. **availability** *n.*

avalanche *n.* a sudden, huge fall of snow and ice down a mountain.

automobile

avenge *v.* to punish somebody in return for something bad that they have done.

avenue *n.* a road, especially one with trees along both sides.

average[1] *n.* the number that you get when you add together several amounts and divide the total by the number of amounts. *The average of 5, 6, and 7 is 6 (5 + 6 + 7 = 18 ÷ 3 = 6).*

average[2] *adj.* **1** figured out as the average. **2** normal; ordinary.

aversion *n.* a dislike. **averse** *adj.*

aviary *n.* a group of large cages where birds are kept.

aviation *n.* the activity of flying in aircraft.

avid *adj.* enthusiastic; eager.

avocado *n.* (*pl.* avocados) a pear-shaped tropical fruit with a dark green skin and a large pit in the middle.

avoid *v.* **1** to stay out of the way of something. **2** to choose not to do something. **avoidance** *n.*

await *v.* (*formal*) to wait for somebody or something. *A surprise awaited her.*

awake[1] *adj.* not asleep.

awake[2] *v.* (awaking, awoke, awoken) to wake up.

award *v.* to give somebody something such as a prize or payment. **award** *n.*

aware *adj.* knowing about something. **awareness** *n.*

away *adv.* **1** at a distance. *The town is two hours away from Boston.* **2** to or in another place. *She walked away.* **3** not present. *Harry is away from school because he is sick.* **4** gradually into nothing. *The music faded away.*

awe *n.* respect mixed with fear.

awful *adj.* very bad; very unpleasant.

awfully *adv.* **1** very badly. **2** (*informal*) very; extremely. *I'm awfully sorry.*

awkward *adj.* **1** uncomfortable or clumsy. **2** not convenient.

awoke *past of* awake.

awoken *past participle of* awake.

ax *n.* a tool for chopping wood.

axis *n.* (*pl.* axes) an imaginary line running through the middle of an object, around which it turns.

axle *n.* the rod on which a wheel turns.

Earth's axis

Bb

babble *v.* to talk quickly in a way that is difficult to understand.

baboon *n.* a large African monkey.

baboon

baby *n.* a very young child.

babysit *v.* (babysits, babysitting, babysat) to take care of a child or children while their guardians are out. **babysitter** *n.*

bachelor *n.* a man who has never been married.

back¹ *n.* **1** the part of your body between your neck and the bottom of your spine. **2** the part of something across from or farthest from the front. **back** *adj.*

back² *adv.* to the same place or person again. *Can I have my pen back?*

back³ *v.* **1** to move backward; to reverse something. *She backed the car out of the garage.* **2** to support and encourage somebody. *Her parents backed her when she decided to apply for drama school.* **back down** to admit that you were wrong. **back out** not to stick to your side of an agreement.

backbone *n.* the bones that run down the back; the spine.

background *n.* **1** the part of a scene or picture that is behind the most important figures or objects. **2** things that happened before an event that help explain it. **3** a person's family, home, and education.

backpack *n.* a type of bag that you carry on your back.

backside *n. (informal)* a person's bottom.

backstage *adj., adv.* behind the scenes in a theater.

backstroke *n.* a style of swimming on your back.

backward *adj.* toward the back; toward where you began.

backward *adv.* **1** toward the back. **2** in the opposite way to the usual way. *Say the alphabet backward.*

bacon *n.* smoked or salted meat that has come from a pig.

bacteria *n. pl. (sing.* bacterium) very small organisms. Some bacteria cause diseases.

bad *adj.* (worse, worst) **1** unpleasant; harmful. **2** (of a problem or illness) serious.

badge *n.* a small object that you wear on your clothes, with a picture, message, or your name on it.

badger¹ *n.* an animal with a gray coat and black-and-white stripes on its head.

badger

badger² *v.* to pester; to keep asking someone for something.

badly *adv.* **1** in a harmful way; not well. **2** seriously. *He wasn't hurt badly.* **3** very much. *She needs help badly.*

badminton *n.* a game similar to tennis, but that is played with a shuttlecock.

baffle *v.* to puzzle somebody.

bag *n.* a container made of cloth, plastic, paper, or leather for carrying things.

baggage *n.* bags and cases; luggage.

baggy *adj.* hanging loosely; not tight.

bagpipes *n. pl.* a musical instrument that is played by blowing air through one pipe into a bag and then squeezing the air out through other pipes.

bail¹ *n.* **1** money paid to a law court to free an accused person until the trial.

bail² *v.* to remove water from a boat using a container.

A
B
C
D
E
F
G
H
I
J
K
L
M
N
O
P
Q
R
S
T
U
V
W
X
Y
Z

bail out 1 to drop from an aircraft by parachute. **2** to get somebody out of a difficult situation.

bait *n.* food put on a hook or in a trap to catch fish or animals. **bait** *v.*

bake *v.* to cook with dry heat in an oven.

baker *n.* a person who makes or sells breads and cakes.

bakery *n.* a place where breads and cakes are made or sold.

balance¹ *v.* to stay steady, without falling. *Can you balance a book on your head?*

balance² *n.* **1** steadiness. **2** a state in which two or more things are equal in weight. **3** the amount of money in a bank account. **4** a device for weighing things.

balcony *n.* **1** a platform on the outside of a building with railings or a wall around it. **2** the top floor of seats in a theater.

bald *adj.* without hair. **baldness** *n.*

bale *n.* a large bundle of hay, paper, or cloth that is tightly tied or wrapped.

balk *v.* to be unwilling or to hesitate before doing something. *Joseph balked at the idea of running the marathon.*

ball *n.* **1** a round object used in games for hitting or throwing. **2** something with a round shape. *a ball of string.* **3** a big, formal party with dancing.

ballad *n.* a long poem or song that tells a story.

ballerina

ballerina *n.* a female ballet dancer.

ballet *(bal-ay)* *n.* a performance of dancing, often telling a story.

balloon *n.* **1** a small bag made of plastic or rubber that can be filled with air or gas. **2** (*also* **hot-air balloon**) a large bag filled with hot air or gas, often with a basket underneath to carry passengers.

ballot *n.* a way of voting in secret.

ballpoint *n.* a pen with a small, metal ball as the writing point.

bamboo *n.* a tropical plant with a hard, hollow stem.

ban *v.* (bans, banning, banned) to forbid something. *Smoking in public places could be banned.* **ban** *n.*

banana *n.* a long tropical fruit that has a yellow skin when it is ripe.

band *n.* **1** a thin, flat strip of cloth, metal, or other material around something. *a rubber band.* **2** a group of people. *a band of robbers.* **3** A music group or a small orchestra.

bandage *n.* a strip of material for covering a wound.

bandit *n.* an armed robber.

bandstand *n.* a platform with a roof where a band can play in a park.

bang *n.* **1** a sudden, loud noise. **2** a blow or knock. **bang** *v.*

bangs *n. pl.* hair that is cut to hang down over the forehead.

banish *v.* to punish somebody by ordering that person to leave a place.

banister *n.* a rail supported by posts along the side of a staircase.

banjo *n.* (*pl.* banjos *or* banjoes) a string instrument with a round body.

bank¹ *n.* a business that takes care of people's money for them. **banker** *n.*

bank² *n.* the raised ground along the edge of a river or lake.

bankrupt *adj.* unable to pay all of your debts. **bankruptcy** *n.*

banner *n.* a flag, especially one with a message on it.

banquet *n.* a fancy dinner for many people; a feast.

baptism *n.* a Christian ceremony in which a person is sprinkled with or dipped in water to show that he or she is a member of the Christian church. They are usually named at the same time. **baptize** *v.*

bar¹ *n.* **1** a block of something hard. *a chocolate bar.* **2** a long piece of metal. *an iron bar.* **3** a counter or room where you can buy drinks. **4** one of the short parts that a piece of music is divided into.

bar² *v.* (bars, barring, barred) to keep somebody out.

barbarian *n.* a rough, uncivilized person.

barbaric *adj.* extremely cruel.

barbecue *n.* **1** a grill for cooking food over a charcoal fire outside. **2** an outdoor party at which food is cooked on a barbecue. **barbecue** *v.*

barbed wire *n.* strong wire with sharp points along it, used for fences and on top of walls.

barber *n.* a person who cuts men's hair.

bar code *n.* a series of thin and thick black lines on an item in a store that can be read by a computer.

bare[1] *adj.* **1** not covered by clothing. *bare feet.* **2** not decorated or covered. *bare walls.* **3** basic; just enough. *the bare necessities of life.*

bare[2] *v.* to uncover or expose something. *The dog bared its teeth.*

barely *adv.* only just.

bargain[1] *n.* **1** an agreement to do something, especially to buy or sell something. **2** something bought cheaply that is good value for money.

bargain[2] *v.* to argue over the price of something.

barge

barge[1] *n.* a flat-bottomed boat that is used on canals and rivers.

barge[2] *v.* to bump into somebody roughly or push your way roughly into a place. *He barged into the room.*

bark[1] *n.* the short, loud noise made by a dog. **bark** *v.*

bark[2] *n.* the rough covering of a tree.

barley *n.* a cereal plant.

bar mitzvah *n.* a religious ceremony for a Jewish boy at the age of 13.

barn *n.* a farm building for animals or for storing crops or animal food.

barnacle *n.* a crustacean that sticks to rocks and to the bottom of boats.

barometer *n.* an instrument that measures air pressure and shows changes in the weather.

baron *n.* a nobleman.

baroness *n.* **1** a woman with the same rank as a baron. **2** the wife of a baron.

barracks *n. pl.* a large building where soldiers live.

barrel *n.* **1** a container for liquids with curved sides. **2** the tube of a gun.

barren *adj.* not able to produce crops, fruit, or children. *barren soil.*

barricade *n.* a barrier that has been built quickly across a road or path to stop people from passing. **barricade** *v.*

barrier *n.* a fence or obstacle.

barrow *n.* **1** a small cart. **2** a mound of soil that covered a grave in prehistoric times.

bartender *n.* a person who serves drinks in a bar.

barter *v.* to exchange goods for other goods without using money.

base[1] *n.* **1** the lowest part of something, which it stands on; the bottom. **2** a headquarters.

base[2] *v.* to develop something from another thing. *The movie is based on a true story.*

baseball *n.* a game played by two teams of nine players with a bat and ball, which takes place during nine innings.

baseball

basement *n.* a level of a building below the ground.

bash *v.* *(informal)* to hit somebody or something hard.

bashful *adj.* shy.

basic *adj.* **1** being the main thing on which something is based. *You need to know these basic facts before you begin.* **2** at the simplest level. *She has a basic knowledge of German.* **basically** *adv.*, **basics** *n. pl.*

basil *n.* an herb used in cooking.

basin *n.* **1** a large bowl. **2** a bowl for washing yourself, attached to a wall or floor. **3** the low, flat area beside a river, drained by the river.

basis *n.* (*pl.* bases) something on which another thing is based. *This idea was the basis of our plan.*

a
b
c
d
e
f
g
h
i
j
k
l
m
n
o
p
q
r
s
t
u
v
w
x
y
z

bask *v.* to lie in warmth or sunshine.

basket *n.* a container for holding or carrying things, made of thin strips of straw or metal that are woven together.

basketball *n.* a game played by two teams, in which points are scored by throwing a ball into a high basket.

bass *(base)* *n.* **1** the lowest male singing voice. **2** the low part in music. **3** an electric guitar that produces very low notes. **4** a double bass.

bassoon *n.* a woodwind instrument that plays low notes.

bat¹ *n.* an animal that is similar to a mouse with

bat

wings, which flies at night.

bat² *n.* a piece of wood that is used for hitting a ball in some games such as baseball. **bat** *v.*

batch *n.* a group of things made or sent at one time. *a batch of cakes.*

bath *n.* **1** a large container that you sit in to wash your entire body. **2** the process of getting washed in a bath.

bathe *v. (baythe)* **1** to take a bath. **2** to wash a part of your body gently. *Let me bathe that cut on your knee.* **3** to go swimming in the ocean, a river, or a lake. **bather** *n.*

bathroom *n.* a room with a bathtub, sink, and toilet

baton *n.* **1** the thin stick used by the conductor of an orchestra. **2** a short stick handed from one runner to the next in a relay race. **3** a truncheon.

battalion *n.* a large group of soldiers.

batter¹ *v.* to hit something many times.

battery¹

She battered the door with her fists.

batter² *n.* a mixture of flour, eggs, and water or milk, used for making pancakes, cakes, or cookies or coating food for frying.

battery *n.* **1** an object that stores and supplies electricity such as for a flashlight or car. **2** a group of large guns.

battle *n.* a fight, especially one fought between armies.

battlements *n. pl.* the top of a castle wall, with openings for shooting through.

battleship *n.* a large ship used in a war.

bawl *v.* to shout or cry loudly.

bay¹ *n.* *(pl.* bays) **1** a part of the sea where the land curves inward. **2** a space or area that is used for a particular activity. **keep at bay** to stop somebody or something from coming any closer or affecting you.

bay² *v.* to bark loudly; to howl.

bayonet *n.* a long, sharp blade attached to the end of a rifle.

bay window *n.* a window that sticks out from the wall of a house.

bazaar *n.* **1** a market, especially in Eastern countries. **2** a sale held to earn money for charity.

B.C. *short for* Before Christ, used with dates before the birth of Christ. *29 B.C.*

be *v.* (am, is, are, being, was, were, been) **1** used to describe people or things. *They are rich.* **2** used with other verbs to describe an action going on. *I was walking in the park when it started to rain.* **3** to exist.

beach *n.* an area of sand or pebbles along the edge of the ocean or a lake.

beacon *n.* a light or fire used as a signal or warning.

bead *n.* a small ball of glass or other material with a hole through it so that it can be threaded onto string to make necklaces or other jewelry.

beak *n.* the hard, pointed part of a bird's mouth.

beaker *n.* a tall, plastic cup without a handle.

beam¹ *n.* **1** a long, straight piece of wood or metal supporting a roof or floor. **2** a ray of light.

beam² *v.* to smile widely.

bean *n.* **1** a plant that has seeds growing in pods. **2** the seed or pod of a bean plant, used as food. **full of beans** *(informal)* very lively.

bear[1] *n.* a large, heavy wild animal with thick fur.

bear[2] *v.* (bearing, bore, borne) **1** to put up with; to stand something. *She could not bear the pain any longer.* **2** to support or carry something. *Will this chair bear my weight?* **3** to produce children, fruit, or flowers. *The tree bears purple flowers in the summer.*

beard *n.* the hair that grows on a man's chin and cheeks.

beast *n.* **1** a wild animal. **beastly** *adj.*

beat[1] *v.* (beating, beat, beaten) **1** to hit many times. *Beat the drum.* **2** to defeat. **3** to stir a mixture with quick movements. *Beat the eggs and sugar well.* **4** to make a regular movement or sound. *My heart was beating fast.*

beat[2] *n.* **1** a regular rhythm, for example of your heart or of music. **2** the regular round of a police officer.

beauty *n.* loveliness in appearance or sound. **beautiful** *adj.*, **beautifully** *adv.*

beaver *n.* a wild animal with a wide, flat tail and sharp teeth that it uses to cut branches to build dams.

became *past of* become.

because *conj.* for the reason that. *I was late because I missed the bus.*

beckon *v.* to make a sign to somebody, asking that person to come.

become *v.* (becoming, became, become) to start to be; to grow to be. *She became sadder and sadder.*

bed *n.* **1** a piece of furniture for sleeping on. **2** a place where flowers are planted. **3** the bottom of the sea or of a river.

bedclothes *n. pl.* sheets, blankets, comforters, and other covers for a bed.

bedding *n.* **1** mattresses and covers for a bed. **2** straw for animals to sleep on.

bedridden *adj.* unable to get out of bed because of an illness.

bedroom *n.* a room for sleeping in.

bee *n.* a flying insect; some species live in large groups and make honey.

beech *n.* a tree with smooth bark and shiny leaves.

beef *n.* the meat from a cow, bull, or ox.

beehive *n.* a box for keeping bees in so that their honey can be collected.

beep *v.* to make a short, high-pitched sound. **beep** *n.*

beer *n.* an alcoholic drink made from malt and flavored with hops.

beet *n.* a dark red root vegetable.

beetle *n.* an insect with hard, shiny covers for its wings.

beetle

before *prep.* **1** earlier than. *Please try to get here before two o'clock.* **2** in front of. *She was before me in the line.* **before** *conj., adv.*

beg *v.* (begs, begging, begged) **1** to ask somebody for money or food on the street. **2** to ask very eagerly or desperately for something. *He begged his captors to let him go.*

beggar *n.* a person who begs for money or food on the street.

begin *v.* (begins, beginning, began, begun) to start. **beginner** *n.*, **beginning** *n.*

behalf *n.* **on behalf of** for somebody. *Eliza thanked our teacher on behalf of the entire class.*

behave *v.* **1** to act in a certain way. *Tim is behaving very strangely.* **2** to act properly; to be good. **behavior** *n.*

behind *prep.* **1** at or toward the back of. *I waited behind Sarah in the line at the post office.* **2** on the other side of. *I hid behind the door.* **3** giving support. *She wants to become a dancer, and her family is right behind her.* **4** making less progress than others. *He is behind the rest of the class with his reading.* **behind** *adv.*

beige *(bayj)* *n.* a pale brown color. **beige** *adj.*

being[1] *form of* be.

being[2] *n.* any living person or thing.

belated *adj.* arriving late.

belch *v.* **1** to burp. **2** to send out fire, smoke, or gases. *The factory's chimneys belched out smoke.*

belief *n.* what somebody believes to be true. *His beliefs are important to him.*

believe *v.* **1** to feel sure that something is true. **2** to think something. **believer** *n.*

bell *n.* **1** a hollow, metal object that makes a ringing sound when it is struck. **2** an electric device that rings as a signal or warning.

bellow *v.* to roar like a bull; to shout very loudly. **bellow** *n.*

a
b
c
d
e
f
g
h
i
j
k
l
m
n
o
p
q
r
s
t
u
v
w
x
y
z

A
B
C
D
E
F
G
H
I
J
K
L
M
N
O
P
Q
R
S
T
U
V
W
X
Y
Z

bellows *n. pl.* an instrument for pumping air to make a fire burn better.

belly *n.* the part of your body between your chest and your legs that contains your stomach.

belong *v.* **1** to be owned by somebody. *This book belongs to me.* **2** to be a member of a club. **3** to have a place somewhere. *That chair belongs in the kitchen.*

belongings *n. pl.* the things that somebody owns. *He cherishes his belongings.*

beloved *adj.* much loved.

below *prep.* **1** in a lower position than. *Your mouth is below your nose.* **2** less than. *temperatures below zero.* **below** *adv.*

belt[1] *n.* **1** a strip of leather or other material that you wear around your waist. **2** a rubber band used in a machine. *a conveyor belt.*

belt[2] *v. (informal)* **1** to hit somebody very hard. **2** to travel very fast. *He belted up the road.*

bench *n.* **1** a long, hard seat for several people to sit on. **2** a table for somebody to work at. *a workbench.*

bend *v.* (bending, bent) **1** to make something into a curved or angled shape. *Bend your arm.* **2** to turn to the right or left. *The road bends just ahead.* **3** to lean your body in a certain direction. *She bent down to pick up the coin.* **bend** *n.*

beneath *prep., adv.* **1** underneath; below. **2** not good enough for. *She felt that cleaning floors was beneath her.*

beneficial *adj.* having good effects.

benefit *n.* something that is good to have; an advantage. **benefit** *v.*

bent *past of* bend.

bequeath *v.* to leave something to somebody when you die. **bequest** *n.*

bereaved *adj.* suffering from a recent death of a relative or friend. **bereavement** *n.*

beret *(buh-ray)* *n.* a flat, round hat.

berry *n.* a small, juicy fruit containing seeds.

berserk *adj.* wild; out of control. *The man suddenly went berserk and started smashing things.*

berth *n.* **1** a sleeping place in a ship or train. **2** a place in a dock where a boat is tied up.

beside *prep.* next to. **be beside yourself**
to lose control of yourself because of strong emotion. *She was beside herself with worry.*

besides[1] *prep.* in addition to. *There are three people in my family besides my mother.*

besides[2] *adv.* also. *These shoes are too expensive, and besides, I don't think I like them.*

besieged castle

besiege *v.* to surround a place with an army, in order to force the people there to surrender.

best *adj., adv.* better than all the rest.

best man *n.* the male friend of a bridegroom who helps him with the arrangements for his wedding.

bet *v.* (bets, betting, bet *or* betted) to risk money on the result of a race or some other event. **I bet . . .** I am sure . . . *I bet I can run faster than you.* **bet** *n.*

betray *v.* **1** to do something that will hurt somebody to whom you should be loyal. *She betrayed her own brother to the enemy.* **2** to show something that you are trying to hide. *His face betrayed his true feelings.* **betrayal** *n.*

better *adj.* **1** more excellent; more suitable. **2** recovered from an illness. **better** *adv.*

between *prep.* **1** in the space dividing two things. *To score, you have to kick the ball between the posts.* **2** in parts; in shares. *Divide the candy between you.* **3** comparing one to the other. *I can't see much difference between Lucy and her sister.*

beverage *n.* a drink.

beware *v.* **beware of** to watch out for or guard against something dangerous. *Beware of the dog!*

bewilder *v.* to confuse or puzzle somebody. *I was bewildered by the huge choice.* **bewilderment** *n.*

beyond *prep.* **1** on the far side of. *Our house is just beyond the school.* **2** more than. *They succeeded beyond all their hopes.* **be beyond somebody** be impossible for somebody to understand or do.

bi- *prefix* two or twice. *biplane, bilingual.*

biased *(bye-ust) adj.* preferring one side over the other.

bib *n.* a piece of cloth or plastic placed under a child's chin to protect the child's clothes from food stains.

Bible *n.* the holy book of the Christian church. **biblical** *adj.*

bicycle

bicycle *n.* a two-wheeled vehicle that you ride by pedaling.

bid *v.* (bidding, bid) to offer a sum of money for something. **bid** *n.*

big *adj.* (bigger biggest) **1** large in size. **2** important.

bigot *n.* a person who has an irrational or strong dislike of people of another race or religion or with different opinions. **bigoted** *adj.*, **bigotry** *n.*

bike *n.* a bicycle.

bikini *n.* a two-piece bathing suit worn by women and girls.

bilingual *adj.* speaking two languages very well.

bill *n.* **1** a piece of paper showing how much money you owe for something. **2** a bird's beak. **3** a draft of a law before it has been discussed by lawmakers. **4** a paper note that is used for currency, as in a dollar bill.

billion *n.* one thousand million (1,000,000,000). **billionth** *adj.*

billy goat *n.* a male goat.

bin *n.* a container for storing something in.

binary *adj.* made up of two parts or units.

binary system *n.* a mathematical system using only the digits 0 and 1.

bind *v.* (binding, bound) **1** to tie. *The robbers bound him to the chair with a rope.* **2** to wrap a length of material around something. *The nurse bound the deep cut with a bandage.* **3** to fasten together the pages of a book and put a cover on it.

bingo *n.* a game in which each player marks numbers on a card as they are called out. The first player to have all, or a row, of his or her numbers called out is the winner.

binoculars *n. pl.* an instrument with two eyepieces that you look through to make distant objects seem closer.

biodegradable *adj.* able to be broken down naturally by bacteria.

biography *n.* the written story of somebody's life. **biographical** *adj.*

biology *n.* the scientific study of all living things. **biological** *adj.*, **biologically** *adv.*, **biologist** *n.*

biplane *n.* an aircraft that has two sets of wings, one set on top of the other.

birch *n.* a forest tree with smooth bark.

bird *n.* a creature with feathers, a beak, two legs, and two wings. Most birds can fly.

birth *n.* the time of coming into life or of being born.

bird

birthday *n.* the anniversary of the day that you were born.

birthmark *n.* a mark on your skin that has been there since you were born.

biscuit *n.* a small cake of bread.

bishop *n.* **1** a senior priest in some Christian churches. **2** a chess piece.

bison *n.* (*pl.* bison) a variety of large, hairy, oxlike animals; buffalo.

bison

bit[1] *past of* bite

bit[2] *n.* **1** a small piece or amount. **2** the metal part of a bridle that the horse holds in its mouth. **3** the smallest unit of information used by a computer. **4** the end part of a drill.

bitch *n.* a female dog, wolf, or fox.

bite *v.* (biting, bit, bitten) **1** to cut something with your teeth. **2** (of an insect) to sting. **bite** *n.*

bitter *adj.* **1** sharp and unpleasant in taste; not sweet. *This coffee is bitter.* **2** angry and upset. **3** (of the weather) very cold. **bitterness** *n.*

bizarre *adj.* very strange.

black¹ *n.* the darkest of all colors. **blacken** *v.*

black² *adj.* **1** black in color. **2** dark-skinned (of people).

blackberry *n.* a small, juicy, black fruit that grows on a thorny bush.

blackbird *n.* a bird with black feathers and a yellow beak.

blackboard *n.* a board with a black surface on which you write with chalk.

black hole *n.* an area in space where a star has collapsed that sucks everything into it, even light.

blackmail *n.* the threat to tell a secret unless somebody pays you money. **blackmail** *v.*, **blackmailer** *n.*

blacksmith *n.* a person who makes or repairs iron goods such as horseshoes.

bladder *n.* the organ of your body where waste liquid is stored before it is passed out of your body.

blade *n.* **1** the sharp cutting edge of a knife, sword, or ice skate. **2** a single leaf of grass.

blame *v.* to say that somebody is the cause of something bad. *I didn't break it—don't blame me!* **blame** *n.*

bland *adj.* mild and dull. *This food tastes bland.*

blank *adj.* with nothing on it. *a blank sheet of paper.*

blanket *n.* **1** a thick, woolen cover for a bed. **2** a thick layer of something. *A blanket of snow covered the ground.*

blare *v.* to make a loud, unpleasant sound. *I can't hear you very well with that radio blaring!*

blaspheme *(blass-feem) v.* to speak about God or religion without respect. **blasphemous** *adj.*, **blasphemy** *n.*

blast *n.* **1** a sudden rush of air. **2** an explosion. **3** a sudden loud noise. **blast** *v.*

blastoff *n.* the moment when a rocket or space shuttle is launched.

blastoff

blaze *v.* to burn with a strong flame. **blaze** *n.*

blazer *n.* a smart jacket, often worn as part of a uniform.

bleach¹ *n.* a strong liquid containing chemicals, normally used for disinfecting and cleaning.

bleach² *v.* to remove the color from something, especially using bleach.

bleak *adj.* **1** cold and bare. *a bleak landscape.* **2** without hope. *The future looks bleak.*

bleat *v.* to cry like a sheep. **bleat** *n.*

bleed *v.* (bleeding, bled) to lose blood.

blend *v.* to mix together. **blend** *n.*

bless *v.* to ask God to take care of somebody or something. *The priest blessed the children.* **blessing** *n.*

blew *past of* blow.

blind¹ *adj.* not able to see. **blindness** *n.*

blind² *v.* to make somebody unable to see.

blind³ *n.* a covering that can be pulled down over a window.

blindfold *n.* a piece of cloth tied over your eyes to prevent you from seeing.

blink *v.* to close and open your eyes very quickly.

bliss *n.* very great happiness. **blissful** *adj.*, **blissfully** *adv.*

blister *n.* a small bubble under your skin, filled with a watery liquid.

blizzard *n.* a heavy snowstorm.

bloated *adj.* swollen, especially as a result of eating too much.

blob *n.* a drop of a thick liquid.

block¹ *n.* **1** a big, solid piece of something. *a block of wood.* **2** a large building of apartments or offices. **3** a group of buildings with streets on four sides. **4** a barrier. *a road block.*

block² *v.* to get in the way so that people or things cannot get past.

block letters *n. pl.* capital letters.

blog *n.* *(informal)* somebody's personal diary or thoughts published on the Internet. Blog *was originally short for* Weblog. **blog** *v.*, **blogger** *n.*

blond *adj.* (of a man or boy) having light-colored hair.

blonde *adj.* (of a woman or girl) having light-colored hair.

blood *n.* the red liquid that flows around our bodies. **bloody** *adj.*

blood vessel *n.* one of the tubes that carries blood around inside your body.

bloom¹ *v.* to produce flowers.

bloom² *n.* a flower.

blossom¹ *n.* the flowers on trees in the spring.

blossom² *v.* **1** to produce blossoms. **2** to develop. *She had begun to blossom into a fine musician.*

blot *n.* a spot or stain made by ink or paint. **blot** *v.*

blouse *n.* a shirt worn by women and girls.

blow¹ *v.* (blowing, blew, blown) **1** (of the wind) to move. **2** to let out air through your mouth. **3** to move by blowing. *The wind blew the fence down.* **4** to be moved by blowing. *The door blew shut.* **blow up 1** to destroy something by an explosion. **2** to fill something up with air; to inflate.

blow² *n.* **1** a hard knock. *a blow to the head.* **2** a sudden event of bad luck. *His wife's death was a terrible blow.*

blubber¹ *n.* the fat of whales and some other sea animals.

blubber² *v. (informal)* to cry noisily.

blue¹ *n.* the color of a clear sky. **out of the blue** suddenly; without warning.

blue² *adj.* **1** of the color of a clear sky. **2** sad or depressed.

blueberry *n.* a small blue berry and the plant on which it grows.

blues *n. pl.* a type of slow, sad jazz. **the blues** a feeling of sadness.

bluff *v.* to try to trick somebody by pretending to be better at something than you really are or by pretending to be somebody else. *Pretending to be a police officer, he bluffed his way into the palace.* **bluff** *n.*

blunder *n.* a stupid mistake. **blunder** *v.*

blunt *adj.* **1** having an edge or point that is not sharp. **2** saying plainly what you think, without being polite. **bluntness** *n.*

blur *v.* (blurs, blurring, blurred) to make something unclear. *The rain blurred our view out of the window.* **blur** *n.*

blurb *n.* a short description of a book, normally written on its back cover or in advertising used to sell the book.

blush *v.* to become red in the face, usually because you are embarrassed. **blush** *n.*

boa constrictor *n.* a large snake that kills its prey by winding itself around the prey and crushing it.

boar *n.* **1** a male pig. **2** a wild pig.

board¹ *n.* **1** a flat piece of wood. **2** a flat piece of stiff cardboard that is used for a particular purpose. *Chess is played on a square board.* **3** a group of people who control a business. *the board of directors.* **4** meals. *He pays for his room and board.* **onboard** on a ship, plane, or train.

board² *v.* **1** to go on to a ship, plane, train, or similar vehicle. **2** to live and have your meals somewhere.

boarding school *n.* a school where you eat and sleep, as well as have classes. **boarder** *n.*

boast *v.* to talk proudly about how good you think you are or about something that you own. **boast** *n.*, **boastful** *adj.*, **boastfully** *adv.*

boat *n.* a vehicle for traveling on water.

bob¹ *v.* (bobs, bobbing, bobbed) to move up and down quickly. *The cork was bobbing around in the water.*

bob² *n.* a short, straight hairstyle.

bobsled *n.* a long sled for two or more people, used for racing.

body *n.* **1** the whole of a person or an animal. **2** a dead person or animal. **3** the main part of a thing. *the body of a car.*

bodyguard *n.* a person whose job is to protect somebody else from attacks.

bog *n.* an area of wet ground. **boggy** *adj.*

bogus *adj.* false. *She entered the country using a bogus passport.*

boil¹ *v.* **1** (of a liquid) to become so hot that it bubbles and produces steam. **2** to cook something in boiling water.

boil² *n.* a painful swelling under the skin.

boiler *n.* a tank in which water is heated to supply a building.

boiling *adj. (informal)* very hot.

boiling point *n.* the temperature at which a liquid boils.

boisterous *adj.* noisy and lively.

boa constrictor

bold *adj.* **1** brave and confident. **2** standing out clearly; easy to see. *The picture had been painted in bold colors.* **boldness** *n.*

bolt¹ *n.* **1** a sliding metal bar used to fasten a door. **2** a thick metal pin used with a nut for fastening things together.

bolt² *v.* **1** to fasten with a bolt. **2** to rush away; to escape. *The horse has bolted.*

bomb *n.* a container filled with explosives, used to blow things up. **bomb** *v.,* **bomber** *n.*

bombard *v.* **1** to attack with bombs or heavy gunfire. **2** to attack with questions or abuse. **bombardment** *n.*

bombshell *n.* **1** a great, usually very unpleasant, surprise. **2** an explosive bomb. **3** an attractive person.

bond¹ *n.* **1** a feeling that unites people or groups. *a bond of friendship.* **2 bonds** the ropes or chains used to hold somebody as a prisoner.

bond² *n.* to stick together.

bondage *n.* slavery.

bone *n.* one of the hard, white parts that make up a skeleton. **bony** *adj.*

bonfire *n* a large, outdoor fire.

bonnet *n.* a baby's or a woman's hat, normally fastened under the chin.

bonus *n.* an extra payment or reward.

booby trap *n.* a hidden bomb or trap intended to hurt people who come close to it.

book¹ *n.* a number of sheets of paper fastened together inside a cover, for reading or writing in.

book² *v.* to order something before the time that you need it. *We have booked a table in the restaurant.*

booklet *n.* a small book with a paper cover.

bookmaker *n.* a person who makes books.

bookworm *n.* a person who loves reading books.

boom *n.* **1** a loud, deep sound. **2** a sudden increase in something. *There has been a boom in sales of ice cream this summer.* **3** a pole on a boat, along which a sail is stretched. **boom** *v.*

boomerang *n.* a curved piece of wood that, when thrown, returns to the thrower. They are used as hunting weapons by Australian Aborigines.

boost *v.* to increase the power or amount of something. *We need to boost our sales figures.* **boost** *n.*

boot¹ *n.* a heavy shoe that covers the foot and lower part of the leg.

boot² *v.* to kick. **boot up** to start a computer working by loading a start-up program.

booty *n.* goods that have been stolen, especially in a war.

border *n.* **1** the line that divides two countries. **2** a decorative strip along the edge of something. **3** a long flower bed.

bore¹ *v.* **1** to make a hole through something, especially with a drill. **2** to make somebody tired and uninterested. *Long car journeys bore me.* **bored** *adj.,* **boredom** *n.,* **boring** *adj.*

bore² *n.* **1** an uninteresting person or thing. **2** the size of the barrel of a gun.

bore³ *past of* bear.

born *v.* **be born** to come into the world. *What year were you born?*

borne *past participle of* bear.

borough *(ber-row) n.* a town or an area that has its own local government.

borrow *v.* to take something away for a while, intending to return it.

bosom *n.* a person's chest.

boss *n.* a manager; the person in charge.

bossy *adj.* (bossier, bossiest) taking pleasure in telling other people what to do. **bossiness** *n.*

botany *n.* the study of plants. **botanical** *adj.,* **botanist** *n.*

both *adj., adv., pron.* the two; the one and the other. *Both of my brothers are older than I am.*

bother¹ *v.* **1** to worry, annoy, or disturb somebody. *Don't bother me now—I'm busy.* **2** to take the time or trouble to do something. *Don't bother to clean up.*

bother² *n.* trouble or inconvenience.

bottle *n.* a narrow-necked glass or plastic container for liquids.

bottom *n.* **1** the lowest part of something. **2** the soft, fleshy part of your body that you sit on. **bottom** *adj.*

bough *(rhymes with* cow) *n.* a tree branch.

bought *past of* buy.

boulder *n.* (*rhymes with* older) a very large stone.

bounce *v.* to spring up again, like a rubber ball does when it hits the ground. **bounce** *n.,* **bouncy** *adj.*

bound¹ *past of* bind.

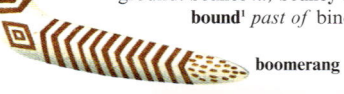

boomerang

bound[2] *v.* to leap or jump. **bound** *n.*

bound[3] *adj.* **bound to** certain to.

boundary *n.* a line that separates one place from another.

bouquet *(bo-kay* or *boo-kay) n.* a bunch of flowers.

bout *n.* **1** a period of illness. *a bout of the flu.* **2** a contest in wrestling or boxing. **3** a short period of something. *a bout of hard work.*

boutique *n.* a small store, especially one selling clothes.

bow[1] *(rhymes with* no) *n.* **1** a weapon for shooting arrows, made of a stick of wood bent by a string. **2** a wooden rod with strings stretched along it, used for playing musical instruments such as the violin. **3** a looped knot, used for tying shoelaces and ribbons.

bow[2] *(rhymes with* now) *v.* to bend your head and the upper part of your body forward, as actors do at the end of a play.

bow[3] *(rhymes with* now) *n.* **1** a lowering of the head and upper body. **2** the front part of a ship.

bowels *n. pl.* the long tubes through which food passes after it leaves your stomach.

bowl[1] *n.* a deep, round dish.

bowl[2] *v.* to throw the ball in the game of bowling.

bowler *n.* **1** a person who bowls. **2** a hat with a rounded top.

bowling *n.* an indoor game in which heavy balls are rolled down a lane to knock down pins.

box[1] *n.* a hollow container, especially one with straight sides, often made of wood or cardboard.

box[2] *v.* to fight with your fists as a sport.

boxer *n.* **1** a person who boxes as a sport. **2** a large dog, similar to a bulldog.

boxing *n.* the sport of fighting with just your fists.

box office *n.* a place in a theater where you can buy tickets.

boxer

boy *n.* (*pl.* boys) a male child.

boycott *v.* to refuse to take part in something or to do business with somebody, as a protest. **boycott** *n.*

bra *n.* a garment that women wear under their other clothes and to support their breasts.

brace[1] *n.* a device that holds things together or in place.

brace[2] *v.* **brace yourself** to prepare yourself for something that might be difficult or unpleasant.

braces *n. pl.* a piece of wire attached over teeth to straighten them.

bracelet *n.* a piece of jewelry that you wear around your wrist.

bracket *n.* a support for a shelf attached to a wall.

brag *v.* (brags, bragging, bragged) to boast.

braid *n.* **1** a length of hair consisting of three pieces that have been twisted together. **2** a narrow strip of woven threads, often used to decorate something. **braid** *v.*

Braille *(brayl) n.* a system of raised dots on paper that blind people can use to read by feeling.

brain *n.* the part of your body inside your head, protected by your skull, that controls the rest of your body and with which you think.

brainwash *v.* to force somebody to have a particular view by repeating something to them over and over again.

cerebrum

cerebellum

brain stem

human brain

brain wave *n.* a sudden, good idea.

brainy *adj.* (brainier, brainiest) intelligent.

brake *n.* a part of a vehicle used for stopping or slowing down. **brake** *v.*

bramble *n.* a thorny bush that blackberries or raspberries grow on.

bran *n.* the outer covering of grain.

branch[1] *n.* **1** one of the armlike parts growing out from the trunk of a tree.

a
b
c
d
e
f
g
h
i
j
k
l
m
n
o
p
q
r
s
t
u
v
w
x
y
z

A
B
C
D
E
F
G
H
I
J
K
L
M
N
O
P
Q
R
S
T
U
V
W
X
Y
Z

2 an office or store belonging to a larger organization. *The bank has four branches in the city.*

branch² *v.* to separate into smaller parts like branches. *The railroad line branches after the next station.*

brand¹ *n.* a particular make of goods.

brand² *v.* **1** to mark cattle with a hot piece of metal to show whom they belong to. **2** to give somebody a bad reputation. *The newspapers branded her a liar.*

brand-new *adj.* completely new.

brandy *n.* a strong, alcoholic drink made from wine.

brass *n.* **1** a yellowish metal made by mixing copper and zinc. **2 the brass** the musical instruments made of brass that form part of an orchestra.

brave *adj.* able to face danger without fear, or to endure pain without complaining. **bravery** *n.*

brawl *n.* a fight. **brawl** *v.*

bray *n.* (*pl.* brays) the harsh sound that a donkey makes. **bray** *v.*

bread *n.* a food made from flour, water, and often yeast and baked in an oven.

breadth *n.* the distance from one side of something to the other.

break¹ *v* (breaking, broke, broken) **1** to divide into pieces, especially with force. *He got in by breaking a window.* **2** to stop working. *My watch broke.* **3** to fail to keep something. *You broke your promise.* **break down 1** (of machinery) to stop working. *Our car broke down.* **2** to become very upset. **breakdown** *n.* **break in** to enter a building by force. *Thieves broke in and stole her jewelry.* **break-in** *n.* **break out** to appear or start suddenly. *War has broken out.*

break² *n.* **1** a rest from working. **2** an opening. *a break in the clouds.* **3** a change. *a break in the weather.*

breaker *n.* a large ocean wave.

breakfast *n.* the first meal of the day.

breakthrough *n.* an important development or discovery.

breakwater *n.* a wall built out into the ocean to protect the shore from strong waves.

breast *n.* **1** one of the two parts on a woman's chest that can produce milk. **2** a person's or an animal's chest.

breaststroke *n.* a style of swimming on your front.

breath *n.* the air taken into and sent out from your lungs.

Breathalyzer *n.* a device used by the police to measure the amount of alcohol in a person's blood.

breathe *v.* to take air into your lungs and let it out again.

breather *n.* (*informal*) a short rest.

breed¹ *v.* (breeding, bred) **1** (of animals) to produce young. **2** to raise animals and allow them to breed in order to sell them.

breed² *n.* a particular type of an animal. *The spaniel is a breed of dog.*

breeze *n.* a gentle wind. **breezy** *adj.*

brew *v.* **1** to make beer. **2** to make tea or coffee. **3** to start to develop. *There's a storm brewing.*

brewery *n.* a place where beer is made.

bribe¹ *n.* money or a gift given to persuade somebody to do something.

bribe² *v.* to offer a person a bribe. **bribery** *n.*

brick *n.* **1** a block of baked clay for building. **2** a rectangular block.

bride *n.* a woman who is about to get married or who has just married.

bridegroom *n.* a man who is about to get married or who has just gotten married.

bridesmaid *n.* a girl or woman who helps a bride at her wedding.

bridge *n.* **1** a structure built to allow people and vehicles to cross a road, river, or railroad track. **2** the captain's platform on a ship. **3** a card game designed to be played by four players. **4** the bony part of your nose. **5** a thin piece of wood over which the strings are stretched on a violin, guitar, or other stringed instrument. **bridge** *v.*

bridle *n.* the harness on a horse's or pony's

bridge

head, to which the reins are attached.

brief[1] *adj.* short. *a brief visit.*

brief[2] *v.* to give somebody instructions so that he or she can do something. **brief** *n.*

briefcase *n.* a flat case, usually used for carrying documents.

briefs *n. pl.* short, snug underpants.

brigade *n.* a large unit in the army.

bright *adj.* **1** shining strongly; full of light. *bright sunshine.* **2** strong and clear. *bright red.* **3** cheerful. *a bright smile.* **4** intelligent. **brightness** *n.*

brighten *v.* to make or become brighter.

brilliant *adj.* **1** very intelligent. **2** very bright. **brilliance** *n.*

brim *n.* **1** the bottom edge of a hat that sticks out. **2** the edge of a cup or glass.

brine *n.* salty water.

bring *v.* (bringing, brought) **1** to come carrying something or accompanying somebody. *Can I bring a friend to your party?* **2** to cause to come. *The news brought great happiness.* **bring about** to cause. **bring up 1** to care for a child until it is an adult; raise. **2** to mention something.

brink *n.* the edge of a cliff or other high area. **on the brink of** just about to do something.

brisk *adj.* moving quickly.

bristle *n.* a short, stiff hair. **bristly** *adj.*

brittle *adj.* hard but easily broken. *Eggshells are brittle.*

broad *adj.* wide. **broaden** *v.*

broadband *n.* a telecommunication system using signals that are sent out over several different frequencies. With broadband, using the Internet is much faster, and you can use several computers and phones at the same time.

broadcast *v.* (broadcasting, broadcast) to send out a program on the radio or television. **broadcast** *n.*

broccoli *n.* a vegetable with small, green flower heads.

brochure *(broh-sher)* *n.* a pamphlet giving information about something. *a tourism brochure.*

broke[1] *past of* break.

broke[2] *adj.* having no money left. *I'm afraid I can't come to the movies; I'm completely broke.*

broken *past participle of* break.

broker *n.* a person who buys and sells stocks and shares for other people.

bronchitis *(bron-kye-tis)* *n.* an illness that makes it difficult to breathe and that makes you cough a lot.

bronze *n.* a golden-brown metal made by mixing copper and tin. **bronze** *adj.*

brooch *(rhymes with coach)* *n.* a piece of decorative jewelry that you pin to your clothes.

brood[1] *v.* **1** (of a bird) to sit on eggs to hatch them. **2** to worry for a long time about something.

brood[2] *n.* a group of birds or other creatures hatched or born at one time.

brook *n.* a small stream.

broom *n.* a long-handled brush used for sweeping.

broth *n.* a thin soup.

brother *n.* a boy or man who has the same parents as you.

brought *past of* bring.

brow *n.* **1** a forehead. **2** an eyebrow. **3** the top of a hill.

brown *n.* the color of coffee and most types of wood. **brown** *adj.*

browse *v.* to look casually, especially at items in a store.

bruise *n.* a dark mark on your skin where it has hit against something. **bruise** *v.*

brush[1] *n.* an object with short, stiff hairs, used for making your hair neat, cleaning something, or painting.

brush[2] *v.* **1** to use a brush. **2** to touch lightly while moving close to something. *She brushed past him.*

brutal *adj.* cruel and violent. *a brutal attack.* **brutally** *adv.*

brute *n.* **1** a cruel, violent person or animal.

bubble *n.* a thin ball of liquid with air or gas inside. *soap bubbles.* **bubble** *v.*, **bubbly** *adj.*

buccaneer *n.* *(historical)* a pirate.

buck[1] *n.* **1** the male of the deer, rabbit, hare, and some other animals. **2** *(informal)* a U.S. dollar.

buck[2] *v.* (of a horse) to jump into the air with all four feet together.

bucket *n.* an open container with a handle.

buckle *n.* a fastening for connecting the ends of a belt or strap. **buckle** *v.*

bud *n.* a shoot on a plant or tree that will develop into a leaf or flower.

a
b
c
d
e
f
g
h
i
j
k
l
m
n
o
p
q
r
s
t
u
v
w
x
y
z

Buddhism *n.* an Asian religion that teaches spiritual purity and freedom from human concerns, founded in India by Buddha in the 400s B.C. **Buddhist** *adj., n.*

statue of Buddha

budge *v.* to move.

budget *n.* a plan of how money will be spent. **budget** *v.*

buffalo *n.* (*pl.* buffaloes) **1** a North American bison. **2** a large Asian ox.

buffer *n.* something that lessens the force of a crash or blow.

buffet (*buh-fay*) *n.* **1** a meal where you can help yourself to different dishes of food, usually set out on a table. **2** a piece of dining-room furniture with shelves and cupboards.

bug *n.* **1** an insect. **2** a minor illness. *a stomach bug.* **3** a mistake in a computer program. **4** a tiny, hidden microphone, usually used for secretly recording conversations. **bug** *v.*

buggy *n.* **1** a one-horse carriage. **2** a baby carriage.

bugle *n.* a brass musical instrument like a small trumpet.

build¹ *v.* (building, built) to make something by putting parts together.

build² *n.* the shape and size of a person's body. *He is of average build.*

building *n.* a structure that has been built with a roof and walls.

bulb *n.* **1** the round part of some plants that grows underground. **2** the round, glass part of an electric light.

bulge *n.* a swelling; a lump. *The apple made a bulge in her pocket.* **bulge** *v.*

bulky *adj.* (bulkier, bulkiest) large and difficult to carry.

bull *n.* the male of the cow, elephant, whale, and some other animals.

bulldog *n.* a type of strong dog with a large head and flat face.

bulldozer *n.* a machine for moving dirt and clearing land.

bullet *n.* a small piece of metal fired out of a gun.

bulletin *n.* a news announcement.

bullfight *n.* a traditional public entertainment in Spain and South America in which people fight bulls and sometimes kill them.

bullion *n.* bars of silver or gold.

bullock *n.* a castrated bull.

bull's-eye *n.* the center of a target.

bully *n.* a person who uses his or her strength or power to hurt or frighten other people. **bully** *v.*

bumblebee *n.* a type of large bee.

bump¹ *v.* to knock against something.

bump² *n.* **1** a lump or swelling. **2** a loud, heavy blow or the sound this makes.

bumblebee

bumper *n.* a bar that is attached to the front and back of a car to protect it from damage.

bumpy *adj.* (bumpier, bumpiest) uneven; having bumps. *a bumpy road.*

bun *n.* **1** a small, round, sweet piece of bread. **2** hair twisted into a round shape and fastened at the back of the head.

bunch *n.* **1** a number of things growing or held together. *a bunch of bananas, a bunch of flowers.* **2** (*informal*) a group of people.

bundle *n.* a number of things tied up together. *a bundle of sticks.*

bungalow *n.* a house built on one level.

bunk beds *n. pl.* a pair of narrow beds one above the other.

bunker *n.* **1** a strongly built

bulb

underground shelter. **2** an area filled with sand on a golf course.

buoy *(boy* or *boo-ee) n.* a floating object used as a guide or warning for ships.

buoyant *adj.* **1** able to float. **2** lively; active. *Sales of new cars were extremely buoyant this year.* **buoyancy** *n.*

burden *n.* **1** a heavy load. **2** something that is difficult to do or bear. *She worried about becoming a burden to her children in her old age.* **burden** *v.*

bureau *(byoor-oh) n. (pl.* bureaus *or* bureaux) **1** an office. **2** a writing desk.

burglar *n.* a person who breaks into a house to steal people's possessions. **burglary** *n.,* **burgle** *or* **burglarize** *v.*

burial *n.* the burying of a dead body.

burn[1] *v.* (burning, burned) **1** to destroy or damage something by heat or fire. **2** to be on fire.

burn[2] *n.* an injury or mark caused by heat or fire.

burp *v.* to make a sudden, loud noise in your throat as air rises up from your stomach, normally after eating.

burrow *n.* a hole or tunnel made in the ground by an animal for use as a shelter. **burrow** *v.*

burst[1] *v.* (bursting, burst) **1** to break open or apart suddenly; to explode. **2** to start doing something very suddenly. *He burst into tears.*

burst[2] *n.* **1** a break. *a burst in the pipe.* **2** a sudden, short period of something. *a burst of applause.*

bury *v.* (buries, burying, buried) **1** to put a dead body in the ground. **2** to hide something under the ground or under something else.

bus *n.* a large road vehicle used for carrying a lot of people.

bush *n.* **1** a large plant with a lot of thick stems. **2 the bush** an area of wild land in Africa or Australia.

bushy *adj.* (bushier, bushiest) growing thickly. *bushy eyebrows.*

business *(biz-nis) n.* **1** the making, selling, or buying of something to get money. **2** a company that makes, buys, or sells things or offers a service. **3** a thing that concerns you. *It is none of your business.*

busker *n.* a person who plays or sings in the street for money. **busk** *v.*

bust[1] *n.* **1** a woman's breasts. **2** a statue of a person's head and shoulders.

bust[2] *v. (informal)* to break.

bustle *v.* to rush around in a busy way. **bustle** *n.*

busy *adj.* (busier, busiest) **1** having a lot to do. **2** full of traffic or people. *a busy street.* **3** engaged. *The phone was busy.* **busily** *adv.*

butcher *n.* a person whose job is cutting up and selling meat.

butler *n.* the chief male servant of a house.

butt[1] *n.* **1** a barrel. *a water butt.* **2** the handle end of a gun. **3** the end of a cigarette left after it has been smoked. **4** *(informal)* a person's buttocks.

butt[2] *v.* to hit with the head or horns. *The goat butted him in the stomach.*

butter *n.* a soft, yellow food made from cream, used for cooking and for spreading onto bread.

buttercup *n.* a small, yellow wildflower.

butterfly *n.* an insect with large, often patterned, wings.

butterfly

buttocks *n. pl.* the two fleshy parts that make up your bottom.

button *n.* **1** a small, round object used for fastening parts of clothing together. **2** a small part of a machine that you press to make it work.

buy *v.* (buying, bought) to get something by paying money for it.

buzz *v.* to make a humming noise like a bee. **buzz** *n.*

buzzard *n.* a large bird of prey.

bypass *n.* a road that goes around a town instead of passing through it.

by-product *n.* a substance or product obtained or formed during the making of something else.

byte *n.* a unit for measuring the amount of memory or information in a computer.

a
b
c
d
e
f
g
h
i
j
k
l
m
n
o
p
q
r
s
t
u
v
w
x
y
z

Cc

cab *n.* **1** a taxicab. **2** the part of a truck, bus, or train where the driver sits.

cabbage *n.* a large, round vegetable with large green or purple leaves.

cabin *n.* **1** a room in a ship or the passenger section of an aircraft. **2** a small, simple house, usually wooden.

cabinet *n.* a cupboard.

cable *n.* **1** strong, thick rope or wire. **2** a set of wires carrying electricity or telephone signals.

cable car *n.* a box-shaped vehicle hanging from a moving cable, for carrying people up and down mountains or across valleys.

cable television *n.* television shows that are sent along cables, rather than transmitted by radio signals.

cackle *n.* **1** the sound made by a hen. **2** a loud, unpleasant laugh. **cackle** *v.*

cactus *n.* (*pl.* cacti *or* cactuses) a prickly desert plant with a thick stem.

cactus

cadet *n.* a person training to become a member of the armed forces or the police.

café *(kaf-ay)* *n.* a type of small restaurant where coffee, tea, and snacks are served.

cage *n.* a box with bars, in which birds or animals are kept.

cake *n.* **1** a sweet food made from flour, butter, eggs, and sugar and baked in an oven. **2** a block of soap.

caked *adj.* covered with a thick layer of something that gets hard when it dries.

calamity *n.* a disaster.

calcium *n.* a chemical element found in minerals such as limestone and chalk, as well as in teeth and bones.

calculate *v.* to figure out an answer using math. **calculation** *n.*

calculator *n.* an electronic machine for doing math.

calendar *n.* a list of the days, weeks, and months of the year.

calf *(rhymes with* half*)* *n.* (*pl.* calves) **1** a young cow, seal, elephant, or whale. **2** the back part of your leg below the knee.

call *v.* **1** to shout to somebody to get that person to come to you. **2** to give somebody a nickname. *They call him Tiny.* **3** to telephone. **call off** to cancel. **call** *n.*, **caller** *n.*

calligraphy *(ka-lig-raf-ee)* *n.* handwriting as an art.

calling *n.* a profession or occupation.

callous *adj.* cruel and heartless.

calm *(rhymes with* arm*)* *adj.* **1** quiet; still. *a calm sea.* **2** relaxed; not excited or anxious. *Stay calm!* **calm** *v.*, **calm** *n.*

calorie *n.* a unit for measuring the amount of energy that is provided by food.

calves *plural of* calf.

camcorder *n.* a portable video camera and sound recorder.

came *past of* come.

camel *n.* an animal with one or two humps on its back, often used to carry goods and people across the desert.

camera *n.* an instrument for taking photographs or filming a movie.

camouflage *v.* to disguise something by making it look like other things that are around it. Animals in the wild are camouflaged to blend in with their surroundings so that they can hide from predators. **camouflage** *n.*

camp[1] *n.* a place where people stay in tents or huts for a while.

camp[2] *v.* to live in a tent for a while.

campaign *n.* an organized series of actions planned in order to achieve a particular result.

camper *n.* **1** a person who camps. **2** a portable dwelling.

campus *n.* the grounds and buildings of a college or university.

can[1] *v.* (could) **1** to be able to. *Can you swim?* **2** to be allowed to. *You can* *borrow my bike.*

can² *n.* a metal container for food or a drink; a tin.

canal *n.* an artificial waterway.

canary *n.* a small, yellow songbird that is often kept in a cage as a pet.

cancel *v.* (canceling, canceled) to stop something that has been arranged from happening. *The football game was canceled.* **cancellation** *n.*

cancer *n.* a serious disease that makes some abnormal body cells grow too fast.

candid *adj.* openly saying what you think; honest. **candor** *n.*

candidate *n.* a person who takes part in a competition, especially for election to the government or for a job.

candle *n.* a stick of wax with a wick through the middle, burned to give light.

candlestick *n.* a holder for a candle.

candy *n.* a sweet food made from sugar and flavoring.

cane *n.* 1 a long, hollow stem of a plant such as bamboo. 2 a walking stick.

canine¹ *adj.* to do with dogs.

canine² *n.* a pointed tooth close to the front of the mouth.

canned *adj.* put in cans; tinned. *canned peas.*

cannibal *n.* *(historical)* a person who eats human flesh. **cannibalism** *n.*

cannon *n.* a big, heavy gun.

cannot can not.

canoe *n.* a light, narrow boat that is moved through the water with paddles.

canopy *n.* a cloth covering hung over a throne or bed.

can't *contr.* can not.

canteen *n.* 1 a snack bar or cafeteria in a factory or other place of work. 2 a container for carrying water.

canter *v.* to gallop at an easy pace. **canter** *n.*

canvas *n.* a coarse cloth used for tents, sails, or shoes and as a surface for painting pictures on.

canvass *v.* to go around asking people to vote for your political party, or to conduct a survey.

canyon *n.* a long valley with very steep sides, usually with a river flowing through it.

cap *n.* 1 a soft, flat hat with a peak at the front. 2 a lid.

capable *adj.* able to do something. **capability** *n.*

capacity *n.* 1 the amount that something can hold, often expressed as cubic feet. 2 the power or ability to do something.

cape *n.* 1 a short cloak. 2 a piece of land that juts out into the ocean.

capital *n.* 1 the city where the government of a country is. 2 (*also* **capital letter**) a large letter. Capitals are used at the beginning of names and sentences. *A, B, and C are capitals.* 3 money invested to make more money or to start a business.

capital punishment *n.* punishment of a crime by legally killing the criminal.

capsize *v.* to turn upside down in the water. *The boat capsized.*

capsule *n.* 1 a small pill containing medicine, which you swallow whole. 2 a part of a spacecraft that is designed to separate and travel on its own.

captain *n.* 1 the officer in charge of a ship or aircraft. 2 a senior army officer. 3 the leader of a sports team.

caption *n.* the words close to a picture that explain what it is.

captivate *v.* to fascinate somebody.

captive *n.* a prisoner; a captured person or animal. **captivity** *n.*

captor *n.* a person who captures another person or an animal.

capture *v.* 1 to take somebody prisoner. 2 to take something by force.

car *n.* 1 a vehicle with an engine and four wheels, for carrying a small number of people. 2 one of the parts of a train in which passsengers or freight are carried.

caramel *n.* 1 a type of chewy candy. 2 burned sugar used as a flavoring.

carat *n.* 1 a unit for measuring the purity of gold. 2 a unit for measuring the weight of precious stones.

caravan

caravan *n.* 1 a home on wheels, pulled by a car. 2 a group of people and animals traveling together across a desert.

A
B
C
D
E
F
G
H
I
J
K
L
M
N
O
P
Q
R
S
T
U
V
W
X
Y
Z

carbohydrate *n.* a substance found in foods such as bread, potatoes, and pasta that provides the body with energy.

carbon *n.* an important chemical element found in diamonds, charcoal, and in all living things.

carbon dioxide *n.* a gas that is present in the air, breathed out by humans and animals. Plants and trees absorb it.

carbon monoxide *n.* a poisonous gas with no smell, found in car exhaust fumes.

carburetor *n.* the part of a vehicle's engine where gasoline is mixed with air.

carcass *n.* the body of a dead animal.

card *n.* **1** a piece of stiff paper with a picture or message on it. *a birthday card.* **2** a piece of plastic with your information on it. *a credit card.* **3** a playing card. **4** a post card.

cardboard *n.* thick, stiff paper.

cardiac *adj.* to do with the heart.

cardigan *n.* a knitted woolen jacket.

cardinal *n.* a senior priest in the Roman Catholic Church.

care¹ *v.* **1** to think that something is important or interesting; to feel concerned about something. **2** to mind or be upset about something. *I don't care what you say.* **care for 1** to take care of someone or something. **2** to love somebody.

care² *n.* **1** the process of caring for someone. **2** great attention. *The label says "Handle with care."* **3** a worry. **take care** to be careful. **take care of** to look after.

career¹ *n.* a job or profession that a person has for a long time. *a career in teaching.*

career² *v.* to move fast and in an uncontrolled way.

careful *adj.* taking great care; paying attention. **carefully** *adv.*

careless *adj.* not paying enough attention to what you do; sloppy. **carelessness** *n.*

caress *v.* to touch gently and lovingly.

caretaker *n.* a person who takes care of a large building such as a school.

cargo *n.* (*pl.* cargoes) goods carried by a ship, truck, train, or aircraft.

caricature *n.* a drawing of somebody with their most distinctive features exaggerated in an amusing way.

carnation *n.* a garden flower.

carnival *n.* a public festival with street processions, colorful costumes, and singing and dancing.

carnivore *n.* an animal that eats meat. **carnivorous** *adj.*

carol *n.* a Christian religious song of joy, especially sung at Christmas.

carp

carp *n.* a large freshwater fish.

carpenter *n.* a person who makes things from wood. **carpentry** *n.*

carpet *n.* a thick, soft floor covering, made of wool or a similar material.

carriage *n.* **1** a vehicle pulled by horses or ponies. **2** posture.

carrion *n.* the dead and decaying body of an animal.

carrot *n.* an orange-colored root vegetable.

carry *v.* (carries, carrying, carried) **1** to hold something and take it to another place. **2** (of a sound) to be able to be heard at a distance. **carry on** to continue. **carry out** to succeed in doing something.

cart *n.* a wooden vehicle pulled by a horse, an ox, or some other animal.

cartilage (*kar*-til-ij) *n.* a strong, flexible material in your body, found especially around your joints.

carton *n.* a plastic or cardboard box, especially for food or drink.

cartoon *n.* **1** a funny drawing in a newspaper or magazine. **2** a movie made by photographing a series of drawings, in which the characters appear to move. **cartoonist** *n.*

cartridge *n.* **1** a case containing the explosive that fires a bullet from a gun. **2** a small, closed container for ink.

cartwheel *n.* a somersault in which you fall sideways, stand on your hands, and then bring your legs over, finally returning to a standing position.

carve *v.* **1** to shape a piece of wood or stone. **2** to slice meat to serve at a meal. **carving** *n.*

cascade¹ *n.* a waterfall.

cascade² *v.* to pour down like a waterfall.

case *n.* **1** a box for carrying things or storing them. **2** an example; an instance. *a case of mistaken identity.* **3** a matter that needs to be investigated, especially one to be decided in a court of law.

cash[1] *n.* money in paper bills and coins.

cash[2] *v.* to exchange a check for money.

cashier *n.* a person who receives and pays out money in a bank, store, or other business.

cashmere *n.* a very fine, soft wool that comes from goats.

casino *n.* (*pl.* casinos) a building where people play gambling games.

cask *n.* a wooden barrel, often used for storing alcoholic drinks.

casket *n.* **1** a small box for jewels. **2** a fancy coffin.

casserole *n.* **1** a dish made by cooking meat or vegetables in liquid inside of an oven. **2** a container with a lid, in which food is cooked.

cassette *n.* a plastic case containing magnetic tape used for recording and playing back sounds and music.

cassock *n.* a long robe, usually black, worn by some Christian priests.

cast[1] *v.* (casting, cast) **1** to throw or direct something. *The Moon cast a pale light over the garden.* **2** to give somebody a part in a play or movie. **3** to pour liquid metal into a mold, where it will set.

cast[2] *n.* **1** all the people who take part in performing a play or movie. **2** something made in a mold.

castanets *n. pl.* a Spanish wooden percussion instrument that makes a clicking sound. Often used in the performance of flamenco.

castaway *n.* (*pl.* castaways) a person whose boat has been shipwrecked.

castle *n.* **1** a large building with thick, high walls, built to be strong against an attack. **2** a chess piece, also called a rook.

castrate *v.* to remove a male animal's testicles so that it cannot reproduce.

casual *adj.* **1** relaxed; careless or not serious. *She has a casual attitude toward work.* **2** informal. *casual clothes.* **3** not planned; happening by chance. *a casual meeting.*

casualty *n.* a person who is killed or injured in a war or an accident.

cat *n.* **1** a furry animal often kept as a pet. **2** one of the group of large wild animals that includes lions and tigers.

catacombs (*kat-a-komes*) *n. pl.* an underground burial chamber.

catalog *n.* a list of things such as the books in a library or the items in a store.

catalyst (*kat-a-list*) *n.* **1** a substance that speeds up a chemical reaction. **2** something that causes a change.

catamaran *n.* a boat that looks like two boats that have been connected together side by side.

catapult *n.* a "Y"-shaped stick with a piece of elastic attached to it, for shooting stones.

cataract *n.* **1** a condition of the eye that causes blindness. **2** a waterfall.

catarrh (*kat-ar*) *n.* the thick liquid that forms in your nose and throat when you have a cold.

catastrophe (*kat-as-trof-ee*) *n.* a great disaster. **catastrophic** (*kat-a-strof-ik*) *adj.*

catch[1] *v.* (catching, caught) **1** to get hold of something that is moving. *I caught the ball.* **2** to be early enough for a bus, train, or other public vehicle. **3** to get an illness. *catch a cold.* **4** to notice somebody doing something wrong. *The store detective caught her stealing the sweater.* **5** to hit something hard. *The ball caught her on the chin.* **6** to hear something. *I didn't catch what he said.* **catch on** to become popular. **catch up 1** to reach or pass somebody in front, after following. **2** to spend time doing something that you should have done before. *She has a lot of homework to catch up on.*

catch[2] *n.* **1** an act of catching something. **2** a small device that is used to keep a door or box closed. **3** a hidden difficulty or problem.

castle

A

B

C

D

E

F

G

H

I

J

K

L

M

N

O

P

Q

R

S

T

U

V

W

X

Y

Z

catching *adj.* (of a disease) spreading very quickly; infectious.

catch phrase *n.* a phrase that becomes popular for a time, usually because a famous person has said it.

catchy *adj.* (catchier, catchiest) easy to remember. *a catchy tune.*

category *n.* a class or group.

caterpillar *n.* the larval stage in the growth of a butterfly or moth.

cathedral *n.* the main church in an area with a bishop in charge of it.

Catholic *n.* a member of the part of the Christian Church that has the Pope as its leader. Also called a Roman Catholic. **Catholic** *adj.*

catkin *n.* the hanging, fluffy flower of willows, birches, and oaks.

cattle *n. pl.* cows, bulls, and oxen.

caught *past of* catch.

cauliflower *n.* a vegetable with large, green leaves surrounding the edible round, white part in the middle.

cause[1] *v.* to make something happen.

cause[2] *n.* **1** what makes something happen. *Have they found the cause of the explosion?* **2** an aim that a person or group supports. *The money was donated to a good cause.*

causeway *n.* (*pl.* causeways) a raised path crossing marshland or water.

caution[1] *n.* care; attention. *Proceed with caution.*

caution[2] *v.* to give somebody a formal warning.

cautious *adj.* careful.

cavalry *n.* **1** soldiers in tanks and armored vehicles. **2** *(historical)* soldiers on horseback.

cave *n.* a large hole in the side of a hill or cliff or underground.

caveman *n.* (*pl.* cavemen) *(historical)* a person who lived in a cave in prehistoric times.

cavern *n.* a large, deep cave.

caviar *n.* the salted eggs of a large fish called a sturgeon, eaten as a delicacy.

cavity *n.* a space or hole located inside of something solid.

CD *short for* compact disk.

CD-ROM *n.* (*short for* compact disk, read-only memory) a disk that stores large amounts of information that you can see on a computer screen but cannot alter.

cease *v.* to stop.

cedar *n.* a large evergreen tree.

ceiling *n.* the inner roof of a room.

celebrate *v.* to have a party or do something else to mark an occasion as special. **celebration** *n.*

celebrity *n.* a famous person.

celery *n.* a vegetable with long, crisp stalks, often eaten raw.

cell *n.* **1** a very small unit of living matter found in animals and plants. **2** a very small room in a prison, monastery, or convent. **cellular** *adj.*

cellar *n.* an underground room, often used for storing things.

cello *(chel-o) n.* (*pl* .cellos) a stringed instrument like a large violin that you sit down to play. **cellist** *n.*

cell phone *n.* a mobile telephone that uses a network of short-range transmitters.

cellulose *n.* the main substance present in the cell walls of plants.

Celsius *adj. another word for* centigrade.

cement *n.* a gray powder that becomes hard when mixed with water. Cement is used in building.

cemetery *n.* a place where the dead are taken to be buried.

censor *v.* to remove from books or movies anything that might offend. **censorship** *n.*

census *n.* an official counting of all the people in a country or in an area.

cent *n.* a coin used in many countries of the world, including the U.S. and many European countries. *There are 100 cents in a dollar.*

centenary *n.* the hundredth anniversary of something.

center *n.* **1** the middle point of something. **2** a building where people meet for a particular activity. *a community center.*

centi- *prefix* one hundred, one hundredth. *centimeter (= one hundredth of a meter).*

centigrade *adj.* a measure on the temperature scale where water freezes at 0 degrees and boils at 100 degrees.

centimeter *n.* a measure of length. *One centimeter is one hundredth of a meter.*

centipede *n.* a small creature with a long body and many legs.

central *adj.* **1** at or near the center. **2** main; most important. **centrally** *adv.*

centurion *n.* *(historical)* an officer in the ancient Roman army.

century *n.* 100 years.

ceramic *adj.* made of baked clay.

ceramics *n. pl.* ceramic objects.

cereal *n.* **1** a grain crop such as corn, rice, or wheat used for food. **2** a breakfast food made from grain.

ceremonial *adj.* with ceremony; formal.

ceremony *n.* a formal event such as a wedding, funeral, or coronation.

certain *adj.* **1** sure. *Are you certain that you locked the door?* **2** particular and, though known, not named. *a certain person I know.* **certainty** *n.*

certificate *n.* a piece of paper that is official proof of something. *a birth certificate.*

CFC *n.* *(short for* chlorofluorocarbon*)* a gas that damages the ozone layer.

chaff *n.* the outer parts of grain that need to be removed before the grain is able to be used as food.

chain *n.* a line of metal rings, called links, that are connected together.

chair *n.* a piece of furniture designed for sitting on.

chalet *(shall-ay)* *n.* a small, wooden house, found especially in alpine regions.

chalk *n.* **1** a soft, white rock. **2** a piece of soft, white rock used for writing on blackboards, usually in schools.

challenge *v.* **1** to invite somebody to take part in a fight or contest. *to challenge somebody to a race.* **2** to question whether something is true. *She challenged my statement.* **challenge** *n.*

chamber *n.* **1** a large, formal room or hall. **2** *(historical)* a room.

chameleon *(ka-mee-lee-un)* *n.* a lizard that is able to change color to match its surroundings.

champagne *(sham-pain)* *n.* white wine with lots of bubbles in it.

champion¹ *n.* a person who has beaten everyone else.

champion² *v.* to strongly support a particular cause.

championship *n.* a competition to find the best person or team.

chance *n.* **1** a possibility of something happening. *They have no chance of winning.* **2** an opportunity to do something. *She had a chance to meet the president.* **3** luck; something that

happens that you cannot control. *We met by chance.* **take a chance** to take a risk.

chancellor *n.* the head of an organization or the name given to the leader of some countries, including Germany.

change¹ *v.* **1** to become different or to make something different. **2** to put on different clothes. *Let me change before we go out.* **3** to get off one train or bus and get onto another.

change² *n.* **1** the money given back when you give too much money for something. **2** something different from what is usual. *We usually go to school by car, but today we're walking, for a change.* **changeable** *adj.*

channel *n.* **1** a narrow stretch of water connecting two larger bodies of water. **2** a narrow passage for water to run through. **3** a television station.

Chanukah *another spelling of* Hanukkah.

chant *v.* **1** to say the same word or group of words over and over again. **2** to sing a religious song or prayer. **chant** *n.*

chaos *(kay-os)* *n.* complete confusion. **chaotic** *adj.*

chapel *n.* a small church or part of a larger church.

chaplain *n.* a clergyman or clergywoman who works in a school, hospital, or prison.

chapter *n.* one section of a book.

char *v.* (charring, charred) to burn something until it is black.

character *n.* **1** the type of person that you are. **2** one of the people in a book or play. *Hagrid is a character in the Harry Potter books.* **3** a letter, number, or other symbol used in printing.

characteristic¹ *n.* a quality or feature that is typical of something and that makes it different from other things.

characteristic² *adj.* typical.

charcoal *n.* a black substance made by burning wood without much air.

charge¹ *v.* **1** to ask a certain price for something. **2** to rush forward in an aggressive way. *She angrily charged into the store and demanded her money back.* **3** to formally accuse somebody of doing something wrong. *He was arrested and charged with murder.* **4** to pass an electrical current through a battery to give it power.

charge[2] *n.* **1** a price or fee. **2** a formal statement accusing somebody of a crime. **3** an attack. **4** the electricity carried by something. **in charge of** having control of and being responsible for something.

chariot *n. (historical)* a horse-drawn vehicle used for fighting and racing.

charity *n.* **1** an organization that raises money to help people in need. **2** help given to people in need. **charitable** *adj.*

charm *n.* **1** the power of attracting or delighting. **2** an object that is believed

chariot

to have magical powers. **charm** *v.*

charming *adj.* pleasant and attractive.

chart *n.* **1** a table that provides information about something. **2** a map for sailors. **chart** *v.*

charter *n.* a written statement of rights or permission to do something.

chase *v.* to run after and try to catch somebody or something.

chasm (*kaz-um*) *n.* a deep gap in the ground.

chat *v.* (chatting, chatted) to talk in a friendly way. **chat** *n.*, **chatty** *adj.*

chat room *n.* an area on the Internet where you can discuss things with other people.

chateau (*sha-toe*) *n.* (*pl.* chateaus or chateaux) a castle or mansion in France.

chatter *v.* **1** to talk quickly and continuously about unimportant things. **2** (of teeth) to knock together repeatedly because you are cold or afraid.

chauffeur (*show-fur*) *n.* a person paid to drive his or her employer's car.

cheap *adj.* not expensive; low in price.

cheat[1] *v.* to act dishonestly in order to get something for yourself.

cheat[2] *n.* a person who cheats.

check[1] *v.* **1** to make sure that something is right. *Check your spelling.* **2** to stop or hold back for a short time. *He almost screamed, but he checked himself in time.*

check[2] *n.* **1** a test to check something. **2** a pattern made up of squares. **3** a piece of paper that, when filled in and signed, tells a bank to pay money to somebody.

checkers *n.* a game played with counters on a board that has black-and-white squares.

check in *n.* a desk at an airport where you go to show your ticket before getting on a plane. **check in** *v.*

check out *n.* a counter in a supermarket where you pay for what you buy.

checkup *n.* an examination by a doctor to make sure that you are healthy.

cheek *n.* the side of your face, below your eye.

cheeky *adj.* (cheekier, cheekiest) rude and disrespectful. **cheekily** *adv.*

cheer *v.* **1** to shout encouragement or approval. **2** to make somebody happier or less worried. **cheer up** to make or become happier.

cheerful *adj.* looking and feeling happy.

cheese *n.* a solid food made from milk.

cheetah *n.* a wild cat with a spotted coat, found in Africa and Asia. Cheetahs can run very fast.

chef (*sheff*) *n.* a head cook in a restaurant or hotel.

chemical[1] *n.* a substance used in chemistry. *Bleach contains a number of dangerous chemicals.*

chemical[2] *adj.* to do with chemistry; made by chemistry.

chemist *n.* a scientist who studies or works in chemistry.

chemistry *n.* a branch of science that is about what substances are made of and how they work together.

cherish *v.* to value highly; to care for something or someone lovingly.

cherry *n.* a small, round, usually red fruit with a pit.

chess *n.* a game for two people, each with 16 pieces, called chess pieces, played on a board with black-and-white squares.

chest *n.* **1** the top part of the front of your body. **2** a large, strong box with a lid. **chest of drawers** a piece of furniture with drawers.

chestnut *n.* **1** a large tree with prickly fruits containing shiny, reddish-brown nuts. **2** this edible nut.

chew *v.* to break up food in your mouth with your teeth.

chewing gum *n.* a type of candy that you chew for a long time but do not swallow.

chick *n.* a very young bird.

chicken *n.* **1** a young hen. **2** the meat from a young hen. **3** a coward.

chickenpox *n.* a disease that causes red, itchy spots on your skin.

chief[1] *n.* a ruler or leader.

chief[2] *adj.* most important; main.

child *n.* (*pl.* children) **1** a young boy or girl. **2** somebody's son or daughter.

childhood *n.* the time in your life when you are a child.

childish *adj.* like a child; silly; immature. **childishness** *n.*

children *plural of* child.

chili *n.* **1** a small, red or green pod from a type of pepper that gives a hot, spicy taste to food. **2** chili con carne.

chill[1] *v.* to make something cold.

chill[2] *n.* **1** a feeling of coldness. **2** a slight cold or fever.

chilly *adj.* (chillier, chilliest) rather cold.

chime *v.* to make a ringing sound, like a bell. **chime** *n.*

chimney *n.* (*pl.* chimneys) a type of pipe in a building that allows the smoke from a fire to escape.

chimpanzee *n.* an African ape.

chin *n.* the part of your face located below your mouth.

china *n.* **1** very thin, fine pottery. **2** cups, plates, and dishes made from this.

chink *n.* **1** a narrow opening; a gap. **2** a light, ringing sound, like that of glasses hitting together; clink.

chip[1] *n.* **1** a potato chip. **2** a tiny electronic device made from silicon, which can hold a lot of information and is used in computers. **3** a small piece broken off something.

chip[2] *v.* (chipping, chipped) to break a small piece off something.

chipmunk *n.* a small member of the squirrel family.

chirp *v.* to make short, high sounds like a bird. **chirp** *n.*

chisel *n.* a sharp tool used for shaping wood or stone. **chisel** *v.*

chivalry (*shiv-ul-ree*) *n.* **1** polite and helpful behavior. **2** (*historical*) the rules of behavior that knights in the Middle Ages were expected to follow.

chivalrous *adj.*

chive *n.* an herb related to the onion.

chlorine (*klor-een*) *n.* a strong-smelling gas that is used to kill germs in water and to make cleaning products.

chlorophyll (*klor-o-fill*) *n.* the green coloring in plants' cells that allows them to absorb energy from sunlight.

chocolate *n.* a brown candy made from the ground, roasted seeds of the cacao tree.

choice *n.* **1** an act of choosing. **2** a thing or person that is chosen. *a good choice*. **3** all the things that you can choose from. *You can buy this car in a wide choice of colors.*

choir (*kwire*) *n.* a group of people trained to sing together.

choke *v.* **1** to be unable to breathe because something is blocking your throat and stopping air from entering your lungs.

cholesterol (*ko-lest-er-ol*) *n.* a fatty substance found in most body tissue, including the blood.

choose *v.* (choosing, chose, chosen) **1** to make a choice between two or more possibilities. **2** to decide.

chop[1] *v.* (chopping, chopped) to cut into pieces with an ax or a knife.

chop[2] *n.* a thick slice of lamb or pork with a piece of bone in it.

chopsticks *n. pl.* a pair of sticks used for eating, especially in China and Japan.

choral (*kor-al*) *adj.* sung by a choir. *choral music.*

chord (*kord*) *n.* **1** a group of musical notes sung or played together. **2** a straight line connecting any two points on a curve. See **circle**.

chore *n.* a boring task.

choreography (*kor-ee-og-ra-fee*) *n.* the art of arranging the steps and movements of a dance. **choreographer** *n.*

chorus (*kawr-us*) *n.* **1** the part of a song that is repeated after each verse. **2** a choir. **3** music for a choir.

christen *v.* to give a name to a baby and accept him or her into the Christian Church in a special ceremony.

christening *n.* a ceremony in which a child is given a name and accepted into the Christian Church.

Christian *n.* a person who believes in and follows the teachings of Jesus Christ. **Christian** *adj.*

a
b
c
d
e
f
g
h
i
j
k
l
m
n
o
p
q
r
s
t
u
v
w
x
y
z

A

B

C

D

E

F

G

H

I

J

K

L

M

N

O

P

Q

R

S

T

U

V

W

X

Y

Z

Christianity *n.* the religion based on the teachings of Jesus Christ.

Christmas *n.* December 25, when Christians celebrate the birth of Jesus.

chrome *n.* a metal coated with chromium.

chromium *n.* a hard, silver-colored metal.

chromosome (*krom-uh-soam*) *n.* a part of a cell in an animal or a plant, containing parts called genes that determine the animal's or plant's characteristics.

chronic *adj.* **1** (of an illness) lasting for a long time. *chronic asthma.* **2** *(informal)* very bad. **chronically** *adv.*

chronicle (*kron-ik-ul*) *n.* a record of events in the order in which they happened. **chronicle** *v.*

chronological *adj.* in the order in which events happened. **chronologically** *adv.*

chrysalis (*kriss-a-liss*) *n.* a stage between caterpillar and adult in the development of a moth or butterfly.

chrysanthemum (*kri-santh-em-um*) *n.* a garden flower.

chubby *adj.* (chubbier, chubbiest) slightly fat.

chuck *v.* **1** *(informal)* to throw something in a careless way. **2** to give up.

chuckle *v.* to laugh quietly.

chunk *n.* a thick piece of something. *chunks of meat.*

church *n.* a building where Christians pray.

churchyard *n.* the land around a church, often where people are buried.

churn *n.* a container in which cream is shaken around to make butter. **churn** *v.* **churn out** to produce something in large amounts. *The factory churns out cheap toys.*

chutney *n.* a food made from fruits or vegetables with vinegar, sugar, and spices. It is usually eaten cold with meat, cheese, or curry.

cider *n.* a drink made from apples.

cigar *n.* tobacco rolled in a tobacco leaf for smoking.

cigarette *n.* tobacco rolled in thin paper for smoking.

cinder *n.* a piece of partially burned coal or wood.

cinnamon *n.* a spice obtained from the bark of an Asian tree.

cipher *n.* a secret code. (*can also be spelled* cypher.)

circa *prep.* the Latin word for "around," used with dates. You can also write circa as "c." *He died circa 1782* or *He died c. 1782.*

circle[1] *n.* **1** a perfectly round, flat shape or a curved line around this shape. **2** anything in the shape of a circle. **3** the upper floor of seats in a theater.

circle[2] *v.* to make a circle around something. *Circle the correct answer.*

circuit *n.* **1** a circular racecourse. **2** the

circle

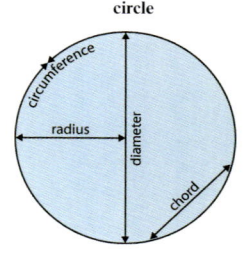

complete path of an electric current.

circular[1] *adj.* **1** in the shape of a circle; round. **2** beginning and ending at the same point. *a circular driveway.*

circulate *v.* to move or send around. *Blood circulates through your body.*

circulation *n.* **1** the movement of blood around the body. **2** the number of copies of a newspaper or magazine that have been sold.

circumcision *n.* the cutting away of loose skin at the end of a boy's or a man's penis for religious or medical reasons.

circumference *n.* the distance around the outside of a circle.

circumstance *n.* a fact or condition connected with something. *He died in mysterious circumstances.*

circus *n.* a traveling show with clowns, acrobats, animals, and other acts, usually performed in a tent.

cistern *n.* a water tank.

citadel *n.* *(historical)* a fortress protecting a city.

citizen *n.* **1** a person who has the legal right to live in a particular country. *She is an American citizen.* **2** a person who lives in a town or city.

citrus fruit *n.* a juicy fruit such as an orange, lemon, or lime.

city *n.* a large or important town.

citrus fruit

civil *adj.* **1** when something has to do with the citizens of a country. **2** to do with ordinary people, not the armed forces. **3** polite. *Please try to be civil.*

civilian *n.* a person who is not in the armed forces. **civilian** *adj.*

civilization *n.* a human society that is highly developed and organized.

civilized *adj.* **1** (of a society) highly developed and well organized. **2** polite; showing good manners.

civil servant *n.* a person who works for any of the government departments that are not legislative, judicial, or military (the **civil service**).

civil war *n.* a war between groups of people within the same country.

claim *v.* **1** to say that something is yours. *You should claim your prize.* **2** to say that something is true. *He claims that he's a millionaire.* **claim** *n.*

clamber *v.* to climb using both your hands and your feet.

clammy *adj.* (clammier, clammiest) damp and sticky.

clamp *n.* a metal object for holding things in place. **clamp** *v.*

clan *n.* a large group of related families.

clap[1] *v.* (clapping, clapped) to hit the palms of your hands together to make a noise, often to show appreciation.

clap[2] *n.* **1** an act of clapping. **2** the sudden loud noise made by thunder.

clarify *v.* (clarifies, clarifying, clarified) to make something easier to understand. **clarification** *n.*

clarinet *n.* a woodwind instrument with a single reed.

clarity *n.* clearness.

clash *v.* **1** to fight or disagree violently. **2** to make a loud, crashing sound like metal objects being hit together. **3** (of colors) not going well together. **4** (of two events) to happen at the same time, so that you cannot attend both. *Suki's birthday party clashes with my violin lesson.* **clash** *n.*

clasp[1] *v.* to hold something tightly.

clasp[2] *n.* a small device for fastening jewelry or a bag.

class *n.* **1** a group of students who are taught together. **2** a school lesson.

3 a group of people or things that are alike in some way.

classic[1] *adj.* generally considered to be very good and important. *classic novels.*

classic[2] *n.* a book, movie, or other work that is generally considered to be very good and important.

classical music *n.* serious music in a style that has been used for a long time.

classify *v.* to arrange things so they are ordered into classes or groups.

classroom *n.* a room where students go to have classes.

clatter *v.* to bang together noisily, making a lot of short, loud sounds.

clause (*klawz*) *n.* **1** a part of a sentence containing a verb. **2** one section in a legal document.

claustrophobia (*klos-tro-foh-bee-yuh*) *n.* the fear of being in enclosed spaces. **claustrophobic** *adj.*

claw *n.* a curved, pointed nail on an animal's foot.

clay *n.* soft, sticky earth that becomes hard when it is baked.

clean *adj.* free from dirt and unwanted

claw

marks. **clean** *v.*

clear[1] *adj.* **1** easy to see, hear, or understand. *a clear message.* **2** easy to see through. *clear glass.* **3** free from obstacles or dangers. *Make sure that the road is clear before you cross.* **4** free of cloud or rain. *a clear sky.*

clear[2] *v.* **1** to make or become clear. **2** to jump or get over something without touching it. *The horse cleared the fence.*

clearing *n.* a small area in a forest where there are no trees growing.

clergy *n.* the people who normally conduct religious services.

clerk *n.* a worker in an office or bank who takes care of the accounts and records or is involved in the clergy.

clever *adj.* (cleverer, cleverest) **1** quick to learn; intelligent; skillful. **2** skillfully made. *a clever plan.*

cliché *(klee-shay) n.* a phrase that has been used so much that it is no longer effective or interesting.

client *n.* a customer.

cliff *n.* a very steep, high rock, especially by the ocean.

climate *n.* the usual weather that a particular place has. *a warm climate.*

climax *n.* the most exciting and important part of something.

climb *v.* to go up, sometimes using both hands and feet to hold on. **climb** *n.*, **climber** *n.*

cling *v.* (clinging, clung) to hold on tightly to something.

clinic *n.* a place where you can go for medical advice or treatment.

clip¹ *n.* **1** a small device for holding things together. *a paper clip.* **2** a short piece from a movie or TV show.

clip² *v.* (clips, clipping, clipped) **1** to fasten something to something else. **2** to cut something with scissors or shears.

clipboard *n.* a board with a clip at the top, for holding papers.

clipper *n.* *(historical)* a fast sailing ship.

clippers *n. pl.* a tool used for cutting things, especially hair.

cloak *n.* a loose coat with no sleeves.

cloakroom *n.* a place to leave your coat and belongings.

clock *n.* an instrument that shows what time it is.

clockwise *adj., adv.* going around in the same direction as the hands of a clock.

clockwork *n.* a mechanism in some clocks or toys, which makes them work when wound up with a key.

clod *n.* a lump of dirt.

clog¹ *v.* (clogs, clogging, clogged) to become blocked up.

clog² *n.* a heavy, wooden shoe, originally from the Netherlands.

cloister *n.* a covered passageway running around a quadrangle in a monastery or other similar building.

clone *n.* an animal or a plant produced in a laboratory from the cells of another animal or plant so that it is identical to the original. **clone** *v.*

close¹ *(rhymes with* doze) *adj., adv.* **1** near.

We stood close together. **2** having a good relationship. *I am close to my sister.* **3** with not much difference between the winner and loser. *a close contest.* **4** careful and thorough. *Have a closer look.* **5** uncomfortably warm; stuffy.

close² *(rhymes with* doze) *v.* **1** to shut. **2** to bring or come to an end. **close down** to close for good.

closure *n.* the closing of something.

cloth *n.* **1** a material woven or knitted from wool or cotton. **2** a piece of material used for cleaning.

clothes *n. pl.* things to wear.

clothing *n.* clothes.

cloud *n.* a gray or white mass floating in the sky, made of tiny drops of water.

clouds

cirrus —
cirrostratus

stratocumulus

cumulus —
cumulonimbus

stratus —

cloudy *adj.* (cloudier, cloudiest) **1** covered with clouds. **2** (of a liquid) not clear.

clout *v. (informal)* to hit something or someone hard, especially with the fist. **clout** *n.*

clover *n.* a very small plant with leaves divided into three parts and pink or white flowers.

clown *n.* a person in a circus who performs funny tricks.

club *n.* **1** a heavy stick with one thicker end, usually used as a weapon. **2** a stick used for hitting the ball in golf. **3** a group that people join to do things together. **4 clubs** one of the four suits in a pack of playing cards, with the symbol ♣ on them.

cluck *v.* to make a noise like a hen.

clue *n.* something that helps solve a puzzle or crime.

clump *n.* a group of things growing close together.

clumsy *adj.* (clumsier, clumsiest) awkward; lacking skill. **clumsily** *adv.*, **clumsiness** *n.*

clung *past of* cling.

cluster *n.* a group of people or things close together; a bunch. **cluster** *v.*

clutch[1] *v.* to seize or hold tightly.

clutch[2] *n.* **1** a firm hold. **2** the control in a car that you press with your foot when you want to change gears. **3** a group of eggs in a nest.

clutter *n.* a lot of things lying around in an untidy mess. **clutter** *v.*

Co. *short for* company.

co- *prefix* together; working with. *cooperate, coauthor.*

coach[1] *n.* **1** a bus used for long journeys. **2** a part of a train that carries passengers. **3** a carriage pulled by horses. **4** a sports instructor.

coach[2] *v.* to teach somebody something, especially a sport.

coal *n.* a black mineral that burns slowly and gives out heat.

coalition *(koh-a-lish-un)* *n.* the joining together of political parties for a period of time.

coarse *adj.* **1** rough in texture; not delicate. **2** rude or indecent; without social refinement. *coarse language.*

coast *n.* the land beside the ocean.

coastguard *n.* a person who watches the ocean for ships in danger.

coat[1] *n.* **1** a piece of outdoor clothing with sleeves that you wear over your other clothes. **2** a covering. *a coat of paint.* **3** an animal's fur.

coat[2] *v.* to cover with a thin layer of something. *raisins coated with chocolate.* **coating** *n.*

coat of arms *n.* a design or pattern on a shield used by some families, institutions, and countries.

coax *v.* to persuade gently. *She coaxed him into giving her the gun.*

cobblestones *n. pl.* rounded stones used for making road surfaces.

cobra *n.* a poisonous, hooded snake.

cobweb *n.* a fine net made by a spider to catch insects for food.

cock *n.* **1** a fully grown male chicken. **2** any male bird.

cockatoo *n.* a type of parrot with a crest on its head.

cockerel *n.* a young cock or rooster.

cockle *n.* a type of shellfish.

cockney *n.* (*pl.* cockneys) **1** a person from the East End of London, England. **2** the dialect spoken by such a person.

cockpit *n.* **1** the part of a plane where the pilot sits. **2** the part of a racing car where the driver sits.

cockroach *n.* a large, black beetle.

cocoa *n.* chocolate powder made from the seeds of the cacao tree.

coconut *n.* the large nut of a tree called the coco palm. Coconuts are hairy on the outside and have white flesh and juice inside.

cocoon *n.* a silky case made by a caterpillar where it turns into a moth or butterfly.

cocoon

cod *n.* (*pl.* cod or cods) a large, edible sea fish.

code *n.* **1** a way to send secret messages. **2** a set of rules.

coeducation *n.* the education of boys and girls together.

coffee *n.* a hot, brown drink made by adding water to the roasted and ground beans of the coffee plant.

coffin *n.* a box in which a dead person is buried or cremated.

cog *n.* **1** a wheel with sharp teeth around the rim, used in machinery to turn another wheel. **2** one of the teeth around the rim of such a wheel.

coil *v.* to wind something around and around to form loops or spirals. **coil** *n.*

coin *n.* a piece of metal money.

coincide *v.* to happen at the same time.

coincidence *n.* a situation when two or more things happen at the same time by chance. *It was a coincidence that Bob and Curtis were wearing the same tie.*

coke *n.* a solid, gray substance made from coal and burned as fuel.

cold[1] *adj.* **1** having a low temperature. **2** unfriendly. **cold** *n.*, **coldness** *n.*

cold[2] *n.* an illness that usually makes you sneeze and gives you a sore throat or runny nose.

a b **c** d e f g h i j k l m n o p q r s t u v w x y z

41

cold-blooded *adj.* **1** cruel and unfeeling. **2** (of fish or reptiles) having a body temperature that changes according to the surroundings.

coleslaw *n.* raw, chopped cabbage and other vegetables mixed in mayonnaise.

collaborate *v.* to work together with somebody. **collaboration** *n.*

collage *(koll-aj)* *n.* a picture made by sticking down small pieces of paper or other materials onto a surface.

collapse *v.* **1** to fall down or inward. **2** to fail completely. *The business has collapsed.* **collapse** *n.*

collapsible *adj.* folding.

collar *n.* **1** the part of a shirt or other clothing that goes around your neck. **2** a band of leather or metal put on an animal's neck.

colleague *n.* a person who works with you.

collect *v.* **1** to gather or bring together. *The teacher collected our books.* **2** to bring a number of things together because you are interested in them. *to collect stamps.* **3** to fetch. *Mom usually collects me from school.* **collection** *n.*, **collector** *n.*

collective noun *n.* a noun that refers to many people, animals, or things in a group. *Flock* and *school* are collective nouns.

college *n.* a place where people can go to study after they have left high school.

collide *v.* to crash together. *The two trucks collided on the expressway.*

collie *n.* a breed of sheepdog.

colliery *n.* a coal mine.

collision *n.* a crash.

colon *n.* **1** the punctuation mark (:) written before a list of things. **2** a section of the large intestine.

colonel *(kern-ul)* *n.* a high-ranking officer in the army, air force, or marines.

colony *n.* **1** a country that has been settled in by people from a foreign country and which is still governed by the colonizing country. **2** a group of insects or animals that live together. *a colony of ants.* **colonial** *adj.*, **colonize** *v.*

color¹ *n.* the way something looks as it reflects light of a particular wavelength. *Red, blue, and yellow are colors.*

color² *v.* to put color on something. *She colors her hair to hide the gray.*

colorful *adj.* **1** having lots of colors; bright **2** lively; full of interesting details.

colossal *adj.* huge; giant.

colt *n.* a young male horse.

column *n.* **1** a tall, round pillar. **2** a long, narrow piece of writing running down a newspaper page.

coma *n.* a state of deep unconsciousness.

combine

comb¹ *n.* a small object with a row of teeth, used for making hair neat.

comb² *v.* **1** to make hair neat with a comb. **2** to search a place thoroughly.

combat *n.* fighting, especially in a war.

combine¹ *v.* to mix together. *Combine the eggs and butter in a bowl.* **combination** *n.*

combine² *n.* a farm machine that cuts and threshes grain.

combustion *n.* burning.

come *v.* (coming, came, come) **1** to move toward a place. *Come here!* **2** to arrive. *A letter came for you today.* **3** to happen. *Friday comes before Saturday.* **4** to become. *His wish came true.* **5** to go with somebody. *I'm going out. Do you want to come too?* **6** to add up to something. *The bill for dinner came to $40.*

comedian *n.* an entertainer who makes people laugh.

comedy *n.* a funny book, play, or movie.

comet *n.* an object with a taillike trail of gas that moves around the Sun.

comfort¹ *v.* to make somebody less worried or upset.

comfort² *n.* **1** a pleasant condition of being relaxed, happy, or warm. **2** a person or thing that makes you feel better.

comfortable *adj.* **1** pleasant to sit in or wear. *a comfortable chair.* **2** at ease; free from pain or worry. *Sit down and make yourself comfortable.*

comic¹ *adj.* funny.

comic² *n.* a children's paper with stories told in pictures.

comical *adj.* funny.

comma *n.* the punctuation mark (,) used in writing to show a pause.

command *v.* **1** to order somebody to do something. **2** to be in charge of something. *He commanded a large army.* **command** *n.*

commandment *n.* an important rule or command given by God.

commemorate *v.* to do something special to remember an important event or person. **commemoration** *n.*

commence *v.* to begin.

comment *n.* a remark about somebody or something. **comment** *v.*

commentary *n.* a description of something, especially a sporting event, as it is happening.

commentator *n.* a person giving a commentary.

commerce *n.* buying and selling; trade.

commercial[1] *adj.* to do with trade.

commercial[2] *n.* an advertisement on the television or radio.

commit *v.* (committing, committed) to do; to carry out. *She committed a crime.*

committee *n.* a group of people who are chosen by others to plan and organize things for the group. *Our club's committee meets once a month to discuss upcoming events.*

common[1] *adj.* **1** found in large numbers. **2** happening often. **3** shared by two or more people or things. *characteristics common to apes and humans.* **4** ordinary; not special.

common[2] *n.* an area of grassy land where anyone can go.

common noun *n.* a noun that refers to things in general. *Table, chair,* and *animal* are examples of common nouns.

common sense *n.* sensible thinking.

communicate *v.* to pass on information, ideas, or feelings to other people.

communication *n.* the passing of information from one person to another.

communications *n. pl.* systems for linking places by transportation, telephone, or radio.

Communion *n.* a ceremony in the Christian Church at which people eat blessed bread and drink wine in memory of the death of Christ.

communism *n.* the political belief that there should be no private property and that everything should be owned by the people. **communist** *n.*

community *n.* all the people who live in a particular place.

commuter *n.* a person who travels every day to and from work. **commute** *v.*

compact *adj.* small; taking up little space.

compact disk *n.* a plastic disc containing digitally stored information or music, played on a stereo or computer.

companion *n.* a person with whom you spend time.

company *n.* **1** a business organization that makes or sells things. **2** the condition of being together with somebody. *She has her daughter for company.* **3** a gathering of people, especially guests.

comparative *n.* the form of an adjective

compass

or adverb that means "more." English comparatives often end in "-er" such as *faster* and *bigger.*

compare *v.* to look at things to see how alike or different they are. *We compared shirts.* **comparison** *n.*, **comparative** *adj.*

compartment *n.* a section separated off inside something. *The drawer has a secret compartment.*

compass *n.* **1** an instrument that shows direction, used for finding the way. **2** an instrument used for drawing circles.

compassion *n.* a feeling of pity or sympathy for somebody who is suffering. **compassionate** *adj.*

compatible *adj.* able to work or live with someone or something else without there being any problems.

compel *v.* (compelling, compelled) to force somebody to do something. *I felt compelled to tell the truth.* **compulsion** *n.*

compensate *v.* to make up for loss or an injury. **compensation** *n.*

compete *v.* to take part in a contest. *compete in a race.*

competent *adj.* able to do things efficiently and effectively. **competence** *n.*

competition *n.* a game or contest in which many people participate to see who is the best.

A
B
C
D
E
F
G
H
I
J
K
L
M
N
O
P
Q
R
S
T
U
V
W
X
Y
Z

competitive *adj.* **1** liking to compete with others. **2** organized as a competition. *competitive sports.*

competitor *n.* a person who is participating in a competition.

complain *v.* to say that you are not pleased with something. *We complained about the food.*

complaint *n.* a statement that you are not pleased with something.

complete¹ *adj.* **1** finished. **2** whole; with no parts missing. **3** total; perfect. *I felt like a complete fool.*

complete² *v.* to finish something. **completion** *n.*

complex¹ *adj.* complicated; made up of many different parts. *He's a very complex person.* **complexity** *n.*

complex² *n.* a group of buildings or a building with several different parts. *an apartment complex.*

complexion *n.* the natural color and appearance of skin on a person's face.

complicated *adj.* made up of many different parts or aspects; difficult to understand. **complication** *n.*

compliment *n.* a remark that expresses admiration. **compliment** *v.*

complimentary *adj.* **1** showing admiration. **2** given free. *complimentary tickets to the movies.*

component *n.* one of the parts that make up something. *computer components.*

compose *v.* to write a piece of music, a story, or a speech. **composed of** made up of. *Water is composed of hydrogen and oxygen.* **composition** *n.*

composer *n.* a person who writes music.

compound *n.* something made up of separate parts or elements.

comprehend *v.* to understand.

comprehensible *adj.* easy to understand.

comprehension *n.* when something has been understood.

comprehensive *adj.* including everything that is needed.

compress *v.* to press or squeeze something into a small space. **compression** *n.*

compromise *n.* an agreement between two people or groups, each giving up part of what they originally wanted. **compromise** *v.*

compulsive *adj.* unable to stop yourself. *a compulsive gambler.*

computer

compulsory *adj.* having to be done; obligatory. *English classes are compulsory in all schools.*

computer *n.* an electronic machine that stores and organizes information, solves problems, or controls other machines. **computing** *n.* **computerize** *v.*

con *v.* (conning, conned) to trick somebody. **con** *n.*

concave *adj.* curving inward, like the inside of a bowl.

conceal *v.* to hide something.

conceited *adj.* too proud of yourself.

conceive *v.* **1** to become pregnant. **2** to think up; imagine. *I can't conceive of how cold it must have been.*

concentrate *v.* **1** to give all your attention to something. **2** to make a liquid thicker or stronger by removing water from it. **concentration** *n*

concept *n.* an idea.

conception *n.* **1** the action of becoming pregnant. **2** an idea or plan.

concern¹ *n.* **1** worry. **2** something of interest to or affecting you. *That's not my concern.*

concern² *v.* **1** to have to do with; to affect. *This news doesn't concern us.* **2** to worry. *His attitude concerns me.*

concerning *prep.* about; on the subject of.

concert *n.* a musical performance.

concise *adj.* saying everything that is necessary in few words.

conclude *v.* **1** to come to an opinion, after looking at the facts. *He concluded that she must have been the thief.* **2** to finish. **conclusion** *n.*

concrete *n.* a hard building material made by mixing cement, sand, small stones, and water.

condemn *v.* **1** to say very strongly that somebody or something is wrong or very bad. **2** to sentence somebody to a punishment. **condemnation** *n.*

condense v. **1** to make something shorter. *She condensed the story into five lines.* **2** to change from a gas into a liquid. **condensation** n.

condition n. **1** the general state that somebody or something is in. *My bike is in good condition.* **2** something that must be agreed to. *You can go, on the condition that you are back for lunch.*

conduct[1] (kon-**dukt**) v. **1** to carry out. *to conduct a survey.* **2** to direct an orchestra or a choir during a performance. **3** to allow heat or electricity to pass through.

conduct[2] (**kon**-dukt) n. behavior. *He was released for good conduct.*

conductor n. **1** a person who directs an orchestra or choir. **2** a person who sells or checks tickets on a bus or train. **3** something that allows electricity or heat to pass through it.

cone n. **1** a shape or object with a circular base and a point at the top. **2** the fruit of a fir or pine tree.

confectionary n. candy.

conference n. a formal meeting at which several matters are discussed.

confess v. to admit to doing something wrong. **confession** n.

confetti n. pl. tiny pieces of colored paper that are thrown at parties and weddings.

confide v. to tell your secrets to somebody. *She confided in her sister.*

confidence n. trust or belief, especially in your own abilities.

confident adj. having confidence. *I'm confident that I can win.*

confidential adj. private; secret. **confidentially** adv.

confine v. **1** to limit; to restrict. *They confined the fire to a small area.* **2** to keep someone in a place. *He was confined to the barracks.* **confinement** n.

confirm v. to say that something is definite. *We confirmed the date of our vacation.* **be confirmed** to be fully accepted as a member of some Christian churches. **confirmation** n.

confiscate v. to take something away from somebody as a punishment. **confiscation** n.

conflict[1] (**kon**-flikt) n. a fight, war, or serious disagreement.

conflict[2] (kon-**flikt**) v. to be so different from something else that the two things cannot both exist or be true. *Joe and I had conflicting plans.*

conform v. to follow the accepted customs and rules.

confront v. to meet somebody face-to-face in order to fight or accuse that person. **confrontation** n.

confuse v. **1** to mix up somebody's ideas so that they cannot think clearly or understand. **2** to mistake one person or thing for another. *I always confuse my friend Hannah with her twin sister.* **confusion** n.

congested adj. **1** blocked up. **2** crowded with traffic. **congestion** n.

congratulate v. to tell somebody that you are glad he or she has succeeded or had good luck. **congratulation** n. **congratulations** n. pl.

congregate v. to come together in a crowd.

congregation n a group of people at a church service.

Congress n. the legislative branch of the U.S. government.

conical adj. cone-shaped.

conifer n. a tree with needlelike leaves that produces cones.

conjunction n. a word that connects two parts of a sentence or phrase. *And* and *but* are conjunctions.

conjure v. to perform clever tricks and make it seem like magic. **conjurer** (conjuror) n.

connect v. to join or fasten together. **connection** n.

conquer v. to defeat an enemy; to overcome. **conquest** n.

conscience (**kon**-shuns) n. your sense of what is right and wrong.

conscientious (kon-shee-**en**-shus) adj. careful and hard-working.

conscious (**kon**-shus) adj. awake; aware of what is happening. **consciousness** n.

consecutive adj. following one after another.

consent v. to agree to; to give permission for something. **consent** n.

consequence n. the result of something.

conservation n. taking care of nature, wildlife, or old buildings so that they are not ruined. **conservationist** n.

conservative adj. not liking great change or new ideas.

conserve v. **1** to keep something as it is without changing it. **2** to avoid wasting something. *conserve energy.*

consider *v.* to think about something.
considerable *adj.* great.
considerate *adj.* kind and thoughtful.
consideration *n.* **1** careful thought. **2** something that must be thought about carefully. **3** thoughtfulness toward other people.
consist *v.* to be made up of something.
consistent *adj.* not changing; steady.
console[1] *(kon-sole) v.* to comfort or cheer up somebody. **consolation** *n.*
console[2] *(kon-sole) n.* a control panel for operating an electronic machine.
consonant *n.* any letter of the alphabet except a, e, i, o, and u.
conspicuous *adj.* very noticeable.
conspire *v.* to plan in secret to do something illegal or wrong. **conspiracy** *n.*, **conspirator** *n.*
constant *adj.* staying the same.
constellation *n.* a group of stars forming a certain shape in the sky.
constipated *adj.* finding it difficult to empty your bowels. **constipation** *n.*
constitution *n.* **1** the laws or rules by which a country or organization is governed. **2** your general health.
construct *v.* to build. **construction** *n.*
constructive *adj.* helpful.
consult *v.* to try to get advice or help from somebody or from a book. **consultant** *n.*, **consultation** *n.*
consume *v.* **1** to eat or drink. **2** to use up. *The car consumes a lot of gas.* **3** to destroy. *Fire consumed the building.* **consumer** *n.*, **consumption** *n.*
contact[1] *n.* **1** touching. **2** communication. *I've lost contact with my old friends.*
contact[2] *v.* to get in touch with somebody.
contact lens *n.* a small, plastic lens worn on the eye to help you see better.
contagious *adj.* caught by being in contact with infected people. *a contagious disease.*
contain *v.* to have something inside. *This jar contains jelly.*
container *n.* a box, jar, or tin in which you put things.
contaminate *v.* to make something dirty or impure. **contamination** *n.*
contemplate *v.* to think about or look at something for a long time. **contemplation** *n.*
contemporary *adj.* **1** of the present time; modern. **2** happening at the same period in history.
contempt *n.* a total lack of respect.

content, contented *(kon-tent) adj.* when you are happy or satisfied.
contents *(kon-tents) n. pl.* the things that are in something.
contest *n.* a competition.
continent *n.* one of the seven main land masses of the world: North America, South America, Asia, Africa, Europe, Australia, and Antarctica. **continental** *adj.*
continual *adj.* happening again and again. *continual warnings.* **continually** *adv.*
continue *v.* to go on; to keep on. **continuation** *n.*
continuous *adj.* going on all the time; never stopping. *a continuous noise.*

continents

contour *n.* **1** an outline. **2** a line on a map connecting points of equal height.
contra- *prefix* against; opposite. *contraflow* (traveling in the opposite direction to normal).
contraception *n.* prevention of pregnancy.
contraceptive *n.* a device or drug that helps prevent pregnancy.
contract[1] *(kon-trakt) v.* to get smaller. **contraction** *n.*
contract[2] *(kon-trakt) n.* a written agreement.
contradict *v.* to say the opposite of what somebody else has said. **contradiction** *n.*
contrary *adj.* opposite.
contrast *(kon-trast) v.* to compare different things and notice the differences. **contrast** *(kon-trast) n.*
contribute *v.* to give money or help. **contribution** *n.*
control *v.* (controls, controlling, controlled) to make somebody or something do what you want. **control** *n.*
controls *n. pl.* the levers and buttons that you use to control a machine.
controversial *adj.* causing a lot of arguments or discussions.
controversy *n.* a long argument.
convalescence *n.* a time when somebody is recovering from an illness. **convalescent** *adj.*

A B C D E F G H I J K L M N O P Q R S T U V W X Y Z

convenient *adj.* **1** easy to use or reach. *Our house is very convenient for the station.* **2** suitable. *When would be a convenient time to meet?* **convenience** *n.*

convent *n.* a place where nuns live, pray, and work.

conventional *adj.* normal; ordinary. **conventionally** *adv.*

converge *v.* to come together from different directions.

conversation *n.* an informal talk between two or more people.

convert *v.* to change from one thing to another. **conversion** *n.*

convex *adj.* curved outward.

convey *v.* **1** to carry from one place to another. **2** to communicate.

convict[1] *(**kon**-vikt) n.* a person who is in prison for committing a crime.

convict[2] *(kon-**vikt**) v.* to find somebody guilty of a crime. **conviction** *n.*

convince *v.* to make somebody believe that something is true.

convoy *n.* (*pl.* convoys) a group of vehicles or ships traveling together.

cook[1] *v.* to make food ready to eat by heating. **cooking** *n.*, **cookery** *n.*

cook[2] *n.* a person who cooks.

cookie *n.* a small, flat cake made of sweetened dough.

cool[1] *adj.* **1** relatively cold. **2** calm. *Keep cool!* **3** unfriendly.

cool[2] *v.* to make or become cool.

cooperate *(koh-**op**-er-ate) v.* to work together to do something. *If we cooperate, we will finish the job sooner.* **cooperation** *n.*, **cooperative** *adj.*

cope *v.* to deal with problems successfully.

copper *n.* a reddish-brown metal.

copy[1] *n.* something made to be exactly like something else.

copy[2] *v.* (copies, copying, copied) **1** to make a copy of something. **2** to do the same as another person.

copyright *n.* the legal right to publish a book, show a movie, or play a piece of music. **copyright** *v.*

coral *n.* a hard material found on the seabed, made from the skeletons of tiny sea creatures.

cord *n.* a thin rope.

core *n.* the central part of something.

cork *n.* **1** a piece of cork used as a stopper for a bottle. **2** the light, tough outer bark of the cork oak tree.

corkscrew *n.* a tool for removing corks from bottles of wine.

corn *n.* **1** the seeds of wheat, oats, or maize, especially the yellow seeds of maize that are eaten as a vegetable. **2** a small lump of hard skin on the foot.

corner *n.* a place where two lines, roads, or walls meet.

cornet *n.* a brass musical instrument similar to a trumpet.

coronation *n.* the ceremony when a king or queen is crowned.

corporal *n.* a soldier of low ranking.

corporal punishment *n. (historical)* punishment by beating or whipping.

corps *(kor) n.* (*pl.* corps) a part of an army.

corpse *n.* a dead human body.

correct[1] *adj.* right or true; with no mistakes. *All my math equations were correct.*

correct[2] *v.* to make something right. **correction** *n.*

correspond *v.* **1** to be similar to or the same as. **2** to exchange letters or E-mails.

correspondence *n.* letters or E-mails.

corridor *n.* a long passage in a building, with rooms leading off it; hallway.

corrode *v.* to wear away by the action of rust or chemicals. **corrosion** *n.*

corrugated *adj.* shaped into regular, narrow ridges. *corrugated iron.*

corrupt *adj.* **1** morally wrong; doing illegal things in return for money. **2** (of computer data) containing errors and so useless. **corrupt** *v.*, **corruption** *n.*

cosmetics *n. pl.* beauty products such as lipstick or eyeshadow.

cosmic *adj.* to do with the universe.

cosmos *n.* the universe.

cost *v.* (costing, cost) **1** to have a certain price. **2** to cause the loss of something. *It cost me my job.* **cost** *n.*

costume *n.* **1** clothes. *18th-century costume.* **2** clothes worn by an actor in a play or movie or unusual clothes that you wear to look like another person or thing.

cot *n.* a small bed with high sides, normally for a baby.

coral

cottage *n.* a small house, usually in the country.

a b c d e f g h i j k l m n o p q r s t u v w x y z

47

cotton *n.* the soft material covering the seeds of the cotton plant. Cotton is made into cloth and thread.

couch *n.* a long, soft seat; sofa.

cough *(koff) v.* to suddenly force air out of your throat and lungs, resulting in a loud sound. **cough** *n.*

could *past of* can.

council *n.* a group of people who are chosen to serve as administrators or advisers.

count[1] *v.* **1** to say numbers in order. *Count to ten.* **2** to add up. *Count the number of people in the room.* **3** to include. *There are six people coming on the trip, if you count me.*

cotton

count[2] *n.* a European nobleman.

counter *n.* **1** a table or flat surface in a store. **2** a small, flat disk used in some board games.

counter- *prefix* against; opposing. *counteract, counterattack.*

counterclockwise *adj., adv.* going around in the opposite direction to the hands of a clock.

counterfeit *adj.* not real; fake. *counterfeit money.* **counterfeit** *n., v.*

countess *n.* **1** a woman who has the same aristocratic ranking as a count. **2** the wife of an earl or a count.

countless *adj.* too many to count.

country *n.* **1** a land with its own people and government. *France and Chile are countries.* **2** (*also* **countryside**) land away from towns and cities.

county *n.* a part of a country with its own local government.

couple *n.* **1** two; a pair. **2** two people who have a romantic relationship.

coupon *n.* a ticket that allows you to pay less for something or that you fill in to apply for something.

courage *n.* bravery.

courageous *adj.* brave.

courier *(ker-ree-er) n.* a messenger.

course *n.* **1** a series of classes. **2** one part of a meal. *the main course.* **3** a piece of ground for some sports. *a racecourse.* **4** the direction that something follows. *the course of the river.*

court *n.* **1** a place where trials are held; a law court. **2** a place where games such as tennis and squash are played. **3** where a king or queen receives visitors.

courteous *(kur-tee-us) adj.* polite. **courtesy** *n.*

courtyard *n.* a space without a roof, enclosed by walls or buildings.

cousin *n.* the child of your aunt or uncle.

cove *n.* a small bay.

cover *v.* to put something over another thing. **cover** *n.*

covering *n.* a layer that covers something.

cow *n.* a farm animal kept for its milk.

coward *n.* a person who is easily frightened and cannot hide fear. **cowardice** *n.,* **cowardly** *adj.*

cowboy, cowgirl *n.* a person who takes care of cattle, especially in the U.S.

cox *n.* a person who steers a rowboat.

cozy *adj.* (cozier, coziest) warm and comfortable. **cozily** *adv.,* **coziness** *n.*

crab *n.* a sea creature with a hard shell and ten legs, two of which have large claws called pincers.

crack[1] *v.* to break without falling into pieces. *I dropped the plate, and it cracked.*

crack[2] *n.* **1** a thin line on something that is almost broken. *There's a crack in the cup.* **2** a sharp noise.

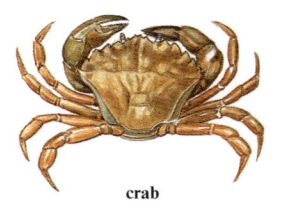

crab

cracker *n.* **1** a thin, crisp, savory wafer. **2** a paper tube that bangs when you pull it apart and that contains a small present.

crackle *v.* to make a lot of short, sharp sounds. *The dry branches crackled under my feet.*

cradle *n.* a bed for a small baby.

craft *n.* **1** skilled work with the hands. **2** a boat, spaceship, or aircraft.

craftsman, craftswoman *n.* a person who is skilled at making something.

crafty *adj.* (craftier, craftiest) cunning; sly.

cram *v.* (cramming, crammed) to push something into a small space.

cramp *n.* a sudden, painful contraction of the muscles.

cramped *adj.* too small for all the people or things that have to fit into it.

crane *n.* **1** a machine that lifts and moves heavy things. **2** a large water bird with long legs that it uses for wading.

crash[1] *v.* to hit something violently and noisily. *The car crashed into a tree, wrecking the car.*

crash[2] *n.* **1** an accident in which a vehicle hits something. **2** a sudden, loud noise. *a crash of thunder.*

crate *n.* a large, wooden box.

crater *n.* **1** the mouth of a volcano. **2** a hole in the ground caused by an explosion.

crave *v.* to have a very great desire for something.

crawl[1] *v.* to move around on your hands and knees.

crawl[2] *n.* a style of swimming in which you bring your hands over your head, one at a time, while kicking your legs.

crayon *n.* a colored wax stick for drawing and coloring.

craze *n.* a fashion that only lasts for a short period of time.

crazy *adj.* (crazier, craziest) foolish; very silly. **crazily** *adv.*

creak *v.* to make a harsh, squeaking sound. *The stairs creak when you walk on them.* **creak** *n.*, **creaky** *adj.*

cream *n.* **1** the thick, fatty part of milk. **2** a thick, smooth liquid that you put on your skin. *face cream.* **3** the yellowish-white color of cream. **creamy** *adj.*

crease *n.* a line in paper or cloth made by folding. **crease** *v.*

create *v.* to make; to bring something into existence. *Authors create characters for their stories.* **creation** *n.*

creative *adj.* good at making or thinking of original things.

creator *n.* a person who has created something. **the Creator** God.

creature *n.* any living thing that is not classified as a plant.

credit *n.* **1** praise or acknowledgment. *She did the work, but her brother got all the credit.* **2** a person or thing that brings honor. *He's a credit to his parents.* **3** being allowed to pay for something later. *They bought the TV on credit.*

credit card *n.* a plastic card used to obtain things and pay for them later.

creek *n.* **1** a small inlet in the coastline. **2** a small stream.

creep *v.* (creeping, crept) to move slowly and quietly.

cremate *v.* to burn a dead body. **cremation** *n.*

crematorium *n.* a place where bodies are taken to be cremated.

crept *past of* creep.

crescent *n.* **1** a curved shape like that of the new moon. **2** a row of houses laid out in the shape of a crescent.

crest *n.* **1** a tuft of feathers or fur on the head of a bird or other creature. **2** the highest point. *the crest of a wave.* **3** a badge on a coat of arms.

crew *n.* the team of people who work on a ship, train, or aircraft.

crib *n.* a baby's cot.

cricket[1] *n.* **1** an outdoor game played with flat bats and a ball by two teams of eleven players.

cricket[2] *n.* a small insect similar in appearance to a grasshopper.

crime *n.* something that is against the law.

criminal *n.* a person who commits a crime.

crimson *n., adj.* deep red.

cringe *v.* to back away or shrink in fear.

cripple *v.* **1** to injure someone so seriously that he or she can't move or walk properly. **2** to damage a machine.

crisis *n.* **1** a deciding moment or a worst point. **2** a difficult or dangerous time.

crisp *adj.* dry, hard, and easy to break.

critical *adj.* **1** very serious or dangerous. *He is in the hospital, and his condition is critical.* **2** criticizing. **critically** *adv.*

criticize *v.* to say what you think is wrong with somebody or something. **criticism** *n.*

croak *v.* to make a low, hoarse sound like a frog makes. **croak** *n.*

crochet *(kro-**shay**) n.* a type of knitting that is done with a hooked needle. **crochet** *v.*

crockery *n.* the collective noun for plates, cups, saucers, and other dishes.

a
b
c
d
e
f
g
h
i
j
k
l
m
n
o
p
q
r
s
t
u
v
w
x
y
z

crocodile *n.* a large, long-tailed tropical reptile that lives in rivers.

crocodile

crocus *n.* a small spring flower.

crook *n.* **1** a dishonest person. **2** a stick with a hooked end, used by shepherds.

crooked *adj.* **1** not straight; bent. **2** dishonest.

crop¹ *n.* **1** a plant grown for food, such as wheat or rice. **2** the plants that are gathered at harvest time.

crop² *v* (cropping, cropped) to cut. **crop up** to happen unexpectedly.

croquet *(krow-kay)* *n.* an outdoor game in which balls are hit through hoops with a wooden hammer.

cross¹ *n.* **1** the mark X or +. **2** the sign † used in the Christian religion. **3** a mixture of two things. *a cross between a spaniel and a poodle.*

cross² *v.* **1** to go from one side to the other. *We crossed the road.* **2** to place two things across each other. *She crossed her legs.* **3** to pass each other. *Our letters must have crossed in the mail.* **cross out** to put a line through something.

crossbow *n.* a weapon for firing arrows.

crossing *n.* a place where people can go across a street or river.

crossroads *n.* a place where two roads meet each other and cross.

cross section *n.* the flat part that you see when you cut straight through an object. *a cross section of an apple.*

crossword *n.* a word puzzle where small squares have to be filled with letters to make words.

crotchet *n.* a note in music equal to two quavers in length.

crouch *v.* to bend your knees and back so that your body is close to the ground.

crow¹ *n.* a large, black bird.

crow² *v.* to make a loud sound like a cockerel or rooster makes in the morning.

crowd *n.* a large group of people who are gathered together in one place.

crowded *adj.* containing too many people or things.

crown *n.* a circular ornament worn by kings and queens on their heads.

crucial *adj.* very important.

crucifix *n.* a model of Christ on the cross.

crucify *v.* (crucifies, crucifying, crucified) *(historical)* to kill somebody by attaching his or her hands and feet to a cross.

crude *adj.* **1** in its natural, unrefined state. *crude oil.* **2** rude and vulgar. *a crude joke.* **crudity** *n.*

cruel *adj.* (crueler, cruelest) causing pain to others in a deliberate manner. **cruelly** *adv.*, **cruelty** *n.*

cruise¹ *n.* a vacation on a ship, stopping at different ports along the way.

cruise² *v.* **1** to go on a cruise. **2** to travel at a steady speed.

crumb *n.* a very small piece of bread, cake, or cookie.

crumble *v.* to break into small pieces. **crumbly** *adj.*

crumple *v.* to make or become creased. *a crumpled piece of paper.*

crunch *v.* to crush noisily, especially with your teeth. **crunchy** *adj.*

crusade *n.* a campaign in support of a cause. **crusader** *n.*

crush¹ *v.* to press something under a heavy weight.

crush² *n.* a strong liking for somebody that usually lasts only a short time.

crust *n.* **1** the hard, outer part of bread or pastry. **2** any hard, outer covering.

crustacean *n.* one of a group of animals, most of which have a hard shell and live in water.

crutch *n.* one of a pair of sticks that people who have an injured leg can use to help them walk.

cry¹ *v.* (cries, crying, cried) **1** to have tears coming from your eyes. **2** to shout.

cry² *n.* **1** a shout. *a cry of pain.* **2** the sound made by some animals. *the cry of the seagulls.* **3** a period of crying.

crypt *n.* an underground room located beneath a church.

crystal *n.* **1** a rock that is clear like glass. **2** a small, symmetrically shaped piece of a substance such as salt or ice. **3** very clear glass of a good quality.

crystal

cub *n.* **1** the young of a bear, lion, fox, tiger, and some other animals.

cube *n.* a solid object with six square sides. **cubic** *adj.*

cubicle *n.* a small compartment.

cuckoo *n.* a gray bird that lays its eggs in the nests of other birds.

cucumber *n.* a long, green vegetable that is eaten in salads.

cud *n.* food that cows or sheep bring up from their stomach to chew again.

cuddle *v.* to hug. **cuddle** *n*

cuddly *adj.* (cuddlier, cuddliest) pleasant to cuddle.

cue *n.* **1** a signal for an actor to say or do something. **2** a long rod for playing pool, billiards, or snooker.

cuff *n.* the end part of a sleeve.

culprit *n.* a person who has done something wrong.

cultivate *v.* to prepare land for growing crops. **cultivation** *n.*

culture *n.* **1** the customs and ways of life of a particular society. **2** music, literature, and painting.

cultured *adj.* having good manners and a good education.

cunning *adj.* good at deceiving; sly.

cup *n.* a small bowl with a handle that you drink from.

cupboard *(kub-erd)* *n.* a piece of furniture where you store things; cabinet.

curb[1] *n.* the edge of the sidewalk.

curb[2] *v.* to keep something under control. *We must curb our spending.*

cure *v.* **1** to make better. **2** to preserve some substances such as leather, tobacco, and meat by drying, smoking, or salting them. **cure** *n.*

curious *adj.* **1** wanting to find out about something. **2** odd; strange. **curiosity** *n.*

curl *n.* a curved length of hair. **curl** *v.*, **curly** *adj.*

currant *n.* a small berry.

currency *n.* the money used in a country.

current[1] *adj.* happening now.

current[2] *n.* **1** a flow of air or water. **2** a flow of electricity through a wire.

curriculum *n.* (*pl.* curricula) a program of study, such as in a school.

curry *n.* a hot-tasting, spicy food, often served with rice.

curse[1] *n.* a spell intended to bring harm or bad luck to somebody.

curse[2] *v.* to swear; to complain angrily about somebody.

cursor *n.* an indicator showing your position on a computer screen.

curtain *n.* a piece of material that is pulled across a window or the front of a theater stage to cover it.

curtsy *n.* a gesture of respect sometimes made by women, for example when meeting an important person, by bending the knees slightly. **curtsy** (*or* curtsey) *v.*

curve[1] *v.* to bend.

curve[2] *n.* a rounded line.

cushion *n.* a soft object, used for making a chair more comfortable.

custard *n.* a sweet, yellow sauce made with milk, sugar, and eggs.

custody *n.* the legal right to take care of a child. **in custody** arrested and waiting for trial.

custom *n.* the way that something is usually done.

customary *adj.* usual.

customer *n.* a person who buys things from a store or business.

customs *n. pl.* the place at an airport or port where officials check to make sure that you are not carrying anything illegal.

cut *v.* (cutting, cut) **1** to use a sharp object such as a knife, scissors, or an ax on something. **2** to reduce. *The store has cut its prices.* **cut** *n.*

cute *adj.* attractive.

cutlery *n.* knives, forks, and spoons; silverware.

cycle[1] *n.* a bicycle. **cycle** *v.*, **cyclist** *n.*

cycle[2] *n.* a series of events happening repeatedly.

cyclone *n.* a violent storm characterized by strong winds.

cygnet *(sig-net)* *n.* a young swan.

cylinder *n.* **1** an object with round ends and straight sides. **2** a piece of machinery with this shape, especially in an engine. **cylindrical** *adj.*

cymbal *n.* a musical instrument like a brass plate that you hit with another cymbal or with a stick to make a clashing sound.

cynic *(sin-ik)* *n.* a person who thinks the worst about everybody. **cynical** *adj.*

cypher *another spelling of* cipher.

czar *(zar)* *n.* (*historical*) an emperor of Russia. (can also be spelled *tsar*.)

Dd

dab *v.* (dabbing, dabbed) to touch something lightly and quickly. *Jenny dabbed the cut with gauze.* **dab** *n.*

dabble *v.* **1** to put your hands or feet in water and move them around. **2** to be involved in something, but not in a serious way. *She dabbles in politics.*

dad, daddy *n.* *(informal)* father.

daffodil *n.* a yellow spring flower.

dagger *n.* a short, two-edged knife used as a weapon.

dahlia *n.* **(*dah-lee-uh*)** a garden flower.

daily *adj., adv.* happening or coming every day. *a daily newspaper.*

dainty *adj.* (daintier, daintiest) small, pretty, and delicate. **daintily** *adv.*, **daintiness** *n.*

dairy *n.* a place where milk is kept and butter and cheese are made.

daisy *n.* a small wildflower with a yellow center and white petals.

dale *n.* a valley.

Dalmatian *n.* a large, spotted dog.

dam *n.* a thick wall built across a river to hold back the water.

damage *v.* to harm something. **damage** *n.*

dam

damp *adj.* slightly wet. **dampness** *n.*

dance[1] *v.* to move about to the rhythm of music. **dancer** *n.*

dance[2] *n.* **1** a series of steps and movements that you do in time to music. **2** a party where people dance.

dandelion *n.* a yellow wildflower.

dandruff *n.* small, white pieces of dead skin in a person's hair.

danger *n.* **1** something that may cause harm or an injury. **2** a situation that is not safe. **dangerous** *adj.*

dangle *v.* to hang or swing loosely.

dank *adj.* unpleasantly damp and cold.

dappled *adj.* marked with patches of dark and light.

dare *v.* **1** to be brave enough to do something. **2** to challenge somebody to show how brave he or she is. **daring** *adj.*

dark *adj.* **1** without light. *a dark night.* **2** not light in color; closer to black than to white. *dark blue.* **3** (of hair, skin, or eyes) brown or black. **the dark** darkness. **darkness** *n.*

darken *v.* to make or become dark.

darn *v.* to mend a hole in cloth by sewing threads across it.

dart[1] *n.* **1** a small arrow that you throw in the game of darts. **2 darts** a game in which players score points by throwing small arrows at a round target with numbers on it.

dart[2] *v.* to move forward suddenly. *Jane darted across the road.*

dash[1] *v.* to rush; to run quickly.

dash[2] *n.* **1** the mark (–) used in writing to show a break in a sentence. **2** a small quantity. *a dash of sauce.*

data (***day**-tuh* or ***dah**-tuh*) *n. pl.* facts or information.

database *n.* a large amount of information stored on a computer.

date *n.* **1** a particular day, month, or year. **2** an appointment to meet somebody, especially a boyfriend or girlfriend. **3** the sweet, sticky fruit that grows on the date palm tree.

daughter *n.* somebody's female child.

daunt *v.* **be daunted** to be discouraged or frightened. *She was daunted by the amount of work that needed to be done.*

dawdle *v.* to waste time by moving slowly.

dawn[1] *n.* sunrise.

dawn[2] *v.* to begin to get light.

day *n.* (*pl.* days) **1** a time of 24 hours, from midnight to the next midnight. **2** the part of the day when it is light. **3** a particular time. *in my granddad's day.*

daydream *n.* pleasant thoughts that take your mind away from what you are doing. **daydream** *v.*

daytime *n.* the time when it is light.

daze[1] *v.* to make somebody confused and unable to think clearly. *The blow to my head dazed me for a moment.*

A B C **D** E F G H I J K L M N O P Q R S T U V W X Y Z

daze² *n.* a state of stunned confusion.

dazzle *v.* **1** to blind somebody for a short time with a very bright light. *The car's headlights dazzled her.* **2** to impress somebody greatly with beauty or charm.

de- *prefix* opposite or negative of. *defrost, derail.*

dead *adj.* no longer alive.

dead end *n.* a road closed off at one end.

deadline *n.* a time by which something must be finished.

deadly *adj.* (deadlier, deadliest) causing or likely to cause death.

deaf *adj.* not able to hear well.

deafen *v.* to make so much noise that nothing else can be heard.

deal¹ *n.* a bargain or agreement.

deal² *v.* (dealing, dealt) **1** to do business. *He deals in stocks and shares.* **2** to give out playing cards. **deal with 1** to take action on something. *You clean this room, and I'll deal with the kitchen.* **2** to be concerned with something. *The book deals with interesting subjects.* **dealer** *n.*

dear *adj.* **1** much loved or valued. *a dear friend.* **2** a word that you use to start a letter. *Dear Tom . . .*

death *n.* the end of life.

deathly *adj.* like death.

debate *v.* to discuss or argue about something in a formal way, often in public. **debate** *n.*

debris *(deb-ree)* *n.* the remains of something broken or destroyed.

debt *(rhymes with yet)* *n.* something one person owes to another.

debut *(day-byoo)* *n.* a first public appearance. *She made her debut on the stage at the age of 14.*

decade *n.* a period of ten years.

decathlon *n.* a sporting competition made up of ten athletic events.

decay *v.* to rot; to decompose. **decay** *n.*

deceased *adj.* dead.

deceive *v.* to make somebody believe something that is not true. **deceit** *n.*, **deceitful** *adj.*, **deception** *n.*

December *n.* the twelfth, and final, month of the year.

decent *adj.* **1** satisfactory; good. *decent quality.* **2** respectable. *a decent way to behave.* **decency** *n.*

deceptive *adj.* making somebody believe something that is not true. *Appearances can sometimes be deceptive.*

decibel *n.* a unit for measuring how loud a sound is.

decide *v.* to make up your mind about something.

deciduous *adj.* losing all of its leaves in the winter. *a deciduous tree.*

decimal¹ *adj.* using units of ten. *decimal currency.*

decimal² *n.* a fraction written as a number, with amounts less than one placed after a dot (a **decimal point**), e.g. *1.25.*

decipher *(di-sigh-fer)* *v.* to figure out the meaning of something that is written in code or that is difficult to read.

decision *n.* **1** the process of deciding something. **2** something that is decided.

decisive *adj.* **1** final; putting an end to a contest. *a decisive battle.* **2** able to decide things quickly and easily.

deck *n.* **1** the floor of a ship. **2** a pack of playing cards.

declare *v.* **1** to announce something publicly. *Great Britain declared war in 1939.* **2** to say very firmly. **declaration** *n.*

decline *v.* **1** to become less strong or less good. *Her health is declining.* **2** to refuse something; to turn down. *I declined his offer.* **decline** *n.*

decompose *v.* to rot.

decorate *v.* **1** to make something more beautiful. **2** to paint or put up wallpaper in a room. **decoration** *n.*, **decorative** *adj.*

decrease *v.* to make or become smaller or less. **decrease** *n.*

decree *n.* an official order. **decree** *v.*

dedicate *v.* **1** to give all your time and energy to something. *She dedicated her life to helping the sick.* **2** to say that a book or song is written in honor of somebody. *I dedicated my novel to my father.* **dedication** *n.*

deduce *v.* to figure out something from the facts that are available. **deduction** *n.*

deduct *v.* to take away something; to subtract. *He deducted $10 from the bill.* **deduction** *n.*

deed *n.* **1** something that is done. **2** an important legal document.

deep *adj.* **1** going down a long way. *a deep hole.* **2** going back a long way from the front. *The shelf was not deep enough.* **3** strong and dark. *deep red.* **4** low. *a deep voice.* **5** intense. *She experienced deep sadness.*

deepen v. to make or become deeper.

deer n. (pl. deer) a wild animal that can run fast. Male deer have antlers.

deface v. to ruin the appearance of something, e.g. by writing on it.

defeat v. to beat somebody in a game, competition, or war. **defeat** n.

defect¹ n. (dee-fekt) a fault.

defect² v. (di-fekt) to leave your country or political party and go to another one. **defection** n., **defector** n.

defective adj. faulty.

defend v. **1** to protect from harm or attack. *The soldiers defended the castle.* **2** to speak in support of somebody or something. **defense** n., **defender** n., **defensive** adj.

defendant n. a person being accused of a crime in a court of law.

defer v. (deferring, deferred) to delay something until later.

defiant adj. standing up to somebody and openly refusing to obey. **defiance** n.

deficient adj. lacking in something. **deficiency** n.

define v. to explain the meaning of a word. **definition** n.

definite adj. **1** clearly stated; already decided. *definite plans.* **2** certain; without doubt. *Are you definite about that?*

deformed adj. with an unnatural shape.

defrost v. to thaw; to remove the ice from something.

defuse (dee-fyooz) v. **1** to make a bomb safe so that it does not explode. **2** to make a situation less dangerous.

defy v. (defies, defying, defied) to disobey somebody openly. *She defied her parents and went out.*

degree n. **1** a unit for measuring temperature or angles. *ninety degrees* (often written *90°*). **2** a qualification given by a college.

dehydrated adj. **1** dried out; with the water removed. **2** having lost too much water from your body. **dehydration** n.

dejected adj. sad or disappointed.

delay v. **1** to make somebody late. **2** to put off something until later. **delay** n.

delete v. to cross out or remove words that are already written. **deletion** n.

deliberate adj. done on purpose.

delicacy n. something that is considered especially delicious to eat.

delicate adj. **1** easily damaged or broken; fragile. *delicate china.* **2** finely made. *delicate lace.* **3** sensitive. *a delicate instrument.* **4** not very strong; easily becoming sick. *a delicate child.*

delicatessen n. a store selling cooked meat, cheese, sandwiches, and unusual foods; deli.

delicious adj. very good to eat.

delight¹ n. great pleasure.

delight² v. to give great pleasure to somebody. **delighted** adj.

delightful adj. very pleasant.

delinquent n. a person who breaks the law.

deliver v. **1** to take things to a place where they are needed. *The mailman delivered two letters.* **2** to help at the birth of a baby. *The doctor arrived in time to deliver the baby.* **delivery** n.

delta n. **1** a triangular area of land at the mouth of a river, where its main stream divides into several smaller streams. **2** the fourth letter of the Greek alphabet (Δ, δ).

delta

demand v. to ask for something very firmly. *She demanded an explanation.* **demand** n.

democracy n. **1** a system of government in which the people of a country elect their own leaders. **2** a country governed in this way. **democrat** n., **democratic** adj.

Democratic Party n. one of the two main political parties in the U.S. **Democrat** n.

demolish v. to knock something down. *They demolished the apartment block at the end of our street.* **demolition** n.

demon n. a devil or an evil spirit.

demonstrate v. **1** to show or explain something. **2** to take part in a protest march or similar gathering. **demonstration** n.

den n. **1** the home of a wild animal. **2** a private or secret place.

denial n. an act of denying something.

denim *n.* strong, cotton fabric used for making jeans.

denounce *v.* to say in public that somebody has done something wrong.

dense *adj.* **1** closely packed together. *a dense forest.* **2** thick. *dense fog.* **density** *n.*

dent *n.* a hollow part in the surface of something, made by hitting or pressing it. **dent** *v.*

dental *adj.* to do with teeth.

dentist *n.* a person who looks after and treats teeth.

dentures *n. pl.* a set of false teeth.

deny *v.* (denies, denying, denied) to say that something is not true.

deodorant *n.* a substance put on the body to prevent or cover up odors.

depart *v.* to leave; to go away. **departure** *n.*

department *n.* one of the parts of a big organization such as a government, a college, or a business.

depend *v.* **1** to rely. *I'm depending on you to help me.* **2** to be controlled or decided by. *It all depends on the weather.* **dependent** *adj.*, **dependence** *n.*

dependant *n.* someone who depends on another person, especially for financial support.

depict *v.* to paint, draw, or describe somebody or something.

deport *v.* to send somebody out of a country. **deportation** *n.*

deposit[1] *v.* **1** to put something somewhere. **2** to put money in a bank.

deposit[2] *n.* **1** an amount of money given as the first part of a payment. **2** an amount of money paid into a bank.

depot *(deep-oh)* *n.* **1** a warehouse. **2** a bus station.

depressed *adj.* sad and gloomy.

depression *n.* **1** sadness and hopelessness. **2** a hollow. **3** a time when businesses are doing badly, and there is more unemployment than usual.

deprive *v.* to take something away from somebody. **deprivation** *n.*

depth *n.* the distance from the top to the bottom of something. **in depth** thoroughly. *an in depth study.*

deputy *n.* **1** second in command. **2** a person appointed to act for someone else.

derelict *adj.* abandoned and in ruins.

descant *n.* a tune that is sung or played above the main tune.

descend *(di-send)* *v.* to go down.

descended from related to somebody who lived a long time ago.

descendant *n.* a person related to somebody who lived a long time ago.

describe *v.* to say what somebody or something is like. **description** *n.*, **descriptive** *adj.*

desert[1] *(dez-ert)* *n.* a large area of land where there is little water or rain.

desert

desert[2] *(di-zert)* *v.* to abandon somebody or something.

deserve *v.* to have earned something by what you have done. *You deserve the prize for all of your hard work.*

design[1] *v.* to prepare a plan or drawing to show how something will be made. **designer** *n.*

design[2] *n.* **1** a plan or drawing of how something will be made. **2** a style or pattern. *The building is modern in design.*

desire[1] *v.* to want something very much.

desire[2] *n.* a strong wish or need.

desk *n.* a piece of furniture for writing at.

desktop publishing *n.* the creation of a book or magazine, ready for printing, using a computer.

despair[1] *v.* to lose all hope.

despair[2] *n.* a feeling of hopelessness.

despatch *another spelling of* dispatch.

desperate *adj.* **1** willing to do anything to get what you want. *She was so desperate for money that she began to steal.* **2** very serious. *a desperate situation.* **desperation** *n.*

despicable *adj.* very unpleasant or evil.

despise *v.* to dislike and have a very low opinion of somebody.

despite *prep.* in spite of.

dessert *(di-zert)* *n.* the sweet course at the end of a meal.

destination *n.* the place where you are going to.

destiny *n.* fate.

destitute *adj.* extremely poor.

destroy *v.* to damage something so it cannot be repaired. **destruction** *n.*, **destructive** *adj.*

a
b
c
d
e
f
g
h
i
j
k
l
m
n
o
p
q
r
s
t
u
v
w
x
y
z

detach

A
B
C
D
E
F
G
H
I
J
K
L
M
N
O
P
Q
R
S
T
U
V
W
X
Y
Z

detach *v* to remove something that was attached to something else.

detached *adj.* standing by itself.

detail *n.* an individual fact or small piece of information.

detailed *adj.* having many details.

detention *n.* to keep somebody somewhere against their will. **detention** *n.*

detect *v.* to discover or notice something. **detection** *n.*

detective *n.* a person, especially a police officer, whose job it is to follow clues in order to find criminals.

deter (*di-ter*) *v.* (deterring, deterred) to discourage or prevent somebody from doing something.

detergent *n.* a liquid or powder used for cleaning.

deteriorate *v.* to become worse. **deterioration** *n.*

determined *v.* having firmly made up your mind. **determination** *n.*

deterrent *n.* something that deters.

detest *v.* to hate something.

detonate *v.* to set off an explosion. **detonator** *n.*

detour *n.* a route away from and longer than the planned route, especially to avoid something such as an obstacle.

deuce *n.* a score of 40-40 in tennis.

devastate *v.* to destroy a place completely. **devastation** *n.*

develop *v.* **1** to grow bigger or better. **2** to make the pictures on a photographic film visible by using chemicals. **3** to get, have, or show something. *He developed a fever.* **development** *n.*

device *n.* something, such as a tool or an instrument, made to do a particular thing. *A saw is a device for cutting wood.*

devil *n.* **1 Devil** in Christianity the supreme evil spirit. **2** any evil spirit.

devious *adj.* cunning and dishonest.

devise *v.* to invent something.

devolution *n.* the transfer of power from central government to a regional government. **devolve** *v.*

devoted *adj.* loyal and loving. *He is a devoted father.*

devour *v.* to eat something up greedily.

devout *adj.* deeply religious.

dew *n.* tiny drops of water that usually form on the ground outside overnight.

diabetes (*die-a-bee-teez*) *n.* a disease in

which there is too much sugar in the blood. **diabetic** *adj.*, *n.*

diagnose *v.* to decide what illness a patient has. **diagnosis** *n.*

diagonal *n.* a straight line across a square or rectangle from one corner to the opposite corner. **diagonal** *adj.*, **diagonally** *adv.*

diagram *n.* a drawing that helps explain something.

dial[1] *n.* the face of a clock, watch, or other similar instrument.

dial[2] *v.* (dialing, dialed) to make a telephone call by pressing buttons.

dialect *n.* a form of a language spoken in a particular region.

dialogue *n.* conversation in a movie or book.

diameter *n.* a straight line across a circle, passing through the center. See **circle**.

diamond *n.* **1** a very hard, colorless precious stone consisting of carbon. **2** a four-sided figure with equal sides but no right angles. **3 diamonds** one of the four suits in a pack of playing cards with the symbol ◆ on them.

diaper *n.* a piece of thick padding worn around a baby's bottom.

diarrhea (*die-uh-ree-uh*) *n.* a stomach illness that makes you need to go to the bathroom often and that makes your feces runny.

diary *n.* a book in which you write down what happens each day.

dice, die *n.* (*pl.* dice) a small cube with one to six dots on its sides, used in games.

dictate *v.* to speak or read aloud so that somebody can write down what you say. **dictation** *n.*

dictator *n.* a ruler who has complete control of a country.

dictionary *n.* an alphabetical book that explains the meanings of words and shows you how to spell them.

did *past of* do.

die *v.* (dying, died) **1** to stop living. **2** to come to an end. **die down** to lose strength or power. *The wind has died down.* **die out** to no longer exist.

diesel engine *n.* a type of engine that burns a special type of oil (**diesel**) to supply power.

diet (*dye-ut*) *n.* **1** the food you usually eat. *a healthy diet.* **2** a controlled eating plan to help you lose weight or stay healthy.

differ *v.* **1** to be different. **2** to disagree.

difference *n.* **1** the way that one thing is

56

not the same as another. **2** the amount by which one number is bigger than another. **3** a disagreement.

different *adj.* not the same.

difficult *adj.* **1** hard; not easy. **2** not easy to please. *a difficult child.*

difficulty *n.* a problem.

dig *v.* (digging, dug) **1** to use a shovel to move dirt or make a hole. **2** to poke something.

digest *v.* to break up food in your stomach and turn it into a form that your body can use. **digestion** *n.*, **digestive** *adj.*

digit *(dij-it) n.* **1** any of the figures 0 to 9. *The number 100 has three digits.* **2** a finger or a toe.

digital *adj.* showing the time or speed in numbers rather than by hands on a dial. *a digital watch.*

dignity *n.* a serious, calm manner.

dike *n.* a wall to stop the ocean or a river from flooding the land.

dilapidated *adj.* falling to pieces.

dilemma *n.* a difficult situation in which you must choose between two or more courses of action.

dilute *v.* to reduce the strength of a liquid by adding water. **dilution** *n.*

dim *adj.* (dimmer, dimmest) badly lit; not bright. **dimness** *n.*

dimension *n.* a measurement of length, width, or height.

diminish *v.* to make or become less.

din *n.* a loud, unpleasant noise.

dine *v.* to have dinner.

dinghy *n.* a small, open boat.

dingy *(din-jee) adj.* (dingier, dingiest) dull and gloomy. *a dark, dingy room.*

dinner *n.* the main meal of the day, usually eaten in the evening.

dinosaur *n.* one of a large number of prehistoric reptiles that became extinct 65 million years ago.

dip¹ *v.* (dips, dipping, dipped) **1** to put something into a liquid for a moment. **2** to go downward. *The road dips ahead.*

dip² *n.* **1** a hollow. **2** a soft, savory mixture in which you dip crackers, chips, and vegetables. **3** a short swim.

diplomacy *n.* **1** the management of relations between countries. **2** tact.

diplomat *n.* a person who works for his or her country in diplomacy. *She is a diplomat in the French Embassy.*

diplomatic *adj.* **1** to do with diplomats. **2** tactful. **diplomatically** *adv.*

dire *adj.* terrible; urgent.

direct¹ *adj.* **1** straight; shortest. *the most direct route.* **2** honest; saying exactly what you think. **direct** *adv.*, **directly** *adv.*

direct² *v.* **1** tell somebody the way to go. **2** to organize people and tell them what to do, especially in a play or movie.

direction *n.* **1** the place or point to which you are moving or facing. **2 directions** instructions on how to do something or get somewhere.

director *n.* **1** a senior manager of a business. **2** a person who directs a play or movie.

directory *n.* a list of names, addresses, and telephone numbers.

dirt *n.* dust, mud, or any other substance that is unclean.

dirty *adj.* (dirtier, dirtiest) not clean; covered in dirt. **dirtiness** *n.*

dis- *prefix* the opposite or negative of. *disappear, disapprove.*

disable *v.* to harm or injure somebody in a way that seriously affects his or her life. **disability** *n.*, **disabled** *adj.*

disadvantage *n.* something that is not helpful; a drawback or problem.

disagree *v.* (disagreeing, disagreed) **1** to have different ideas about something. **2** to have a bad effect on somebody. *Rich food often disagrees with me.* **disagreement** *n.*

disagreeable *adj.* unpleasant.

disappear *v* to go out of sight; to vanish. **disappearance** *n.*

disappoint *v.* to make someone sad by not being or doing what that person had hoped for. **disappointment** *n.*

disapprove *n.* to think that something is bad or wrong. **disapproval** *n.*

dinosaurs

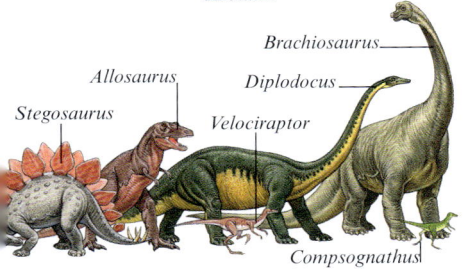

Brachiosaurus

Allosaurus

Diplodocus

Stegosaurus

Velociraptor

Compsognathus

A
B
C
D
E
F
G
H
I
J
K
L
M
N
O
P
Q
R
S
T
U
V
W
X
Y
Z

disaster *n.* an event that causes great damage or suffering. **disastrous** *adj.*

discard *v.* to throw something away.

disciple *(di-sigh-pul) n.* a follower.

discipline *n.* punishment or training that makes people obey rules.

disk jockey *n.* a person who plays recorded music on the radio or at a party. Often shortened to D.J.

disco *n.* (*short for* discotheque) a place where people dance to pop music; club.

discomfort *n.* lack of comfort; slight pain or worry.

discount *n.* a reduction in the original price of something.

discover *v.* to find out something new. **discovery** *n.*

discriminate *v.* **1** to see the differences between things. **2** to treat one person or group differently from another, often unfairly. **discrimination** *n.*

discus *n.* a type of heavy disk used in a throwing competition.

discuss *v.* to talk about something. **discussion** *n.*

disease *n.* an illness.

disgrace *n.* **1** shame. **2** something to be ashamed of. *Your clothes are a disgrace!* **in disgrace** out of favor.

disguise *v.* to change somebody's appearance so that they will not be recognized. *He was disguised as a police officer.* **disguise** *n.*

disgust *n.* a feeling of strong dislike. *He looked away in disgust.* **disgust** *v.*, **disgusted** *adj.*, **disgusting** *adj.*

dish *n.* **1** a plate or bowl for cooking or serving food. **2** one course of a meal.

dishonest *adj.* deceitful; not honest. **dishonesty** *n.*

disinfect *v.* to make something free from germs. **disinfectant** *n.*

disintegrate *v.* to break into many small pieces. **disintegration** *n.*

disk *n.* **1** any flat, circular object. **2** a compact disk. **3** a musical record. **4** in computing a device used to store information. (can also be spelled disc.)

dislike *v.* not to like something; to find something unpleasant. **dislike** *n.*

dismal *adj.* gloomy and sad. *a dismal, gray day.* **dismally** *adv.*

dismantle *v.* to take something apart.

dismay *n.* a strong feeling of shock, worry, or disappointment. *She reacted to the bad news with dismay.* **dismay** *v.*

dismiss *v.* **1** to send somebody away. **2** to order somebody to leave a job. **3** to refuse to consider something. **dismissal** *n.*

disobey *v.* to refuse to obey somebody. **disobedience** *n.*, **disobedient** *adj.*

disorder *n.* **1** confusion; lack of order. **2** rioting. **3** an illness.

dispatch *v.* to send something. **dispatch** *n.* (*can also be spelled* despatch.)

display[1] *v.* to put something where people can look at it.

display[2] *n.* (*pl.* displays) an exhibition or show.

disposable *adj.* intended to be thrown away after use.

dispose *v.* to get rid of something. **disposal** *n.*

dispute[1] *(dis-pyoot) v.* to argue about something.

dispute[2] *(dis-pyoot) n.* an argument.

disqualify *v.* to stop somebody from taking part in a competition or an exam because he or she has broken the rules. **disqualification** *n.*

disregard *v.* to deliberately pay no attention to something.

disrespect *n.* a lack of respect.

disrupt *v.* to stop something from progressing normally. **disruption** *n.*, **disruptive** *adj.*

dissect *v.* to cut something into pieces to examine it. **dissection** *n.*

dissolve *v.* to mix something with a liquid so that it becomes part of the liquid. *Salt dissolves easily in water.*

distance *n.* the amount of space between two places. **in the distance** far away.

distant *adj.* faraway.

distil *v.* (distilling, distilled) to purify a liquid by turning it into steam and then cooling it until it becomes a liquid again. **distillation** *n.*

distinct *adj.* **1** easily seen or heard. **2** obviously different.

distinction *n.* **1** a difference. **2** excellence. *a man of distinction.*

distinguish *v.* **1** to tell the difference between things. *Can you distinguish between a butterfly and a moth?* **2** to see or hear something clearly; to identify. *I could barely distinguish the figure in the distance.*

distinguished *adj.* famous and well respected. *a distinguished novelist.*

distract *v.* to take attention away from

what someone was doing. **distraction** n.

distress n. great pain or sorrow. **distress** v.

distribute v. to share something out. **distribution** n., **distributor** n.

district n. a part of a country or city.

disturb v. **1** to interrupt somebody when that person is doing something. **2** to upset or worry somebody. **3** to move something from its usual position. **disturbance** n.

ditch n. a long, narrow channel for draining away water.

dive v. **1** to plunge headfirst into water. **2** to drop down suddenly. **dive** n.

diver n. a person who works or explores underwater using breathing equipment.

diverse adj. varied; assorted.

diversion n. something that takes your attention away from something else.

divert v. **1** to change the direction of something. **2** to take somebody's attention away from something.

divide v. **1** to separate into parts; to share. **2** to find out how many times one number goes into another. *If you divide eight by two, you get four.* **dividable** or **divisible** adj., **division** n.

divine adj. of or like God or a god.

divorce n. the legal ending of a marriage. **divorce** v.

Diwali n. a Hindu and Sikh festival of lights in October or November.

dizzy adj. (dizzier, dizziest) feeling that everything is spinning and that you are going to fall. **dizziness** n.

D.J. *short for* disk jockey.

do v. (does, doing, did, done) **1** to carry out an action. **2** to finish or deal with something. **3** to be acceptable. *There isn't any coffee. Will tea do?* **4** a word used in questions and negative statements. *Do you like it?*

docile adj. easily controlled; obedient.

dock n. **1** a place in a harbor where ships are loaded and unloaded.

doctor n. a person who treats sick or injured people.

document n. a piece of paper with official or important information.

documentary n. a movie about real situations and people.

dodge v. to get quickly out of the way.

doe n. a female deer or rabbit.

does *form of* do.

doesn't *contr.* does not.

dog n. a four-legged mammal, often kept by people as a pet.

doll n. a toy in the shape of a small person, usually a baby.

dollar n. the unit of money in many countries, including Australia, Canada, and the U.S.

dolphin n. an intelligent sea mammal with a snout like a beak.

dome n. a rounded roof.

domestic adj. **1** to do with the home.

dolphin

2 kept as pets. *domestic animals.*

dominate v. **1** to control powerfully. **2** to be the most important or noticeable feature. *The castle dominates the town.* **dominant** adj., **domination** n.

dominoes n. pl. small, rectangular tiles with dots, used for playing the game dominoes.

donate v. to give something, especially to a charity. **donation** n., **donor** n.

done *past participle of* do.

donkey n. (pl. donkeys) an animal of the horse family, with long ears.

don't *contr.* do not.

doodle v. to draw without concentrating. **doodle** n.

doom n. a terrible fate that is impossible to prevent.

door n. a flat piece of wood or glass that swings on hinges and that opens and closes the entrance to a building, room, or cupboard.

dormant adj. not active; sleeping.

dormitory n. **1** a bedroom that has enough room for several people. **2** a building that houses several people, as in a college dormitory.

dose n. an amount of medicine to be taken at one time.

dot n. small spot.

dotted adj. made of dots. *a dotted line.*

double[1] adj. **1** twice as much or as many. **2** made up of two parts. **double** v.

double[2] n. a person who looks exactly like somebody else.

a
b
c
d
e
f
g
h
i
j
k
l
m
n
o
p
q
r
s
t
u
v
w
x
y
z

double bass *n.* a large stringed instrument that you play standing up.

double-cross *v.* to betray somebody.

doubt¹ (*rhymes with* out) *v.* to feel uncertain about something.

doubt² *n.* a feeling of uncertainty. **doubtful** *adj.*

dough (*rhymes with* go) *n.* a mixture of flour, water, and other ingredients for making bread or cake.

doughnut *n.* **1** a small, ring-shaped fried cake. **2** something that is ring shaped. (can also be spelled *donut*.)

dove *n.* a bird related to the pigeon.

down¹ *prep., adv.* **1** from a higher to a lower level or amount. **2** from standing to sitting or lying. *lie down.*

down² *n.* very soft feathers.

down³ *adj.* sad; depressed.

download *v.* to copy data from the Internet into a computer's memory.

downward *adv.* toward a lower place.

doze *v.* to sleep lightly. **doze** *n.*

dozen *n.* twelve.

Dr. *a short way of writing* Doctor.

drab *adj.* dull; not colorful.

draft¹ *n.* an early version of a piece of writing before it has been edited.

draft² *n.* a flow of cold air inside. **drafty** *adj.*

drag *v.* (dragging, dragged) **1** to pull something roughly along the ground. **2** to pass very slowly. *The class really dragged.*

Chinese dragon

dragon *n.* a fierce, fire-breathing creature in stories and legends.

dragonfly *n.* a large, often brightly colored insect with long wings.

drain¹ *n.* a pipe that takes waste water away from where it has been used.

drain² *v.* **1** to allow liquid to flow away. *Wash and drain the dishes.* **2** to flow away.

drained *adj.* exhausted; lacking energy.

drake *n.* a male duck.

drama *n.* **1** a play. **2** acting and the theater. **3** exciting events.

dramatic *adj.* **1** to do with acting and the theater. **2** noticeable; striking. *a dramatic improvement.* **3** exciting; impressive. *dramatic events.* **dramatically** *adv.*

drank *past of* drink.

drastic *adj.* extreme; severe.

draw¹ *v.* (drawing, drew, drawn) **1** to make a picture with a pen, pencil, or crayon. **2** to pull something. *to draw the curtains.* **3** to attract something. *The show drew a large crowd.*

draw² *n.* the selecting of winning tickets in a lottery or raffle. *a prize draw.*

drawback *n.* a disadvantage or problem.

drawbridge *n.* *(historical)* a bridge across a moat that could be pulled up when a castle was being attacked.

drawer *n.* a box-shaped part of a chest or cupboard that can be pulled open.

drawing *n.* a picture made with a pen, pencil, or crayon.

drawn *past participle of* draw.

dread *v.* to be afraid of something. **dread** *n.*

dreadful *adj.* terrible; unpleasant. **dreadfully** *adv.*

dreadlocks *n. pl.* hair twisted into long, thin ringlets.

dream *n.* **1** a series of things that seem to happen to you when you are asleep. **2** a hope or ambition. **dream** *v.*

dreary *adj.* (drearier, dreariest) very dull; gloomy.

dredge *v.* to clear away sand and mud from a riverbed or harbor.

drench *v.* to make something very wet.

dress¹ *n.* **1** a piece of clothing, usually worn by women and girls, that covers the body from the shoulders to the legs. **2** clothing for formal occasions. *dress shoes.*

dress² *v.* to put on clothes.

dresser *n.* a piece of furniture like a cupboard with shelves above it.

dressing *n.* **1** a covering for a wound. **2** a sauce for salads.

drew *past of* draw.

dribble *v.* **1** to let saliva fall from your mouth. **2** in sports to bounce a ball or push forward a puck.

drift *v.* to be carried slowly along by the wind or water.

drill *n.* **1** a pointed tool that is used for

making holes. *She used the electric drill to put screws in the wall.* **2** exercises that are part of a soldier's training or sports. **3** an exercise intended to train people in what to do in a dangerous situation. *a fire drill.* **drill** *v.*

drink[1] *v.* (drinking, drank, drunk) to swallow a liquid.

drink[2] *n.* **1** any liquid that you swallow. **2** an alcoholic drink.

drill

drip *v.* (dripping, dripped) to fall in drops. **drip** *n.*

drive[1] *v.* (driving, drove, driven) **1** to be in control of a vehicle. **2** to take somebody somewhere in a car. **3** to force something along. *They drove the herd of cattle across the road.* **4** to make something work. *The engine was driven by steam.* **driver** *n.*

drive[2] *n.* **1** a journey in a car. **2** a path or road leading from the street to a house.

drizzle *n.* light rain. **drizzle** *v.*

dromedary *n.* a camel with one hump.

drone[1] *v.* to make a continuous, low, humming noise.

drone[2] *n.* a male bee or ant, one of a colony of bees or ants that does no work.

drool *v.* **1** to let saliva drip from your mouth. **2 drool over** to show in an obvious way that you want something.

droop *v.* to hang down limply.

drop[1] *n.* a small amount of a liquid.

drop[2] *v.* (drops, dropping, dropped) to fall or let something fall. **drop in** to visit somebody casually.

drought (*rhymes with* out) *n.* a long period of dry weather.

drove *past of* drive.

drown *v.* to die or to kill somebody by suffocation in water.

drowsy *adj.* (drowsier, drowsiest) sleepy. **drowsily** *adv.*

drug *n.* **1** a medicine. **2** an illegal substance swallowed, smoked, or injected by people to produce an effect such as happiness or excitement. **drug** *v.*

drum[1] *n.* a round, hollow musical instrument with a skin stretched over a frame, which you beat.

drum[2] *v.* (drumming, drummed) **1** to play a drum. **2** to beat on a surface with your fingers. **drummer** *n.*

drunk[1] *adj.* having drunk too much alcohol.

drunk[2] *past participle of* drink.

dry[1] *adj.* (drier, driest) not wet; without water. **dryness** *n.*

dry[2] *v.* (dries, drying, dried) to make or become dry.

dry-clean *v.* to clean clothes using special chemicals instead of water.

dual *adj.* double; consisting of two parts.

dubious (*doo-bee-us*) *adj.* **1** doubtful. **2** suspicious; not reliable.

duchess *n.* **1** a woman with the same ranking as a duke. **2** the wife of a duke.

duck[1] *n.* a common water bird with a broad beak and webbed feet.

duck[2] *v.* to bend down quickly to get out of the way of something.

duckling *n.* a young duck.

due *adj.* **1** expected to arrive or happen. *What time is the bus due to arrive?* **2** owing; to be paid. *Payment is due.* **3** suitable. *After due consideration, she took the job.* **due to** caused by something.

duel *n.* (*historical*) a fight that often took place between two people.

duet (*doo-et*) *n.* a piece of music that can be performed by two performers.

dug *past of* dig.

duke *n.* a nobleman of the highest rank.

dull *adj.* **1** gloomy; not bright. *a dull, gray day.* **2** boring. *a dull book.* **3** not sharp. *a dull ache.*

dumb *adj.* **1** not able to speak. *She was struck dumb at the sight.* **2** (*informal*) stupid.

dummy *n.* **1** a model of a human figure. **2** a rubber pacifier for a baby to suck.

dump[1] *n.* a place where garbage is left.

dump[2] *v.* **1** to get rid of something or throw something away. **2** to put something down carelessly. *She dumped her bag on the floor.*

dune *n.* a low hill of sand.

dung *n.* feces from large animals.

dungarees *n. pl.* trousers with a top part that covers your chest and with straps that go over your shoulders; overalls.

dungeon (**dun**-jun) n. an underground prison in a castle.

duplicate (**doo**-pli-kate) v. to make an exact copy of something. **duplicate** (**doo**-pli-kut) n.

durable adj. lasting a long time.

during prep. 1 throughout. Groundhogs hibernate during the winter. 2 at some time in. They arrived during the night.

dusk n. the time of evening when it is starting to get dark.

dust¹ n. tiny particles of dirt. **dusty** adj.

dust² v. to remove dust with a cloth.

duster n. a soft cloth that you use for dustin furniture.

duty n. 1 something that you must do. 2 tax on goods that you buy. **on duty** working. **off duty** not working.

duvet (doo-**vay**) n. a thick blanket filled with feathers or other soft material.

DVD (short for digital versatile disk) n. a disk used for storing movies.

dwarf n. (pl. dwarfs or dwarves) a very small person, animal, or plant.

dwell v. (dwelling, dwelled or dwelt) to inhabit a place.

dwelling n. a place to live in.

dwindle v. to become smaller or less.

dye¹ n. a substance used to change the color of something.

dye² v. (dyeing, dyed) to change the color of something by soaking it in a dye.

dynamic adj. full of energy.

dynamite n. an explosive.

dynamo n. (pl. dynamos) 1 a machine that uses movement to make electricity; generator. The light on my bike is powered by a small dynamo. 2 an extremely energetic person.

dynasty n. a series of kings and queens belonging to the same family.

dyslexia (dis-**lek**-see-a) n. a special difficulty with reading and spelling. **dyslexic** adj.

Ee

each adj., pron. every person or thing.

eager adj. enthusiastic. **eagerness** n.

eagle n. a large bird of prey.

ear n. the part of the body that is used for hearing.

earache n. a pain in the ear.

earl n. a British nobleman.

early adj., adv. 1 close to the beginning of a period of time. early morning. 2 before the expected or usual time. We went to bed early. **earliness** n.

earn v. 1 to get something by working for it. 2 to deserve something.

eagle

earnest adj. serious; sincere.

earnings n. pl. money that is earned.

earring n. a piece of jewelry that you wear on your ear.

earth n. 1 **Earth** the planet on which we live. 2 soil. 3 the hole where a fox or badger lives.

earthquake n. a violent shaking of the surface of Earth.

earthquake

earthwork *n. (historical)* a mound of earth used as a fortification.

earwig *n.* an insect with pincers at the end of its abdomen.

ease[1] *n.* comfort; freedom from pain.

ease[2] *v.* **1** to make or become less difficult or unpleasant. *The drugs eased the pain.* **2** to move something gently and carefully. *We eased the lid off the box.*

easel *n.* a special stand designed for supporting a picture or blackboard.

east *n.* **1** the direction from which the Sun rises each morning. **2 the East** the countries in Asia such as Japan and China. **east** *adj., adv.*

Easter *n.* the day when Christians remember the resurrection of Jesus Christ.

eastern *adj.* in or of the east part of a place. *eastern England.*

easy *adj.* (easier, easiest) **1** able to be done without much effort or ability. **2** free from pain, trouble, or worry. *an easy life.* **easily** *adv.*

easygoing *adj.* not easily upset or worried.

eat *v.* (eating, ate, eaten) **1** to take in food through your mouth. **2** to destroy something by chemical action.

ebb *v.* **1** (of the tide) to move away from the land. **2** to become less.

ebony *n.* a hard, black wood.

eccentric *(ek-sen-trik) adj.* odd; strange.

echo *(ek-oh) n. (pl.* echoes) a sound that is heard again when it bounces back off something. **echo** *v.*

eclipse *n.* **1** a time when the Sun's light is blocked because the Moon passes between Earth and the Sun. **2** a time when the Moon's light is blocked because Earth passes between the Sun and the Moon. **eclipse** *v.*

ecology *n.* the study of living things, the places where they live, and how they are dependent on each other. **ecological** *adj.,* **ecologist** *n.*

economical *adj.* using as little of something as necessary; not wasteful. *This car is extremely economical to run.*

economize *v.* to save money by being careful about what you spend.

economy *n.* the management of a country's money. **make economies** to save money by being careful.

ecosystem *n.* a community of plants and animals and how they interact with each other and their environment.

eczema *(ek-za-ma) n.* a disease of the skin that makes it rough and dry.

edge *n.* the part along the side or end of something. **on edge** nervous.

edible *adj.* suitable to be eaten.

edifice *n.* a large, impressive building.

edit *v.* **1** to prepare writing or a movie by changing and arranging it. **2** to prepare a newspaper or magazine for publication.

edition *n.* all the copies of a book or newspaper printed at one time.

editor *n.* a person who edits.

educate *v.* to teach or train somebody. **education** *n.,* **educational** *adj.*

eel *n.* a long, snakelike fish.

effect *n.* **1** a result. **2** an impression made by something.

effective *adj.* doing a job very well.

efficient *adj.* doing a job well, without wasting time or effort. **efficiency** *n.*

effort *n.* **1** the use of energy; a state of trying hard. **2** hard work. **effortless** *adj.*

e.g. *short for* for example. *Please wear comfortable shoes, e.g. sneakers.*

egg *n.* **1** one of the oval or rounded objects that young birds, insects, fish, and reptiles live inside before they are born. **2** a hen's egg, which is used as food. **3** in a female animal

egg

the cell from which a baby is formed.

eggplant *n.* a vegetable with a smooth, dark purple skin.

Eid *n.* a Muslim festival, specifically one at the end of Ramadan.

either[1] *conj., pron., adj.* one or the other; one of two. *You can have either milk or lemonade.*

either[2] *adv.* also. *If you don't go, I won't go either.*

eject *v.* to push or send something out with force. **ejection** *n.,* **ejector** *n.*

elaborate *adj.* very detailed or complicated. *an elaborate design.*

elastic *n.* a material that stretches and then goes back to the same size. **elastic** *adj.*

a b c d **e** f g h i j k l m n o p q r s t u v w x y z

elated *adj.* extremely happy. **elation** *n.*

elbow *n.* the joint where your arm bends.

elder *adj.* older.

elderly *adj.* rather old.

eldest *adj.* greatest in age or seniority.

elect *v.* to choose somebody by voting.

election *n.* a time when people vote to choose the people who will lead their town, country, or club.

elector *n.* a person who can vote.

electric *adj.* worked by electricity.

electrical *adj.* 1 to do with electricity. 2 worked by electricity.

electrician *n.* a person who works with electrical equipment.

electricity *n.* a form of energy that is used to make heat and light and to power machines.

electrocute *v.* to kill or badly injure someone by putting an electrical current through his or her body. **electrocution** *n.*

electrode *n.* a metal conductor through which an electrical current enters or leaves a battery.

electron *n.* a very small particle within an atom, carrying an electric charge.

electronic *adj.* operated by silicon chips or transistors that carry and control electrical currents. Many pieces of equipment, such as computers and televisions, contain electronic devices. **electronically** *adv.*

electronics *n. pl.* the science or technology that deals with electronic devices.

elegant *n.* graceful and stylish. **elegance** *n.*

element *n.* 1 in chemistry a substance that cannot be divided into simpler substances. 2 a single part of

something. **3 the elements** the weather.

elementary *adj.* simple; basic.

elementary school *n.* a school where children go between the ages of 6 and 12.

elephant *n.* a very large mammal with thick skin, a trunk, and tusks.

elf *n.* (*pl.* elves) a small mischievous creature with magical powers.

eligible *adj.* qualified. *You are not eligible to drive until you are 16.* **eligibility** *n.*

eliminate *v.* to remove somebody or something. **elimination** *n.*

elm *n.* a tall tree with broad leaves.

elongated *adj.* long and thin.

elope *v.* to run away to get married. **elopement** *n.*

eloquent *adj.* able to express your ideas well. **eloquence** *n.*

else *adv.* 1 more; extra. *Would you like anything else to eat?* 2 other; different. *He took someone else's book instead of his own.* **or else** otherwise.

E-mail *n.* (*short for* electronic mail) a message or messages sent and received using a computer. (*can also be spelled email.*)

embankment *n.* a wall of dirt built to carry a railroad or to hold back water.

embark *v.* to go on board a ship.

embarrass *v.* to make somebody feel uncomfortable or ashamed. **embarrassment** *n.*

embassy *n.* the building used by an ambassador and his or her staff.

emerald

African elephants

emblem *n.* a badge or symbol.

embrace *v.* to put your arms around somebody. **embrace** *n.*

embroider *v.* to sew pictures or designs onto cloth. **embroidery** *n.*

embryo (*em-bree-oh*) *n.* (*pl.* embryos) an unborn animal or human in the early stages of development.

emerald *n.* a green precious stone.

merge *v.* to come out; to appear.

emergency *n.* a sudden, dangerous situation needing quick action.

emigrate *v.* to leave your own country

and go live in another. **emigrant** *n.*, **emigration** *n.*

eminent *adj.* well known and highly respected. *an eminent lawyer.*

emir *n.* the title of the ruler in some Muslim countries. (*can also be spelled* amir). **emirate** *n.*

emit *v.* (emits, emitting, emitted) to send out something. **emission** *n.*

emotion *n.* a strong feeling, including love, joy, or grief. **emotional** *adj.*, **emotionally** *adv.*

emperor *n.* a man who rules an empire.

emphasis *(em-fa-sis)* *n.* stress, e.g. on words, to show special importance.

emphasize *v.* to stress something to show that it is especially important.

empire *n.* a group of countries under one ruler. *the Roman Empire.*

employ *v.* **1** to pay somebody to work. **2** to use something. **employment** *n.*

employee *n.* a person who works for someone else; a worker.

employer *n.* a person or company that employs others.

empress *n.* a woman who rules an empire or the wife of an emperor.

empty[1] *adj.* (emptier, emptiest) with nothing inside.

empty[2] *v.* (empties, emptying, emptied) to make or become empty. **emptiness** *n.*

emu

emu *n.* (*pl.* emus) a large Australian bird that cannot fly.

enable *v.* to make something possible for somebody. *The Internet enables us to find facts quickly.*

enamel *n.* **1** a very hard, shiny coating on things such as metal pans, pottery, and glass. **2** the hard, white surface of teeth.

enchant *v.* **1** to delight somebody. **2** to put a spell on somebody or something. **enchantment** *n.*

enclose *v.* **1** to surround something on all sides. **2** to put something inside a letter or envelope. *I enclose a check for $20.*

enclosure *n.* an area with a fence or wall around it.

encounter *n.* **1** an unexpected meeting. **2** a fight or contest between people. **encounter** *v.*

encourage *v.* to give somebody the confidence to do something. **encouragement** *n.*

encyclopedia *(en-sye-klo-pee-dee-uh)* *n.* a book, or set of books, containing information on many different topics, usually arranged in alphabetical order. (*can also be spelled* encyclopaedia).

end[1] *n.* the last or farthest part of something. *the end of the road.*

end[2] *v.* to bring or come to an end.

endanger *v.* to put something in danger.

endangered species *n.* a species of animal in danger of becoming extinct.

endeavor *v.* to try to do something.

endless *adj.* without an end.

endure *v.* **1** to suffer through something. **2** to last; to continue. **endurance** *n.*

enemy *n.* **1** the people that you fight against in a war. **2** someone who hates you and wants to harm you.

energetic *adj.* strong and active. **energetically** *adv.*

energy *n.* **1** the strength or power to do work. **2** power from gas or electricity that gives light and heat or powers machines.

engage *v.* **1** to employ somebody. **2** to involve or occupy somebody. *She engaged him in conversation.*

engaged *adj.* busy. **get engaged** to agree to get married. **engagement** *n.*

engine *n.* a machine that changes energy into movement.

engineer *n.* a person who designs and builds things such as bridges, roads, or machines. **engineering** *n.* the work of an engineer.

engrave *v.* to cut a picture or writing into metal or glass. **engraving** *n.*

enigma *n.* a mystery or puzzle.

enjoy *v.* to get pleasure from something. **enjoyable** *adj.*, **enjoyment** *n.*

enlarge *v.* to make or become bigger. **enlargement** *n.*

enormous *adj.* very big.

enough *adj.*, *adv.*, *n.*, *pron.* as much as you need. *Have you had enough to eat?*

enrol *v.* (enrols, enrolling, enrolled) to put your name on a list to join something. **enrolment** *n.*

ensure *v.* to make certain.

a
b
c
d
e
f
g
h
i
j
k
l
m
n
o
p
q
r
s
t
u
v
w
x
y
z

65

A
B
C
D
E
F
G
H
I
J
K
L
M
N
O
P
Q
R
S
T
U
V
W
X
Y
Z

enter *v.* **1** to go into a place. **2** to type something into a computer or write something down in a book or list. **3** to take part in a competition.

enterprise *n.* **1** something you try to do that is new and challenging. *We wish you success in your enterprise.* **2** a business or company.

entertain *v.* **1** to amuse and interest people. **2** to have people as guests in your home. **entertainment** *n.*

enthusiasm *n.* a lively interest. **enthusiastic** *adj.*, **enthusiastically** *adv.*

entire *adj.* whole; complete.

entrance[1] *(en-truns)* *n.* **1** an act of entering. **2** the place where you enter.

entrance[2] *(en-traans)* *v.* to delight somebody very much.

entry *n.* **1** a way in; an entrance. **2** something that you send in or enter for a competition. *a winning entry.*

envelope *n.* a paper cover for a letter.

envious *adj.* feeling envy. *He was envious of his friend's happiness.*

environment *n.* **1** the surroundings and conditions in which a person or an animal lives. **2** the natural world. **environmental** *adj.*

envy *n.* a feeling of wanting what somebody else has. **envy** *v.*

epic *n.* a long story, poem, or movie that tells about great adventures and heroic deeds.

epidemic *n.* an outbreak of a disease that affects a large number of people at the same time.

epilepsy *n.* a brain condition that can cause unconsciousness and often seizures. **epileptic** *adj.*

episode *n.* **1** one program in a television or

equator

radio series. **2** one in a series of events.

epitaph *n.* words written on a tomb.

equal[1] *adj., n.* the same in size, number, or value. **equality** *n.*, **equally** *adv.*

equal[2] *v.* (equals, equaling, equaled) to be the same in size, number, or quality.

equation *n.* a mathematical formula stating that two values are equal.

equator *n.* an imaginary line around Earth, exactly halfway between the North and South poles. **equatorial** *adj.*

equilateral *adj.* with all sides of equal length. *an equilateral triangle.* See **triangle**.

equinox *n.* one of only two days during the year, in spring and fall, when day and night are of equal length.

equip *v.* (equips, equipping, equipped) to provide somebody or something with everything that is needed.

equipment *n.* the things that are needed for a particular purpose.

equivalent *adj.* equal in value, size, or meaning. **equivalent** *n.*

era *n.* a period of history.

eradicate *v.* to get rid of something completely. **eradication** *n.*

erase *v.* to rub something out. **eraser** *n.*

erect[1] *v.* to put up or build something. *They erected a war memorial.* **erection** *n.*

erect[2] *adj.* standing upright.

erode *v.* to gradually wear away.

erosion *n.* the slow wearing away of soil or rock by wind, water, or ice.

err *v.* to make a mistake.

errand *n.* a small job that somebody is sent away to do.

erratic *adj.* irregular; not having or behaving according to a set pattern.

volcano erupting

error *n.* a mistake.

erupt *v.* **1** (of a volcano) to burst out violently and shoot out lava. **2** to break out suddenly and violently. *The demonstration started quietly, but violence suddenly erupted.* **eruption** *n.*

escalator *n.* a moving staircase.

escape *v.* to get away from somebody or something; to get free. **escape** *n.*

escort[1] *(ess-kort)* *v.* to go with somebody, especially to protect or guard that person.

escort[2] *(ess-kort)* *n.* a person who accompanies somebody.

especially *adj.* specially; particularly.

espionage (*esp-ee-on-ajh*) *n.* spying.

essay *n.* (*pl.* essays) a piece of writing on a particular subject.

essence *n.* **1** the most important part or quality of something. **2** a concentrated liquid from a plant, used to flavor food or in perfume.

essential *adj.* absolutely necessary. **essentially** *adv.*

essentials *n. pl.* things that are essential.

establish *v.* **1** to set something up. *The firm was established in 1902.* **2** to show something with the facts. *establish the cause of death.* **establishment** *n.*

estate *n.* **1** an area of land on which houses or factories have been built. **2** an area of land owned by one person. **3** all of the

estuary

money and property left by somebody when he or she dies.

estimate (*ess-tim-ate*) *v.* to guess something; to calculate roughly. **estimate** (*ess-tim-ut*) *n.*

estuary *n.* the wide part of a river, where it flows into the sea.

et cetera (*shortened to* etc.) and so on; and other things. *We need basic food items: milk, bread, rice, etc.*

eternal *adj.* without end; lasting forever. **eternally** *adv.*

eternity *n.* time without end.

ethnic *adj.* associated with a particular race of people.

EU *n.* (*short for* European Union) a group of European countries that have joined to promote trade and industry.

euro *n.* the unit of currency in several European countries, including Ireland, France, and Germany.

euthanasia (*yooth-an-ay-juh*) *n.* the painless killing of somebody suffering from an illness that cannot be cured.

evacuate *v.* to move somebody away from an area for a time because it is dangerous. *We*

were told to evacuate from our homes after the explosion. **evacuation** *n.*

evade *v.* to avoid something. *She evaded the question.* **evasion** *n.*, **evasive** *adj.*

evaporate *v.* to turn from a liquid into a gas, usually because of heat. **evaporation** *n.*

eve *n.* the day before an event or special day. *New Year's Eve.*

even[1] *adv.* a word that you use to point out the unexpected in what you are saying. *He's not my friend—I don't even know him!* **even if** no matter that.

even[2] *adj.* **1** smooth and level. *an even surface.* **2** equal. *The scores are even.* **3** that can be divided exactly by two.

evening *n.* the time in the day between afternoon and night.

event *n.* a happening.

eventually *adv.* in the end; at last.

ever *adv.* at any time; at all times.

evergreen *n.* a tree that has green leaves all year round.

every *adj.* all of the people or things.

everybody, everyone *pron.* every person.

everything *pron.* all things; each thing.

everywhere *adv.* in every place.

evict *v.* to force somebody to move out of his or her home. **eviction** *n.*

evidence *n.* information that makes somebody believe that something is true.

evident *adj.* clear and obvious.

evil *adj.* very bad; wicked. **evil** *n.*

evolution *n.* the process by which animals and plants develop and change over thousands of years.

evolve *v.* to gradually develop over a period of time.

ewe *n.* a female sheep.

ex- *prefix* former. *ex-president.*

exact *adj.* just right; perfectly correct.

exaggerate *v.* to make something sound bigger or more impressive than it really is. **exaggeration** *n.*

examination *n.* **1** (*also* **exam**) an important test to find out how much you know. **2** a close look at something. *The doctor gave her a thorough examination.*

examine *v.* to look at something closely.

example *n.* **1** something that shows what other things of the same type are like. *This poem is a fine example of the poet's work.* **2** a model for other people to copy. *You should set an example for the boys.*

exasperate *v.* to irritate and frustrate somebody. **exasperation** *n.*

excavate *v.* to uncover something by digging. **excavation** *n.*

exceed *v.* to go beyond or be greater than something. *Don't exceed the speed limit.*

excel *v.* (excels, excelling, excelled) to be very good at something.

excellent *adj.* extremely good.

except *prep.* not including.

exception *n.* somebody or something that is not included.

exceptional *adj.* unusual; remarkable.

excerpt *n.* a short piece taken from a book, play, or movie.

excess *n.* a larger amount than is needed or usual. **excessive** *adj.*

exchange *v.* to give one thing and get another for it. **exchange** *n.*

excite *v.* to make somebody have very strong feelings of happiness about something that he or she is looking forward to. **excitement** *n.*

exclaim *v.* to say something suddenly and loudly. **exclamation** *n.*

exclamation point, exclamation mark *n.* the punctuation mark (!) used to show that the writer is expressing strong feelings.

exclude *v.* 1 to stop somebody from taking part or joining in. 2 to leave something out; not to include. **exclusion** *n.*

exclusive *(ex-klooss-iv) adj.* 1 available to only a small number of people because it is very expensive. 2 not shared with others.

excrete *v.* to get rid of waste from the body.

excruciating *adj.* very painful.

excursion *n.* an outing.

excuse¹ *(ex-kyooss) n.* a reason that you give for doing something wrong.

excuse² *(ex-kyooz) v.* 1 to allow somebody not to do something. 2 to forgive somebody; to let somebody off.

execute *v.* to kill somebody legally as a punishment. **execution** *n.*

executive *n.* one of the senior employees of a company.

exhaust²

exercise¹ *n.* 1 physical activity that you do to stay strong and healthy. 2 a piece of work that you do to practice a skill.

exercise² *v.* 1 to do physical exercises. 2 to use something. *exercise your judgment.*

exhale *v.* to breathe out. **exhalation** *n.*

exhaust¹ *(ig-zawst) v.* 1 to make somebody very tired. 2 to use up something completely. **exhaustion** *n.*

exhaust² *n.* a pipe through which waste gases from an engine are sent out.

exhibit¹ *v.* to show something in public.

exhibit² *n.* something that is shown, especially in an exhibition.

exhibition *n.* a public display, especially of works of art.

exhilarating *adj.* very exciting.

exile *v.* to send somebody away his or her own country, often as a punishment. **exile** *n.*

exist *v.* to be real; to live. **existence** *n.*

exit *n.* 1 a way out of a place. 2 an act of going out. *He made a quick exit.* **exit** *v.*

expedition

exotic *adj.* when something is strange and interesting because it comes from a distant place. *exotic plants.*

expand *v.* to make or become larger. **expansion** *n.*

expanse *n.* a wide area. *an expanse of sky.*

expect *v.* 1 to think that something will happen or that somebody or something will come. *I'm expecting a letter today.* 2 to require something. *Mom expects us to clean our rooms.* **be expecting** to be pregnant.

expedition *n.* a long journey for a special reason such as climbing a mountain.

expel *v.* (expels, expelling, expelled) to force out somebody or something. *She was expelled from school for stealing.*

expense *n.* the cost of doing something.

expensive *adj.* costing a lot of money.

experience[1] *n.* **1** something that happens to you or something that you do. *Getting lost in the woods was a frightening experience.* **2** knowledge and skill gained by doing something. *She has gained a lot of teaching experience.*

experience[2] *v.* to have experience of or to feel something. *We are experiencing some difficulties with our Web site at the moment.*

experiment *n.* a test done in order to find out something. **experiment** *v.*

expert *n.* a person who knows a lot about a particular subject.

expire *v.* **1** to come to an end. *My membership at the tennis club expires at the end of this month.* **2** (*literary*) to die. **expiry** *n.*

explain *v.* to make the meaning of something clear. **explanation** *n.*

explode *v.* to burst with a loud bang. **explosion** *n.*

exploit[1] (*ex-ployt*) *v.* **1** to use somebody unfairly for your own advantage. **2** to use something fully.

exploit[2] (*ex-ployt*) *n.* a daring action.

explore *v.* to look carefully around a place. **exploration** *n.*, **explorer** *n.*

explosive[1] *n.* a substance that can explode.

explosive[2] *adj.* likely to explode.

export (*ex-port*) *v.* to sell goods to another country.

export (*ex-port*) *n.* something that is exported.

expose *v.* **1** to uncover or leave unprotected. **2** to reveal the truth about somebody. **3** to allow light to hit film as you take a photograph. **exposure** *n.*

express[1] *v.* to show something by words or actions. **expressive** *adj.*

express[2] *adj.* fast. *an express train.*

expression *n.* **1** the look on a person's face. **2** the act of expressing something. **3** a phrase that has a special meaning.

extend *v.* **1** to make something longer or larger. **2** to stretch out.

extension *n.* **1** the process of making something longer or larger. **2** an extra room or rooms added to a building. **3** one of several telephones connected to the same line and number.

extensive *adj.* covering a large area.

extent *n.* the size or level of something.

exterior *n.* the outside of something.

exterminate *v.* to kill large numbers of people or animals. **extermination** *n.*

external *adj.* outside. **externally** *adv.*

extinct *adj.* **1** no longer in existence. *The dodo is an extinct bird.* **2** no longer active. *an extinct volcano.*

extinguish *v.* to put out a fire.

human eye

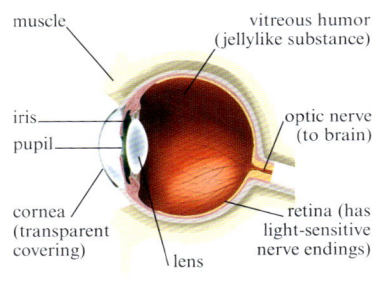

muscle
iris
pupil
cornea (transparent covering)
lens
vitreous humor (jellylike substance)
optic nerve (to brain)
retina (has light-sensitive nerve endings)

extra *adj.* more than is usual.

extra- *prefix* **1** beyond; outside. *extraordinary.* **2** very. *extraspecial.*

extract[1] (*ik-strakt*) *v.* to pull something out, especially by force.

extract[2] (*ek-strakt*) *n.* a short piece taken from a book or movie.

extraordinary *adj.* very unusual. **extraordinarily** *adv.*

extravagant *adj.* spending or costing too much. **extravagance** *n.*

extreme *adj.* **1** great or strong. *extreme cold.* **2** farthest. *the extreme southern tip of Chile.* **extremely** *adv.* very.

eye *n.* **1** the part of the body that we use for seeing. **2** the small hole of a needle. **3** the center of a storm.

eyebrow *n.* the curve of hair above the eye.

eyelash *n.* one of the short, curved hairs that grow on your eyelids.

eyelid *n.* the flap of skin that covers your eye when it is closed.

eyesight *n.* the ability to see.

eyewitness *n.* a person who saw an event happen and can describe it.

a b c d **e** f g h i j k l m n o p q r s t u v w x y z

Ff

fable *n.* a story that teaches a lesson, usually with animals as characters.

fabric *n.* cloth.

fabulous *adj.* **1** wonderful; marvelous. **2** occurring only in stories and legends. *fabulous creatures.*

face¹ *n.* **1** the front part of your head. **2** the front surface of something. *a mountain face.*

face² *v.* **1** to look toward something; to be across from something. *Our house faces north.* **2** to deal with or accept something bravely. *We have to face the truth.*

facial *adj.* of, or affecting, the face.

facility *n.* a building, service, or piece of equipment for a particular purpose. *Our school has very good sports facilities.*

fact *n.* something that is known to be true or to have happened. **in fact** actually; really.

factor *n.* **1** one of the things that may affect an outcome. **2** a number that divides exactly into another. *3 and 2 are factors of 6.*

factory *n.* a building where machines are used to make things.

factual *adj.* containing facts; real.

fad *n.* a fashion that does not last long.

fade *v.* **1** to become gradually paler. *Our curtains have faded in the Sun.* **2** to become gradually weaker or fainter.

Fahrenheit *(fa-ren-hite) adj.* measured on the temperature scale where water freezes at 32° F and boils at 212° F.

fail *v.* **1** not to pass a test. *He failed his spelling test again.* **2** not to succeed in something. *She failed to convince me.*

failing *n.* a weakness or fault.

failure *n.* **1** a lack of success. **2** an unsuccessful person or thing. **3** the fact of not doing something. *I was surprised by his failure to reply to my letter.*

faint¹ *adj.* weak; not clear. *We could hear a faint sound when we listened carefully.*

faint² *v.* to lose consciousness for a short period of time.

fair¹ *adj.* **1** reasonable; treating people equally. **2** (of hair or skin) light-colored. **3** relatively good or relatively large. *I have a fair amount of work.* **4** fine; without rain or clouds. *fair weather.*

fair² *n.* a group of outdoor amusements, with rides, games, and stalls.

fairly *adv.* relatively. *I know him fairly well.*

fairy *n.* an imaginary magical creature, like a very small person with wings.

fairy tale *n.* a traditional story for children, with fairies, giants, or magic.

faith *n.* **1** trust. *I have complete faith in you.* **2** a religion.

faithful *adj.* loyal and true. **faithfully** *adv.*, **faithfulness** *n.*

fake *n.* a copy of something that is made to fool people. **fake** *adj., v.*

falcon *n.* a bird of prey.

fall¹ *v.* (falling, fell, fallen) **1** to drop to the ground. **2** to become lower or less. *The temperature falls at night.* **3** to happen. *My birthday falls on a Tuesday this year.*
fall through to fail to happen as expected.

fall² *n.* **1** an act of dropping or falling down. **2** the season between summer and winter; autumn. **3 falls** a waterfall.

fallout *n.* radioactive dust settling after a nuclear explosion.

false *adj.* **1** not true; wrong. **2** artificial; not real.

falsehood *n.* a lie.

falter *v.* to move or speak in an unsteady, hesitant way.

falcon

fame *n.* the state of being famous.

familiar *adj.* already well known. *Her face was familiar to me.* **be familiar with** to know about something. **familiarity** *n.*

family *n.* **1** a group of people who are all related to each other. **2** a group of related animals or plants.

family tree *n.* a chart showing a person's ancestors and relations.

famine *n.* a serious shortage of food.

famous *adj.* known to a lot of people.

fan¹ *n.* an enthusiastic supporter.

fan² *n.* a machine or object that moves the

air in order to make you cooler. **fan** *v.*

fanatic *n.* a person who is overly enthusiastic about something.

fancy[1] *adj.* (fancier, fanciest) elaborate and highly decorated. *a fancy cake.*

fancy[2] *v.* (fancies, fancying, fancied) *(informal)* **1** to like. **2** to imagine.

fanfare *n.* a short tune played loudly on trumpets, often to welcome someone.

fang *n.* a long, sharp tooth.

fantastic *adj.* **1** wonderful. **2** strange; like a fantasy. *a fantastic story.*

fantasy *n.* something, usually pleasant, that you imagine or dream about, but that is not real.

far[1] *adv.* (farther *or* further, farthest *or* furthest) **1** a long way away. *Our house isn't far from the corner.* **2** much. *It's far colder than it was yesterday.*

far[2] *adj.* distant; opposite. *They live on the far side of the lake.*

farce *n.* a funny play, full of ridiculous events. **farcical** *adj.*

fare *n.* the price of traveling on a bus, train, or other public vehicle.

Far East *n.* China, Japan, and other countries in eastern Asia.

farewell goodbye. *a farewell speech.*

farm[1] *n.* land and buildings where crops are grown and animals are raised.

farm[2] *v.* to manage a farm. **farmer** *n.*

fascinate *v.* to interest and attract somebody strongly. **fascination** *n.*

fashion *n.* **1** a way of dressing or doing things that is very popular for a while. **2** a way of doing things. **fashionable** *adj.*, **fashionably** *adv.*

fast[1] *adj.* **1** quick. **2** showing a time later than the right time. *My watch is fast.*

fast[2] *adv.* **1** quickly. **2** thoroughly. *Lucy is fast asleep.* **3** firmly set. *My boot was stuck fast in the mud.*

fast[3] *v.* to give up food for a time. *He was fasting because it was Ramadan.* **fast** *n.*

fasten *v.* to tie or attach something firmly. **fastener** *n.*, **fastening** *n.*

fat[1] *n.* **1** the soft, oily substance found in humans and animals that stores energy and generates warmth. **2** an oily substance used in cooking such as butter or margarine. **fatty** *adj.*

fat[2] *adj.* (fatter, fattest) **1** having too much flesh on the body. **2** thick.

fatal *adj.* **1** causing death. *a fatal accident.* **2** causing disaster. *The pilot of the*

airplane made a fatal decision. **fatally** *adv.*

fate *n.* **1** a power that some people believe controls events. **2** an outcome or the thing that will happen to somebody or something in the future. *A terrible fate awaited her.*

father *n.* a male parent.

fathom *n.* a unit for measuring the depth of water, equal to 6 ft., or 1.8m.

fatigue *(fat-eeg)* *n.* tiredness; weakness.

fault *n.* a mistake; something wrong. **faulty** *adj.*

fauna *n.* the animal life of an area.

favor[1] *n.* **1** a helpful or kind action. **2** approval or preference. **be in favor of** to like or support something.

favor[2] *v.* to like something more than anything else.

favorite *adj.* liked more than any other. **favorite** *n.*

fawn *n.* **1** a young deer. **2** a light yellowish-brown color.

fax *n.* **1** a machine that sends a copy of a document along telephone lines and then allows it to be printed at the other end. **2** a document sent in this way. **fax** *v.*

fear[1] *n.* the feeling of being afraid.

fear[2] *v.* to feel afraid of something.

fawn

fearful *adj.* **1** afraid. **2** awful.

fearless *adj.* brave; without fear.

fearsome *adj.* frightening; terrible.

feast *n.* a large and special meal. *a wedding feast.*

feat *n.* an achievement that is difficult and impressive.

feather *n.* one of the light coverings that grows on a bird's body.

feature *n.* **1** one of the parts of the face such as the nose or the mouth. **2** an important part of something. **3** a newspaper article or part of a television show about a particular subject.

February *n.* the second month of the year.

feces (*fee-seez*) *n.* the solid waste matter that people and animals get rid of from their bodies.

feather

fed *past of* feed.

fed up *adj.* unhappy or bored.

fee *n.* a payment made to somebody in return for a service.

feeble *adj.* weak.

feed *v.* (feeding, fed) **1** to give food to a person or an animal. **2** to eat. **3** to put something into a machine. *The information is fed into a computer.*

feel *v.* (feeling, felt) **1** be aware of something by touch. *She felt his hand on her shoulder.* **2** to experience an emotion or sensation. *I felt angry.* **feeling** *n.*

feeler *n.* one of the two long, thin parts on the heads of insects and some other creatures, used for feeling with.

feet *plural of* foot.

feline (*fee-line*) *adj.* to do with cats.

fell *v.* **1** *past of* fall. **2** to cut or knock something down. *They felled the tree.*

fellow¹ *n.* a man or boy.

fellow² *adj.* belonging to the same group. *He doesn't know many of his fellow students.*

felt¹ *past of* feel.

felt² *n.* thick cloth made from pieces of wool that are pressed together rather than woven.

felt-tip pen *n.* a pen, often brightly colored, whose writing point is made of felt or fiber.

female *adj.* of the sex that gives birth to children or produces eggs. **female** *n.*

feminine *adj.* when something is to do with or is typical of women.

feminist *n.* a supporter of women's rights. **feminism** *n.*

fen *n.* low, marshy land.

fence¹ *n.* a wooden or wire barrier.

fence² *v.* to fight with special swords called foils. **fencing** *n.*

fend *v.* **fend for yourself** to take care of yourself. **fend off** to defend yourself against attacks.

ferment *v.* to change chemically, as bread dough does when yeast is added and as grape juice does when it turns into wine. **fermentation** *n.*

fern *n.* a plant with feathery leaves.

ferocious *adj.* fierce; savage. *a ferocious beast.* **ferocity** *n.*

ferret *n.* a small mammal that can be trained to hunt rabbits and rats.

ferry *n.* a boat that carries people and cars for short distances. **ferry** *v.*

fertile *adj.* **1** able to produce babies. **2** able to produce a lot of good crops. **fertility** *n.*

fern

fertilize *v.* to make fertile. Fertilize the soil with manure. **fertilization** *n.*

fervent *adj.* showing great emotion.

fervor *n.* strong enthusiasm for something. *religious fervor.*

festival *n.* **1** a time when people celebrate something, especially a religious day. **2** an organized series of events such as concerts or movies.

fetch *v.* to go to get something or somebody.

fetching *adj.* attractive; pretty.

fetus (*feet-us*) *n.* an unborn animal or human in its mother's womb.

feud (*fyood*) *n.* a long-lasting, bitter fight between people or groups.

feudal system *n.* the social system of Europe in the Middle Ages, by which people served a nobleman in return for land and protection.

fever *n.* a much higher body temperature than normal, due to

fetus

illness. **feverish** *adj.*

few *adj.* not many; a small number of things or people. *There were only a few people there.*

fiancé *(fee-on-say)* *n.* a man that a woman is engaged to marry.

fiancée *(fee-on-say)* *n.* a woman that a man is engaged to marry.

fiasco *n.* (*pl.* fiascos) a complete failure.

fib *n.* a small lie. **fib** *v.*, **fibber** *n.*

fiber *n.* **1** a fine thread. **2** the substances in plants that cannot be digested by our bodies when we eat them, but which help our digestive system work properly.

fickle *adj.* changing your mind often.

fiction *n.* stories about imaginary people and events. **fictional** *adj.*

fictitious *adj.* not true or real. *a fictitious account of events.*

fiddle[1] *n.* a violin.

fiddle[2] *v.* **1** to keep touching or playing around with something. **2** to cheat.

fidget *v.* to move around restlessly.

field[1] *n.* **1** a piece of land used for growing crops or keeping animals, often with a fence or hedge around it. **2** a piece of land used for something in particular. *a sports field.* **3** an area of study or interest. *She's an expert in her field.*

field[2] *v.* to catch or stop the ball in games such as baseball. **fielder** *n.*

fiend *(feend)* *n.* a devil or an evil person.

fierce *adj.* violent and aggressive.

fiery *adj.* **1** like fire. **2** easily made angry. *a fiery temper.*

fig *n.* a sweet fruit full of small seeds.

fight *v.* (fighting, fought) **1** to try to hurt somebody using your hands or a weapon. **2** to try hard to do or get

fig

something. *We must fight for our nation's freedom.* **3** to argue. **fight** *n.*

fighter *n.* **1** a person who fights. **2** a type of small warplane.

figure *n.* **1** a sign used for a number such as 1, 2, or 6. **2** the shape of someone's body. **3** a well-known person. *a public figure.* **4** a diagram or picture in a book.

file[1] *n.* **1** a box or folder for keeping papers neat. **2** in computing a collection of data. **3** a metal tool with a rough surface for making things smooth. **4** a line of people walking one behind another.

file[2] *v.* **1** to put papers in a file. **2** to use a file to make something smooth. **3** to walk in a line.

fill *v.* to make or become full.

fillet *n.* a piece of meat or fish with the bones removed.

filling *n.* **1** a substance that a dentist uses to fill a hole in a tooth. **2** the mixture inside of a pie or sandwich.

film[1] *n.* **1** a roll of material used in a camera to make photographs. **3** a thin coating of something. *a film of oil on the water.*

film[2] *v.* to use a camera to make a movie or television program.

filter *n.* a device that cleans liquids or gases that pass through it. **filter** *v.*

filthy *adj.* (filthier, filthiest) very dirty.

fin *n.* one of the parts on the outside of a fish's body that help it swim and balance. See **fish**.

final[1] *adj.* last. **finally** *adv.*

final[2] *n.* the last game or match of a competition. **finalist** *n.*

finance[1] *n.* money affairs. **financial** *adj.*, **financially** *adv.*

finance[2] *v.* to provide money for someone or something.

find *v.* (finding, found) **1** to discover or come across something. **2** to know something by experience or have an opinion about something. *I found the movie funny.* **find out** to discover something.

fine[1] *adj.* **1** very good. *a fine view.* **2** (of weather) good and clear. *a fine day.* **3** very thin or delicate. *fine wire.* **4** in very small pieces. *fine sand.*

fine[2] *n.* an amount of money that has to be paid as a punishment.

fine[3] *v.* to make somebody pay a fine. *She was fined for parking in the wrong place.*

finger *n.* one of the long, thin end parts of the hand.

fingernail *n.* one of the nails at the end of your fingers.

fingerprint *n.* the mark left on something by the tip of your finger.

finicky *adj.* fussy. *He's really finicky about what he eats.*

finish[1] *v.* to bring or come to an end.

finish[2] *n.* the end; the last part.

fir *n.* an evergreen tree with cones and needlelike leaves.

fire[1] *n.* **1** the light and heat that is produced when something is burning. **2** a device for heating. *an electric fire.* **3** shooting; gunfire. *enemy fire.*

fire[2] *v.* **1** to shoot a gun or other weapon. **2** to dismiss somebody from his or her job.

fire engine *n.* a vehicle that carries firefighters and their equipment.

fire extinguisher *n.* a container full of chemicals for putting out a fire.

firefighter *n.* a person whose job is to put out fires.

fireplace *n.* a space in the wall of a room for a fire.

fire station *n.* a place where fire engines are kept.

fireworks *n. pl.* small, exploding devices that make colored sparks or a loud noise when they are lit.

firm[1] *adj.* **1** strong and steady. *The castle was built on firm ground.* **2** not changing your mind. *a firm decision.*

firm[2] *n.* a business company.

first *adj., adv.* number one in order; before all others. **first** *n.,* **firstly** *adv.*

first aid *n.* emergency medical treatment given to a sick or injured person before a doctor arrives.

fish[1] *n.* (*pl.* fish *or* fishes) a water creature with gills, fins, and scales.

fish[2] *v.* to try to catch fish.

fist *n.* a tightly closed hand.

fit[1] *adj.* (fitter, fittest) **1** healthy and strong. **2** suitable.

fit[2] *v.* (fits, fitting, fitted) **1** to be the

fish[1]

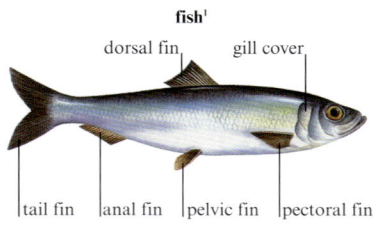

dorsal fin gill cover

tail fin | anal fin | pelvic fin | pectoral fin

right size and shape. *These shoes don't fit me.* **2** to put something in place. *She fit a new lock on the door.*

fit[3] *n.* **1** a sudden loss of consciousness with uncontrolled movements of the body; seizure. **2** a sudden, uncontrolled outburst. *a coughing fit.*

fitness *n.* being healthy and strong.

fix[1] *v.* **1** to mend something. **2** to attach or make something firm. **3** to decide on something.

fixture *n.* **1** a sporting event that has been arranged. **2** an object in a building that has been fixed in position such as a cupboard or a sink.

fizz *v.* to produce a lot of small bubbles. **fizzy** *adj.*

fjord (*fee-ord*) *n.* a long, narrow inlet found on high, rocky coasts. (*can also be spelled* fiord.)

flabby *adj.* (flabbier, flabbiest) having loose, soft flesh.

flag[1] *n.* a piece of colored cloth with a pattern on it, often representing a country or an organization.

flag[2] *v.* (flags, flagging, flagged) to become tired.

flair *n.* a natural ability. *She has a flair for writing.*

flake *n.* a small, thin, light piece of something such as snow. **flaky** *adj.*

flamboyant *adj.* bold and showy.

flame *n.* the burning gas from a fire in a long, thin shape.

flamingo *n.* (*pl.* flamingos or flamingoes) a large wading bird with pink feathers.

flammable *adj.* able to burn easily.

flan *n.* a flat, open pie.

flank *n.* the side of an animal's body.

flannel *n.* **1** light, woolen cloth. **2** a piece of cloth used for washing yourself; washcloth.

flap[1] *n.* a piece of material that hangs down over an opening. *a tent flap.*

flap[2] *v.* (flaps, flapping, flapped) to move up and down. *The bird flapped its wings.*

flare[1] *v.* **flare up** to suddenly become stronger, brighter, or more violent. *The fire flared up when the oil dripped onto it.*

flare[2] *n.* a flame or light used as a signal.

flash[2] *n.* a sudden burst of light. **in a flash** very quickly; suddenly.

flash[2] *v.* **1** to shine brightly and quickly.

2 to move quickly. *A car flashed past.*

flask *n.* a bottle, especially one for keeping liquids hot or cold; thermos.

flat[1] *adj.* (flatter, flattest) **1** level and smooth. **2** (of a tire) having lost most of its air. **3** (of a drink) no longer fizzy.

flat[2] *n.* **1** a sign in music indicating that a note should be played lower by half a tone.

flatten *v.* to make something flat.

flatter *v.* to praise somebody more than he or she deserves. **flattery** *n.*

flavor *n* the taste of something. **flavor** *v.*

flaw *n.* a fault or weakness.

flea *n.* a small, jumping insect that feeds on blood.

fledgling *n.* a young bird that is just ready to fly.

flee *v.* (fleeing, fled) to run away.

fleece *n.* **1** a sheep's wool coat. **2** a warm, woolen jacket.

fleet *n.* a group of ships or trucks.

flea

flesh *n.* **1** the soft part of humans and animals, between the bones and the skin. **2** the soft part of fruits.

flew *past of* fly.

flexible *adj.* bending or changing easily.

flick *v.* to make a quick, sharp movement. **flick** *n.*

flicker *v.* to shine unsteadily. *The candle flickered.* **flicker** *n.*

flight *n.* **1** the action of flying. **2** a journey in an aircraft. **3** running away from danger. **4** a set of steps.

flimsy *adj.* (flimsier, flimsiest) thin or easily broken.

fling *v.* (flinging, flung) to throw something with great force.

flint *n.* a very hard type of stone.

flip *v.* (flips, flipping, flipped) to toss or turn something over quickly.

flipper *n.* **1** an armlike limb that seals and walrus uses for swimming. **2** a type of large, flat, rubber shoe that helps you swim underwater.

flirt *v.* to talk to somebody to show that you are attracted to him or her but not in a serious way. **flirt** *n.*

float[1] *v.* to be held up in water or air.

float[2] *n.* a light object attached close to the end of a fishing line.

flock[1] *n.* a large group of animals, particularly sheep or birds.

flock[2] *v.* to move in a large group.

flog *v.* (flogs, flogging, flogged) **1** to beat or whip a person or an animal. **2** *(informal)* to sell something.

flood[1] *n.* **1** a lot of water that spreads over land that is usually dry. **2** a large number of people or things that keep coming. *There has been a flood of new products onto the market.*

flood[2] *v.* **1** to cover something with a flood. **2** to overflow.

floor *n.* **1** the part of a room that you walk on. **2** one level or story of a building. *We live on the second floor.*

flop[1] *v.* (flops, flopping, flopped) **1** to fall limply. **floppy** *adj.* **2** *(informal)* to be a complete failure.

flop[2] *n.* *(informal)* a complete failure.

floppy disk *n.* *(old-fashioned)* a magnetic disk for storing data from a computer, now being replaced by CDs, memory sticks, or flash drives.

florist *n.* a person who sells flowers.

flour *n.* a powder made from grain, used for baking.

flourish *(flur-ish)* *v.* to grow well; to become successful.

flow *v.* to move along smoothly, as water does in a river. **flow** *n.*

flower[1] *n.* the colored part of a plant that produces seeds.

flower[2] *v.* to produce flowers.

flown *past participle of* fly.

flu *n.* *(short for* influenza) an illness that

flower

stigma (receives pollen grains)

anther (stores pollen)

petal

style

ovule

stamen (male part)

sepal (protects flower bud)

stem

ovary (female part)

gives you a high temperature, headache, and aching muscles.

fluctuate *v.* to change all the time. *Her mood fluctuates between delight and despair.* **fluctuation** *n.*

a
b
c
d
e
f
g
h
i
j
k
l
m
n
o
p
q
r
s
t
u
v
w
x
y
z

A
B
C
D
E
F
G
H
I
J
K
L
M
N
O
P
Q
R
S
T
U
V
W
X
Y
Z

fluent *adj.* able to speak or write easily and well.

fluff *n.* small pieces of soft, woolen material from blankets or clothes.

fluffy *adj.* (fluffier, fluffiest) soft and furry. *a fluffy kitten.*

fluid *n.* a liquid or, less commonly, a gas.

flung *past of* fling.

fluorescent *adj.* when something is so bright that it seems to give out light. *fluorescent colors.*

fluoride *n.* a mixture of chemicals that is added to water and toothpaste to prevent tooth decay.

flush *v.* **1** to blush. **2** to clean something by a rush of water. **flush** *n.*

flustered *adj.* nervous and confused.

flute *n.* a wind instrument, in the shape of a long tube with holes in it, which you hold horizontally.

flutter *v.* to move up and down or from side to side with small, quick movements.

fly[1] *v.* (flies, flying, flew, flown) **1** to move through the air. **2** to travel in or pilot an aircraft. **3** to move very quickly.

fly[2] *n.* a flying insect.

foal *n.* a young horse.

foam *n.* a mass of small bubbles. **foam** *v.*

focus *v.* (focuses, focusing, focused) **1** to adjust the lens of a camera in order to get a clear picture. **2** to concentrate on something. **focus** *n.*

fodder *n.* food for cows or horses.

foe *n.* an enemy.

fog *n.* a thick mist that is difficult to see through. **foggy** *adj.*

foil[1] *n.* **1** metal in the form of very thin sheets; tin foil. **2** a light, slender sword with a button at the tip, used in fencing.

foil[2] *v.* to stop somebody from succeeding.

fold[1] *v.* to bend part of a thing back on itself.

fold[2] *n.* **1** a folded part of something. **2** an enclosure for sheep.

folder *n.* a cover for keeping papers in.

foliage *n.* the leaves of plants.

folk, folks *n. pl.* people.

follow *v.* **1** to go along behind somebody or something. **2** to go along a road or

path. **3** to understand something.

folly *n.* a foolish act.

fond *adj.* **be fond of** to like something. **fondly** *adv.*, **fondness** *n.*

fondle *v.* to touch or stroke a person or an animal gently.

font *n.* **1** a stone basin in a church that holds water for baptism. **2** a set of letters and symbols used in desktop publishing and printing.

food *n.* anything that is eaten.

fool[1] *n.* a silly person.

fool[2] *v.* to trick somebody.

foolish *adj.* stupid; silly.

foot *n.* (*pl.* feet) **1** the part of the leg that you stand on. **2** the lower part of something. *the foot of the page.* **3** a measure of length, equal to 12 inches.

footnote *n.* a note at the bottom of a printed page.

footprint *n.* a mark left by a foot on the ground, especially on soft ground.

footsteps *n. pl.* the sound of somebody's feet as he or she walks.

forbid *v.* (forbids, forbidding, forbade, forbidden) to tell somebody that he or she should not do something.

force[1] *v.* **1** to make somebody do something against his or her will. **2** to push something with violence.

force[2] *n.* **1** power; strength. **2** a group of people who work together, such as the air force.

ford *n.* a shallow place where a river can be crossed.

forecast *v.* **1** to say what is likely to happen in the future. **2** to report on what the weather will be like in the future. **forecast** *n.*

forehead *n.* the part of your face above your eyebrows.

foreign *adj.* from or of another country. **foreigner** *n.*

foresight *n.* the ability to know about something in advance.

forest *n.* a large area of land thickly covered with trees.

forfeit *v.* to lose the right to something because of something that you have done wrong. **forfeit** *n.*

forge[1] *v.* to make a copy of something in order to trick people. *forged dollar bills.* **forgery** *n.*

forge[2] *n.* a furnace used by a blacksmith to heat metal for shaping.

foil

forget *v.* (forgets, forgetting, forgot, forgotten) to not remember.

forgive *v.* (forgiving, forgave, forgiven) to stop being angry with somebody for what he or she has done wrong. **forgiveness** *n.*

fork *n.* **1** a tool with prongs for eating with or for digging earth. **2** a place

medieval forge

where something divides. *We came to a fork in the road.* **fork** *v.*

forlorn *adj.* lonely and unhappy.

form¹ *n.* **1** the shape of something. **2** a printed paper with spaces where answers have to be filled in.

form² *v.* **1** to make into a certain shape. *Please stand up and form a circle.* **2** to take shape.

formal *adj.* **1** following the accepted rules; official. **2** suitable for important and serious occasions. **formally** *adv.*

format¹ *v.* (formats, formatting, formatted) **1** to arrange text on a computer into a particular form or style. **2** to prepare a computer disk for use.

format² *n.* the size, form, or shape that something takes.

former *adj.* previous; earlier. **the former** the first of two things just mentioned. *We visited France and Italy, spending longer in the former.*

formerly *adv.* in past times.

formula *n.* (*pl.* formulas *or* formulae) a rule or fact in science or math, written in signs or numbers.

fort *n.* a building that is strongly defended against attacks.

forthcoming *adj.* coming soon.

fortify *v.* to make a place stronger against attacks. **fortification** *n.*

fortress *n.* a castle or fortified town.

fortunate *adj.* lucky.

fortune *n.* **1** luck. **2** a lot of money.

forward *adv.* toward the front.

fossil *n.* the remains of a prehistoric animal or plant that has been preserved in rock.

foster *v.* **1** to raise a child who is not your own, without becoming his or her legal parent. **2** to encourage something.

foster parent *n.* a person who fosters a child who can no longer be cared for by the birth parents.

fought *past of* fight.

foul¹ *adj.* dirty; disgusting; bad.

foul² *n.* an action that breaks the rules of a sport. **foul** *v.*

fossil

found *v.* **1** *past of* find. **2** to establish something. *She founded the school in 1898.* **foundation** *n.*, **founder** *n.*

foundations *n. pl.* the strong base of a building below the ground.

foundry *n.* a place where metals or glass are melted and molded.

fountain *n.* a structure producing a jet of water that rises into the air.

fountain pen *n.* a pen with a nib and a supply of ink inside.

fowl *n.* (*pl.* fowl *or* fowls) a bird, eg. a chicken, that is kept for its eggs or meat.

fox *n.* a wild animal with reddish-brown fur and a bushy tail.

foyer *(foy-er)* *n.* the entrance hall of a theater or other large building.

fraction *n.* **1** a part of a whole number. *1/2 (one half) and 1/4 (one fourth) are fractions.* **2** a small amount.

fox

fracture *v.* to break or crack something, especially a bone. **fracture** *n.*

fragile *adj.* delicate; easily damaged.

fragment *n.* a small, broken piece.

a b c d e **f** g h i j k l m n o p q r s t u v w x y z

A
B
C
D
E
F
G
H
I
J
K
L
M
N
O
P
Q
R
S
T
U
V
W
X
Y
Z

fragrance *n.* a nice smell. **fragrant** *adj.*

frail *adj.* weak; feeble. **frailty** *n.*

frame *n.* **1** the main, hard structure around which something is built. *The aircraft has a steel frame.* **2** the border around the edge of a picture.

framework *n.* the basic supporting structure of something.

frank *adj.* open and honest. **frankness** *n.*

frantic *adj.* very upset or excited because of worry or fear. **frantically** *adv.*

fraud *n.* **1** the crime of taking money by deceit. **2** a person who pretends to be something that he or she is not.

fraught (*frawt*) *adj.* **1** full of possible problems or dangers. *fraught with danger.* **2** stressed; anxious.

freckle *n.* a small, brown mark on the skin. **freckly** *adj.*

free¹ *adj.* **1** costing no money. **2** loose; not tied up or shut in. **3** able to do what you want. **4** available. **freedom** *n.*

free² *v.* (freeing, freed) to set a person or an animal free.

freeze *v.* (freezing, froze, frozen) **1** to change into ice; to become solid because of cold. **2** to make food very cold so that it can be kept for a long time. **3** to stand completely still.

freezer *n.* a large, metal box where it is possible to store food below freezing point, in order to preserve it.

freezing point *n.* the temperature at which a liquid freezes.

freight (*frate*) *n.* cargo.

frenzy *n.* wild excitement or anger.

frequency *n.* **1** the number of times that something happens. **2** the rate at which a radio wave vibrates.

frequent *adj.* happening often.

fresh *adj.* **1** recently made or picked. *fresh bread, fresh flowers.* **2** not canned or preserved. *fresh fruit.* **3** cool and clean. *fresh air.*

freshwater *adj.* (of a fish) living in rivers and lakes, not in the sea.

fret *v.* (frets, fretting, fretted) to worry.

friction *n.* the natural resistance an object meets with when it is rubbed against something else.

Friday *n.* the sixth day of the week.

fridge *n.* a type of cupboard in which food is kept very cold (*short for* refrigerator).

friend *n.* a person that you know well and that you like. **friendship** *n.*

friendly *adj.* (friendlier, friendliest) kind and helpful.

frieze (*rhymes with* squeeze) *n.* a decorated

frigate *n.* a small, fast warship.

fright *n.* a sudden feeling of fear.

frighten *v.* to make somebody afraid.

frill *n.* a strip of cloth or other material with many small folds, attached to something as decoration.

frisk *v.* **1** to search somebody for something

ancient Greek frieze

illegal. **2** to jump around in a playful way.

frisky *adj.* playful.

frivolous *adj.* silly; not serious.

frock *n.* a girl's or woman's dress.

frog *n.* a small amphibian with long back legs and webbed feet.

front *n.* **1** the part of something that faces forward. **2** in a war the place where the fighting is; front line. **front** *adj.*

frontier *n.* a border between countries.

frost *n.* powdery ice that forms on the ground when it gets very cold. **frosty** *adj.*

froth *n.* a mass of small bubbles found on top of a liquid.

frown *v.* to pull your eyebrows together and wrinkle your forehead when you

frog

are angry, sad, or thinking hard.

froze *past of* freeze.

frozen *past participle of* freeze.

fruit *n.* **1** the part of a plant with seeds inside, often used as food. **2** the result of something. *the fruit of all your labors.*

frustrate *v.* **1** to make somebody feel

disappointed or angry because that person cannot do what he or she wanted to. **2** to prevent something from succeeding. **frustration** *n.*

fry[1] *v.* (fries, frying, fried) to cook food in hot oil.

fry[2] *n.* (*pl.* fries) a fried, cut potato; French fry.

fudge *n.* a soft, brown candy.

fuel *n.* anything that is burned to make heat or energy, including coal, oil, wood, or gas.

fulfill *v* (fulfills, fulfilling, fulfilled) to carry out a task or promise.

full *adj.* **1** with no room left inside. **2** complete. *a full explanation.*

fumble *v.* to use your hands clumsily.

fumes *n. pl.* strong-smelling or poisonous smoke or gases.

fun *n.* amusement; a good time.

function[1] *n.* the special work of a person or thing.

function[2] *v.* to work.

fund[1] *n.* an amount of money for a charity or other purpose.

fund[2] *v.* to provide the money for someone to do something.

fundamental *adj.* basic and important. **fundamentally** *adv.*

funeral *n.* the ceremony at which somebody who has died is buried or cremated.

fungus *n.* (*pl.* fungi *or* funguses) a soft, spongy plantlike growth such as a mushroom or toadstool.

funnel *n.* **1** a cone-shaped object, used to pour liquid into a narrow container. **2** a chimney on a ship.

funny *adj.* (funnier, funniest) **1** amusing. **2** strange; odd. *a funny noise.* **funnily** *adv.*

fur *n.* the soft, hairy covering on some animals. **furry** *adj.*

furious *adj.* extremely angry.

furnace *n.* a very hot oven.

furnish *v.* to equip a room or building with furniture.

furniture *n.* chairs, tables, beds, desks, and other similar things.

furrow *n.* a straight, narrow cut made in the ground by a plow.

further *adj., adv.* **1** more far. **2** more; extra. *I have one further question.*

furthermore *adv.* in addition.

furthest *adj., adv.* the most.

fury *n.* violent anger.

fuse[1] *n.* **1** a safety device in an electrical circuit. **2** a lead that sets off the explosion of a bomb.

fuse[2] *v.* **1** to connect by heat. **2** to stop working because a fuse has melted. **fusion** *n.*

fuselage *(fyoo-zel-ajh) n.* the body of an aircraft.

fuss *n.* unnecessary excitement or worry. **fuss** *v.*

fussy *adj.* (fussier, fussiest) difficult to please; too concerned with details.

future *n.* the time to come.

fuzzy *adj.* (fuzzier, fuzziest) **1** having a soft, hairy texture. *a fuzzy blanket.* **2** blurred; not clear. *fuzzy photographs.*

fuselage

fungus

Gg

gabble v. to talk very quickly and not very clearly.

gadget n. a small device or tool. *A can opener is a gadget.*

gag[1] n. **1** a piece of cloth tied over somebody's mouth to stop him or her from speaking. **2** a joke.

gag[2] v. (gags, gagging, gagged) to tie a piece of cloth over somebody's mouth to stop him or her from speaking.

gain v. to get something; to get more of something. *The baby has gained weight.* **gain** n.

galaxy n. a very large group of stars and planets. **galactic** adj.

gale n. a very strong wind.

gallant adj. **1** brave and daring. **2** courteous, especially to women.

gallbladder n. the organ in your body next to your liver, containing a greenish liquid, called bile, that helps digestion.

galleon n. (historical) a large Spanish sailing ship from history.

gallery n. **1** a building where pictures or other works of art are displayed. **2** the highest part in a theater where people sit.

galleon

galley n. (pl. galleys) **1** the kitchen on a ship or aircraft. **2** (historical) a long ship with one deck that is propelled by oars and sails.

gallon n. a measure for liquids equal to 4 quarts (3.8 liters).

gallop n. the fastest a horse can go. **gallop** v.

gallows n. (historical) a wooden frame on which criminals used to be hanged.

galore adv. in large quantities. *There was food galore at the party.*

gamble v. **1** to bet money on the result of a game or race. **2** to take a risk on something. **gambler** n., **gambling** n.

game n. **1** an activity with rules, for one or more players. *Tennis and checkers are both games.* **2** wild animals and birds that are hunted for food or for sport.

gammon n. a type of ham or bacon.

gander n. a male goose.

gang[1] n. a group of people who do things together. *one of the gang.*

gang[2] v. **gang up on** to join in with others against somebody.

gangster n. a member of a gang made up of violent criminals.

gangway n. (pl. gangways) **1** a passage between rows of seats. **2** a movable bridge between a ship and the shore.

gap n. a space between things.

gape v. **1** to stare in surprise at something, with your mouth open. *Drivers stopped to gape at the accident.* **2** to be wide open. *His mouth gaped open.*

garage n. **1** a building where vehicles are kept. **2** a place where vehicles are taken to be repaired.

garbage n. trash.

garden n. a piece of land where flowers, fruits, and vegetables are grown. **gardener** n., **gardening** n.

gargle v. to wash your mouth and throat with a liquid without swallowing it.

gargoyle n. an ugly stone carving of the head of a human or animal, for carrying water away from the roof of a building for decoration.

garish (*gair-ish*) adj. too brightly colored.

garland n. a ring or thread of leaves or flowers.

garlic n. a plant with a strong-tasting bulb that is used in cooking.

garment n. a piece of clothing.

garnish v. to decorate food with small amounts of another food. *Garnish the dish with sprigs of parsley.*

garter n. an elastic band used to hold up a sock or stocking.

gas n. **1** a substance that is neither solid nor liquid. Oxygen and helium are gases. **2** the gas used for heating and cooking in homes. **3** fuel that makes a vehicle run; gasoline.

gash n. a long, deep cut.

gasp *v.* **1** to take a sudden, sharp breath. **2** to breathe with difficulty. **gasp** *n.*

gastric *adj.* to do with the stomach.

gate *n.* a type of door, usually located in a wall, fence, or hedge.

gâteau *(ga-toe)* *n.* (*pl.* gâteaux) a rich, creamy cake, often chocolate.

gatecrash *v.* to go to a party that you have not been invited to.

gateway *n.* (*pl.* gateways) an opening that contains a gate; an entrance.

gather *v.* **1** to collect or pick something. **2** to bring or come together.

gathering *n.* a meeting of people.

gaudy *(gaw-dee)* *adj.* (gaudier, gaudiest) too brightly colored or elaborate.

gauge[1] *(rhymes with rage)* *v.* **1** to measure something with a gauge. **2** to estimate something, often its size or weight.

gauge[2] *n.* **1** an instrument for measuring something. *a gas gauge.* **2** the distance between the two rails of a railroad track.

gauntlet *n.* a long, thick, protective glove.

gauze *(gawz)* *n.* thin, woven cloth, normally used as a bandage.

gave *past of* give.

gay *adj.* **1** homosexual. **2** *(old-fashioned)* cheerful; happy.

gaze *v.* to look at something for a long time. **gaze** *n.*

gazelle *n.* a type of small antelope that is found in parts of Africa and Asia.

gear *n.* **1** one of a set of toothed wheels that works together to send power to the wheels of a car or bicycle.

geese *plural of* goose.

gel *n.* a thick substance, like jelly.

gem *n.* a precious stone.

gender *n.* **1** the sex of a person or an animal. **2** the class of a noun in many languages such as Spanish or French, e.g. masculine, feminine, or neuter.

gene *(jeen)* *n.* a tiny part of the cells of all living things. Genes are responsible for the way living things look and develop. They pass from parents to their children.

general[1] *adj.* **1** to do with most people or things. *The general feeling is that the manager should resign.* **2** not detailed or specific. *a general description of events.* **in general** usually; mostly.

general[2] *n.* a senior officer in the army, navy, or air force.

generally *adv.* usually; mostly.

generate *v.* to produce something, especially electricity.

generation *n.* **1** all the people of around the same age. *People of my generation listen to different music than our parents.* **2** the generating of something. *the generation of electricity.*

generator *n.* a machine that is able to produce electricity.

generous *adj.* ready to give money or help freely and happily. **generosity** *n.*

genetic *adj.* to do with genes.

genetics *n.* the study of the way that characteristics are passed on from one generation to the next through genes.

genitals *n. pl.* the sex organs on the outside of the body.

genius *(jeen-yus)* *n.* a person who is extremely intelligent.

genre *(jhan-ra)* *n.* a type or style of book, movie, or music, e.g. comedy, horror, or classical.

gentle *adj.* **1** quiet and kind; not rough. *Be gentle with the kitten.* **2** not harsh or strong; soft. *a gentle breeze.* **3** rising gradually. *a gentle slope.* **gentleness** *n.*, **gently** *adv.*

gentleman *n.* (*pl.* gentlemen) **1** a polite word to describe a man. **2** a man with good manners.

genuine *adj.* real and true; not fake.

geography *n.* the study of Earth and its countries, physical features, weather, and people. **geographer** *n.*, **geographical** *adj.*

geology *n.* the study of Earth's rocks and soil and how they were formed. **geological** *adj.*, **geologist** *n.*

geometric, geometrical *adj.* **1** to do with geometry. **2** consisting of regular lines or shapes. *a geometric design.*

geometry *n.* the study in mathematics of lines, angles, and shapes.

geranium *n.* a garden plant with red, pink, white, or purple flowers.

gerbil *n.* a small rodent that is often kept as a pet.

geriatric *adj.* to do with older people. *The hospital has a geriatric ward.*

gerbil

germ *n.* a very small living thing that can cause diseases.

germinate *v.* (of a seed) to begin to develop into a plant. **germination** *n.*

gesture *n.* **1** a movement of your hands or head to express a feeling or idea. **2** something that you do to express your feelings. *She sent him some flowers as a gesture of friendship.*

get *v.* (getting, got, gotten) **1** to receive or obtain. *I got a bike for my birthday.* **2** to buy or bring. *Will you get me some fruit from the store?* **3** to go somewhere; to arrive. *How do we get across the river?* **4** to become. *He's getting fat.* **5** to persuade. *Can you get him to agree?* **6** to catch an illness. *I'm getting a cold.* **7** to understand. *She didn't get the joke.* **get along with** to have a friendly relationship with somebody. **get away with** to do something bad but not be punished for it. **get by** to manage. *She gets by on a very low salary.* **get on** to make progress. **get out of** to avoid doing something. **get over** to recover from something. *She's getting over her cold.* **get through 1** to pass an exam or test. **2** to contact somebody on the telephone.

geyser (*gy-zer*) *n.* a natural hot spring from which extremely hot water and steam shoot out.

ghastly *adj.* horrible; terrible.

ghost *n.* the spirit of a dead person that

geyser

appears to somebody who is still living. **ghostly** *adj.*

giant[1] *n.* a huge, usually frightening, person in fairy tales.

giant[2] *adj.* unusually large. *a giant fish.*

gibberish *n.* nonsense.

gibbon *n.* an ape with long arms and no tail.

giddy *adj.* (giddier, giddiest) dizzy; lighthearted. **giddiness** *n.*

gift *n.* **1** a present; something that is given by someone to somebody. **2** a natural ability or talent. *He has a real gift for music.*

gibbon

gifted *adj.* with great natural ability; exceptionally intelligent.

gig *n.* (*informal*) a performance by a musician or band; show.

gigantic (*jy-gan-tik*) *adj.* very large.

giggle *v.* to laugh in a silly way. **giggle** *n.*, **giggly** *adj.*

gill *n.* one of the parts of a fish's body, through which it breathes. See **fish**.

gilt *adj.* covered thinly with gold.

gimmick *n.* something unusual used as a way of attracting attention. *an advertising gimmick.*

gin *n.* a colorless, alcoholic drink made from grains.

ginger *n.* a hot-tasting root of a plant, used as a flavoring.

gingerbread *n.* a type of cake flavored with ginger.

gingham *n.* checkered cotton cloth.

giraffe *n.* an African mammal with very long legs and a long neck, which it uses to eat leaves from the tops of trees.

girder *n.* a large iron or steel bar supporting a floor or wall.

girl *n.* a female child.

gist (*jist*) *n.* the main points. *Just give me the gist of what she said.*

give *v.* (giving, gave, given) **1** to hand something over to somebody else. *She gave me a present for my birthday.* **2** to let somebody have something. *Can you give me some advice?* **3** to make a sound or a movement. *He gave a shout.* **4** to bend or break. *We pushed hard against the door, and at last the lock gave.* **give in** to finally agree to something that you do not want to do. *Her dad finally gave in and said she could have ice cream.* **give out** to distribute. *Can you give out these books to the class?*

A B C D E F G H I J K L M N O P Q R S T U V W X Y Z

give up to stop doing or using something. *My uncle is trying to give up smoking.* **give way 1** to let other people go in front of you. **2** to break or collapse. *the bridge gave way.*

glacier *(glay-sher) n.* a huge mass of ice that moves extremely slowly down a mountain valley.

glad *adj.* (gladder, gladdest) pleased.

gladiator *n. (historical)* in ancient Rome

glacier

a man trained to fight for the entertainment of spectators.

glamour *n.* attractiveness and excitement. *the glamour of Hollywood in the 1920s.* **glamorous** *adj.*

glance *v.* to look quickly at something. **glance** *n.*

gland *n.* an organ in the body that stores substances that are used or gotten rid of.

glare *v.* **1** to look angrily at somebody. **2** to shine with an unpleasantly bright light. **glare** *n.*

glass *n.* **1** a hard, transparent material that is used to make windows and a variety of types of containers such as bottles. **2** a container made of glass, used for drinking from. **3** a mirror.

glasses *n. pl.* lenses in a frame, worn over your eyes to improve your sight; spectacles.

glaze[1] *v.* **1** to fit glass into a window. **2** to cover something with a shiny coating. *The potter glazed the vase.*

glaze[2] *n.* a shiny coating painted onto pottery before it is baked.

glazier *n.* a person whose profession is to fit glass into windows.

gleam *v.* to shine brightly. **gleam** *n.*

glee *n.* great joy. **gleeful** *adj.*

glen *n.* a narrow valley.

glide *v.* to move smoothly and easily.

glider *n.* a small, light aircraft that doesn't have an engine.

glimmer *n.* to shine faintly. **glimmer** *n.*

glimpse *v.* to see something for only a moment. **glimpse** *n.*

glisten *v.* to shine like a wet surface.

glitter[1] *v.* to shine with a lot of tiny,

bright flashes of light; to sparkle.

glitter[2] *n.* tiny, sparkly pieces used for decoration.

global *adj.* concerning the whole world. **globally** *adv.*

global warming *n.* a gradual increase in Earth's temperature caused by the greenhouse effect.

globe *n.* an object shaped like a ball, especially a map of Earth shaped like this.

gloomy *adj.* (gloomier, gloomiest) **1** dark and dull. **2** sad. *Don't look so gloomy.* **gloom** *n.*, **gloomily** *adv.*

glorious *adj.* magnificent; beautiful.

glory *n.* **1** fame; honor. **2** beauty; splendor.

gloss *n.* a shine on a surface. *Her hair has a lovely gloss.* **glossy** *adj.*

glossary *n.* a list of special words and their meanings, often found in books.

glove *n.* a covering for your hand.

glow *v.* to send out a steady heat or light without flames. *The barbecue is ready when the coals start to glow.* **glow** *n.*

glowworm *n.* a beetle whose tail glows green in the dark.

glucose *n.* a natural sugar found in plant and animal tissue.

glue *n.* a sticky substance used for connecting things. **glue** *v.*

glum *adj.* (glummer, glummest) extremely sad and gloomy. *Why are you so glum?*

glut *n.* too large a supply of something. *a glut of apples.*

gnat *(nat) n.* a small, flying insect that bites.

gnaw *(naw) v.* to keep chewing or biting at something. *The dog gnawed on his bone.*

gnome *(nome) n.* a small creature in fairy tales that lives underground.

go[1] *v.* (goes, going, went, gone) **1** to walk, travel, or move somewhere. *We went to the movies.* **2** to lead somewhere. *Where does this road go?* **3** to become. *The banana went black.* **4** to work properly. *My watch doesn't go.* **5** to disappear. *Your bike is gone!* **going to** intending to; about to. *I'm going to phone Bob.* **go off 1** to explode. *A bomb went off.* **2** to become rotten. *The meat went off.* **go on** to continue.

goal *n.* **1** the space into which a ball must go to score in games such as soccer and hockey. **2** the point scored by doing this. **3** something that you are trying to achieve. *Her goal in life is to become a ballet dancer.*

A
B
C
D
E
F
G
H
I
J
K
L
M
N
O
P
Q
R
S
T
U
V
W
X
Y
Z

goat *n.* a type of farm animal with horns and a beard.

gobble *v.* to eat quickly and greedily.

goal

goblin *n.* a small, ugly, and usually evil creature in fairy tales.

god *n.* **1** a supernatural being that is worshipped because people believe that it has control over their lives. **2 God** in the Christian, Jewish, and Muslim religions the creator and ruler of everything in the universe.

goddess *n.* a female god.

godparent, godfather, godmother *n.* a person who promises at a child's baptism to make sure that the **godchild (goddaughter** or **godson)** is raised according to Christian beliefs.

goggles *n. pl.* large glasses that protect the eyes from water, dust, or other substances.

gold *n.* **1** a precious, shiny, yellow metal, often used for making jewelry. **2** a yellow color. **gold** *adj.*

golden *adj.* **1** made of gold. **2** with the color of gold.

goldfish *n.* (*pl.* goldfish) an orange fish often kept as a pet.

golf *n.* a game in which a small ball is hit across open ground and into small holes with a stick (called a **golf club**). **golfer** *n.*

gondola *n.* a long, narrow boat used in the canals in Venice, Italy.

gondolier *n.* a person who moves a gondola through the water.

gondola

gone *past participle of* go.

gong *n.* a large, round metal disk that makes a ringing note when it is hit with a hammer.

good *adj.* (better, best) **1** of a high quality or standard. *a good book.* **2** well behaved. *Be a good dog.* **3** pleasant. *I'm in a good mood today.* **4** kind; virtuous. *You've been very good to me.* **5** suitable. *She's a good person for the job.* **6** skillful. *a good swimmer.* **7** healthy; beneficial. *Fresh fruit is very good for you.* **goodness** *n.*

goodbye a word that you say when leaving somebody.

Good Friday *n.* the Friday before Easter, when Christians commemorate the day that Jesus was crucified.

goods *n. pl.* **1** things that are bought and sold. **2** things that are carried on trains or trucks.

goose *n.* (*pl.* geese) a large water bird with a long neck and webbed feet.

gooseberry *n.* a sour-tasting green berry with a hairy skin.

goose bumps *n. pl.* small bumps that sometimes appear on your skin when you are cold or afraid.

gorge[1] *n.* a steep, narrow valley.

gorge[2] *v.* **gorge yourself** to eat greedily.

gorgeous *adj.* extremely beautiful or attractive.

gorilla *n.* the largest type of ape, found on the continent of Africa.

gory *adj.* (gorier, goriest) full of violence and blood. *a gory movie.* **gore** *n.*

gosling *n.* a young goose.

gospel *n.* one of the four books of the New Testament, containing accounts of the life and teachings of Jesus.

gossip *n.* talk about other people that is often unkind or untrue. **gossip** *v.*

got *past of* get.

govern *v.* to rule or control, especially a country. **governor** *n.*

government *n.* the people who are in charge of and govern a country.

gown *n.* a woman's formal dress.

grab *v.* (grabs, grabbing, grabbed) to take something quickly and roughly.

grace *n.* **1** beauty of movement. *The dancer moved with incredible grace.* **2** mercy. *the grace of God.* **3** decency; politeness. *He didn't have the grace to apologize.* **4** a short prayer said before a meal.

graceful *adj.* moving beautifully and elegantly. **gracefully** *adv.*

gracious *adj.* polite and kind.

grade *n.* **1** one level in a scale of qualities or sizes. **2** a mark on a test or school work.

gradient *n.* the steepness of a slope.

gradual *adj.* happening slowly; little by little. **gradually** *adv.*

graduate[1] *(**graj**-yoo-ate)* *v.* to successfully complete a course of study, especially at a college or high school. **graduation** *n.*

graduate[2] *(**graj**-yoo-ut)* *n.* a person who has graduated.

graffiti *n. pl.* words or drawings that are scribbled on a wall.

graft *v.* **1** to cut part of one plant and connect it to another so that it grows. **2** to take skin or bone from one part of the body to help repair a damaged part. **graft** *n.*

grain *n.* **1** the seeds of plants such as wheat, rice, and oats. **2** a very small, hard piece of something. *a grain of sand.* **3** the natural pattern in wood.

gram *n.* a measure of weight. *There are 1,000 grams in a kilogram.*

grammar *n.* the rules for using words and putting them together. **grammatical** *adj.*

granary *n.* a building where grain is stored.

grand *adj.* **1** important; splendid; large; impressive. **2** *(informal)* very pleasant.

grandchild, granddaughter, grandson *n.* the child of your daughter or son.

grandparent, grandfather, grandmother *n.* the parent of one of your parents.

grandstand *n.* a covered structure with rows of seats at a sports stadium or field.

granite *(**gran**-it)* *n.* a hard, gray or reddish rock often used in building.

grant[1] *v.* to allow or give something. *The genie granted her three wishes.* **take something for granted 1** to assume that something is true without checking. **2** to have something without appreciating it.

grant[2] *n.* an amount of money that is awarded for a particular purpose.

grape *n.* a green or purple berry that grows in bunches on a vine and from which wine and grape juice are made.

grapefruit *n.* *(pl.* grapefruit) a large, yellow citrus fruit, similar to an orange.

graph *n.* a diagram used to show changes in a quantity or value.

graphic *adj.* **1** clear and detailed. *a graphic description.* **2** to do with drawing and designing. *a graphic artist.*

graphics *n. pl.* drawings, pictures, or designs. *computer graphics.*

grape

grasp *v.* **1** to take hold of something firmly. **2** to understand something. **grasp** *n.*

grass *n.* a plant with thin, green leaves that grows on lawns and in fields.

grasshopper *n.* a small, jumping insect that makes a noise by rubbing its wings together.

grate[1] *v.* to shred food into small, thin pieces by rubbing it against a metal tool (a **grater**) that has a rough surface full of small holes.

grate[2] *n.* a framework of metal bars in a fireplace, for holding coal or wood.

grateful *adj.* thankful. **gratefully** *adv.*

gratitude *n.* the quality of being grateful.

grave[1] *n.* a hole in the ground in which a dead body is buried.

grave[2] *adj.* serious; solemn.

gravel *n.* small stones used in the making of roads and paths.

graveyard *n.* a place, often close to a church, where dead people are buried.

gravity *n.* **1** the natural force that attracts things toward Earth. **2** the quality of seriousness; dignity.

gravy *n.* a hot sauce, usually made with meat juices.

gray *n.* a color halfway between black and white. **gray** *adj.*

graze *v.* **1** to eat grass that is growing. **2** to scrape your skin. **graze** *n.*

grease *n.* a thick, oily substance. **greasy** *adj.*

great *adj.* **1** very large. **2** important, famous. **3** *(informal)* very good, wonderful.

greedy *adj.* (greedier, greediest) wanting more of something than you need. **greed** *n.*, **greedily** *adv.*

green[1] *n.* **1** the color of grass or leaves. **2** an open, grassy area.

green[2] *adj.* **1** having the color green. **2** to do with care for the environment.

greenhouse *n.* a glass building where plants are grown.

greenhouse effect *n.* the warming up of Earth's surface, due to gases such carbon dioxide in the atmosphere trapping the Sun's heat.

greet v. to welcome somebody. *She greeted me with a kiss.* **greeting** n.

grenade n. a small bomb that is thrown by hand.

grew past of grow.

grid n. a set of straight lines that cross each other to make squares.

grief n. great sadness.

grieve v. to feel grief, especially because somebody has died.

greenhouse effect

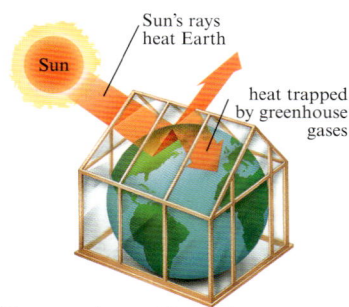

Sun

Sun's rays heat Earth

heat trapped by greenhouse gases

grill¹ v. to cook something under direct heat.

grill² n. the part of an oven that is used for grilling food.

grim adj. (grimmer, grimmest) **1** serious; stern. **2** very unpleasant.

grime n. dirt. **grimy** adj.

grin n. a broad smile. **grin** v.

grind v. (grinding, ground) to crush something into a powder.

grip v. (grips, gripping, gripped) to hold something firmly. **grip** n.

gripping adj. keeping your attention because it is so exciting.

gristle n. a tough, rubbery substance that is found in meat.

grit n. tiny pieces of stone.

groan v. to make a long, deep sound showing pain or sorrow. **groan** n.

groceries n. pl. the things bought in a grocery store.

groom¹ n. **1** a person who takes care of a horse. **2** a bridegroom.

groom² v. to brush and clean an animal's coat.

groove n. a long, thin cut in a surface.

grope v. to feel your way by touch.

gross¹ *(grohs)* adj. **1** very bad. *a gross error.* **2** rude; coarse. **3** total; with nothing taken away. *gross salary* (= before tax and other deductions). **4** unpleasantly fat or large.

gross² n. *(old-fashioned)* 12 dozen; 144.

grotesque *(grow-tesk)* adj. very unnatural or strange-looking.

grotto n. (pl. grottoes or grottos) a small cave.

grotty adj. (grottier, grottiest) *(informal)* unpleasant; in bad condition.

ground¹ n. **1** the surface of Earth. **2** a sports field.

ground² past of grind.

grounds n. pl. **1** the land around a large building. *the castle grounds.* **2** good reasons. *What grounds do you have for calling him a liar?*

group n. **1** a number of people or things gathered together or belonging together. **2** a number of musicians who play or sing together. **group** v.

grove n. a group of trees.

grovel v. (grovels, groveling, groveled) to behave too humbly toward somebody.

grow v. (growing, grew, grown) **1** to develop; to get bigger or taller. **2** to plant something in the ground and take care of it. **3** to become. *She grew tired.* **grow up** to become an adult.

growl v. to make a low, rough sound in the throat. **growl** n.

grownup n. an adult. **grown-up** adj.

growth n. **1** the process of growing. **2** a lump growing on or inside a living thing.

grub n. **1** the young of some insects after they hatch. **2** *(informal)* food.

grubby adj. (grubbier, grubbiest) dirty. **grubbiness** n.

grudge¹ n. anger or resentment toward somebody because of a past event.

grudge² v. to be unhappy that somebody has something (usually in a negative sentence); begrudge. *I don't grudge him his wealth.*

grueling adj. difficult and exhausting.

gruesome adj. horrible.

grumble v. to complain in an angry way.

grumpy adj. (grumpier, grumpiest) bad-tempered **grumpily** adv.

grunt v. to make a low, rough noise, like a pig. **grunt** n.

guarantee n. a promise, especially to fix or replace an item that breaks after it is bought. **guarantee** v.

guard¹ v. **1** to protect something from being attacked or stolen. **2** to watch a person to stop him or her from escaping.

guard² n. **1** a person who guards. **2** a

railroad employee in charge of a train. **3** the duty of guarding.

guardian *n.* a person who is legally responsible for taking care of a child but who is not the child's parent.

guerrilla *(guh-**ril**-uh)* *n.* a member of a small, unofficial army that makes surprise attacks, especially against official government troops. (*can also be spelled* guerilla.)

guess *v.* to give an answer or opinion without knowing if it is exactly right. **guess** *n.*

guest *n.* a person who is visiting another person's house or staying in a hotel.

guide[1] *v.* to show somebody the way; to lead.

guide[2] *n.* a person or thing that guides.

guidebook *n.* a book of information used by tourists.

guide dog *n.* a dog that has been specially trained to guide blind people.

guillotine *(**gil**-uh-teen)* *n.* *(historical)* an instrument for cutting off people's heads, especially in France during the French Revolution.

guilty *adj.* having done something wrong. **guilt** *n.,* **guiltily** *adv.*

guinea pig *n.* **1** a small, furry rodent without a tail, often kept as a pet. **2** a person who is used in an experiment.

guitar *n.* a musical instrument with strings that you pluck. **guitarist** *n.*

gulf *n.* a large bay.

gull *n.* a large sea bird.

gullible *adj.* easily persuaded or deceived; too willing to believe anything that people say.

gulp *v.* to swallow noisily and quickly.

gum *n.* **1** the pink flesh in which your teeth are set. See **tooth**. **2** glue. **3** chewing gum.

gun *n.* a weapon that fires bullets from a long tube that is open at one end.

gunfire *n.* the firing of guns.

gurdwara *n.* a building where people of the Sikh religion go to pray.

guide dog

gurgle *v.* to make a bubbling sound.

guru *n.* **1** a Hindu or Sikh religious leader. **2** a teacher or expert. *a fashion guru.*

gush *v.* to flow out suddenly. *Blood gushed from the wound.*

gust *n.* a sudden blast of wind.

guts *n. pl.* **1** the intestines. **2** (*informal*) courage. *to have guts.*

gutter *n.* a small channel for carrying away rainwater.

gull

guy *n.* (*pl.* guys) (*informal*) a man or boy.

gym *n.* **1** a room or building with equipment for physical exercise (*short for* gymnasium). **2** exercises to strengthen your body and make you more agile, often using equipment such as bars and ropes (*short for* gymnastics).

gymnasium *n.* see **gym**.

gymnast *n.* a person who does gymnastics.

gymnastics *n. pl.* see **gym**.

gypsy *n.* a member of a race of people who live and travel around in caravans.

a
b
c
d
e
f
g
h
i
j
k
l
m
n
o
p
q
r
s
t
u
v
w
x
y
z

Hh

habit *n.* **1** something that you do so often, you do not think about it. **2** a monk's or nun's robe. **habitual** *adj.*, **habitually** *adv.*

habitable *adj.* to be of a condition to be lived in.

habitat *n.* the natural home of an animal or plant.

hack *v.* **1** to chop something roughly. **2** to get into a computer system illegally to get information from it. **hacker** *n.*

had *past of* have.

haddock (*pl.* haddock) *n.* an edible sea fish.

haggard *adj.* looking tired and sick because of pain or worry.

haiku *n.* a Japanese three-lined poem containing exactly 17 syllables.

hail¹ *n.* frozen rain falling as small balls of ice. **hail** *v.*

hail² *v.* to call or wave to somebody or something. *We hailed a taxi.*

hair *n.* **1** one of the threadlike growths on the skin of mammals. **2** a mass of these on a person's head.

haircut *n.* the cutting of somebody's hair, or the style in which it is cut.

hairdresser *n.* a person who cuts and styles people's hair.

hair-raising *adj.* very frightening.

hairy *adj.* (hairier, hairiest) **1** covered in hair. **2** (*informal*) frightening.

hajj *n.* the pilgrimage to Mecca that Muslims are expected to make at leasat once in their lives.

halal *n.* meat from animals that have been killed according to Muslim law.

half¹ *n.* (*pl.* halves) one of the two equal parts of something.

half² *adv.* partly; not completely. *She left her dinner half eaten.*

halfhearted *adj.* without energy or enthusiasm. *a halfhearted attempt.*

hall *n.* **1** the entrance room of a house.

the Kaaba in Mecca, part of the Muslim hajj

2 a large public room for meetings, concerts, or other events.

Halloween *n.* the evening of October 31 when, in the past, people believed that witches and ghosts roamed. Today children dress up in costumes and go door-to-door for tricks or treats.

hallucinate *v.* to see something in your mind that does not really exist. **hallucination** *n.*

halo *n.* (*pl.* halos *or* haloes) a circle of light around something, especially around the head of a saint or holy person.

halt *v.* to stop. **halt** *n.*

halve *v.* **1** to divide into two equal parts. **2** to reduce something by half.

halves *plural of* half.

ham *n.* the salted or smoked meat of a pig's leg.

hamburger *n.* a round, flat cake of minced beef, eaten in a hamburger bun.

hamlet *n.* a very small village.

hammer¹ *n.* a tool with a heavy metal head used for hitting nails into things.

hammer² *v.* **1** to hit with a hammer. **2** to hit loudly and repeatedly. *He hammered on the door.*

hammock *n.* a long piece of cloth hung up at the corners and used as a bed.

hamper¹ *n.* a large basket with a lid.

hamper² *v.* to make it difficult to do something. *Heavy rain hampered the search for survivors.*

hammock

hamster *n.* a small rodent with a short tail and pouches in its mouth for storing food, often kept as a pet.

hand¹ *n.* **1** the part at the end of your arm, with four fingers and a thumb. **2** a pointer on a clock or watch. **3** the set of playing cards that you hold in your hand during a card game. **give somebody a hand** to help somebody. **out of hand** out of control.

hand² *v.* to pass something with your hand. *Please could you hand me the salt.*

handbag *n.* a small bag in which you carry personal belongings.

handcuffs *n. pl.* steel rings connected by a short chain, used for locking a prisoner's hands together.

handful *n.* **1** as much of something as

you can hold in your hand. **2** a small number or amount. **3** *(informal)* a person who is difficult to control. *Her youngest son is a handful!*

handicap *n.* **1** anything that makes it more difficult to do things; a disadvantage. **2** *(old-fashioned)* a physical or mental disability. **handicapped** *adj.*

handicraft *n.* an activity that requires skillful use of your hands such as pottery or embroidery.

handkerchief *(hang-ker-chief) n.* a piece of cloth or paper used for wiping your nose or eyes.

handle[1] *n.* the part of an object that you can hold it by.

handle[2] *v.* **1** to touch something with your hands. **2** to deal with something. *You handled the situation very well.*

handlebars *n. pl.* the bars at the front of a bicycle or motorcycle that the rider holds and uses to steer.

handsome *adj.* good-looking.

handwriting *n.* writing done by hand.

handy *adj.* (handier, handiest) **1** easy to reach; in a convenient place. *The house is handy for the mall.* **2** easy to use; useful. *a handy tool.* **3** skillful with your hands. *She's handy with a screwdriver.*

hang *v.* **1** (hanging, hung) to fix or be attached from above so that the lower part is free. **2** (hanging, hanged) to kill somebody by hanging that person by a rope around his or her neck. **hang around** to wait in a place without having anything specific to do there. **hang on 1** to wait. **2** to hold on to something firmly. **hang up** to end a telephone call by putting down the receiver.

hangar *n.* a large building in which aircraft are kept.

hanger *n.* a shaped wooden, metal, or plastic object with a hook, used to hang clothes.

hang glider *n.* a type of kite to which you strap yourself and use to fly from the

hang glider

top of a cliff or hill in the sport of **hang-gliding** *v.*

Hanukkah *n.* the Jewish festival of lights that takes place in December. *(can also be spelled* Chanukah*)*.

happen *v.* to take place; to occur. **happen to** to do something by chance. *My friend and I happen to have the same birthday.*

happening *n.* an event.

happy *adj.* (happier, happiest) **1** feeling or showing pleasure. **2** willing. *I'd be happy to help you.* **happily** *adv.*, **happiness** *n.*

harass *v.* to annoy or trouble somebody constantly. **harassment** *n.*

harbor[1] *n.* a place where ships shelter or unload their cargo.

harbor[2] *v* to give shelter or a hiding place to somebody.

hard[1] *adj.* **1** solid or firm; not soft. *The ground was too hard to dig.* **2** difficult. *Yesterday's homework was really hard.* **3** harsh; tough; not kind or gentle. *Don't be too hard on the children.* **harden** *v.*, **hardness** *n.*

hard[2] *adv.* **1** with great effort. **2** with great force.

hard copy *n.* information from a computer printed on paper.

hard disk *n.* a part inside a computer that holds large amounts of data.

hardly *adv.* only just; almost not.

hare

There's hardly any money left.

hardship *n.* difficult living conditions that cause suffering.

hardware *n.* **1** computer equipment. **2** household tools and equipment.

hare *n.* a type of animal that is similar to a large rabbit but with longer ears than a rabbit and with a short tail.

harm *v.* to hurt or damage somebody or something. **harm** *n.*

harmful *adj.* causing harm or injuries.

harmless *adj.* safe; not dangerous.

harmonica *n.* a musical instrument played by blowing and sucking; mouth organ.

harmony *n.* **1** a pleasant combination of musical notes played at the same time. **2** peaceful agreement. *The two companies work together in harmony.* **harmonize** *v.*

harp

harness *n.* the leather straps by which a horse is attached to the cart that it is pulling. **harness** *v.*

harp *n.* a large musical instrument played by plucking strings with your fingers. **harpist** *n.*

harpoon *n.* a large spear, often used for hunting whales.

harpsichord *n.* *(historical)* a stringed instrument with a keyboard, similar in appearance to a piano.

harsh *adj.* **1** cruel; stern. **2** rough and unpleasant to see or hear. *a harsh voice.*

harvest *n.* **1** the time for cutting and bringing in grains and other crops. **2** the crops brought in. **harvest** *v.*

has *form of* have.

hassle¹ *n.* something that is a nuisance and difficult to do. *It was a real hassle finding someone to fix our car.*

hassle² *v.* to bother somebody all the time. *Stop hassling me!*

haste *n.* speed; doing things quickly.

hasten *v.* to hurry.

hasty *adj.* (hastier, hastiest) **1** done in a hurry. **2** done without thinking carefully. **hastily** *adv.*

hat *n.* a covering for the head.

hatch¹ *n.* an opening in a wall or floor, often covered by a small door.

hatch² *v.* **1** to break out of an egg. **2** to plan something secretly.

hatchback *n.* a car with a back door that opens upward.

hatchet *n.* a small ax.

hate¹ *v.* to dislike something very much.

hate², hatred *n.* a strong dislike.

haughty *adj.* (haughtier, haughtiest) too proud and thinking that you are better than other people.

haul *v.* to pull a heavy load.

haunt *v.* (of a ghost) to visit a place often. **haunted** *adj.*

have *v.* (has, having, had) **1** to own or possess. *Katie has a new bike.* **2** to feel or experience. *I have a bad cold.* **3** to get or take. *We had burgers for lunch.* **4** to cause to be done. *Have you had your hair cut?* **have to** must. *I have to go home now.*

haven *n.* a safe place.

havoc *n.* destruction; great disorder.

hawk *n.* a bird of prey.

hay *n.* grass that has been cut and dried and is used as food for animals.

hay fever *n.* an allergy to pollen that affects some people in the summer. It causes sneezing and sore eyes.

haystack *n.* a large pile of hay.

hazard *n.* a danger or risk. **hazardous** *adj.*

haze *n.* a thin mist. **hazy** *adj.*

hazel *n.* **1** a small tree that produces hazelnuts. **2** the brownish-green color of some people's eyes.

head¹ *n.* **1** the top part of your body, containing your eyes, mouth, and brain. **2** the chief person; the person in charge. **3** the top or front part of something.

head² *v.* **1** to lead something. *He heads up a team of scientists.* **2** to move in a certain direction. *We're heading home.* **3** to hit a ball with your head.

headache *n.* a pain in your head.

headdress *n.* a type of covering or band for the head.

heading *n.* words written above a piece of writing; a title.

headlight *n.* one of the main lights on the front of a vehicle.

headline *n.* **1** words in larger print at the top of a story in a newspaper. **2 the headlines** the most important items of news on the TV or radio.

headphones *n. pl.* a pair of small speakers that you wear over your ears, for listening, in private, to a stereo system—specifically a personal stereo.

headquarters *n.* the main office of an organization, from which the entire organization is controlled.

headway *n.* progress.

heal *v.* to make or become well or healthy again. *Fortunately, the cut on my arm healed very quickly.*

health *n.* a person's physical or mental condition. *The old man fell and is in poor health.*

healthy *adj.* (healthier, healthiest) **1** well and strong. **2** good for your health. *healthy food.* **healthily** *adv.*

A B C D E F G H I J K L M N O P Q R S T U V W X Y Z

heap *n.* a pile of things. **heap** *v.*

hear *v.* (hearing, heard) **1** to take in sounds through your ears. *Can you hear that noise?* **2** to receive information. *Have you heard the good news?*

hearing *n.* the ability to hear.

hearing aid *n.* a small device worn by a person with bad hearing to make sounds louder.

hearse *(rhymes with nurse) n.* a car that carries a coffin to a funeral.

human heart

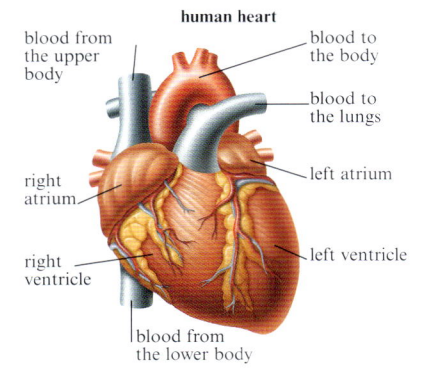

blood from the upper body

blood to the body

blood to the lungs

left atrium

right atrium

left ventricle

right ventricle

blood from the lower body

heart *n.* **1** the organ that pumps blood around your body. **2** the central or most important part. **3** feelings; emotions. *She had a change of heart.* **4** courage. **5** a shape like this ♥. **6 hearts** one of the four suits in a pack of playing cards.

heart attack *n.* a sudden failure of the heart to work properly, sometimes causing death.

heartbreak *n.* great sadness; regret. **heartbreaking** *adj.*, **heartbroken** *adj.*

hearth *(harth) n.* the floor of a fireplace.

heartless *adj.* without feeling or pity.

hearty *adj.* (heartier, heartiest) **1** cheerful and enthusiastic. *a hearty welcome.* **2** large and strong. *a hearty appetite.* **heartily** *adv.*

heat[1] *n.* **1** the quality of being hot. **2** the warmth from something hot. **3** one of the stages in a competition, to decide who will take place in the final.

heat[2] *v.* to make or become hot. *We heated up the soup.*

heater *n.* something that produces heat.

heather *n.* a low-growing purple or white shrub that grows on moors and hills.

heat wave *n.* a period of very hot weather.

heave *v.* to lift, push, or throw something with effort. *They heaved the dresser up into the van.*

heaven *n.* in some religions, the home of God, where good people are believed to go when they die.

heavy *adj.* (heavier, heaviest) **1** weighing a lot. *a heavy box.* **2** having a particular weight. *How heavy is that box?* **3** great in amount or force. *heavy rain.* **heavily** *adv.*, **heaviness** *n.*

heavy metal *n.* a type of very loud rock music played especially on electric guitars and drums.

hectare *n.* a measure of area equal to 100 acres.

hectic *adj.* very busy; rushed.

hedge *n.* a row of bushes making a boundary around a field or garden.

hedgehog *n.* a small animal that is covered in spikes. It defends itself by rolling up into a ball.

heel *n.* **1** the back part of your foot. **2** the part of a sock or shoe under your heel.

hefty *adj.* (heftier, heftiest) big and strong.

heifer *(hef-er) n.* a young cow that has not had a calf.

height *n.* **1** the measurement of how high something is. **2** the very highest,

helicopter

tail fin

rotor blade

landing skid

greatest. or strongest point. *The storm was at its height.*

heir *(air) n.* the person who will inherit somebody's property or position.

heiress *(air-ess) n.* a female heir.

held *past of* hold.

helicopter *n.* an aircraft with a horizontal rotor that acts as a propeller and wings.

helium *n.* a very light gas, used in balloons and airships.

hell *n.* the place where the Devil is believed to live and where evil people are believed to be punished when they die.

helm *n.* a wheel or handle used to steer a boat or a ship.

helmet *n.* a type of hard protective hat, often worn by the police or firefighters.

help *v.* **1** to do something useful for somebody. *He helped me carry the bags.* **2** to improve something. *Good test results will help her get a job.* **3** to prevent something from happening. *I couldn't help laughing.* **help** *n.*, **helper** *n.*

helpful *adj.* useful; giving help. **helpfully** *adv.*, **helpfulness** *n.*

helping *n.* a share of food at a meal.

helpless *adj.* not able to take care of yourself. **helplessness** *n.*

hem *n.* the edge of a piece of cloth that is turned over and sewn. **hem** *v.*

hemisphere *n.* one half of Earth. *France is in the Northern Hemisphere.*

hen *n.* **1** a female chicken. **2** a female bird.

hence *adv.* **1** for this reason. *She has just lost her job, hence, her lack of money.* **2** from this time. *a few days hence.*

heptagon *n.* a shape with seven sides.

herald *v.* to be a sign that something is about to happen. *The darkening clouds heralded a storm.*

heraldry *n.* the study of coats of arms.

herb *n.* a plant used for flavoring food or for making medicines. **herbal** *adj.*

herbivore *n.* an animal that only eats plants. **herbivorous** *adj.*

herd¹ *n.* a group of animals grazing or moving together. *a herd of cattle.*

herd² *v.* to gather together in a group. *The dogs herded the sheep together.*

here *adv.* in, at, or to this place.

hereditary *adj.* capable of being passed on from parents to their children. *hereditary diseases.*

heritage *n.* things that are passed on from one generation to another.

hermit *n.* a person who lives alone.

hero *n.* (*pl.* heroes) **1** a person admired for his or her bravery. **2** the most important male character in a play, movie, or story. **heroic** *adj.*, **heroism** *n.*

heroine *n.* **1** a woman admired for her bravery. **2** the most important female character in a play, movie, or story.

heron *n.* a long-legged wading bird.

herring *n.* a small sea fish.

hesitate *v.* to pause before doing something, due to uncertainty. **hesitant** *adj.*, **hesitation** *n.*

hexagon *n.* a shape with six sides. **hexagonal** *adj.*

heyday *n.* the time when a person or thing is most successful or popular.

hibernate *v.* to spend the winter in a type of deep sleep. *Bears hibernate.* **hibernation** *n.*

hiccup (*hik-up*) *n.* a sudden and repeated jumping feeling in your throat that makes you let out a sharp noise. **hiccup** *v.* (*can also be spelled* **hiccough**, *which is pronounced the same.*)

hide¹ *v.* (hiding, hid, hidden) **1** to put something where others cannot find it. **2** to go somewhere where you cannot

hieroglyphics

be seen by other people.

hide² *n.* the skin of an animal.

hideous *adj.* very ugly.

hieroglyphics (*hy-ruh-glif-iks*) *n. pl.* ancient Egyptian writing using small pictures instead of words or letters. *The hieroglyphics are of the name Cleopatra.*

high *adj.* **1** rising a long way above the ground. *high mountains.* **2** having a particular height. *The wall is 10 ft. high.* **3** more than the normal level in amount, strength, or importance. *high speed, high winds, high rank.* **4** not deep in sound. *a high voice.* **high, highly** *adv.*

highlight¹ *v.* **1** to draw special attention to something. **2** to mark important parts of a piece of writing with a brightly colored pen called a highlighter.

highlight² *n.* the best part of something. *The highlight of our vacation was a ride in a helicopter.*

high-tech *adj.* using modern equipment and methods. (*can also be spelled* hi-tech.)

highway *n.* (*pl.* highways) a wide road with several lanes for fast traffic.

highwayman *n.* (*pl.* highwaymen) (*historical*) in earlier times a robber on horseback.

hijack *v.* to take control of a plane or car and force the pilot or driver to take you somewhere. *Terrorists have hijacked a plane in Japan.* **hijack** *n.*, **hijacker** *n.*

hike *n.* a long walk in the country. **hike** *v.*, **hiker** *n.*

hill *n.* an area of high land, smaller than a mountain. **hilly** *adj.*

hilt *n.* the handle of a sword.

hind *adj.* at the back. *hind legs.*

hinder *v.* to delay or prevent the progress of something. **hindrance** *n.*

Hinduism *n.* the main religion of India that involves the worship of many gods and the belief that people return to life in a different form after death. **Hindu** *adj., n.*

hinge *n.* a moving joint that attaches a door to a doorway or a lid to a box.

hint *v.* to suggest something without really saying it. *Ben hinted that he wanted a new bike.* **hint** *n.*

hippopotamus

hip *n.* one of the two joints at the sides of your body between the tops of your legs and your waist.

hip-hop, hip hop *n.* a type of rap music.

hippopotamus *n.* (*pl.* hippopotamuses *or* hippopotami) a large, thick-skinned African animal that lives close to rivers. Often shortened to hippo.

hire *v.* to hire someone, such as for a job. **hire** *n.*

hiss *v.* to make a sound rather like a long letter *s.* **hiss** *n.*

historian *n.* a person who studies history.

historic *adj.* famous in history. *We learned about the historic battles that took place between France and England.*

historical *adj.* of or about people and events from history. *a historical novel.* **historically** *adv.*

history *n.* the study of things that happened in the past.

hit¹ *v.* (hits, hitting, hit) to strike or knock something.

hit² *n.* **1** the action of hitting. **2** a popular or successful thing. *The song was a hit.*

hitch¹ *v.* **1** to attach something to something else. *He hitched his horse to the post.* **2** to hitchhike. **hitch up** to pull up. *He hitched up his trousers.*

hitch² *n.* a small, temporary problem.

hitchhike *v.* to travel by getting a free ride in somebody else's car.

hi-tech *another spelling of* high-tech.

HIV *n.* (*short for* human immunodeficiency virus) a virus that can cause the disease AIDS.

hive *n.* a beehive.

hoard *n.* a secret store of treasure, food, or other things. **hoard** *v.*

hoarse *adj.* (of the voice) rough, harsh, and croaking, especially because of a sore throat or too much shouting.

hoax *n.* a deceptive trick; a practical joke. *There wasn't really a bomb—it was just a hoax.* **hoax** *v.*

hobble *v.* to walk with difficulty, taking small, unsteady steps, because your feet hurt, for example.

hobby *n.* something that you enjoy doing in your spare time.

hockey *n.* a game played by two teams with a puck (ice hockey) or a ball (field hockey). *ice hockey. field hockey. street hockey.*

hoe *n.* a gardening tool used for digging up weeds.

hog¹ *n.* a castrated male pig.

hog² *v.* (hogs, hogging, hogged) to use more than your fair share of something.

hold¹ *v.* (holding, held) **1** to have in your hand. **2** to support or keep firmly in one position. *Could you hold the door open, please?* **3** to contain. *How much does this bottle hold?* **4** to make something take place. *We are holding a party.* **5** to keep somebody prisoner. *The police are holding a man for questioning.* **6** to possess. *She holds the world record.* **hold on** to wait. **hold up** to delay.

hold² *n.* the part of a ship or aircraft where cargo is stored.

hole *n.* **1** an opening or gap. *a hole in my sock.* **2** an animal's burrow.

holiday *n.* (*pl.* holidays) **1** a day off from work or school. **2** a religious feast day.

hollow¹ *adj.* having an empty space inside; not solid. *a hollow tree.*

holly

hollow² *n.* **1** a hollow place. **2** a very small valley.

hollow³ *v.* to make something hollow.

holly *n.* an evergreen shrub or tree with shiny, prickly leaves and red berries.

hologram *n.* an image created by lasers that appears to be three-dimensional.

holster *n.* a leather case for carrying a pistol, worn on a belt.

holy *adj.* to do with God or a god. **holiness** *n.*

home *n.* the place where you live.

homeless *adj.* having nowhere to live.

homeopathy *(ho-mee-op-ath-ee)* *n.* a way of treating an illness by giving tiny quantities of medicines that cause symptoms similar to those of the illness itself. **homeopathic** *adj.*

homesick *adj.* sad because you are away from your home.

homework *n.* schoolwork that you have to do at home.

homosexual *adj.* sexually attracted to people of your own sex. **homosexual** *n.*, **homosexuality** *n.*

honeycomb

bee   honey

honest *(on-ist)* *adj.* truthful; not likely to cheat or steal. **honesty** *n.*

honey *n.* a sweet, sticky food that is made naturally by bees.

honeycomb *n.* a wax structure made by bees. It has many six-sided holes in which bees store their honey and eggs.

honeymoon *n.* a vacation for a couple who have just gotten married.

honeysuckle *n.* a climbing plant with sweet-smelling flowers.

honor¹ *(on-er)* *n.* **1** great respect or public regard. **2** a privilege. *It would be an honor to accompany you.* **3** an official award received for doing something special.

honor² *v.* **1** to respect somebody greatly. **2** to give an award or praise to somebody or something.

honorable *adj.* good; deserving respect. *She*

behaved in an honorable way by refusing to betray her friend. **honorably** *adv.*

hood *n.* **1** a part of a coat or jacket that goes over your head. **2** the folding cover of a stroller or similar thing. **3** the lid over the engine of a car. **4** slang for "neighborhood."

hoodwink *v.* to trick somebody.

hoof *n.* (*pl.* hooves or hoofs) the hard part of the foot of a horse or similar animal.

hook *n.* a curved piece of metal, plastic, or wood, used for catching or holding things. *Hang your coat on the hook.* **hooked** *adj.*

hooligan *n.* a person who behaves violently and noisily. **hooliganism** *n.*

hoop *n.* a large wooden or metal ring.

hoot *v.* to make a sound like a car horn or the cry of an owl. **hoot** *n.*

hooves *plural of* hoof.

hop¹ *v.* (hops, hopping, hopped) **1** to jump on one leg. **2** (of an animal, bird, or insect) to jump with both or all feet placed together.

hop² *n.* a plant used in making beer.

hope¹ *v.* to want something to happen. *I hope you can come.*

hope² *n.* **1** the feeling that what you want may happen. **2** a person or thing that you are relying on for help. *She's my last hope—there's nobody else I can ask.*

hopeful *adj.* full of hope; optimistic that something will happen. **hopefully** *adv.*, **hopefulness** *n.*

hopeless *adj.* **1** without hope. **2** very bad at something. *I'm hopeless at math.*

horizon *n.* the line where the land and the sky seem to meet.

horizontal *adj.* lying level or flat; parallel to the horizon. *a horizontal line.* **horizontally** *adv.*

hormone *n.* a chemical produced in your body that has a specific effect on the way that your body works.

horn *n.* **1** a hard, bony growth on the head of some animals. **2** a brass musical instrument that you blow. **3** the device in a vehicle for making warning sounds.

hornet *n.* a type of large wasp.

horoscope *n.* a prediction about somebody's future, based on the position of the stars and planets.

horrible *adj.* very unpleasant. *a horrible smell.* **horribly** *adv.*

horrid *adj.* horrible.

horrific *adj.* terrifying or shocking.

horrify *v.* (horrifies, horrifying, horrified) to shock somebody greatly. **horrifying** *adj.*

A B C D E F G H I J K L M N O P Q R S T U V W X Y Z

horror *n.* **1** great fear or shock. **2** something that causes great fear or shock to someone.

horse *n.* **1** a four-legged animal with a long mane and a tail. **2** an object in a gym that you use for jumping over; vaulting horse.

horse chestnut *n.* a tree with large brown seeds.

horsepower *n.* a unit for measuring the power of engines.

horseshoe *n.* a "U"-shaped piece of iron that is nailed to a horse's or pony's hoof to protect it.

horticulture *n.* the growing of flowers, fruits, and vegetables. **horticultural** *adj.*

hose *n.* a long, flexible tube through which water can pass.

hospitable *adj.* showing kindness to guests or strangers. **hospitality** *n.*

hospital *n.* a building where people who are sick or injured are taken care of.

host *n.* **1** a person or organization that receives and entertains guests. **2** the person who introduces the performers on a TV or radio show. **3** a large number of something. **host** *v.*

hostage *n.* a person who is held captive by people who will not let him or her go until they have what they want.

hostel *n.* a building where people can stay cheaply for a short time.

hostile *adj.* unfriendly; behaving like an enemy. **hostility** *n.*

hot *adj.* (hotter, hottest) **1** having a high temperature. **2** having a sharp, burning taste. *hot curry.*

hot dog *n.* a hot sausage served in a soft roll. (can also be spelled hotdog.)

hotel *n.* a building where you pay to sleep and eat.

hound[1] *n.* a domestic dog with drooping ears.

hound[2] *v.* to chase somebody ceaselessly. *The photographers hounded the actress for many weeks.*

hour *n.* a period of 60 minutes. *There are 24 hours in a day.*

hourly *adj., adv.* happening or coming every hour. *an hourly bus.*

house[1] (*rhymes with* mouse) *n.* **1** a building where people, especially a single family, live. **2** a building that is used for a particular purpose.

house[2] (*rhymes with* cows) *v.* to provide a place for somebody to live or for something to take place.

household *n.* all the people who live together in a house.

housekeeper *n.* a person who is paid to take care of a house.

housework *n.* the work of keeping a house neat and tidy.

hovel *n.* a small, dirty house or hut.

hover *v.* **1** to stay in the air in one place. *A dragonfly hovered above the boat.* **2** to move around while staying close to a person or thing. *Julie hovered by the phone, waiting for it to ring.*

hovercraft *n.* a vehicle that can move over land or water, supported by a cushion of air. (also called ACV, or air-cushion vehicle.)

hovercraft

however *adv.* **1** but; nevertheless. *I'd like to go—however, I can't afford it.* **2** no matter how. *I can't do it, however hard I try.* **3** how. *However did you find me?*

howl *v.* to make a long, sad noise like a dog makes when it is hurt. **howl** *n.*

hub *n.* the center of a wheel.

hue *(hyoo) n.* a color or shade.

huff *n.* **in a huff** in a bad mood.

hug *v.* (hugs, hugging, hugged) to hold somebody tightly in your arms. **hug** *n.*

huge *adj.* extremely large; enormous.

hull *n.* the body of a ship.

hum *v.* (hums, humming, hummed) **1** to sing with your lips closed. **2** to make a low, buzzing noise. **hum** *n.*

human, human being *n.* a person. **human** *adj.*

humane *(hyoo-**main**) adj.* kind; not cruel. *the humane treatment of prisoners.*

humanity *n.* **1** all human beings. **2** the quality of being humane.

humble *adj.* modest and not proud. **humbly** *adv.*

humid *adj.* damp and warm. *a humid climate.* **humidity** *n.*

humiliate *v.* to make a person feel ashamed or look ridiculous. **humiliation** *n.*

a b c d e f g **h** i j k l m n o p q r s t u v w x y z

hummingbird

hummingbird *n.* a small, brightly colored bird that makes a humming sound by beating its wings very fast.

humor[1] *n.* the ability to make people laugh or smile or to see when something is funny. *She has a good sense of humor.*

humor[2] *v.* to try to keep somebody happy by agreeing with that person or doing what he or she wants. *Don't tell him he's wrong—just humor him.*

humorous *adj.* funny.

hump *n.* **1** a small hill. **2** a rounded lump, for example, on a camel's back.

hunch[1] *n.* an idea about something, based on a feeling rather than fact. *I have a hunch that something is wrong.*

hunch[2] *v.* to bend your shoulders forward and your head down. *He sat at the desk with his shoulders hunched.*

hung *past of* hang.

hunger *n.* the feeling of wanting food.

hungry *adj.* (hungrier, hungriest) feeling like you want food. **hungrily** *adv.*

hunk *n.* **1** a large, thick piece. *a hunk of bread.* **2** *(informal)* a good-looking man.

hunt[1] *v.* **1** to chase and kill wild animals as a sport or for food. **2** to search for something. **hunter** *n.*

hunt[2] *n.* **1** the act of hunting animals. **2** a search.

hurdle *n.* **1** a small obstacle that you jump over in a running race. **2** an obstacle; a difficulty.

hurl *v.* to throw something with force.

hurricane *n.* a violent, windy storm.

hurry *v.* (hurries, hurrying, hurried) **1** to move or do something quickly. **2** to make somebody hurry. **hurry** *n.*

hurt *v.* (hurting, hurt) **1** to cause pain or unhappiness. *He hurt his leg.* **2** to be painful. *My tooth hurts.*

hurtle *v.* to move very fast.

husband *n.* the man that a woman is married to. *Her husband is a doctor.*

hush[1] a warning to be quiet.

hush[2] *n.* a sudden silence.

husky[1] *adj.* (huskier, huskiest) low and rough in sound. *a husky voice.* **huskily** *adv.*

husky[2] *n.* a dog that is used to pull sleds in Arctic regions.

hut *n.* a small house or shelter, often made out of wood or local stones.

hutch *n.* a wooden box with a wire front for rabbits or other small pets.

hybrid *n.* plant or animal produced from two different species.

hydrant *n.* an outdoor water tap.

hydraulic *adj.* using the pressure produced by water or some other liquid being forced along pipes. *hydraulic brakes.*

hydroelectricity *n.* electricity produced from the power of running water.

hydrofoil *n.* a fast, light boat that rests on special supports and skims the surface of the water. (also called hydroplane.)

hydrogen *n.* a very light, colorless gas that burns easily. Hydrogen and oxygen together make water.

hyena *(hi-yeen-a)* *n.* a doglike animal found in Africa and Asia, with a howl that sounds like human laughter.

hygiene *(high-jeen)* *n.* cleanliness and healthiness. **hygienic** *adj.*

hymn *(pronounced the same as* him*)* *n.* a religious song praising God.

hype *n.* *(informal)* excessive publicity about something in order to sell it. *There has been a lot of hype on TV about the band's new album.* **hype** *v.*

hyphen *n.* a mark (-) used in writing to separate parts of a word, as in *grown-up*, or to show that a word continues over to the next line.

hypnosis *n.* a state like deep sleep in which somebody's actions can be controlled by another person.

hypnotize *v.* to put somebody into hypnosis. **hypnotic** *adj.,* **hypnotism** *n.*

hypocrite *(hip-a-krit)* *n.* a person who pretends to believe or feel something that is different from his or her actual feelings or beliefs. **hypocrisy** *(hip-ok-ra-see)* *n.,* **hypocritical** *adj.*

hypodermic needle *n.* a medical instrument with a hollow needle for injecting medication under the skin.

hypotenuse *(hi-pot-uh-nooz)* *n.* the longest side of a right-angled triangle, across from the right angle. See **triangle**.

hypothermia *n.* a dangerous medical condition caused by exposure to cold, when the body's temperature becomes abnormally low.

hysterical *adj.* in a state of uncontrolled excitement, grief, panic, or other strong emotion. **hysteria** *n.,* **hysterically** *adv.*

Ii

ice *n.* **1** frozen water. **2** a frozen dessert.

iceberg *n.* a huge mass of ice that floats in the sea.

ice cream *n.* a soft, very cold, sweet food.

ice cube *n. a* small block of ice that is used for cooling down drinks.

iced *adj.* **1** very cold. **2** covered with ice.

ice hockey *n.* a form of hockey played on ice by skaters using a rubber puck; hockey.

ice hockey

ice rink *n.* a building or area with a floor of ice for skating on.

ice skate *n.* a boot with a blade underneath for moving on ice. **ice-skate** *v.*, **ice skating** *n.*

icicle *n.* a hanging, pointed piece of ice, made of dripping water that has frozen.

icon *n.* **1** a small picture on a computer screen representing a program. **2** a picture of Christ or a saint, often painted on wood, found especially in Russian churches.

icy *adj.* (icier, iciest) like or covered with ice; very cold.

idea *n.* a thought; a plan in your mind.

ideal[1] *adj.* perfect; just what you want. *This box is ideal for storing your toys.* **ideally** *adv.*

ideal[2] *n.* the person, thing, or situation that is the best possible.

identical *adj.* exactly the same.

identify *v.* (identifies, identifying, identified) to recognize or name somebody or something. **identification** *n.*

identity *n.* the qualities of a person; who somebody is. *The police do not know the dead man's identity.*

idiom *n.* a group of words that, when used together, have a meaning other than the one that they appear to have.

idiot *n.* a silly or foolish person.

idiotic *adj.* foolish. **idiotically** *adv.*

idle *adj.* **1** lazy. **2** not being used. *Ships were lying idle in the harbor.* **3** with no purpose; not really meant. *idle threats.* **idleness** *n.*, **idly** *adv.*

idol *n.* **1** somebody or something that people worship as a god. **2** somebody who is greatly admired. *a pop star.*

idolize *v.* to admire or love somebody very much.

i.e. *short for* that is; that is to say. *Young children, i.e. those under five years of age, travel for free.*

igloo *n.* a dome-shaped hut made of blocks of snow or ice, traditionally built by the Eskimos and the Inuit people in the Arctic.

igloo

ignite *v.* **1** to set something on fire. **2** to catch fire.

ignition *n.* the device in a car that ignites the fuel and starts the engine.

ignorant *adj.* not knowing about something. **ignorance** *n.*

ignore *v.* to pay no attention to something. *The man simply ignored us and walked straight past.*

iguana *(ig-wah-na)* *n.* a large tropical lizard that lives in trees.

il- *prefix* not. *illegal; illogical.*

ill *adj.* **1** not well; sick. **2** bad or harmful. *ill effects.*

illegal *adj.* against the law.

illegible *adj.* impossible to read. *Your writing is illegible.*

illegitimate *adj.* **1** born to parents who are not married to each other. **2** against the law. **illegitimacy** *n.*

A
B
C
D
E
F
G
H
I
J
K
L
M
N
O
P
Q
R
S
T
U
V
W
X
Y
Z

illiterate *adj.* not able to read and write. **illiteracy** *n.*

illuminate *v.* to light something up. *The gardens were illuminated by rows of lights.* **illumination** *n.*

illusion *n.* something that seems to be real or true but is not. **illusory** *adj.*

illustrate *v.* to add pictures to help explain something in a book or report.

illustration *n.* a picture that appears in a book or magazine.

im- *prefix* not. *immoral; impatient.*

image *n.* **1** a picture or statue. **2** a picture in your mind. **3** the way that you appear to other people.

imaginary *adj.* not real; existing only in your mind. *an imaginary friend.*

imagination *n.* the ability to imagine things.

imaginative *adj.* using your imagination; able to be creative.

imagine *v.* to create a picture in your mind.

imam *n.* a person who leads the prayers in a mosque.

imitate *v.* to copy somebody or something. **imitation** *n.*

immature *adj.* **1** not fully grown or developed. **2** acting in a childish way. **immaturity** *n.*

immediately *adv.* now; at once. **immediate** *adj.*

immense *adj.* very large. **immensely** *adv.*, **immensity** *n.*

immerse *v.* to put something in a liquid so that it is completely covered. **immersion** *n.*

immigrant *n.* a person who comes to live permanently in a country from another country.

immigrate *v.* to come to live permanently in a country. **immigration** *n.*

imminent *adj.* about to happen.

immobile *adj.* not able to move or be moved. *After he broke his ankle, he was immobile for several weeks.*

immoral *adj.* morally wrong, wicked. **immorality** *n.*

immune *adj.* safe from the danger of catching a disease. *She has had chickenpox so she is now immune to it.* **immunity** *n.*

immunize *v.* to make somebody safe from the danger of catching a disease, especially by giving him or her an injection. **immunization** *n.*

impact *n.* **1** the force of an object hitting another. **2** a strong effect. *The movie had a huge impact on me.*

impatient *adj.* soon bored or irritated;

not wanting to wait. **impatience** *n.*

imperfect *adj.* having some faults; not perfect. **imperfection** *n.*

imperial *adj.* to do with an empire or with an emperor or empress.

impersonate *v.* to pretend to be somebody else. **impersonation** *n.*

impertinent *adj.* rude; not showing respect. **impertinence** *n.*

impetuous *adj.* tending to act without thinking first.

implement *n.* a tool or an instrument. *Chopsticks are eating implements.*

imply *v.* (implies, implying, implied) to suggest something without really saying it. *She implied that I was lying.* **implication** *n.*

impolite *adj.* not polite; rude.

import *(im-port)* *v.* to bring goods from abroad to sell in your own country. **import** *(im-port)* *n.*

important *adj.* **1** mattering a lot; to be taken seriously. *It is important that you all know the rules.* **2** having great power or influence. *The queen is a very important woman.* **importance** *n.*

impose *v.* to force somebody to accept something. *Don't impose your ideas on other people.* **imposition** *n.*

impossible *adj.* not possible; not able to be done. **impossibility** *n.*, **impossibly** *adv.*

impostor *n.* a person who pretends to have the identity of someone else. (*can also be spelled* imposter).

impress *v.* to make somebody think positively of you. *I was impressed by the clear way that he spoke.* **impressive** *adj.*

impression *n.* **1** the effect that something has on you. *That book made a deep impression on me.* **2** an idea or feeling. *I got the impression that he was bored.* **3** a hollow mark made by pressing. *an impression of the dog's paw in the cement.* **4** an impersonation.

imprison *v.* to put somebody in prison. **imprisonment** *n.*

improve *v.* to make or become better. *My teacher says that my work has improved a lot this term.* **improvement** *n.*

improvise *v.* **1** to do the best you can with what you have. *We didn't have any shelves, so we improvised with bricks and planks of wood.* **2** to make something up as you go along. *She improvised a tune on the piano.*

improvisation *n.*

impudent *adj.* rude. **impudence** *n.*

impulse *n.* a sudden desire to do something. **impulsive** *adj.*

in- *prefix* not. *insensitive, informal, incorrect.*

inborn *adj.* natural; present since your birth. *an inborn ability.*

incense *n.* a substance that gives off a sweet smell when it is burned.

incentive *n.* something that encourages you to do something. *They offered huge prizes as an incentive to enter the competition.*

inch *n.* a measure of length. *There are 12 inches in one foot.*

incident *n.* something that happens.

incidentally *adv.* by the way. *Incidentally, when's your birthday?*

incinerator *n.* a container in which garbage is burned.

incision *n.* a cut.

incite *v.* to provoke or urge somebody to do something bad.

inclination *n.* a tendency; a slight desire or preference.

incline *v.* to lean or slope toward something. **be inclined** to be likely to behave in a certain way. *She is inclined to be lazy.*

include *v.* to contain or count something as part of the whole. *Does the price of the hotel room include breakfast?* **inclusion** *n.*

incognito *adj., adv.* in disguise so that people do not know who you are.

income *n.* the money that somebody earns or receives regularly.

income tax *n.* money paid regularly to the government from a person's earnings.

incongruous *adj.* seeming out of place.

incorporate *v.* to include something so that it is part of the whole.

increase[1] *(in-krees) v.* to make or become greater in size or amount.

increase[2] *(in-krees) n.* growth.

incredible *adj.* hard to believe; amazing. **incredibly** *adv.*

incriminate *v.* to suggest that somebody is responsible for a crime or fault.

incubate *v.* (of a bird) to sit on eggs to keep them warm before they hatch. **incubation** *n.*

incubator *n.* a piece of hospital equipment in which babies who are born too early are kept warm and safe until they are strong and well.

incurable *adj.* not able to be cured. *incurable diseases.*

indecent *adj.* rude or shocking; not decent. *an indecent joke.*

indeed *adv.* **1** really; certainly. *"She's very smart." "She is, indeed!"* **2** used for emphasis. *Thanks very much indeed.*

indefinite *adj.* not clear; not set. *The workers have gone on strike for an indefinite period.*

indelible *adj.* not easily rubbed out.

independent *adj.* not controlled by or needing help from others. **independence** *n.*

indestructible *adj.* not able to be destroyed.

index *n.* an alphabetical list at the end of a book, giving all the subjects in the book and the pages where they are mentioned.

index finger *n.* the finger located next to your thumb.

indicate *v.* **1** to point out or show something. *There is an arrow painted on the tree to indicate the right path.* **2** to signal. *Drivers must always indicate before turning.* **indication** *n.,* **indicator** *n.*

indifferent *adj.* **1** not caring or not interested. *He was indifferent to the feelings of others.* **2** mediocre; not very good. **indifference** *n.*

indigestion *n.* pain caused by difficulty in digesting food.

indignant *adj.* angry, especially at something wrong that has been done to you. **indignation** *n.*

indigo *n.* a deep color between blue and purple.

indispensable *adj.* essential; not very easy to replace.

individual[1] *adj.* **1** to do with, or for, one person only. *Each of the children had an individual lunch box.* **2** single; separate. *Put price labels on each individual item.* **individually** *adv.*

individual[2] *n.* a person.

indoors *adv.* inside a building. *Let's go indoors.* **indoor** *adj.*

indulge *v.* to let somebody have what he or she wants. **indulgence** *n.,* **indulgent** *adj.*

indigo

industrious *adj.* hard-working. *an industrious worker.*

industry *n.* **1** the work of making things in factories. **2** a trade or business. **industrial** *adj.*

inevitable *adj.* certain to happen.

inexplicable *adj.* impossible to explain.

infamous (*in-fuh-mus*) *adj.* well known, or famous, for being bad or evil. *an infamous murderer.*

infancy *n.* the time when you are a very young child.

infant *n.* a very young child or baby.

infantry *n.* soldiers who fight on foot.

infect *v.* to give a disease to somebody.

infection *n.* an illness caused by germs.

infectious *adj.* (of a disease or illness) easily passed on from one person to another.

inferior *adj.* lower in rank or quality.

infested *adj.* full of insects, mice, rats, or other pests.

infinite (*in-fin-it*) *adj.* without end or limits. *We believe that the universe is infinite.* **infinitely** *adv.*

infinitive *n.* a basic form of a verb, for example, *to be*, *to live*, and *to find*.

infinity *n.* space, time, or an amount that is without end or limits.

infirmary *n.* a hospital.

inflammable *adj.* easily set on fire.

inflate *v.* to fill something with air. **inflatable** *adj.*

inflation *n.* a general rise in prices.

inflict *v.* to make a person suffer something.

influence *v.* to have an effect on someone or something. **influence** *n.*

inform *v.* to tell somebody. *Please inform us of your decision.*

informal *adj.* friendly and relaxed; not formal. **informality** *n.*, **informally** *adv.*

information *n.* facts or knowledge.

information technology *n.* the use of computers to store and send information.

inflate

informative *adj.* providing information.

infrastructure *n.* the basic facilities in a country such as roads and transportation.

infuriate *v.* to make somebody very angry.

ingenious (*in-jeen-ee-yus*) *adj.* **1** skillful and good at making things. **2** Well made.

ingredient *n.* one of several things that go into a mixture, especially in cooking.

inhabit *v.* to live in a place.

inhabitant *n.* a person who lives in a place.

inhale *v.* to breathe in. **inhalation** *n.*

inherit *v.* **1** to receive money or property from somebody who has died. **2** to

have qualities that are the same as your parents. *She has inherited her mother's intelligence.* **inheritance** *n.*

inhuman *adj.* extremely cruel and brutal. **inhumanity** *n.*

initial[1] *adj.* first; at the beginning. **initially** *adv.*

initial[2] *n.* the letter that begins a word, especially a name. *John Paton's initials are J. P.*

initiative *n.* the ability to lead the way and make decisions for yourself.

inject *v.* to use a needle and syringe to put medicine into somebody's body. **injection** *n.*

injure *v.* to hurt somebody. *Two people were injured in the accident.*

injury *n.* the damage done to a person's body, often in an accident.

injustice *n.* unfairness; lack of justice.

ink *n.* a colored liquid used for writing, drawing, or printing.

inland *adj.* away from the coast. *Kansas City is an inland city.*

inlet *n.* a small bay.

inmate *n.* a person who lives in an institution, especially a prison.

inn *n.* a small hotel, especially in the country.

inner *adj.* inside; central.

inning *n.* a duration of time in a sport. *Baseball has nine innings.*

innocent *adj.* not guilty of a crime or of doing anything wrong. **innocence** *n.*

inoculate *v.* to protect somebody from a disease by giving him or her an injection. **inoculation** *n.*

input *n.* **1** what you put into something; your contribution. **2** the information that is fed into a computer. **input** *v.*

inquest *n.* an official investigation to find out why somebody died.

inquire *v.* to ask about something. (*can also be spelled* enquire).

inquiry *n.* **1** a question or a request for information. **2** an official investigation. (*can also be spelled* enquiry).

inquisitive *adj.* eager to find out about things; curious. **inquisitiveness** *n.*

insane *adj.* crazy; not sane. **insanity** *n.*

inscribe *v.* to carve or write words on an object. **inscription** *n.*

insect *n.* a small creature with six legs and no backbone.

insecticide *n.* a chemical used to kill insects.

insert *v.* to put something inside

something else. *She inserted the key into the lock.* **insertion** *n.*

inside[1] *n.* the inner part of something.

inside[2] *adj.* in or close to the inner part.

inside[3] *prep., adv.* in or to the inside. *It's raining—let's go inside.*

insect

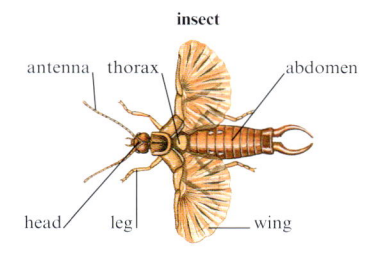

antenna thorax abdomen

head leg wing

insist *v.* to say very firmly that you must do or have something. *Paul insisted on paying for the ice cream.* **insistence** *n.*, **insistent** *adj.*

insomnia *v.* an inability to sleep.

inspect *v.* to examine something carefully. **inspection** *n.*

inspector *n.* a person whose job is to inspect something. *a food inspector.*

inspire *v.* to encourage somebody by filling him or her with enthusiasm or confidence. *The exhibition inspired me to paint a picture.* **inspiration** *n.*

install *v.* to put equipment in a place, ready for use. *The engineer installed a new telephone line.*

installment *n.* **1** one of a series of payments. *We are paying for our new car in installments.* **2** an episode of a story.

instance *n.* an example. **for instance** for example.

instant[1] *n.* a moment; a very short time.

instant[2] *adj.* immediate. **instantly** *adv.*

instead *adv.* in place of something. *I don't like ice cream—can I have an apple instead?*

instinct *n.* a natural habit that does not need to be learned. *Birds build nests by instinct.* **instinctive** *adj.*

institute *n.* an organization that has been set up for a special purpose, especially teaching or research.

institution *n.* **1** a large organization where people can live or work together. **2** a custom or tradition.

instruct *v.* to teach or direct somebody. **instruction** *n.*, **instructor** *n.*

instrument *n.* **1** a delicate tool for doing

a specific job. *medical instruments.* **2** an object used for making music.

insulate *v.* to cover something with a material so that heat or electricity cannot pass through it. *Plastic is used for insulating electric cables.* **insulation** *n.*

insult[1] (*in-sult*) *v.* to upset somebody by being rude to him or her.

insult[2] (*in-sult*) *n.* a remark or action that insults somebody.

insurance *n.* an agreement with a company that if you pay them a regular sum, they will give you money if something of yours is lost or damaged or if you become sick. **insure** *v.*

intact *adj.* whole; not damaged.

integrate *v.* to combine several people or things into one whole. **integration** *n.*

integrity *n.* honesty; trustworthiness.

intellectual *adj.* involving your mind and thoughts. *an intellectual problem.*

intelligent *adj.* smart and able to understand things easily. **intelligence** *n.*

intend *v.* to mean or decide to do something.

intense *adj.* very strong. *intense heat.* **intensity** *n.*

intensive *adj.* thorough. *an intensive search.*

intention *n.* the thing you mean to do or action you mean to take.

intentional *adj.* done on purpose.

inter- *prefix* among or between. *intercontinental* (= between or connecting different continents).

interactive *adj.* allowing two-way communication, e.g. between a computer program and its user. **interact** *v.*

intercept *v.* to stop somebody or something that is moving from one place to another.

intercom *n.* a system that people use for communicating with each other when they are in different rooms.

interest[1] *n.* **1** a feeling of wanting to know or learn about something. **2** something that you like doing or learning about. **3** extra money that you pay back if you have borrowed money.

interest[2] *v.* to make somebody want to know more about something; to keep somebody's attention. **interested** *adj.*, **interesting** *adj.*

interfere *v.* **1** to involve yourself in something that does not concern you. *Please do not interfere.* **2** to get in the way of something.

a b c d e f g h **i** j k l m n o p q r s t u v w x y z

A

B

C

D

E

F

G

H

I

J

K

L

M

N

O

P

Q

R

S

T

U

V

W

X

Y

Z

interference *n.* **1** the act of interfering in something. **2** interruption of radio signals so that they cannot be received properly.

interior *n.* the inside of something. **interior** *adj.*

intermediate *adj.* in the middle; between two stages or levels.

intermission *n.* a time between two events or between parts of a play or concert.

internal *adj.* on the inside of something. **internally** *adv.*

international *adj.* involving different countries. *The United Nations is an international organization.*

Internet *n.* a global computer network that allows you to communicate with other people and exchange information.

interpret *v.* **1** to translate a speaker's words from one language to another. **2** to decide what something means. *She interpreted his smile as a sign of approval.* **interpretation** *n.*

interrogate *v.* to question somebody thoroughly. **interrogation** *n.*

interrupt *v.* **1** to disturb somebody who is in the middle of speaking or doing something. **2** to stop something for a while. **interruption** *n.*

intervene *v.* to interrupt a quarrel or fight and try to stop it. **intervention** *n.*

interview *n.* a meeting at which somebody is asked questions. *She has an interview for a job.* **interview** *v.*

intestines *n. pl.* the long tubes through which food passes after it leaves your stomach. See **digestion**.

intimate *(in-tim-ut) adj.* **1** close; very friendly. **2** private and personal. *The newspaper published intimate details about her life.*

intimidate *v.* to frighten somebody so that he or she will do what you want. **intimidation** *n.*

into *prep.* **1** to the inside of something. *Come into my room.* **2** against. *The car drove into a wall.* **change into; turn into** to become. *Tadpoles turn into frogs.*

intrepid *adj.* brave; fearless.

intricate *adj.* complicated and detailed.

intrigue[1] *(in-treeg) n.* a secret plan.

intrigue[2] *(in-treeg) v.* to make somebody curious. *The story intrigued me.*

introduce *v.* **1** to make people known to each other. *Ben introduced me to his sister.* **2** to bring in something new. **3** to say a few words at the start of a TV or radio show, explaining what it is about.

introduction *n.* **1** introducing somebody or something. **2** words at the beginning of a book telling you what it is about.

intrude *v.* to enter somewhere where you are not wanted or invited. **intrusion** *n.*

intuition *n.* the power of understanding or realizing something without thinking it through. **intuitive** *adj.*

invade *v.* to enter and attack another country. **invasion** *n.*

invalid[1] *(in-va-lid) n.* a person who is sick and needs care.

invalid[2] *(in-val-id) adj.* not able to be used legally; not valid.

invaluable *adj.* extremely useful.

invent *v.* **1** to think of or make something for the first time. **2** to make up a story. **invention** *n*

inventor *n.* a person who invents things.

invertebrate *n.* an animal with no backbone, e.g. an insect, worm, or snail.

quotation marks *n. pl.* the marks " " most often used in writing before and after speech.

invest *v.* to put money into something in order to make a profit. **investment** *n.*

investigate *v.* to try to find out all about something. *The police are investigating the robbery.* **investigation** *n.*

invisible *adj.* not able to be seen. **invisibility** *n.*

invite *v.* to ask somebody to come somewhere. **invitation** *n.*

invoice *n.* a document showing goods or services received, asking for payment.

involve *v.* **1** to require something as a necessary part. *The job involvestravel.* **2 to be involved** to participate. *I'm involved in the concert.* **involvement** *n.*

ir- *prefix* not. *irregular; irrelevant.*

irate *(eye-rate) adj.* very angry.

iris *n.* **1** a tall, flowering plant. **2** the colored part of the eye. See **eye**.

iron[1] *n.* **1** a heavy, gray metal. **2** a piece of electrical equipment with a flat bottom that heats up and is used for making clothes smooth and wrinkle free.

iron[2] *v.* to smooth something with an iron.

irony *(eye-ron-ee) n.* the use of

language that says the opposite of what you really mean; to make a deliberate contrast.

irregular *adj.* **1** not regular. **2** not balanced or even. **3** (of verbs) not obeying the usual rules.

irresistible *adj.* too attractive or tempting to resist.

irrigate *v.* to supply water to land by canals or other means. **irrigation** *n.*

irritable *adj.* bad-tempered; easily annoyed.

irritate *v.* to make somebody annoyed. **irritation** *n.*

Islam *n.* the Muslim religion founded by the prophet Muhammad and based on the teachings of the Koran. **Islamic** *adj.*

island *n.* a piece of land surrounded on all sides by water.

isle (*rhymes with* mile) *n.* an island. The word "isle" is mostly used in literature and poetry or in the name of islands. *The Isle of Man.*

isolate *v.* to separate somebody or something from others. **isolation** *n.*

isosceles (*eye-sos-il-eez*) *adj.* (of a triangle) with two sides of equal length. See **triangle**.

issue[1] *v.* to send out or give out something.

issue[2] *n.* **1** one edition of a newspaper or magazine. **2** a subject for discussion.

IT *short for* information technology.

italics *n. p.l* letters printed so that they are angled to the right.

itch *n.* a feeling in your skin that makes you want to scratch. **itchy** *adj.*

item *n.* one of a number of things. *He crossed off each item on the list.*

itinerary *n.* a detailed plan of a journey.

its *adj.* belonging to it. *The cat hurt its paw.*

it's *short for* "it is" or "it has."

ivory *n.* the hard, creamy-white substance that elephants' tusks are made of.

ivy *n.* a climbing evergreen plant with shiny, pointed leaves.

jab *v.* (jabs, jabbing, jabbed) to poke with something sharp. *He jabbed me with the end of his umbrella.*

jack *n.* **1** a device for raising part of a vehicle off the ground so that it can be repaired. **2** the playing card between the ten and the queen.

jack

jackal *n.* a type of wild dog.

jacket *n.* **1** a short coat. **2** an outer covering. *a book jacket.*

jackpot *n.* the top prize in a game or lottery.

jade *n.* a precious, usually green, stone used for making jewelry and ornaments.

jagged *adj.* having sharp, uneven edges.

jaguar *n.* a large wild cat, similar to a leopard, found in South America.

jail *n.* a prison. **jail** *v.*

jam[2] *v.* (jams, jamming, jammed) **1** to squeeze into place. *He jammed his belongings into a suitcase.* **2** to get stuck or make something get stuck. *My key got jammed in the lock.*

jam[3] *n.* **1** a situation in which vehicles cannot move. *a traffic jam.* **2** (*informal*) a difficult situation.

jangle *v.* to make a loud, ringing sound.

January *n.* the first month of the year.

jar[1] *n.* a glass container with a lid, used for storing food.

jar[2] *v.* (jars, jarring, jarred) **1** to have a harsh, unpleasant effect on somebody. *Her voice jarred on my ears.* **2** to jolt.

jargon *n.* the special or technical language of a group of people.

jaunt *n.* a short pleasure trip.

A
B
C
D
E
F
G
H
I
J
K
L
M
N
O
P
Q
R
S
T
U
V
W
X
Y
Z

javelin *n.* a short, light spear, thrown in an athletics competition.

jaw *n.* **1** one of the two bones that hold your teeth. **2** the lower part of your face.

jazz *n.* a type of lively music that has a strong rhythm, first played and sung by African Americans.

jealous *adj.* **1** wanting what somebody else has. **2** angry because the person you love seems to love, or be loved by, somebody else. **jealousy** *n.*

jeans *n. pl.* pants made out of denim.

Jeep *n. (trademark)* a motor vehicle used for traveling over rough ground, especially an army vehicle.

jeer *v.* to speak or shout unkindly at somebody. **jeer** *n.*

jelly *n.* **1** a soft, wobbly food flavored with fruit juice. **2** a substance like this.

jellyfish *n. (pl.* jellyfish *or* jellyfishes) a sea creature with tentacles and a jellylike body.

jeopardy *(jep-er-dee) n.* **in jeopardy** in danger; under threat. *Her job is in jeopardy.* **jeopardize** *v.*

jerk[1] *n.* a short, sudden movement. *We felt a jerk as the train started to move.*

jerk[2] *v.* to move with a jerk.

jest *n.* a joke. **jest** *v.*

jester *n. (historical)* in the Middle Ages an entertainer in the courts of kings.

jet *n.* **1** a strong, fast stream of liquid or gas. **2** an aircraft with an engine that sucks in air and pushes it out at the back, so pushing the aircraft forward.

jet lag *n.* a feeling of extreme tiredness caused by a long plane journey.

jetty *n.* a small pier.

Jew *n.* **1** a person descended from the ancient Hebrew people of Israel. **2** a person who practices the religion of Judaism. **Jewish** *adj.*

jewel *n.* a precious stone such as a diamond, ruby, or emerald.

jeweler *n.* a person who makes or sells items of jewelry.

jewelry *n.* ornaments that you wear such as rings, necklaces, and bracelets.

jig *n.* a fast, lively dance.

jigsaw puzzle *n.* a puzzle made up of wooden or cardboard pieces of various shapes that fit together to make a picture.

jigsaw puzzle

jingle[1] *v.* to make a short, sharp ringing sound like small bells or keys.

jingle[2] *n.* **1** the sound of something jingling. **2** a simple song or tune, used in TV and radio advertising.

jinx *n.* something that brings bad luck.

job *n.* **1** the work that somebody does for money. **2** a task.

jockey *n. (pl.* jockeys) a person who rides horses in races.

jodhpurs *(jod-purs) n. pl.* pants that fit tightly from your knee to your ankle, worn for horse riding.

jog *v.* (jogs, jogging, jogged) **1** to run at a slow, steady pace. **2** to knock gently. *She jogged my arm, and I spilled my drink.* **jog somebody's memory** to remind somebody of something.

join[1] *v.* **1** to become a member of a group or club. *She wants to join the army.* **2** to come together with somebody. *Will you join us for dinner?* **3** to put things together; to connect or unite. *All join hands, please.*

joint[1] *n.* **1** a point where two parts join. *The knee is the joint between the upper and lower bones of the leg.* **2** a big piece of meat.

joint[2] *adj.* shared. *a joint bank account.*

joke *n.* something that you do or say to make people laugh. **joke** *v.*

joker *n.* **1** a person who jokes. **2** in a pack of playing cards an extra card with a picture of a jester on it.

jolly[1] *adj.* (jollier, jolliest) happy; cheerful.

jolt *v.* to move or shake with sudden jerks. **jolt** *n.*

jostle *v.* to push somebody roughly. *He was jostled by the crowd.*

jot *v.* (jots, jotting, jotted) to write something quickly. *Let me jot down your phone number.*

journal *n.* **1** a diary in which you write what you have done each day. **2** a magazine, especially on a particular subject. *He applied for a job on the science journal.*

journalist *n.* a writer for a newspaper or magazine. **journalism** *n.*

journey *n. (pl.* journeys) an act of traveling from one place to another. *His journey to work by bus takes around an hour every day.*

joust *n. (historical)* a contest between two knights on horses, armed with lances. **joust** *v.*

joy *n.* great happiness.

joyful *adj.* filled with joy. *joyful celebrations.* **joyfully** *adv.*

joust

jumbo jet

joy ride *v. (informal)* reckless driving. **joy ride** *n.,* **joy rider** *n.*

joystick *n.* a control lever that can be moved in different directions.

jubilee *n.* a celebration of a special anniversary, for example, the start of a king's or queen's reign.

Judaism *(joo-dee-iz-um) n.* the religion of the Jewish people, based on teachings of the Torah and the Old Testament.

judge[1] *n.* **1** a person who hears and decides cases in a law court. **2** a person who decides the winner in a competition.

judge[2] *v.* **1** to act as a judge. **2** to make a guess about something. **judgment** (*or* judgement) *n.*

judo

judo *n.* a form of wrestling, from Japan, in which two people try to throw each other to the ground.

jug *n.* a container for liquids, usually with a handle and a lip for pouring.

juggle *n.* to keep throwing several balls or other objects up into the air and catching them. **juggler** *n.*

juice *n.* liquid from fruits, vegetables, or other food. **juicy** *adj.*

jukebox *n.* a machine that plays music when you put coins into it.

July *n.* the seventh month of the year.

jumble[1] *v.* to mix things up so that they are messy or in the wrong order.

jumble[2] *n.* an untidy collection of things.

jumbo *adj.* very large.

jumbo jet *n.* a very large jet aircraft.

jump *v.* **1** to spring off the ground; to leap. **2** to get over something by leaping. **3** to move suddenly and quickly. **jump** *n.*

junction *n.* a place where roads or railroad tracks meet.

June *n.* the sixth month of the year.

jungle *n.* a thick forest in a hot country.

junior *adj.* **1** less important in rank. *a junior officer in the navy.* **2** younger. **3** a student in eleventh grade in high school.

junk *n.* **1** things that are worthless or useless. **2** a Chinese sailing boat.

junk food *n.* food that is not very good for your health, but that is easy and quick to get or prepare.

jury *n.* people who are chosen to decide whether an accused person is guilty or not guilty in a law court.

just[1] *adv.* **1** exactly. *That's just what I wanted.* **2** very recently. *I have just arrived.* **3** almost not. *There is just enough money.* **4** only. *She wrote just a brief note.* **5** at this moment. *I'm just going out.*

junk food

just[2] *adj.* fair; right. *a just law.*

justice *n.* **1** fairness and rightness. *a sense of justice.* **2** the law.

justify *v.* (justifies, justifying, justified) to prove or show that something is just or right. **justification** *n.*

jut *v.* (juts, jutting, jutted) to stick out.

juvenile *adj.* **1** to do with young people. **2** childish. **juvenile** *n.*

Kk

kaleidoscope *n.* a tube that you look through and turn to see changing patterns of colors.

kangaroo *n.* an Australian marsupial with strong back legs for jumping.

karaoke *(ka-ree-oh-kee) n.* a form of entertainment, originally from Japan, in which people sing the words along to recorded music.

karate *(ka-rah-tee) n.* a very old form of fighting, originally from Japan, using blows and kicks.

kayak *(kye-ak) n.* a covered canoe.

kebob *n.* small pieces of meat or vegetables cooked on a metal or wooden stick called a skewer.

keel *n.* the long piece of a ship's frame that runs along the bottom.

keen *adj.* **1** eager; enthusiastic. **2** strong; sharp. *Many animals have a very keen sense of smell.*

keep¹ *v.* (keeping, kept) **1** to have something and not give it away. **2** to stay the same; to remain. *Please keep still!* **3** to go on doing something. *He keeps interrupting me.* **4** to make somebody or something stay the same. *This coat should keep you warm.* **5** to have something in a particular place. *Where do you keep your bike?* **6** to provide a home and food for people or animals. *My grandma keeps chickens.*

keep² *n.* a strong tower in a castle.

keeper *n.* a person who takes care of something such as a collection of animals in a zoo.

keg *n.* a small barrel.

kennel *n.* **1** a small hut for a dog. **2** a place where dogs can be taken care of while their owners are away.

kept *past of* keep.

kernel *n.* the inner part of a nut.

kestrel *n.* a small type of falcon.

ketchup *n.* a thick tomato sauce.

kettle *n.* a container with a lid, handle, and spout, used when boiling water.

key¹ *n.* (*pl.* keys) **1** a metal object for opening a lock. **2** one of the small parts of a musical instrument or computer keyboard that you press with your fingers. **3** a list of symbols and other information that helps you understand a map or table. **4** a clue that helps solve a code or explain a mystery. **5** a scale of musical notes starting on a specific note.

key

key² *adj.* very important. *Churchill was a key figure of the 1900s.*

keyboard *n.* **1** the keys of a piano, computer, or typewriter. **2** an electronic musical instrument like a small piano.

khaki *(ka-kee) n.* a brownish-green color.

kick *v.* to hit something with your foot. **kickoff** to start a soccer game by kicking the ball. **kick** *n.*

kid¹ *n.* **1** a young goat. **2** *(informal)* a child.

kid² *v.* (kids, kidding, kidded) to fool somebody for fun. *I'm just kidding.*

kidnap *v.* (kidnaps, kidnapping, kidnapped) to capture somebody and often to demand money for his or her release. **kidnapper** *n.*, **kidnapping** *n.*

kidney *n.* (*pl.* kidneys) one of two internal organs that clean blood and make urine.

kill *v.* to end the life of a person or animal.

kiln *n.* an oven for baking bricks or pottery pieces to make them hard.

kilo *n.* (*pl.* kilos) a kilogram.

kilogram *n.* a measurement of weight, equal to 2.2 lbs. Often referred to as a "kilo."

kilometer *n.* a measure of length, equal to 0.62 miles.

kilowatt *n.* a measure of electrical power, equal to 1,000 watts.

kilt *n.* a type of skirt often made of plaid cloth, traditionally worn by Scottish men.

kimono *n.* (*pl.* kimonos) a loose gown with wide sleeves, traditionally worn

kayak

A B C D E F G H I J K L M N O P Q R S T U V W X Y Z

by Japanese women.

kin *n.* relatives. **next of kin** your closest relatives. *He notified my next of kin.*

kind[1] *adj.* friendly and good to people. **kindness** *n.*

kind[2] *n.* a type or sort.

kindergarten *n.* a type of school for very young children.

king *n.* **1** a male ruler who has inherited the position. **2** the playing card with a picture of a king on it. **3** the important chess piece that must avoid capture.

kingdom *n.* a country that is ruled by either a king or queen.

kingfisher *n.* a small bird with bright blue and orange feathers that lives close to rivers and dives for fish.

kiosk *(kee-osk) n.* a small hut where you can buy a variety of things.

kiss *v.* to touch somebody with your lips to show love or friendship. **kiss** *n.*

kit *n.* **1** a set of equipment or tools that you need in order to do something. *Have you seen my tool kit?* **2** a set of all the things that you need to make something. *a model-airplane kit.*

kitchen *n.* a room in a house where you prepare and cook food.

kite *n.* a toy that flies in the wind and is made of a light frame covered with cloth or paper and attached to a string.

kitten *n.* a young cat.

kiwi *(kee-wee) n. (pl.* kiwis) a New Zealand bird that cannot fly.

kiwi fruit *n.* a green fruit with a brown, hairy skin and black seeds.

knack *n.* the ability someone has to do something easily.

knave *n.* another word for the jack in a pack of playing cards.

knead *v.* to press and squeeze dough with your hands to make it ready for baking.

kimono

knee *n.* the joint located in the middle of your leg.

kneecap *n.* the hard bone located at the front of your knee.

kneel *v.* (kneeling, knelt) to go down on your knees.

knew *past of* know.

knife *n. (pl.* knives) a tool with a blade and a handle, used for cutting.

knight *n.* **1** *(historical)* in the Middle Ages a nobleman who fought on horseback to serve a king or lord. **2** a man with the title "sir." **3** a chess piece shaped like a horse's head.

knit *v.* (knits, knitting, knitted) to make clothes or other things out of yarn, using two long needles or a machine.

knob *n.* a round handle.

knock *v.* **1** to hit something to make a noise. *He knocked on the door.* **2** to hit somebody or something, causing a fall. *I knocked the vase off the table.* **knock out** to hit somebody hard enough to make him or her unconscious. **knock** *n.*

knocker *n.* a metal object that is attached to a door, used for knocking.

knot[1] *n.* **1** a join made in string or rope by tying and pulling it tight. **2** a hard lump in wood, where a branch was connected to the tree trunk. **3** a measure of speed, usually of ships or aircraft, equivalent to just over one mile per hour.

knot[2] *v.* (knots, knotting, knotted) to tie something in a knot.

know *v.* (knowing, knew, known) **1** to be aware of or have something correctly in your mind. *Do you know what time it is?* **2** to be familiar with or to recognize something.

knowledge *n.* the facts and information that you know and understand. **knowledgeable** *adj.*

knuckle *n.* one of the joints of your fingers.

koala *n.* a furry Australian marsupial that lives in trees.

Koran *(ko-rahn) n.* the holy book of Islam. *(can also be spelled* Quran *or* Qur'an.*)*

kosher *(koh-sher) adj.* (of food) prepared in the way that is required by Jewish law.

koala

a
b
c
d
e
f
g
h
i
j
k
l
m
n
o
p
q
r
s
t
u
v
w
x
y
z

L l

label *n.* a piece of paper, card, or cloth with writing on it, attached to something to give information about it. **label** *v.*

labor¹ *n.* **1** work, especially physical work. **2** the process of giving birth to a baby.

labor² *v.* to work hard.

laboratory *n.* a room or building used for scientific experiments.

laborer *n.* a person who does hard physical work.

Labrador retriever *n.* a large black or golden-colored dog.

lace¹ *n.* **1** a thin, delicate material with a pattern of small holes. **2** a shoelace.

lace² *v.* to fasten with laces.

lack *v.* to be without something. *Steve lacked the strength to trek farther up the mountain.* **lack** *n.*

lacquer *(lack-er)* *n.* a clear, shiny paint.

ladder *n.* a set of steps between two long pieces of wood, metal, or rope.

laden *adj.* carrying a lot of heavy things. *He returned from his shopping trip laden with bags.*

ladle *n.* a large, deep spoon.

lady *n.* **1** a polite word for a woman. **2** a special title given to a woman, especially the wife of a knight or lord.

ladybug *n.* a small, flying beetle, usually red with black spots.

lag *v.* (lags, lagging, lagged) to move too slowly and get left behind.

lagoon *n.* a shallow saltwater lake separated from the sea by a sandbank.

laid *past of* lay².

lain *past participle of* lie².

lair *n.* a wild animal's den.

lake *n.* a large area of water completely surrounded by land.

ladybug

lamb *n.* **1** a young sheep. **2** the meat from a young sheep.

lame *adj.* **1** not able to walk without difficulty, because of an injury to the foot or leg. **2** not good enough; weak. *That's a lame excuse.* **lameness** *n.*

lamp *n.* an object that produces light by using electricity or burning oil or gas.

lance *n.* *(historical)* a type of spear with a long handle and sharp point, used in the past by soldiers on horseback.

land¹ *n.* **1** the parts of Earth's surface that are not covered by water. **2** a country. *foreign lands.* **3** a piece of ground owned by somebody.

land² *v.* to come on to land from the sea or the air. *Our plane landed on time.* **landing** *n.*

landing *n.* a flat area of floor at the top of a flight of stairs.

landlady, landlord *n.* **1** a person who owns a house or apartment and rents it out to other people for a period of time.

landmark *n.* a clearly visible building or object that helps you find the way.

landscape *n.* **1** everything you can see when you look across an area of land. *a beautiful landscape.* **2** a picture of an area of countryside.

landslide *n.* a fall of rocks or dirt down the side of a hill or cliff.

lane *n.* **1** a narrow road, usually in the country. **2** one of the strips that a wide road, a racetrack, or a swimming pool is divided into.

language *n.* **1** the system of words that we use continually to talk or write to each other. *Many different languages are spoken in Africa.* **2** any other way of communicating. *sign language.*

lanky *adj.* tall and thin.

lantern *n.* a box with glass sides for holding a candle or oil lamp so that it does not blow out.

lap¹ *n.* **1** the top part of your legs when you are sitting down. **2** the distance around a racetrack.

lap² *v.* (laps, lapping, lapped) **1** to drink by licking with the tongue, like a cat. **2** (of a liquid) to move gently against something. *Waves lapped against the rocks.*

lapel *n.* the part of a coat or jacket that is connected to the collar and folded back across your chest.

lapse¹ *n.* **1** a small mistake. **2** a length of time that has passed. *after a lapse of almost ten years.*

lapse² *v.* **1** to expire; to become invalid. *My membership has lapsed.* **2 lapse into** gradually pass or change into. *We started speaking in French but then lapsed into English.*

laptop *n.* a small, light, portable computer.

lard *n.* the fat of a pig, melted and then solidified, used in cooking.

larder *n.* a small room or cupboard where food is kept cool; pantry.

large *adj.* big. **largeness** *n.*

lark *n.* **1** a small, brown bird that sings beautifully. **2** *(informal)* something done for fun. *We only did it for a lark.*

larva *n.* (*pl.* larvae or larvas) an insect in the first stage after coming out of the egg.

lasagne *(la-zan-yuh* or *la-san-yuh)* *n.* **1** wide, flat strips of pasta. **2** an Italian dish made with this pasta in a meat or vegetable and cheese sauce.

laser *n.* an instrument that produces a very narrow and powerful beam of light, called a **laser beam**.

lash¹ *v.*
1 to strike a person or an animal with a whip. *They used the leather whip to lash the mutineer.* **2** to make sudden, violent movements like a whip. *The shark's tail lashed from side to side.* **3** to fasten tightly with a rope.

mosquito larva

lash² *n.* an eyelash.

lasso *(la-so* or *la-soo)* *n.* (*pl.* lassos or lassoes) a long rope with a loop that tightens when the rope is pulled, mostly used for catching animals. **lasso** *v.*

last¹ *adj., adv.* **1** at the end; after all the others. **2** most recent. *last week.*

last² *v.* **1** to go on for a length of time. *How long does this movie last?* **2** to continue or to remain in good condition for a certain length of time. *His good mood won't last.*

latch *n.* a type of fastening that is used for a gate or door.

late *adj., adv.* **1** coming after the usual or right time. *They were late for school.* **2** near the end of a time. *the late afternoon.* **3** no longer alive. *the late prime minister.*

lately *adv.* recently; not long ago.

lather *n.* a mass of small soap bubbles.

Latin *n.* the language of ancient Rome.

latitude *n.* the distance, measured in degrees, that a place is north or south of the equator.

latter *adj.* toward the end. *the latter part of the year.* **the latter** *n.* the second of two things just mentioned.

laugh *v.* to make a sound to show that you think that something is funny. **laugh** *n.*, **laughter** *n.*

launch¹ *v.* **1** to put a boat into water for the first time. **2** to send a rocket up into space. **3** to start something new.

launch² *n.* **1** an act of launching something. **2** a large boat with a motor.

laundromat *n.* a place with machines where people can wash their clothes.

laundry *n.* **1** clothes that are waiting to be washed. **2** a place where you send clothes to be washed.

lava *n.* hot, liquid rock that flows from an active volcano.

lavatory *n.* a bathroom.

lavender *n.* **1** a small shrub with purple flowers that have a pleasant smell. **2** a pale bluish-purple color.

law *n.* **1** a set of rules in a society that people must obey. **2** one of these rules. **3** a rule in science. *the law of gravity.*

law court *n.* a place where it is decided whether somebody is guilty of a crime and where disagreements between people are judged.

lawful *adj.* allowed by law. **lawfully** *adv.*

lawn *n.* an area of short, cut grass.

lawn mower *n.* a machine that you use to cut grass.

lawn

lawyer *n.* a person who advises on laws and speaks for people in a law court.

lax *adj.* careless; not strict.

lay[1] *past of* lie[2].

lay[2] *v.* (lays, laying, laid) **1** (of a bird) to produce an egg. **2** to put something down carefully.

layer *n.* a thickness or covering. *The ground was covered with a layer of ice and snow.*

lazy *adj.* (lazier, laziest) not wanting to do work or exercise. **lazily** *adv.*, **laziness** *n.*

lead[1] (*rhymes with* bed) *n.* **1** a soft, heavy, gray metal. **2** the part of a pencil that makes a mark.

lead[2] (*rhymes with* reed) *v.* (leading, led) **1** to go in front, especially to show others the way. *She led me to the door.* **2** to be in first place. **3** to be in charge. **4** to go to a place. *Where does this road lead?* **leader** *n.*, **leadership** *n.*

lead[3] (*rhymes with* reed) *n.* **1** a leading position. *The Kenyan runner has moved into the lead.* **2** a clue. *Do the police have any leads yet?*

leaf *n.* (*pl.* leaves) **1** one of the flat, usually green, parts of a plant or tree. **2** a page of a book.

leaflet *n.* a printed paper, often folded over, giving information about something; pamphlet.

league (*leeg*) *n.* **1** a group of sports teams that play games against each other. *The Detroit Red Wings play in the National Hockey League.* **2** a group of people or countries that work together to help each other. *The League of Arab States is an organization of Middle Eastern countries.*

leaf

leak[1] *n.* **1** an unwanted hole through which liquid or gas escapes. *a leak in the water pipe.* **2** liquid or gas that has escaped through such a hole.

leak[2] *v.* **1** to pass through a leak. *Gas was leaking from the cracked pipe.* **2** to have a leak. *This bucket leaks.*

lean[1] *v.* (leaning, leaned) **1** to be in a sloping position. *She leaned over the cot.* **2** to rest against or on something. *He leaned the ladder against the shed.*

lean[2] *adj.* **1** slim and healthy. **2** having little fat. *lean meat.*

leap *v.* (leaping, leaped) to jump. **leap** *n.*

leap year *n.* a year with 366 days instead of 365 that occurs once every four years.

learn *v.* (learning, learned) **1** to get knowledge or skill. *Are you learning French in school?* **2** to get to know. *We learned that Julie was sick.*

learned (*ler-ned*) *adj.* knowing a lot.

lease *n.* a legal document giving use of land, a building, or a car in exchange for rent.

leash *n.* a long strap that you attach to a dog's or other pet's collar so that you can take it for walks.

least *adj.* smallest in size or amount. **least** *adv.*, *pron.*

leather *n.* the skin of an animal made smooth by tanning and used to make bags, shoes, and clothes.

leave[1] *v.* (leaving, left) **1** to go away. **2** to let something or somebody stay or remain. *I left my books on the bus.* **leave out** not to include. *Daisy was left out of the team because of her injury.*

leaves *plural of* leaf.

lecture[1] *n.* a formal talk given to a group of people to teach them something, for example at a college.

lecture[2] *v.* to give a lecture. **lecturer** *n.*

led *past of* lead.

ledge *n.* a narrow, horizontal shelf on a wall or cliff.

leek *n.* a long, white vegetable with thick, green leaves at one end.

left[1] *past of* leave.

left[2] *adj.* of, on, or toward the side opposite to the right. *Raise your left hand.* **left** *adv.*, *n.*

left-handed *adj.* using your left hand more easily than your right.

leftovers *n. pl.* food that remains after a meal is finished.

left-wing *adj.* in politics having socialist political views.

leg *n.* **1** one of the parts of your body that you use for standing and walking. **2** one of the supports of a chair or table. **3** one stage of a

leek

A B C D E F G H I J K L M N O P Q R S T U V W X Y Z

journey. *The first leg is from Chicago to Los Angeles.*

legal *adj.* **1** allowed by the law. **2** to do with the law. **legally** *adv.*

legend *n.* an old, traditional story.

legendary *adj.* **1** told about in old stories. **2** very famous.

leggings *n. pl.* tight-fitting pants made from a stretchy material.

legible *adj.* clear and easy to read. *Your handwriting is barely legible!* **legibility** *n.*, **legibly** *adv.*

legion *n.* **1** *(historical)* a division within the Roman army of between 3,000 and 6,000 soldiers. **2** a large group of soldiers.

legislation *n.* laws or a set of laws.

leisure *n.* free time.

leisurely *adj.* not hurrying; done at a relaxed pace.

lemon *n.* a citrus fruit with a thick, yellow skin and very sour juice.

lemonade *n.* a drink made from the juice of lemons.

lend *v.* (lending, lent) to give somebody the use of something for a time. *I lent her my coat.*

length *n.* **1** the distance from one end of something to the other. **2** the time that something lasts.

lemon

lengthen *v.* to make or become longer.

lengthy *adj.* (lengthier, lengthiest) long.

lenient *adj.* merciful; not strict.

lens *n.* **1** a piece of curved glass for focusing or magnifying, used in cameras and glasses. **2** the part of your eye that focuses light. See **eye**.

Lent *n.* in the Christian religion the 40 days before Easter.

lent *past of* lend.

lentil *n.* a small, dried seed that can be cooked and eaten.

leopard *(lep-erd)* *n.* a large wild cat with black spots on a yellowish coat, found in Africa and Asia.

leotard *(lee-a-tard)* *n.* a tight, one-piece garment worn for dancing or gymnastics.

lesbian *n.* a homosexual woman. **lesbian** *adj.*

less *adj.* smaller in size or amount. less *adv.,* pron. I wasn't very hungry, so I asked for less pasta.

lessen *v.* to make or become less or smaller.

lesson *n.* **1** a time during which something is taught and learned; class. *I am having guitar lessons after school.* **2** something learned by experience. **3** a piece from the Bible, read in church.

let *v.* (lets, letting, let) **1** to allow somebody to do something. *Billy let me ride his bike.* **2** used for giving orders or making suggestions. *Let us pray.* **let down** to disappoint somebody. **let off** to allow somebody to go without punishment.

lethal *adj.* causing death. **lethally** *adv.*

letter *n.* **1** a symbol that we use in writing to make up words. **2** a written message, often sent by mail in an envelope.

lettuce *n.* a salad vegetable with large, green leaves.

leukemia *(loo-kee-mee-a)* *n.* a very serious blood disease.

level[1] *adj.* **1** flat and even; horizontal. *a level surface.* **2** of the same height, standard, or amount. *The scores of the two teams are level.*

level[2] *n.* **1** a height or position. *sea level.* **2** a standard.

level[3] *v.* (levels, leveling, leveled) to make something level.

lever *n.* **1** a bar used for lifting something heavy or for forcing something open. **2** a handle that you use to make a machine work. **lever** *v.*

liable *adj.* responsible for something by law. **liable to** likely to. *She's liable to make careless mistakes.*

liar *n.* a person who tells lies.

liberal *adj.* **1** tolerant and respectful of other people and their ideas. **2** generous. **liberally** *adv.*

liberate *v.* to set a person or an animal

lever

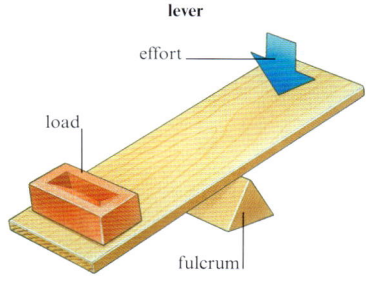

effort

load

fulcrum

free; to release. **liberation** *n.*

liberty *n.* freedom.

librarian *n.* person who works in a library.

library *n.* a place where you can go to read or borrow books or DVDs.

lice *plural of* louse.

license *n.* an official document giving you permission to do something. *a driver's license.*

license *v.* to give a licence to somebody. *Restaurants are licensed to sell food.*

lichen *(lie-ken) n.* a tiny plant that grows in patches on rocks and trees.

lick *v.* to pass your tongue over something. **lick** *n.*

licorice *(lik-er-ish) n.* a strong-tasting, black candy made from a plant root.

lid *n.* **1** a cover for a pot, box, or jar. **2** an eyelid.

lie¹ *v.* (lies, lying, lied) to say something that you know is not true. **lie** *n.*

lie² *v.* (lies, lying, lay, lain) **1** to be in, or get into, a flat position. *She lay down and went to sleep.* **2** to be situated somewhere. *The island lies off the coast.*

lice

pan lid

lieutenant *(loo-ten-int) n.* an officer in the army or navy.

life *n.* (*pl.* lives) **1** the state of being able to grow, develop, and change that makes plants and animals different from stones, water, or minerals. *The doctor saved the man's life.* **2** the time between birth and death. **3** liveliness; energy.

lifeboat *n.* a boat for rescuing people at sea.

life jacket *n.* a sleeveless, inflatable jacket that will keep you afloat in water; life vest.

lift¹ *v.* **1** to raise something. *The box was so heavy that I couldn't lift it.* **2** to rise. *The fog lifted.*

lift² *n.* a ride in somebody else's car or another vehicle; ride. *Our neighbor gave me a lift to school this morning.*

light¹ *n.* **1** the brightness from the Sun, a flame, or a lamp that makes it possible for us to see things. **2** an object, such as

an electric lamp, that gives out light. **3** a flame from a match or a lighter.

light² *v.* (lighting, lit *or* lighted) **1** to start something burning. **2** to give light to something. *The room was lit by lamps.*

light³ *adj.* **1** with a lot of light; not dark. **2** (of a color) pale. *light green.* **3** weighing little; not heavy. **4** gentle. *light rain.* **lighten** *v.,* **lightness** *n.*

lighter *n.* a device for lighting cigarettes or other items.

lighthearted *adj.* **1** happy; cheerful. **2** amusing; not serious.

lighthouse *n.* a tower by or in the sea, with a flashing light to guide or warn ships.

lightning *n.* a flash of light in the sky during a thunderstorm.

light-year *n.* the distance that light travels in one year (approximately six trillion miles); a measure used in astronomy.

like¹ *v.* to enjoy something; to find somebody or something pleasant. **likable** (*or* **likeable**) *adj.*

like² *prep.* **1** the same as or similar to. *She looks a lot like her sister.* **2** in the same or a similar way to. *She sang like a bird.* **3** typical of. *It's really not like Dan to be late.* **like** *conj.*

likely *adv.* (likelier, likeliest) expected to happen. *They said on the weather forecast that it is likely to rain today.* **likelihood** *n.*

likewise *adv.* the same; in the same way.

lilac *n.* a shrub with sweet-smelling, pale purple or white flowers.

lily *n.* a tall plant with white or colored flowers, grown from a bulb.

limb *n.* **1** a leg or an arm. **2** the branch of a tree.

lime *n.* **1** a small, green, sour-tasting citrus fruit similar to a lemon. **2** the color of this fruit. **3** a white substance, calcium oxide, left after heating limestone, often used to make cement.

limerick *n.* a funny five-line poem.

limestone *n.* a type of rock containing the chalky substance calcium carbonate.

limit¹ *n.* a line or point that you cannot or should not go beyond. *The speed limit in the town is 25 miles per hour.*

limit² *v.* to keep something from going beyond a certain point or amount. **limitation** *n.*

limp¹ *adj.* soft; not stiff. *limp lettuce leaf.*

limp² *v.* to walk unevenly, usually because you have hurt your foot or leg.

limpet *n.* a small, cone-shaped mollusk that clings to rocks.

line¹ *n.* **1** a long, thin mark. **2** a piece of rope, string, or wire. **3** a row of people, things, or words. **4** a railroad or a railroad track. **5 lines** the words spoken in a play.

line² *v.* to cover something, e.g. a garment or curtains, on the inside.

linen *n.* a type of cloth that is heavier than cotton, used to make things such as tablecloths and clothing.

liner *n.* a big passenger ship.

linesman *n.* a person who decides if the ball has gone over the line in sports such as football and tennis.

linger *v.* to wait around; to stay.

linguist *n.* a person who studies language or is good at languages.

lining *n.* a layer of material inside of something. *Her coat has a silk lining.*

link¹ *n.* **1** one loop of a chain. **2** a connection.

liner

link² *v.* to connect things together.

linoleum *n.* a shiny, synthetic floor covering.

lion *n.* a large wild cat, found in Africa and India. The male has a thick mane.

lioness *n.* a female lion.

lip *n.* **1** one of the edges of the mouth. **2** the specially shaped part of a jug from which liquid is poured.

lipstick *n.* a type of makeup used for coloring your lips.

liquid *n.* a substance that flows such as water or oil. **liquid** *adj.*

liquor *n.* any strong, alcoholic drink.

lisp *v.* to speak using a *th* sound instead of an *s.*

list¹ *n.* a number of names or things written down or said one after the other. *Did you put milk on the grocery list?* **list** *v.*

list² *v.* (of a ship) to lean to one side.

listen *v.* to pay attention so that you hear something. **listener** *n.*

lit *past of* light.

liter *n.* a measure for liquids, equal to approximately one quart.

literacy *n.* the ability to read and write.

literally *adv.* exactly as stated. *She was literally too tired to walk any farther.*

literary *adj.* **1** to do with literature. **2** (of language) formal and more likely to be found in books than in conversation.

literate *adj.* able to read and write.

literature *n.* **1** novels, poetry, and plays. **2** any written material.

litter *n.* **1** garbage that is dropped on the ground or anywhere else, other than in a garbage can. **2** all the animals born at one time to the same mother. *Our cat had a litter of four kittens.*

little *adj.* **1** small in size. **2** not much. **little** *adv., pron.*

live¹ (*rhymes with* give) *v.* **1** to have life; to be alive. **2** to have your home somewhere. *They live in Boston.*

live² (*rhymes with* hive) *adj.* **1** living; not dead. *They found a live mouse in the closet.* **2** when something is heard or seen on the radio or television as it is actually happening. **3** carrying an electrical current. *a live wire.*

lively *adj.* (livelier, liveliest) full of life and energy. **liveliness** *n.*

liver *n.* an organ in your body that does several important jobs, including cleaning the blood.

lives (*rhymes with* hives) *plural of* life.

livestock *n.* farm animals such as cattle, sheep, and pigs.

living¹ *adj.* having life; alive.

living² *n.* the money that you need in order to be able to live. *She earns a living as a taxi driver.*

living room *n.* a sitting room.

lizard *n.* a four-legged, often small, reptile with a tail.

liver

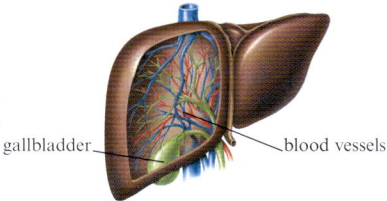

gallbladder   blood vessels

A
B
C
D
E
F
G
H
I
J
K
L
M
N
O
P
Q
R
S
T
U
V
W
X
Y
Z

llama *(lah-ma)* *n.* a mammal, native to South America, that resembles a small camel with no hump.

load¹ *n.* something that is carried, especially something heavy. **a load of, loads of** *(informal)* a lot of.

load² *v.* **1** to put a load onto or into the thing that will carry it. *We loaded the boxes into the van.* **2** to put bullets into a gun. **3** to put data or a program

llama

onto a computer.

loaf *n.* (*pl.* loaves) a large piece of bread baked in one piece.

loan¹ *n.* something that has been lent, especially an amount of money.

loan² *v.* to lend something.

loathe *v.* to hate something.

loaves *plural of* loaf.

lob *v.* (lobs, lobbing, lobbed) to throw or hit a ball high up into the air. **lob** *n.*

lobby *n.* an entrance hall.

lobster *n.* an edible shellfish with a hard shell and large claws.

local *adj.* belonging to a particular area. *a local newspaper.* **local** *n.*, **locally** *adv.*

locality *n.* an area; a neighborhood.

lobster

locate *v.* to find the position of something. *Can you locate your street on this map?* **be located** be in a particular place. *The kitchen is located in the basement.*

location *n.* a place; a position.

lock¹ *n.* **1** a device for fastening a door or box so that it cannot be opened without a key. **2** a section of a canal where the water levels can be changed by opening and shutting large gates.

lock² *v.* to fasten with a lock.

locker *n.* a small cupboard that can be locked to keep things safe.

locket *n.* a small case worn on a chain around the neck, sometimes containing a photograph.

locks *n. pl.* *(literary)* hair.

locomotive *n.* a railroad engine.

locust *n.* a type of large grasshopper that destroys crops by eating them.

lodge¹ *n.* **1** a small house, often

locust

at the entrance to a larger building. **2** a beaver's home.

lodge² *v.* **1** to live in a room in somebody's house, usually paying him or her money to do so. **2** to get stuck. *The bone lodged in his throat.*

lodger *n.* a person who pays to live in a room in somebody's house.

loft *n.* a room or space just under the roof of a building such as a warehouse.

log *n.* **1** a piece of wood cut from a tree that has been felled. **2** a written record, specifically detailing the journey of a ship or an airplane.

logic *n.* correct reasoning. **logical** *adj.*, **logically** *adv.*

logo *n.* (*pl.* logos) a symbol representing a company or other organization.

loiter *v.* to stand around doing nothing in particular. *The children were loitering in the mall.*

lollipop *n.* a candy on a stick.

lonely *adj.* (lonelier, loneliest) **1** sad because you are alone. **2** far away from busy places. *a lonely island off* *the coast of Scotland.* **loneliness** *n.*

long¹ *adj.* **1** not short; measuring a lot from end to end. **2** measuring a certain amount. *Make a cut five inches long.* **3** taking a lot of time. *It was a long, boring movie.* **long** *adv.*

long² *v.* to wish for something very much. *She longed to go home.*

longitude *n.* the distance measured in degrees east or west of a line that runs through Greenwich in London, England, and the North and South poles.

look *v.* **1** to use your eyes to see. **2** to appear or seem. *You look tired.* **look after** to take care of somebody or something. **look for** to search for something. **look forward to** to wait with pleasure for something. **Look out!** Be careful! **look up** to search for something in a book or computer.

lookout *n.* a person who keeps watch for possible danger.

loom¹ *n.* a machine for weaving cloth.

loom² *v.* **1** to appear as a large, frightening shape. *A tall figure loomed out of the darkness.* **2** (of a worrying or unpleasant event) seem likely to happen. *The threat of a new Internet virus has been looming for several days.*

loop *n.* a shape formed by a curve that bends around and crosses over itself. **loop** *v.*

loose *adj.* **1** not tight. *loose pants.* **2** not firmly attached. *One of my teeth is loose.* **3** not tied up. *The horses are loose in the field.* **4** not in a bag or fastened together. *loose candies.*

loosen *v.* to make or become loose.

loot¹ *n.* stolen money or goods.

loot² *v.* to steal goods in a riot or war.

lop *v.* (lops, lopping, lopped) to cut something off. *Dad lopped off the dead branches of the oak tree.*

lopsided *adj.* with one side higher than the other; crooked.

lord *n.* **1** a nobleman. **2** a title for a male member of the aristocracy. **3 Lord** a title for God or Christ.

lose *v.* (losing, lost) **1** to no longer have something; not to be able to find something. **2** to be beaten in a game, argument, or fight. **loser** *n.*

loss *n.* **1** an act of losing something. **2** something that is lost.

lost *adj.* **1** not able to be found. **2** puzzled or confused. **3** not knowing where you

are or in which direction you should go.

lot *n.* **1** a large number or amount. **2** a piece of land with a specific purpose. *a parking lot.*

lotion *n.* a thick liquid that you rub on your skin to clean or heal it.

lottery *n.* an event in which people buy tickets to try to win prizes or money.

loud *adj.* making a lot of sound. **loudness** *n.*

loudspeaker *n.* a part of a radio or CD player that turns electrical signals into sound.

lounge¹ *n.* a sitting room.

lounge² *v.* to sit around lazily.

louse *n.* (*pl.* lice) a small, wingless insect with a fat body and short legs that lives on the bodies of animals or

loudspeaker

humans and sucks their blood.

love¹ *v.* to like somebody or something very much. **lovable** (*or* **loveable**) *adj.*, **lover** *n.*

love² *n.* a strong feeling of liking somebody or something very much.

love³ *n.* in tennis no score.

lovely *adj.* (lovelier, loveliest) **1** attractive; beautiful. *Those flowers are lovely!* **2** pleasant; enjoyable. *We had a lovely time.*

low¹ *adj.* **1** situated close to the ground; not high. *The Sun was low in the sky.* **2** not reaching up to a high level. *They sat on a low wall.* **3** of less than average amount. *This cheese is low in fat.* **4** making little sound; soft. *She spoke in a low voice.* **5** (of notes) having a deep pitch. *The double bass is one of the lowest instruments in the orchestra.* **low** *adv.*

low² *v.* to make a sound like a cow.

lower *v.* to move something down.

loyal *adj.* faithful; not betraying your friends or country.

lubricate *v.* to put oil or grease on something to make it move more easily or smoothly. **lubrication** *n.*

luck *n.* **1** things that happen by chance that you cannot control. *There is no skill involved in this game—it's just luck whether you win or not.* **2** something good that happens by chance.

lucky *adj.* (luckier, luckiest) **1** having good luck. **2** bringing good luck. **luckily** *adv.*

luggage *n.* the cases and bags that you take with you when you travel.

lukewarm *adj.* slightly warm.

lull[1] *v.* to make somebody calm or quiet. *The music lulled him to sleep.*

lull[2] *n.* a short period of calm.

lullaby *n.* a song that is sung to help send a baby to sleep.

lumberjack *n.* a person who cuts down, saws, and moves trees.

luminous *adj.* shining in the dark.

lump *n.* **1** a small, solid mass. **2** a swelling.

lunacy *n.* **1** very stupid behavior. **2** *(historical)* insanity; mental illness.

lumberjack

lunar *adj.* to do with the Moon.

lunatic *n.* **1** a person who is behaving foolishly. **2** *(historical, today offensive)* a mentally ill person.

lunch *n.* a meal that you eat in the middle of the day.

lung *n.* one of the two organs inside your chest that you use for breathing. See **respiration**.

lunge *v.* to move forward quickly and suddenly. **lunge** *n.*

lurch *v.* to make a sudden, jerky movement, often to one side. *The car lurched forward.*

lure *v.* to tempt a person or an animal to do something or go somewhere. *The hunter lured the wild animal into the trap.* **lure** *n.*

lurk *v.* to wait in hiding. *Somebody was lurking in the shadows.*

lush *adj.* growing thickly and strongly. *The tropical rain forest in India is full of lush vegetation.*

lute *n.* *(historical)* an ancient guitarlike instrument with a pear-shaped body and a long neck.

luxury *n.* **1** something that is pleasant to have but that you do not really need. **2** the enjoyment of luxuries. **luxurious** *adj.*

lynx *n.* an animal of the cat family, with long legs, a short tail, and tufted ears.

lyre *n.* a U-shaped, harplike instrument.

lyrics *n. pl.* the words of a song.

Mm

macaroni *n.* short tubes of pasta. *macaroni and cheese.*

machine *n.* a piece of mechanical equipment with parts that move together to do something.

machine gun *n.* a gun that can fire bullets very quickly without being reloaded.

machinery *n.* **1** machines. **2** the working parts of machines.

mackerel *n.* an edible sea fish.

mad *adj.* (madder, maddest) very angry.

madam *n.* a polite way of speaking to a woman, instead of using her name.

made *past of* make.

magazine *n.* **1** a thin book that is published regularly, containing pictures, stories, and news. **2** the part of a gun that holds the bullets.

maggot *n.* the larva of some types of flies, similar to a small worm.

magic *n.* **1** in stories the power of supernatural forces to do amazing things that cannot be explained. **2** amazing tricks that seem like magic. **magical** *adj.*

magician *(ma-ji-shun) n.* a person who does magic tricks.

magnet *n.* a piece of metal that has the power to attract iron or steel. **magnetic** *adj.*, **magnetism** *n.*

magnificent *adj.* extremely impressive; amazing. **magnificence** *n.*

magnet

magnify *v.* (magnifies, magnifying, magnified) to make something appear bigger by using special lenses. **magnification** *n.*

magpie *n.* a large, long-tailed, black-and-white bird that is known to like collecting shiny objects.

mahogany *n.* a hard, reddish-brown wood.

magpie

maid *n.* **1** a female servant in a hotel or private home. **2** *(historical* or *literary)* a girl; maiden.

mail¹ *n.* **1** the system for sending and receiving letters and packages. **2** letters and packages that you send or receive. **mail** *v.*

mail² *n.* armor made of metal rings.

mailbox *n.* a box where you send letters.

maim *v.* to injure somebody badly, so that he or she is permanently disabled.

main *adj.* most important or largest.

mainland *n.* a large piece of land, not including the islands nearby.

mainly *adv.* mostly.

maintain *v.* **1** to keep something in good working condition. *The machinery is maintained regularly.* **2** to continue something. *We must maintain high standards.* **3** to give money to support something. *He has a family to maintain.* **4** to say firmly. *He maintains that he is innocent.* **maintenance** *n.*

maize *n.* a type of cultivated plant that produces corn.

majesty *n.* impressive dignity; splendor. **Your Majesty** the polite way of speaking to a king or queen. **majestic** *adj.*, **majestically** *adv.*

major¹ *adj.* great in size or importance.

major² *n.* a high rank in the army, air force, or marine corps.

majority *n.* the greater number; more than half. *the majority of people.*

make¹ *v.* (making, made) **1** to create or produce something. **2** to force or cause something to happen. *She made me laugh.* **3** to do something. *Can I make a call?* **4** to add up to. *Two plus six make eight.*

a b c d e f g h i j k l **m** n o p q r s t u v w x y z

make² *n.* a brand or type.

makeshift *adj.* built or made very quickly and intended to last only for a short time. *We built a makeshift shelter.*

makeup *n.* colored powders and creams that mostly women and actors put on their faces.

mal- *prefix* bad or badly. *malfunction, malnourished, maltreated.*

malaria *n.* a tropical disease that you can get from mosquito bites.

male *adj.* of the sex that does not give birth to children or produce eggs. **male** *n.*

malicious *adj.* hurting people on purpose; spiteful. *a malicious remark.*

mall *n.* a shopping area.

mallard *n.* a wild duck, the male of which has a green head.

mallet *n.* a wooden or rubber hammer.

malnutrition *n.* a disease caused by not getting enough nutritious food.

malt *n.* barley or other grain that has been prepared by soaking and drying, for making beer, whiskey, or vinegar.

mammal *n.* any animal of which the female gives birth to live young and

mammoth

feeds them with milk from her body.

mammoth¹ *n. (historical)* a very large animal, like a big, hairy elephant, that is now extinct.

mammoth² *adj.* huge; enormous.

man *n. (pl. men)* **1** a fully grown male human. **2** human beings in general; human.

manage *v.* **1** to succeed in doing something even if it is difficult. *I just managed to finish the work on time.*

2 to have control or charge of something. *She manages the store.* **management** *n.*, **manager** *n.*

mane *n.* the long hair on the head and neck of a horse or lion.

mango

maneuver *(man-oo-ver) n.* **1** a movement performed with care and skill. **2 maneuvers** training exercises for large numbers of troops. **maneuver** *v.*

manger *n.* a box designed for horses or cattle to eat from.

mangle *v.* to crush or damage something badly. *The car was mangled in the accident.*

mango *n. (pl.* mangoes *or* mangos) a type of tropical fruit with juicy, orange-colored flesh.

maniac *n.* a person who is behaving wildly and dangerously.

manic *adj.* very energetic or excited.

manicure *n.* a treatment of the hands and nails to make them look attractive.

manipulate *v.* **1** to use or control something skillfully. **2** to influence somebody in a cunning way so that he or she does what you want.

mankind *n.* all people; humankind.

man-made *adj.* artificial.

manner *n.* **1** the way in which you do something. *He greeted me in a friendly manner.* **2** the way in which you behave. *I don't like her manner.* **3 manners** polite behavior.

manor *n.* a large, old country house surrounded by land.

mansion *n.* a large, fancy house.

manslaughter *n.* the crime of killing a person without planning to do it.

mantelpiece *n.* a shelf over a fireplace.

manual¹ *adj.* done or worked with your hands. *manual labor.* **manually** *adv.*

manual² *n.* a book that gives you instructions about how to do something. *The washing machine came with an operating manual.*

manufacture *v.* to make things with machinery in a factory.

manure *n.* dung from animals, spread on soil to help produce better crops.

many *adj.* a great number. **many** *pron.*

map *n.* a stylized drawing of part of Earth's

surface, showing rivers, mountains, countries, towns, roads, and other features.

map *v.* to plot out a journey by drawing or using a map. *We mapped out our hike before we set off.*

maple *n.* a type of tree with large, five-pointed leaves.

mar *v.* (mars, marring, marred) to spoil or ruin something. *The day was marred by terrible weather.*

marathon *n.* a race for runners covering approximately 26 miles.

marble *n.* **1** hard stone that can be carved and polished. **2** a small glass ball used in games.

march[1] *v.* to walk with regular steps.

march[2] *n.* **1** a distance marched. **2** a piece of music for marching to. **3** an organized walk by a group of people to protest against, or support, something.

March *n.* the third month of the year.

mare *n.* a female horse.

margarine *n.* a yellow substance, like butter, made from vegetable fat.

margin *n.* **1** the blank space around the edge of a page of writing or print. **2** the amount by which a contest is won or lost. *We won by a margin of four points.*

marigold *n.* a garden plant with bright yellow or orange flowers.

marina *n.* a harbor where yachts and other boats can moor.

marine[1] *adj.* to do with the sea.

marine[2] *n.* a type of special soldier who serves on a ship.

marionette *n.* a puppet that is moved by pulling strings.

mark[1] *n.* **1** a stain, spot, or scratch on something. **2** a shape or sign on something.

mark[2] *v.* **1** to put a mark on something. **3** to guard an opposing player in a game.

market[1] *n.* a place where things are bought and sold, usually in the open air. *a fruit and vegetable market.*

market[2] *v.* to promote and sell goods or services. **marketing** *n.*

marmalade *n.* a jam made from oranges or other citrus fruits.

maroon[1] *n.* a brownish-red color. **maroon** *adj.*

maroon[2] *v.* to leave somebody in a lonely place from which they cannot escape. *The rebellious pirates were marooned on a desert island.*

marquee *(mar-kee) n.* a large tent.

marriage *n.* **1** the relationship between a husband and wife. **2** a wedding ceremony.

marrow *n.* **1** the soft substance in the hollow part of bones. **2** a large, long, green vegetable; marrow squash.

marry *v.* (marries, marrying, married) **1** to become husband and wife. **2** to perform a marriage ceremony. *We got married on a beach.*

marsupials

marsh *n.* an area of low, wet land. **marshy** *adj.*

marsupial *n.* an animal such as a kangaroo that carries its young in a pouch on the female's stomach.

martial *(mar-shul) adj.* to do with war or battle.

martial arts *n. pl.* self-defense techniques, such as judo and karate, that come from the Far East.

martyr *(mar-ter) n.* a person who suffers or dies for his or her beliefs. **martyrdom** *n.*

marvel *n.* an astonishing or wonderful thing. **marvel** *v.*

marvelous *adj.* wonderful; excellent.

marzipan *n.* a sweet paste made from ground almonds and sugar.

mascot *n.* a person, animal, or thing that is supposed to bring good luck.

masculine *adj.* to do with men, or typical of men.

masks

mash *v.* to crush food until it becomes a soft mass.

mask[1] *n.* a covering for the face that hides or protects it.

mask[2] *v.* to cover up or disguise something.

mason *n.* a person who carves stone.

mass *n.* **1** a large quantity or a lump. **2** (in science) weight. **3 Mass** a Roman Catholic church service.

a
b
c
d
e
f
g
h
i
j
k
l
m
n
o
p
q
r
s
t
u
v
w
x
y
z

massacre *n.* the killing of a very large number of people. **massacre** *v.*

massage *n.* the rubbing of parts of the body to remove pain or to help relaxation. **massage** *v.*

massive *adj.* huge or heavy.

mast *n.* the pole that holds a ship's sails.

master[1] *n.* **1** a person who controls

Michaelangelo painting his masterpiece, the ceiling of the Sistine Chapel

others. **2** a person who is very skilled at something. **3** the male owner of a dog, horse, or other animal.

master[2] *v.* **1** to become skilled at something. **2** to control something.

masterpiece *n.* a work of art done with great skill.

mat *n.* a flat piece of material for wiping shoes on, covering a floor, or putting dishes on (placemat).

mat, **matte** *adj.* not shiny; dull. *a mat finish.*

match[1] *n.* **1** a game or contest between two players or teams. *a tennis match.* **2** a thing that is similar to or the same as another. **3** a small, thin piece of wood used for lighting fires.

match[2] *v.* to be similar to something; to go well with something. *Does this scarf match my gloves?*

mate[1] *v.* (of animals) to come together to breed.

mate[2] *n.* **1** (*informal*) a companion. **2** an animal's breeding partner.

material *n.* **1** any substance from which something is made. *Bricks, wood, and cement are all building materials.* **2** any type of cloth.

maternal *adj.* of or like a mother.

maternity *adj.* for or to do with a woman who is having, or about to have, a baby. *maternity clothes.*

math *short for* mathematics.

mathematics *n.* the study of measurements, numbers, and quantities. **mathematical** *adj.*

matinee *(ma-***tin***-ay)* *n.* an afternoon performance of a play, movie, or show.

matrimony *n.* marriage. **matrimonial** *adj.*

matter[1] *n.* **1** any substance or material that takes up space. **2** a subject.

matter[2] *v.* to be important.

mattress *n.* a soft, thick layer of padding on a bed for sleeping on.

mature *adj.* **1** fully grown or developed. *She is mature for her age.* **2** ripe. *mature cheese.* **maturity** *n.*

mauve

maul *v.* to severely injure somebody by treating him or her roughly or savagely.

mauve *(mawv)* *n.* a purple color. **mauve** *adj.*

maxi- *prefix* very large or very long.

maximum *n.* the greatest possible number or amount or the highest point. *The temperature reached its maximum at noon.* **maximum** *adj.*

may *v.* (might) **1** indicates possibility. *I may see you tomorrow.* **2** indicates asking or giving permission. *May I go now?* **3** indicates expressing a wish. *May you live a long and happy life.*

May *n.* the fifth month of the year.

maybe *adv.* perhaps.

mayonnaise *n.* a thick sauce for sandwiches, made from eggs, oil, and vinegar.

mayor *(rhymes with* player) *n.* the leader of a town or district.

maze *n.* a confusing network of paths that is deliberately difficult to find your way through; labyrinth.

meadow *n.* a field of grass.

meal *n.* the food eaten at one time.

mean[1] *v.* (meaning, meant) **1** to intend to do something. *I didn't mean to upset you.* **2** to express or explain something. *"Begin" means the same as "start."*

mean[2] *adj.* **1** unwilling to share things; not generous. **2** not kind; nasty. **meanness** *n.*

mean[3] *n.* the average of a group of numbers.

meaning *n.* an explanation; what something means.

meanwhile *adv.* at the same time.

measles *n.* an infectious disease causing red spots on the skin.

measure[1] *v.* to find out the size or amount of something. **measurement** *n.*

measure[2] *n.* **1** a unit used for measuring. *A foot is a measure of length.*

2 an instrument or container used for measuring. **3** an action that is intended to achieve something. *measures to prevent poverty.*

meat *n.* the flesh of an animal, used as food.

mechanic *n.* a person who is skilled at repairing or operating machinery.

mechanical *adj.* **1** to do with machinery. **2** worked by machinery. **3** done without thinking. *a mechanical action.* **mechanically** *adv.*

mechanism *n.* a set of working parts found in a machine.

medal *n.* a piece of metal, usually similar to a large coin, given as a reward, e.g. for bravery in war or for sporting achievements. **medalist** *n.*

media *n. pl.* the ways of communicating with the public, especially radio, television, and newspapers.

medical *adj.* to do with doctors or medicine. **medically** *adv.*

medicine *n.* **1** a substance, usually a liquid, that you swallow to treat an illness. **2** the treatment of illnesses. **medicinal** *adj.*

medieval jester

medieval *adj.* to do with the Middle Ages.

mediocre *(mee-dee-oh-ker) adj.* not very good; of average quality. *The hotel that we stayed in during our summer vacation was really mediocre.* **mediocrity** *n.*

meditate *v.* to think deeply in silence in order to relax or for spiritual reasons. **meditation** *n.*

medium[1] *adj.* average or middle in size or quality. *The boxes came in three sizes—small, medium, and large.*

medium[2] *n.* **1** (*pl.* media) a way of communicating something or producing an effect. **2** (*pl.* mediums) a person who claims to be able to communicate with the spirits of dead people.

meek *adj.* quiet, gentle, and obedient.

meet *v.* (meeting, met) **1** to come face to face with someone. **2** to come together; join. **3** to be introduced to someone. *Have you two met?*

meeting *n.* a time when people come together to discuss something.

mega- *prefix* **1** one million. **2** huge; very large.

megabyte *n.* a unit of computer memory (about one million bytes).

melancholy *adj.* sad.

mellow *adj.* **1** (of colors and sounds) soft; not strong or unpleasant. **2** (of food) ripe and pleasant to taste. **3** relaxed and unhurried.

melody *n.* a tune.

melon *n.* a large, juicy fruit containing a lot of seeds.

melt *v.* **1** to become liquid when heated. **2** to make something liquid by heating. *The ice melted in the Sun.*

member *n.* a person who belongs to a club or group. **membership** *n.*

memorable *adj.* easy to remember or worth remembering.

memorial *n.* a monument that is built to remind people of a historical event or a person who has died.

memorize *v.* to learn something so well that you can remember and repeat it later.

memory *n.* **1** the power to remember. *You have a good memory!* **2** a thing that you remember. *happy memories of childhood.* **3** the part of a computer that stores and retrieves information.

memory stick *n.* a portable device for storing computer data that you plug into a special opening in the computer; memory key.

men *plural of* man.

menace *n.* a person or thing that is likely to cause injuries or damage. **menace** *v.*, **menacing** *adj.*

mend *v.* **1** to repair something that is broken; fix. **2** to heal. *Her broken leg is mending well.*

menstruation *n.* the bleeding from a woman's womb that happens every month between puberty and middle age, except during pregnancy. **menstruate** *v.*

mental *adj.* to do with the mind. **mentally** *adv.*

mention *v.* to speak or write briefly about something.

menu *n.* (*pl.* menus) **1** a list of food to choose from in a restaurant. **2** a list of choices shown on a computer screen.

meow *n.* the sound that a cat makes. **meow** *v.*

mercenary[1] *n.* a soldier paid by a foreign country to fight in its army.

mercenary[2] *adj.* concerned more with money than with anything else.

merchant *n.* a person whose job is buying and selling things.

mercury *n.* a poisonous, silver-colored, liquid metal, used in thermometers.

mercy *n.* kindness and forgiveness toward somebody that you have the power to punish. **merciful** *adj.*, **mercifully** *adv.*

merely *adv.* only; simply. *I am merely telling you what I saw.*

merge *v.* to combine or join together.

merit *n.* a good point or quality.

mermaid

mermaid *n.* in stories a sea creature with the upper body of a woman and the tail of a fish.

merry *adj.* (merrier, merriest) happy and cheerful; full of fun. **merrily** *adv.*

merry-go-round *n.* a revolving platform found in an amusement park or at a park.

mesh *n.* a net.

mess[1] *n.* an untidy or unpleasant state. **messy** *adj.*

mess[2] *v.* **mess up** to make something untidy or muddled.

message *n.* a piece of information sent from one person to another.

messenger *n.* a person carrying a message.

met *past of* meet.

metal *n.* any one of a group of substances, such as gold, iron, or copper, that conduct heat and are often shiny. **metallic** *adj.*

metaphor *n.* the use of words in a way that is not literal. *Your room is a pigsty* is a metaphor.

meteor *n.* a small piece of rock moving rapidly through space and burning up as it enters Earth's atmosphere.

meteorite *n.* a meteor that falls to Earth as a piece of rock.

meteorologist *n.* a person who studies or forecasts the weather. **meteorological** *adj.*, **meteorology** *n.*

meter[1] *n.* an instrument for measuring amounts or speeds. *a gas meter.*

meter[2] *n.* a measure of length, equal to 3.28 ft.

method *n.* a way of doing something.

methodical *adj.* careful and well organized.

metric system *n.* the system of weights and measures based on units of ten. Meters, kilograms, and liters are all units in the metric system.

mice *plural of* mouse.

micro- *prefix* very small.

microbe *n.* a tiny living thing that cannot be seen without a microscope.

microchip *n.* a tiny piece of silicon that has an electronic circuit printed on it, used in electronic equipment.

microphone *n.* an instrument that picks up sound waves so that they can be broadcast, recorded, or made louder.

microscope *n.* an instrument with lenses that makes very small objects look much larger so that they can be studied, usually by scientists.

microscopic *adj.* too small to be seen without a microscope.

microwave *n.* an oven that cooks food very quickly.

mid- *prefix* in the middle of. *midway through.*

midday *n.* 12:00; twelve o'clock; in the middle of the day.

middle *n.* the part of something that is halfway between its ends or edges; the center. **middle** *adj.*

middle-aged *adj.* (of a person) between the ages of about 45 and 60.

Middle Ages *n. pl.* the period in history between around A.D. 1100 and 1500.

Middle East *n.* the region east of the Mediterranean Sea, including Iran, Egypt, and the countries in between.

midge *n.* a small, biting insect.

midnight *n.* twelve o'clock in the evening; 12:00 A.M.

midwife *n.* (*pl.* midwives) a person who is trained to help when a baby is born.

might *n.* power; strength.

mighty *adj.* (mightier, mightiest) very powerful. **mightily** *adv.*

migraine *(my-grain)* *n.* a very bad headache that makes you feel sick.

migrate *v.* to move from one place to another to live, as birds do at a particular time of year. **migrant** *n.*, **migration** *n.*, **migratory** *adj.*

mild *adj.* **1** (of a person) gentle; not aggressive. *a mild-mannered man.* **2** not harsh or severe. *She got a mild warning.* **3** (of weather) moderately warm; not cold. **4** (of food or drink) having a flavor that is not strong or spicy. *a mild curry.* **mildness** *n.*

mildew *n.* a tiny, white fungus that grows in warm, damp conditions.

mile *n.* a measure of distance.

militant *adj.* ready to fight.

military *adj.* to do with soldiers and war.

milk[1] *n.* a white liquid produced by female mammals as food for their young.

milk[2] *v.* to take milk from a cow or other animal such as a sheep or goat.

mill *n.* **1** a building with machinery for grinding grain into flour. **2** a factory. *a paper mill.* **3** a device for grinding something. *a pepper mill.*

millennium *n.* (*pl.* millennia) a period of one thousand years.

millet *n.* a grasslike plant with edible seeds.

milli- *prefix* one thousandth part of. *millisecond.*

million *n.* one thousand thousand (1,000,000). **millionth** *adj.*

millionaire *n.* a rich person who has at least a million dollars.

millipede *n.* a small creature with many legs and a long body.

mime *n.* a form of acting in which you use actions and facial expressions instead of words. **mime** *v.*

millipede

mimic *v.* (mimics, mimicking, mimicked) to copy somebody's speech or actions. **mimic** *n.*

minaret *n.* a tall, thin tower on a mosque.

mince *v.* to chop food into extremely small pieces.

minaret

mind[1] *n.* the part of you that thinks, understands, and remembers. **make up your mind** to decide.

mind[2] *v.* **1** to look after something. *Please mind my bag.* **2** to be careful of something. *Mind the step.* **3** to be bothered about something. *I don't mind if you can't come to my party.*

mine[1] *n.* a deep hole in the ground, out of which coal, metals, or diamonds are dug. **mine** *v.*

mine[2] *n.* a type of bomb hidden under the ground or at sea, designed to destroy enemy tanks or ships, for example.

mineral *n.* a solid substance, such as coal, salt, or diamonds, that forms naturally in the rocks in the ground.

mineral water *n.* water from a spring in the ground, containing a variety of mineral salts and gases.

mineral

mingle *v.* to become blended or mixed; to associate with.

mini- *prefix* smaller than average. *A minivan is a small van.*

miniature[1] *adj.* very small.

miniature[2] *n.* a small copy or model of something.

minim *n.* a note in music equal to two crotchets in length.

minimum *n.* the smallest possible number or amount or the lowest point. *Tickets are a minimum of $10 each.* **minimum** *adj.*

a b c d e f g h i j k l **m** n o p q r s t u v w x y z

A
B
C
D
E
F
G
H
I
J
K
L
M
N
O
P
Q
R
S
T
U
V
W
X
Y
Z

minister *n.* **1** a member of the clergy. **2** a government official, below the rank of ambassador.

ministry *n.* **1** the work of a member of the clergy **2** a government department. *The ministry issued a statement.*

minnow *n.* a small freshwater fish.

minor *adj.* small in size or importance. *a minor operation.*

minority *n.* a smaller part or number of people or things.

minstrel *n. (historical)* a traveling musician in medieval times.

mint[1] *n.* **1** a plant with strong-smelling, purplish-green leaves used as a flavoring. **2** a candy flavored with these leaves.

mint[2] *n.* a place where coins are made under government authority.

minus *prep.* used in math to show subtraction. *Six minus two is four* $(6 - 2 = 4)$.

minute[1] (*min*-it) *n.* **1** a unit of time. There are 60 minutes in an hour. **2** a very short time. *See you in a minute.*

minute[2] (*my*-noot) *adj.* very small.

miracle (*mir*-ik-ul) *n.* an amazing event that breaks the laws of nature and which is therefore thought to be caused by a supernatural force. **miraculous** *adj.*

mirage (mi-**rajh**) *n.* something that you think you see but that is not really there, such as a pool of water in the road, caused by hot weather conditions.

mirror *n.* a piece of special glass, coated with metal, that reflects anything placed in front of it.

mis- *prefix* wrong or bad; wrongly or badly. *misbehave* (= to behave badly), *miscalculate* (= to figure something out incorrectly).

miscarriage *n.* the loss of a fetus from its mother's womb before it is able to survive in the outside world.

miscellaneous (mis-uh-**lay**-nee-us) *adj.* made up of several types; mixed.

mischief *n.* troublesome behavior. **mischievous**

mirror

(**miss**-chiv-os) *adj.*

miser (*my*-zer) *n.* a very greedy person; one who hoards money. **miserly** *adj.*

miserable *adj.* very unhappy. **miserably** *adv.*

misery *n.* great unhappiness.

misfortune *n.* **1** bad luck. **2** unlucky event.

mishap (*miss*-hap) *n.* an unlucky accident.

mislay *v.* (mislays, mislaying, mislaid) to lose something because you have put it somewhere where you cannot find it.

mislead *v.* (misleading, misled) to give somebody the wrong idea.

miss *v.* **1** to fail to hit or catch something. *The arrow missed the target.* **2** to fail to see or hear something. *The bank is at the end of the road—you can't miss it.* **3** to feel sad because you are not with somebody. *I'll miss you!*

Miss *n.* a title that can be put before the name of a girl or an unmarried woman.

missile *n.* an object or weapon that is thrown or fired through the air.

missing *adj.* lost or not present.

mission *n.* a task that somebody is sent to carry out.

missionary *n.* a person sent to another country to teach and spread a religion, especially Christianity.

mist *n.* a cloud of water in the air; a thin fog. **misty** *adj.*

mistake[1] *n.* a wrong action or statement.

mistake[2] *v.* (mistaking, mistook, mistaken) **1** to think that one person or thing is another. *I mistook you for my sister.* **2** to be wrong about something. *She mistook what I said.*

mistletoe (*miss*-il-toe) *n.* an evergreen plant with white berries, used as a Christmas decoration.

mistreat *v.* to treat somebody badly.

mistress *n.* the female owner of a dog, horse, or other animal.

mistrust *v.* not to trust somebody.

misunderstand *v.* (misunderstanding, misunderstood) to understand something incorrectly. *He misunderstood the rules.*

mitten *n.* a type of glove without separate parts for the four fingers.

mix *v.* **1** to put things together to form one mass. **2** to come together to form one mass. **mix up** to confuse.

mixture *n.* something made by mixing things together.

moan *v.* **1** to make a long, deep sound

showing pain or sadness. **2** *(informal)* to complain. **moan** *n.*

moat *n.* a deep ditch around a castle, often filled with water.

mob *n.* a noisy or violent crowd.

mobile[1] *(mo-bil or mo-bile) adj.* able to move or be moved easily. *a mobile home.* **mobility** *n.*

mobile[2] *(mo-beel) n.* a hanging decoration with parts that move in currents of air.

mock[1] *v.* to make fun of somebody or something in an unkind way. **mockery** *n.*

mock[2] *adj.* false; not real. *a mock battle.*

model *n.* **1** a copy of something that is much smaller than the real-life object. **2** a person whose job is to wear clothes to show to possible buyers. *a fashion model.* **3** a person who poses for an artist or photographer. **4** a particular type of product. *Our car is the latest model.* **model** *v.*

modem *n.* a device that sends information from one computer to another along telephone lines.

moderate *adj.* not extreme; average. **moderation** *n.*

modern *adj.* new; not old or old-fashioned.

modernize *v.* to make something more modern.

modest *adj.* **1** humble; not boastful. **2** not excessive; moderate. *She is modest about her achievements.* **modesty** *v.*

module *n.* **1** a section that can be connected with other sections to form something such as a spacecraft or a building. *a lunar module.* **2** one part of a course of study. **modular** *adj.*

moist *adj.* slightly wet. **moisten** *v.*, **moisture** *n.*

molasses *n.* thick, dark syrup, produced from sugar when it is being refined.

mold[1] *n.* **1** a hollow container that you can pour a liquid into so that the liquid takes on the shape of the mold when it hardens. **2** a fungus that grows on damp things or stale food. **moldy** *adj.*

mold[2] *v.* to shape something.

mole *n.* **1** a small, furry animal that digs

and lives in tunnels underground. **2** a small, dark mark on the skin. **3** a spy working secretly for a long time.

molecule *n.* the smallest part that a substance can be divided into without changing its basic nature.

mollusk *n.* a creature with a soft body, no backbone, and usually a hard shell. *Snails and oysters are mollusks.*

mollycoddle *v.* to take care of and protect somebody too much.

molt *v.* (of an animal or bird) to lose hair or feathers. *Our cat is molting.*

molten *adj.* melted. *molten rock.*

mom *n.* *(informal)* mother.

moment *n.* a very brief period of time. *Wait a moment.* **momentary** *adj.*, **momentarily** *adv.*

monarch *(mon-ark) n.* a king, queen, emperor, or empress. **monarchy** *n.*

monastery *n.* a place where monks live and work. **monastic** *adj.*

Monday *n.* the second day of the week.

money *n.* the coins and bills that people use to buy things.

mongrel *n.* a dog of mixed breeds; mutt.

monitor[1] *n.* **1** the screen of a computer. **2** an instrument, usually with a screen, used for keeping a check on something. *a heart monitor.* **3** a student with certain responsibilities or duties.

monitor[2] *v.* to check on something over a period of time. *The radar monitors the plane's progress.*

monkeys

monk *n.* a member of a religious group of men who live, work, and pray together in a monastery.

monkey *n.* *(pl.* monkeys) a small, long-tailed mammal that climbs trees and walks on four legs.

mono- *prefix* one; single.

monopoly *n.* the right to be the only person or company to sell or supply a product or service.

monotonous *adj.* going on and on in a dull way. *a monotonous song.* **monotony** *n.*

mobile

A
B
C
D
E
F
G
H
I
J
K
L
M
N
O
P
Q
R
S
T
U
V
W
X
Y
Z

monsoon *n.* **1** a wind that blows in the Indian Ocean. **2** a season of heavy rain caused by the summer monsoon.

monster *n.* **1** a huge, frightening creature. **2** an evil person.

month *n.* one of the twelve parts in a year.

monthly *adj.*, *adv.* happening or coming once a month or every month.

monument *n.* a building or statue, built to remind people of a person or an event.

mood *n.* the way that you are feeling. *I'm in a really good mood today.*

moon

moody *adj.* (moodier, moodiest) **1** often bad-tempered. **2** having moods that change often. **moodily** *adv.*, **moodiness** *n.*

moon *n.* **1** a natural satellite of a planet. **2 Moon** the natural satellite that travels around Earth once every month.

moonlight *n.* light reflected by the Moon.

moor[1] *n.* a large area of open land, often covered with heather.

moor[2] *v.* to tie up a boat.

moose *n.* (*pl.* moose) a large, brown deer with large antlers, usually found in Alaska and Canada.

mop[1] *n.* a sponge pad or a bunch of thick strings or cloths on a long handle, used for cleaning floors.

mop[2] *v.* (mops, mopping, mopped) to wipe a surface with a mop or cloth.

mope *v.* to be sad and depressed.

moped (*moh-ped*) *n.* a type of small motorcycle with pedals.

moral[1] *adj.* **1** to do with right and wrong behavior. **2** good; behaving in the right way. **3 morals** rules or standards of behavior. **morality** *n.*, **morally** *adv.*

moral[2] *n.* the point taught by a story.

morale (*mor-ahl*) *n.* confidence and enthusiasm.

more *adj.* larger in size or amount. **more** *adv.*, *pron.*

morning *n.* the early part of the day; before noon.

Morse code *n.* a way of sending messages using long and short sounds or flashes of light or sound to represent letters.

mortal[1] *adj.* **1** unable to live forever. **2** causing death. *a mortal injury.* **mortality** *n.*, **mortally** *adv.*

mortal[2] *n.* a human being.

mortar *n.* **1** a mixture of cement, lime, sand, and water, used to hold bricks together. **2** a container in which spices are crushed using a pestle.

mortgage (*mor-gij*) *n.* a loan from a bank in order to buy a home.

mortuary *n.* a room where dead bodies are kept before burial or cremation.

mosaic *n.* a picture or design made up of small pieces of colored stone or glass.

mosque (*mosk*) *n.* a building where Muslims worship.

mosquito (*mah-skee-toe*) *n.* (*pl.* mosquitoes or mosquitos) a small insect that sucks blood.

moss *n.* a very small plant that grows in damp places, forming a soft, green covering. **mossy** *adj.*

most *adj.* largest in size or amount. **most** *adv.*, *pron.*

mostly *adv.* mainly; generally.

motel *n.* a hotel for motorists, with parking spaces close to the rooms, usually located directly off a main road.

moth *n.* a winged insect, similar to a butterfly, usually seen at night.

mother *n.* a female parent.

motion *n.* movement.

motive *n.* a reason for doing something.

motor *n.* an engine that uses electricity, gasoline, or other fuel to produce movement.

motorcycle *n.* a two-wheeled vehicle with a gasoline engine.

motorist *n.* a car driver.

mottled *adj.* marked with spots of different colors.

mound *n.* a small hill or pile.

mount[1] *v.* **1** to climb up on to something. *She mounted her horse and rode off across the field.* **2** to rise or increase. *Excitement is mounting.* **3** to put something into a frame or stick it on cardboard to display it.

mount[2] *n.* a mountain, especially in names of mountains. *Mount Everest.*

mountain *n.* a very tall hill.

mountain bike *n.* a bicycle with a strong frame and several gears, for riding over rough ground.

mountaineer *n.* a person who climbs mountains. **mountaineering** *n.*

mourn v. to feel great sadness because someone has died. **mourning** n.

mountaineer

mouse n. (*pl.* mice) **1** a small, furry animal with a long tail. **2** a device that you move with your hand to control the cursor on a computer screen.

mousse *(mooss)* n. a cold food, usually sweet, made with cream and eggs.

mouth n. **1** the opening in your face into which you put food and through which you make sounds. **2** the part of a river where it flows into the sea.

move v. **1** to change place or position. **2** to change houses. **3** to affect the feelings of somebody. *The play moved me to tears.* **moving** adj.

movement n. **1** an act of moving. **2** a section of a piece of classical music. **3** a group of people united for a purpose. *the peace movement.*

movie n. a moving picture shown at a movie theater or on television; film.

movie theater n. a place where people watch movies.

mow *(rhymes with toe)* v. (mowing, mowed, mown) to cut grass. **mower** n.

MP3 player n. a small digital music player that can store and play thousands of songs.

Mr. *(mis-tur)* a title put before a man's name; Mister.

Mrs. *(mis-iz)* a title put before the name of a married woman.

Ms. *(miz)* a title put before the name of a woman that does not show whether or not she is married.

much adj. a great amount of. **much** adv., pron.

muck n. dirt or dung. **mucky** adj.

mud n. soft, wet earth. **muddy** adj.

muddle¹ n. an untidy mess.

muddle² v. to confuse or mix things up.

muesli *(myoos-lee)* n. a mixture of grains, dried fruits, and nuts eaten with milk or yogurt.

mug¹ n. a large cup used without a saucer.

mug² v. (mugs, mugging, mugged) to attack and rob somebody in the street. **mugger** n.

muggy adj. (muggier, muggiest) (of the weather) warm and damp.

mule n. an animal whose parents are a horse and a donkey.

multi- *prefix* many. *multicolored.*

multimedia adj. involving different forms of communication such as sound, pictures, and video.

multiple adj. involving many parts or items.

multiply v. (multiplies, multiplying, multiplied) to increase a number a given number of times. *Two multiplied by three is six (2 x 3 = 6).* **multiplication** n.

mumble v. to speak so that the words are difficult to hear.

mummy n. **2** *(historical)* a dead body preserved by wrapping it in bandages and treating it with special oils and spices, most commonly found in ancient Egypt.

Egyptian mummy

mumps n. an infectious disease that makes your neck and face swell up.

munch v. to chew noisily.

mural n. a picture painted on a wall.

murder v. to kill somebody on purpose. **murder** n., **murderer** n.

murmur n. a low, quiet sound, especially of voices. **murmur** v.

muscle *(mus-ul)* n. one of the parts of your body that tighten and relax to make you move. **muscular** adj.

A
B
C
D
E
F
G
H
I
J
K
L
M
N
O
P
Q
R
S
T
U
V
W
X
Y
Z

museum *(myoo-zee-um)* *n.* a building where interesting objects are kept and shown to the public.

mushroom *n.* a type of fungus. Many mushrooms are edible.

music *n.* an arrangement of sounds, played on an instrument or sung.

musical[1] *adj.* to do with music.

musical[2] *n.* a play or movie with a lot of singing and dancing.

mushrooms

musician *n.* a person who plays music.

musket *n.* a gun that was once used by soldiers.

Muslim *n.* a follower of the Islamic religion, which was founded by the prophet Muhammad. **Muslim** *adj.*

mussel *n.* an edible shellfish that has a black shell.

must *v.* **1** used to express need. *We must go.* **2** used to express a rule, duty, or order. *You must not walk on the grass.* **3** used to express what is definite or likely. *You must be tired.*

mustard *n.* a hot-tasting, yellow paste eaten with food, especially sandwiches.

mutilate *v.* to injure or damage somebody or something badly. **mutilation** *n.*

mutiny *n.* a refusal to obey the people in charge, especially in the armed forces. **mutineer** *n.*, **mutinous** *adj.*

mutter *v.* to speak in a low voice so that people cannot hear you well.

mutton *n.* the meat from a sheep.

muzzle *n.* **1** an animal's nose and mouth. **2** a cover for an animal's mouth, to stop it from biting. **3** the open end of a gun barrel.

mystery *n.* something that is hard to explain or understand. **mysterious** *adj.*

myth *n.* a story from ancient times about gods, heroes, or supernatural beings. **mythical** *adj.*

Nn

nag *v.* (nags, nagging, nagged) to talk to somebody constantly in a complaining or criticizing way.

nail[1] *n.* **1** a thin, pointed piece of metal for hammering into wood. **2** the hard covering at the tip of a finger or toe.

nail[2] *v.* to attach something with nails.

naked *adj.* without clothes on; bare.

name *n.* a word that indicates what a person, place, or thing is called. **name** *v.*

nanny *n.* a person who takes care of children, usually in the children's own home.

nanny goat *n.* a female goat.

nap *v.* (naps, napping, napped) to sleep for a short time. **nap** *n.*

napkin *n.* a piece of cloth or paper for wiping your mouth and hands at meals.

narrate *v.* to tell a story. **narrator** *n.*

narrow *adj.* **1** not far from side to side; not wide. **2** only just managed. *I had a narrow escape.*

nasal *adj.* to do with the nose.

nasty *adj.* (nastier, nastiest) unpleasant; not nice. **nastily** *adv.*, **nastiness** *n.*

nation *n.* a country and the people who live in it. **national** *adj.*, **nationally** *adv.*

nationalist *n.* a person who wants his or her country or province to become independent. **nationalism** *n.*

nationality *n.* membership of a particular nation. *He is of French nationality.*

native *n.* a person born in a particular place. **native** *adj.*

Nativity *n.* the birth of Jesus Christ.

natural[1] *adj.* **1** found in nature; not caused or made by people. **2** ordinary, normal. *It's natural to feel afraid of going to the doctor.* **naturally** *adv.*

natural[2] *n.* a sign (♮) in music indicating that a note should be played neither as a sharp nor a flat.

nature *n.* **1** all the things that make up the world, such as trees, animals, and rivers, but not the things that are made by people. **2** the character of a person or thing. *She has a kind nature.*

naught *n.* nothing; zero; the figure 0.

naughty *adj.* (naughtier, naughtiest) badly behaved. **naughtily** *adv.*, **naughtiness** *n.*

nausea (*naw-zee-uh* or *naw-jah*) *n.* a feeling of sickness. **nauseous** *adj.*

nautical *adj.* to do with ships or sailors.

navel *n.* the small hollow on your stomach, just below your waist; bellybutton.

navigate *v.* to figure out the way that a ship, plane, or car should go, using maps or instruments to guide you. **navigation** *n.*, **navigator** *n.*

navy *n.* a country's warships and sailors. **naval** *adj.*

navy blue *n.* a very dark blue.

near *prep.* at a very short distance from something; close. **near** *adj., adv.*

nearby *adj.,* close by. **near.** *adv.*

nearly *adv.* almost; not quite.

nearsighted *adj.* seeing clearly only the things that are close to you.

neat *adj.* tidy; having everything in the right place. **neatness** *n.*

necessary *adj.* needed; essential. **necessarily** *adv.*

necessity *n.* something that is necessary.

neck *n.* **1** the narrow part between your head and shoulders. **2** a narrow part of something. *the neck of a bottle.*

necklace *n.* a piece of jewelry worn around your neck.

nectar *n.* a sweet liquid in flowers, collected by bees to make honey.

nectarine *n.* a type of peach that has a smooth skin.

need *v.* **1** to have to have something. *I need a snack!* **2** to have to do something. *You need to clean your bike.* **need** *n.*

needle *n.* **1** a small, pointed piece of steel used for sewing. **2** a long, thin stick used for knitting. **3** the moving pointer of a meter or compass. **4** a long, thin, pointed leaf of a pine tree. **5** the sharp metal part that is attached to a syringe for giving injections.

needlework *n.* sewing or embroidery.

negative[1] *adj.* **1** meaning or saying "no"; not positive. **2** less than zero.

negative[2] *n.* a photographic film showing light areas as dark and dark areas as light.

neglect *v.* to fail to take care of something. *The new owners have neglected the garden.* **neglect** *n.*, **neglectful** *adj.*

negotiate *v.* to discuss something to try to reach an agreement. **negotiation** *n.*

neigh *v.* to make the sound that a horse makes. **neigh** *n.*

neighbor *n.* a person who lives close to you.

neighborhood *n.* the area that you live in.

neither *adj., pron.* not one and not the other.

neon light *n.* a light containing the gas neon, which shines when electricity is passed through it.

nephew *n.* the son of your brother or sister.

nerve *n.* **1** one of the fibers that carries feelings and messages between your body and your brain. **2** courage and calmness. *You need a lot of nerve to be a racecar driver.* **3** (*informal*) rudeness. *He has some nerve, asking me for $100!*

nervous *adj.* **1** to do with the nerves. *the nervous system.* **2** anxious or easily frightened. **nervousness** *n.*

nest[1] *n.* a home built by birds and some animals and insects, in which they hatch or give birth to their young and raise them.

nest[2] *v.* to build a nest and live in it.

net *n.* **1** a material made of loosely woven thread, string, or rope, with holes between the threads. **2** a piece of net used for catching fish. **3 the net** (*informal*) the Internet.

nettle *n.* a weed that has stinging hairs on its leaves.

nest

network *n.* **1** an arrangement of lines crossing each other. **2** a system with lots of lines or connections. **3** a number of computers that are connected to each other.

neuter *v.* to remove part of the sex organs of an animal so that it is unable to produce young.

neutral *adj.* **1** not taking sides in a war or argument. **2** (of colors) not strong or bright. *Beige and gray are neutral colors.*

neutron *n.* one of the parts that make up the nucleus of an atom, carrying no electrical charge.

never *adv.* not ever; at no time.

nevertheless *adv.* in spite of that. *The team played well but lost nevertheless.*

A
B
C
D
E
F
G
H
I
J
K
L
M
N
O
P
Q
R
S
T
U
V
W
X
Y
Z

new *adj.* **1** in the original condition; not used or worn. *new sneakers.* **2** made or discovered only recently; not seen or done before. *new ideas.* **3** different; changed. *The children are starting at a new school in September.*

news *n.* recent or up-to-date information about events.

newspaper *n.* printed sheets of paper containing news, which are published daily or weekly.

newt *n.* a small, lizardlike animal that lives on land and in water.

next *adj.* **1** immediately following. **2** nearest. **next** *adv.*

nib *n.* the metal point of a pen.

nibble *v.* to eat in very small bites.

nice *adj.* good or pleasant.

nickname *n.* a name that you call somebody instead of that person's real name.

nicotine *n.* a poisonous substance that is found in tobacco.

niece *n.* the daughter of your brother or sister.

night *n.* the time between sunset and sunrise; when it is dark.

nightingale *n.* a small bird that is known to sing beautifully.

nightmare *n.* **1** a frightening dream. **2** a very frightening or unpleasant situation.

nil *n.* nothing; zero.

nimble *adj.* quick and light in movement. **nimbly** *adv.*

nip *v.* (nips, nipping, nipped) **1** to pinch or bite something. *A crab nipped her toe.*

nipple *n.* the round, pink part in the middle of a breast.

nitrogen *n.* a colorless gas that makes up four fifths of the air that we breathe.

no. *a short way of writing* number.

noble *adj.* **1** aristocratic; of high social rank. *a noble family.* **2** acting in a good, unselfish way. **nobility** *n.*, **nobleman** *n.*, **noblewoman** *n.*, **nobly** *adv.*

nobody *pron.* not a single person.

nocturnal *adj.* happening or active at night. *Owls are nocturnal birds.*

nod *v.* (nods, nodding, nodded) to move your head quickly up and down, as a way of saying yes. **nod** *n.*

noise *n.* a sound, especially a loud, unpleasant one.

noisy *adj.* making a lot of noise; full of noise. **noisily** *adv.*

nomad *n.* a member of a group of people who wander from place to place. **nomadic** *adj.*

non- *prefix* not. *nonsmoker (= a person who does not smoke).*

none *pron.* not one; not any.

nonsense *n.* **1** words that do not mean anything. **2** silly talk or behavior.

noodles *n. pl.* long, thin strips of pasta.

nomads

noon *n.* midday; 12:00 P.M.

no one *pron.* nobody.

noose *n.* a loop of rope that gets tighter when one end is pulled.

nor *conj.* and not. *neither young nor old.*

normal *adj.* usual or ordinary. **normality** *n.*, **normally** *adv.*

north *n.* one of the points of the compass. When you face the rising Sun, north is on your left. **north** *adj.*, *adv.*

northern *adj.* in or of the north part of a place. *northern Europe.*

nose *n.* the part of your face that you use for smelling and breathing.

nostril *n.* one of the two openings at the end of your nose.

nosy *adj.* (nosier, nosiest) too interested in things that do not concern you. *(can also be spelled* nosey*).* **nosily** *adv.*

notch *n.* a small, "V"-shaped cut.

note¹ *n.* **1** words written down to help you remember something. **2** a short letter or message. **3** a piece of paper used as money; bill. **4** a musical sound or the sign that represents it.

note² *v.* **1** to write something down. *I noted his phone number.* **2** to notice something.

notebook *n.* **1** a book for making notes in. **2** a very small portable computer.

nothing *pron.* not anything.

notice¹ *n.* **1** a written message where people can read it. *The notice on the door said "STAY OUT."* **2** attention. *The color attracted my notice.* **3** a statement that you are going to leave a job at a particular time. *John has handed in his notice.*

notice² *v.* to see something. *I noticed that Leila had a new coat.*

notify *v.* (notifies, notifying, notified) to

tell somebody about something formally. **notification** *n.*

notorious *n.* well known for bad reasons. *a notorious criminal.*

noun *n.* a word used as the name of a person, place, or thing. *Tim, card,* and *laughter* are all nouns.

nourish *v.* to give a person, an animal, or a plant the food needed for health and growth. **nourishment** *n.*

novel[1] *n.* a book that tells a story.

novel[2] *adj.* new and unusual.

novelist *n.* a writer of novels.

novelty *n.* **1** newness. **2** something new and unusual.

November *n.* the eleventh month of the year.

novice *(nov-iss)* *n.* a beginner.

nowadays *adv.* at the present time.

nowhere *adv.* not anywhere.

nuclear *adj.* **1** to do with a nucleus. **2** using the power produced by the splitting of the nuclei of atoms. *nuclear weapons.*

nucleus *n.* (*pl.* nuclei) **1** the central part of an atom. See **atom**. **2** the part of a plant or animal cell that controls growth and development.

nude *adj.* naked; without clothes. **nudity** *n.*

nudge *v.* to push something gently with your elbow. **nudge** *n.*

nugget *n.* a lump, especially of gold.

nuisance *n.* a person or thing that annoys you or causes you trouble.

numb *(num)* *adj.* not able to feel anything. *Her fingers were numb from the cold.* **numbness** *n.*

nucleus

cell

nucleus

number *n.* **1** a word or figure showing how many. **2** a quantity. *A large number of people disagreed.*

numeral *n.* a figure, for example 1, 2, or 3, used to express a number.

numerous *adj.* many.

nun *n.* a member of a religious group of women who live, work, and pray together in a convent.

nurse *n.* a person who is trained to take care of people who are sick or injured, especially in a hospital. **nurse** *v.*

nursery *n.* **1** a place where young children are looked after while their parents are at work. **2** a room where a young child sleeps and plays. **3** a place where plants are grown for sale.

nursery rhyme *n.* a short poem or song for young children.

nursery school *n.* a type of school for very young children between the ages of three and five.

nut *n.* **1** a type of fruit with a hard shell and a softer part inside. *a hazelnut.* **2** a piece of metal with a hole in it that screws onto a bolt to fasten it.

nutritious *adj.* (of food) good for you. **nutrition** *n.*

nylon *n.* an artificial fiber used for making clothes, brushes, ropes, and other things.

nuts

hazelnut   Brazil nut

walnut   peanut

a
b
c
d
e
f
g
h
i
j
k
l
m
n
o
p
q
r
s
t
u
v
w
x
y
z
131

Oo

oak *n.* a large tree that produces acorns; the wood produced from this tree.

oar *n.* a pole with a flat end used for moving a rowboat through water.

oasis *(oh-ay-sis) n. (pl.* oases) a place in the desert where water is found and trees grow.

oath *n.* a serious promise.

oats *n. pl.* grains from a certain type of cereal plant, used as food. Oats are often used to make porridge.

obedient *adj.* doing what you are told to do. **obedience** *n.*

obelisk *n.* a tall pillar with four sides and a pointed top.

obese *(oh-beess) adj.* very fat. **obesity** *n.*

obey *v.* to do what you are told to do.

obituary *n.* an announcement of a person's death in a newspaper.

object¹ *(ob-jekt) n.* **1** anything that can be touched or seen, but that is not a living thing. **2** a purpose or aim.

object² *(ob-jekt) v.* to say that you dislike or do not agree with something. *She objects to people smoking in her house.* **objection** *n.*

objective *n.* something that you are trying to achieve.

obligation *n.* a duty.

obligatory *adj.* compulsory.

obelisk

oblige *v.* **1** to make somebody do something. **2** to do something in order to help somebody.

obliged *adj.* **1** having to do something. **2** feeling grateful. *I am much obliged to you for your help.*

oblong *n.* a shape with four sides and four right angles, with two opposite sides longer than the other two.

obnoxious *adj.* extremely unpleasant or offensive.

oboe *n.* a woodwind instrument.

obscene *(ob-seen) adj.* shocking; indecent. **obscenity** *n.*

obscure *adj.* **1** difficult to understand or see. **2** not famous. *an obscure painter.* **obscurity** *n.*

observatory *n.* a building with large telescopes for watching the sky and stars.

observe *v.* **1** to watch something carefully. **2** to notice something. **3** to obey something. *We must observe the rules.* **4** to make a remark. **observation** *n.*

obsessed *adj.* thinking about something the whole time. **obsession** *n.*

obsolete *adj.* no longer used; out of date. *Gas lamps are obsolete now that we have electricity.*

obstacle *n.* something that gets in the way and prevents you from going forward.

obstinate *adj.* refusing to give in or change your mind. **obstinacy** *n.*

obstruct *v.* to block something. **obstruction** *n.*

obtain *v.* to get something. *Tickets can be obtained from the box office.*

obtuse angle *n.* an angle of more than 90 degrees. See **triangle**.

obvious *adj.* easy to see or understand.

occasion *n.* a particular time or event.

occasional *adj.* happening or appearing every once in a while. **occasionally** *adv.*

occupant *n.* a person who lives in or uses a building or room.

occupation *n.* **1** a job. **2** a way of spending time. **3** the capturing of a town or country by an army.

occupy *v.* (occupies, occupying, occupied) **1** to live in or use a room or building. **2** to fill somebody's time. **3** to capture a town or country.

occur *v.* (occurs, occurring, occurred) to happen, to take place. **occur to** to come into somebody's mind. **occurrence** *n.*

ocean *n.* one of the large seas that surround the continents.

o'clock *adv.* used with numbers to show an exact hour on the clock. *nine o'clock.*

octagon *n.* a flat shape with eight straight sides. **octagonal** *adj.*

octave *n.* in music, a range of eight notes, for example from one C to the next C above or below it.

October *n.* the tenth month of the year.

octopus *n.* (*pl.* octopuses or octopi) soft-bodied sea creature with eight tentacles.

octopus

odd *adj.* **1** strange; unusual. **2** (of a number) not able to be divided exactly by two. **3** not one of a pair. *odd socks.*

odds *n. pl.* chances; probability. *The odds are that they will lose again.*

odor *n.* a smell.

offend *v.* **1** to hurt somebody's feelings. **2** to break a law. **offense** *n.*, **offensive** *adj.*

offer *v.* **1** to ask somebody if he or she would like something. *She offered me candy.* **2** to say that you are willing to do something for somebody. *She offered to drive us to the airport.* **offer** *n.*

office *n.* a place where work is normally done, often containing desks, telephones, and computers.

officer *n.* **1** a senior person in the army, air force, or navy. **2** a person in some other job who has the power to tell others what to do. *a police officer.*

official[1] *adj.* done or given out by people in authority. *The president made an official announcement.* **officially** *adv.*

official[2] *n.* a person in a position of authority. *a customs official.*

offside *adj.* in sports in a position in front of the ball where, according to the rules, it may not be played. **offside** *adv.*

offspring *n.* (*pl.* offspring) an animal's young or a human's children.

often *adv.* many times; frequently.

ogre *(oh-ger)* *n.* a cruel giant in stories.

oil *n.* a greasy liquid that does not mix with water, used for many different purposes such as cooking and helping machines run smoothly.

oil rig *n.* a structure that contains equipment used to drill wells from which oil is obtained.

ointment *n.* a creamy substance that you rub on your skin to heal sores and cuts.

old *adj.* **1** having lived for a long time. *an old man.* **2** having a certain age. *I'm 12 years old.* **3** having existed for a long time. *an old building.* **4** not recent; belonging to the past. *In the old days things were different.*

old-fashioned *adj.* out of date; in a style not worn or used nowadays.

olive *n.* a small, black or green, oval fruit with a hard pit. Olives can be eaten or crushed to make olive oil for cooking.

omelet, omelette *n.* a food made from eggs that are beaten and fried.

omen *n.* a sign or warning of something that is going to happen.

ominous *adj.* giving a sign or warning that something bad is going to happen.

omit *v.* (omits, omitting, omitted) to leave something out. *You can omit the last chapter of the book.* **omission** *n.*

omnivore *n.* an animal that feeds on plants and meat. **omnivorous** *adj.*

once[1] *adv.* **1** a single time. *I have met him once.* **2** at a time in the past. *She once lived here.* **at once** immediately.

once[2] *conj.* as soon as; when. *Once you're finished, you can go.*

onion *n.* a strong-tasting bulb, which can be eaten as a vegetable.

online *adj.* connected to the Internet. *an online database.* **online** *adv.*

only[1] *adv.* **1** no more than; just. *There is only one piece of cake left.* **2** alone. *Only you can do it!*

only[2] *adj.* without any others of the same type. *This is the only pair of black shoes that I have.*

only child *n.* a child who has no brothers or sisters.

onion

onward *adv.* forward.

ooze *v.* to flow slowly. *The glue oozed out of the tube.*

opaque *(oh-pake)* *adj.* cloudy; not able to be seen through. *an opaque liquid.*

open[1] *adj.* **1** not closed so that people and things can pass in and out. *an open window.* **2** allowing the inside to be seen. *an open book.* **3** not enclosed or covered. *open country.* **4** honest. *She was open about her feelings.*

a b c d e f g h i j k l m n **o** p q r s t u v w x y z

A B C D E F G H I J K L M N O P Q R S T U V W X Y Z

open² *v.* **1** to make or become open. *She opened the door.* **2** to begin. *The story opens in a ruined castle.* **opening** *n.*

openly *adv.* **1** honestly. **2** in public; not secretly.

open-minded *adj.* open to new ideas.

opera *n.* a play in which the words are sung. **operatic** *adj.*

operate *v.* **1** to work. *Do you know how to operate the machine?* **2** to perform a surgical operation.

operation *n.* **1** the cutting of a patient's body by a surgeon. **2** a carefully planned action. **in operation** working.

operator *n.* **1** a person who works a machine. **2** a person who works on a telephone switchboard, connecting calls.

opinion *n.* your personal thoughts and beliefs about something.

opponent *n.* a person who is against you in a contest or game.

opportunity *n.* a chance to do something.

oppose *v.* to be against something. *I am opposed to the testing of cosmetics on animals.* **opposition** *n.*

opposite¹ *adj.* **1** facing; across from. *They live on the opposite side of the street from us.* **2** entirely different. *We were going in opposite directions.* **opposite** *prep.*

opposite² *n.* something that is as different as possible from another thing. *Good is the opposite of bad.*

opt *v.* to make a choice. **opt out** to choose not to do something.

optical *adj.* to do with the eyes.

optician *n.* a person who tests your eyesight and sells glasses.

optimist *n.* a person who tends to believe that things will turn out well. **optimism** *n.*, **optimistic** *adj.*, **optimistically** *adv.*

option *n.* a choice.

optional *adj.* that may be chosen or not; as you want; not compulsory.

oral *adj.* **1** to do with the mouth. **2** spoken. *an oral test.* **orally** *adv.*

orange *n.* a round, juicy citrus fruit with a thick skin. **2** the color of this fruit. **orange** *adj.*

orangutan *n.* a large ape with reddish-brown fur, found in Indonesia.

orbit *n.* the path followed by an object in space around a planet or around the Sun. **orbit** *v.*, **orbital** *adj.*

orchard *n.* where fruit trees are grown.

orchestra *n.* a group of musicians who play together. **orchestral** *adj.*

orchid *(or-kid)* *n.* a plant with unusually shaped and often colorful flowers.

ordeal *n.* a difficult, painful experience.

order¹ *v.* **1** to tell somebody that he or she must do something. **2** to ask somebody to supply something. *When the waiter came, we ordered two salads.*

order² *n.* **1** a command. **2** a request to somebody to supply something. **3** an arrangement of things. *Put the names in alphabetical order.* **4** tidiness. **5** a peaceful state. *law and order.* **out of order** not working. *The phone is temporarily out of order.*

orchid

orderly *adj.* well behaved; quiet. *Please form an orderly line.*

ordinary *adj.* normal; usual.

ore *n.* rock or dirt from which metal can be taken.

organ *n.* **1** a part inside the body that does a particular job. *The heart is the organ that pumps blood around the body.* **2** a large musical instrument with a keyboard and pipes.

organic *adj.* **1** (of plants) grown without the use of artificial fertilizers or pesticides. **2** to do with living things. **organically** *adv.*

organism *n.* a living animal or plant.

organization *n.* **1** a group of people working together for a purpose. *a charitable organization.* **2** the organizing of something.

organize *v.* to arrange or prepare for something.

oriental *adj.* to do with Eastern countries such as China and Japan. *She bought a book on oriental cooking.*

orienteering *n.* the sport of finding your way across the countryside with the help of a compass and map.

origin *n.* the place or point where something began or first came from. *What is the origin of this word?*

original¹ *adj.* **1** earliest or first. *The original town hall burned down and was rebuilt.* **2** new; not copied. *Matthew had an original idea.* **originality** *n.*, **originally** *adv.*

original² *n.* the earliest version; not a copy. *This painting is an original.*

originate *v.* to begin.

ornament *n.* an object used to decorate a room. *The mantelpiece was full of ornaments.* **ornamental** *adj.*

ornate *adj.* richly decorated.

ornithology *n.* the study of birds. **ornithologist** *n.*

orphan *n.* a child whose parents are dead. **orphaned** *adj.*

orphanage *n.* a home for orphans.

ostrich *n.* a very large bird that runs quickly but cannot fly.

other *adj., pron.* **1** the second of two. *I found one shoe—do you know where the other one is?* **2** the rest. *Susie is here, but where are the others?* **3** different. *The road is closed because of flooding, so we'll have to go some other way.*

otherwise *adv.* **1** if not; or else. *Hurry up, otherwise we'll be late.* **2** in all other ways. *She's a little moody, but otherwise, she's very nice.*

ostrich

otter *n.* an animal that lives close to rivers and eats fish.

ought *(awt)* *v.* **ought to** should.

ounce *n.* a measure of weight equal to 28.35 grams.

outback *n.* the wild, inland parts of the continent of Australia.

outbreak *n.* the sudden appearance of something unpleasant. *There was an outbreak of fighting.*

outburst *n.* a sudden expression of a strong feeling, especially anger.

outcast *n.* a person who has been driven away from friends, family, or others.

outcome *n.* a result.

outdo *v.* (outdoes, outdoing, outdid, outdone) to do better than somebody.

outdoors *adv.* outside; in the open air. **outdoor** *adj.*

outer *adj.* far from the center, farthest away.

outer space *n.* the universe outside of Earth's atmosphere.

outfit *n.* a set of clothes you wear together.

outgrow *v.* (outgrowing, outgrew, outgrown) to get too big or too old for something.

outing *n.* a trip.

outlaw¹ *n. (historical)* a person who has broken the law.

outlaw² *v.* to ban something or make it illegal. *Their government has outlawed smoking in public places.*

outline *n.* a line that shows the shape or edge of something.

outlive *v.* to live longer than somebody.

outlook *n.* **1** your attitude to things. **2** a situation that seems likely to happen in the future.

outnumber *v.* to be greater in number than something else. *Men outnumbered women at the conference.*

output *n.* **1** the amount produced by a factory, business, or person. **2** information produced by a computer.

outrageous *adj.* shocking or unacceptable. *outrageous behavior.*

outright *adv.* at once; completely.

outside¹ *n.* the outer part of something. **outside** *adj.*

outside² *prep., adv.* at or to the outside of something.

outskirts *n. pl.* the edges of a town.

outspoken *adj.* saying exactly what you think, even if it upsets people.

outstanding *adj.* **1** extremely good. **2** still needing to be paid. *outstanding debts.*

outwit *v.* (outwits, outwitting, outwitted) to defeat somebody by being smarter than that person is.

oval *n.* a shape like an egg. **oval** *adj.*

ovary *n.* one of the two organs in females that produce eggs.

oven *n.* an enclosed space in which food is baked or roasted.

over¹ *prep.* **1** above. *The number is over the door.* **2** across. *We went over the bridge.* **3** more than. *She has won over $100.* **4** on top of. *He put the blanket over the sleeping child.* **5** about. *They argued over money.*

over² *adv.* **1** finished. **2** down, from an upright position. *I fell over.* **3** so that a different side is on top. *Turn the meat over to cook the other side.* **4** remaining; not used. *There is a piece of bread left over from lunch.*

over- *prefix* too; too much. *overexcited, overcooked, overweight.*

overall *adj.* including or considering everything. *What will the overall cost of the trip be?*

overalls *n. pl.* a piece of clothing worn over other clothes to keep them clean; dungarees.

overboard *adv.* over the side of a boat.

overcast *adj.* cloudy.

overcome *v.* (overcoming, overcame, overcome) **1** to defeat or conquer something. *He has overcome his fear of the dark.* **2** to affect somebody so strongly that he or she becomes helpless. *Eleanor was overcome by grief when she heard the news.*

overdue *adj.* late.

overflow *v.* to flow over the edges of something. *I left the bath running, and it overflowed.*

overhaul *v.* to examine something carefully and carry out repairs. **overhaul** *n.*

overhead *adj., adv.* above; over your head. *overhead lighting.*

overheads *n. pl.* the general costs involved in running a business such as wages, rent, and electricity.

overhear *v.* (overhearing, overheard) to hear something that you were not supposed to hear.

overlap *v.* (overlaps, overlapping, overlapped) to have one part partially covering another part. *Each roof tile overlaps the one underneath it.*

overleaf *adv.* on the other side of a piece of paper.

overlook *v.* **1** to ignore or not punish something. *He overlooked my mistake.* **2** to miss or fail to notice something. *I think that you have overlooked something.* **3** to look down on something. *Our house overlooks the lake.*

overnight *adj., adv.* **1** for the night. *Do you want to stay at my house overnight?* **2** sudden or suddenly. *She became a star overnight.*

overpass *n.* a bridge that carries one road over another road.

overseas *adj., adv.* across the sea; abroad.

oversight *n.* a mistake, especially due to a failure to notice something.

overtake *v.* (overtaking, overtook, overtaken) to go past another moving vehicle to get in front of it.

overthrow *v.* (overthrowing, overthrew, overthrown) to defeat and force somebody out. *The army attempted to overthrow the government.*

overtime *n.* time spent working after your normal hours.

overture *n.* a piece of music played as an introduction to an opera or ballet.

overwhelm *v.* **1** to defeat somebody completely. **2** to load somebody with too great of an amount. *The students were overwhelmed with data.* **3** to have a strong and sudden effect on somebody. *He was overwhelmed with despair.*

overweight *adj.* too heavy.

owe *v.* **1** to need to pay money back to somebody. **2** to have somebody or something to thank for something. *He owes his life to the man who pulled him out of the river.* **owing to** because of.

owl *n.* a bird of prey that hunts at night.

own[1] *v.* to possess or have something. **own up** to confess; to admit that you have done something wrong. **owner** *n.*

own[2] *adj., pron.* belonging to you. *This is our own house.* **on your own** alone.

ox *n.* (*pl.* oxen) a male animal of the cattle family, often used for pulling heavy loads.

oxygen *n.* a colorless gas found in air.

oyster *n.* a flat shellfish. Some oysters are edible, and others contain pearls.

owl hunting mice

ozone *n.* a poisonous form of oxygen with a strong smell.

ozone layer *n.* a layer of ozone in the upper atmosphere that protects Earth from the Sun's rays.

pace[1] *n.* **1** a step or stride. *She took a pace forward.* **2** a speed of movement. *We were walking at a brisk pace.*

pace[2] *v.* to walk backward and forward.

pacifist *n.* a person who believes that wars are wrong and that you should not fight in them. **pacifism** *n.*

pacify *v.* (pacifies, pacifying, pacified) to make somebody who is angry or upset become calm.

pack[1] *n.* **1** a packet. *a pack of envelopes.* **2** several things tied or wrapped up together or put in a bag, especially for carrying. **3** a group of wild animals. *a pack of wolves.* **4** a set of playing cards.

pack[2] *v.* **1** to put things into a bag or other container ready for a journey. **2** to press or crowd together closely. *They packed into the room to hear his speech.*

package *n.* things wrapped up or packed in a box to be sent.

packet *n.* a small paper or cardboard container in which items are sold.

pact *n.* a formal agreement.

pad[1] *n.* **1** a thick piece of soft material, used for protection or to absorb liquids. **2** sheets of paper that have been connected on one edge.

pad[2] *v.* (pads, padding, padded) **1** to walk along softly. **2** to fill or cover something with a pad. **padding** *n.*

paddle[1] *n.* a short oar for moving a boat through water.

paddle[2] *v.* to walk around in shallow water.

paddle steamboat *n.* a steam-powered boat propelled by two large wheels that are made up of paddles.

paddock *n.* small field for horses.

paddy field *n.* a very wet field where rice is grown.

padlock *n.* a type of lock with a metal loop on one end that you open with a key or a code number. **padlock** *v.*

pagan *(**pay**-gun) n.* a person who does not believe in any of the world's main religions. **pagan** *adj.*

page *n.* **1** a sheet of paper or one side of a sheet of paper in a book or magazine. **2** an individual document on the Internet. **3** a small boy who accompanies a bride at a wedding; pageboy. **4** *(historical)* a boy servant.

pageant *(**paj**-ent) n.* a type of parade or show in which people wear colorful costumes and sometimes act out scenes from history or participate in a competition.

pagoda *n.* an Asian temple in the form of a tower with many stories.

paid *past of* pay.

pail *n.* a bucket.

pain *n.* suffering, in your body or mind. **take pains** to make a great effort. *She took great pains over the preparations for the party.* **painful** *adj.*, **painfully** *adv.*

painstaking *adj.* very careful.

pagoda

paint[1] *n.* a liquid used for coloring surfaces or for making pictures.

paint[2] *v.* to use paint to color a surface or make a picture. **painter** *n.*

painting *n.* a painted picture.

pair *n.* **1** two things that match or go together. *a pair of socks.* **2** a thing made up of two parts. *a pair of scissors.*

pajamas *n. pl.* a loose jacket and pants that you wear in bed.

pal *n.* *(informal)* a friend.

palace *n.* a large, impressive house, especially the home of a king, a queen, or a bishop.

palate *n.* the top of the inside part of your mouth.

paddle steamboat

a
b
c
d
e
f
g
h
i
j
k
l
m
n
o
p
q
r
s
t
u
v
w
x
y
z

137

pale *adj.* **1** light or whitish in color. *pale blue.* **2** not bright or strong. *a pale light.*

palette *n.* a board, often made from wood or plastic, on which an artist mixes paints.

pallid *adj.* (of a person's face) pale.

palm *n.* **1** the inner surface of your hand. **2** a tree that grows in hot countries, with broad, spreading leaves at the top of its tall trunk; palm tree.

pamper *v.* to make somebody comfortable and devote a lot of attention to him or her.

pamphlet (*pam-flit*) *n.* a small, thin book with a paper cover used for distributing information; leaflet.

pan *n.* a metal container with a handle, used for cooking food in.

pancake *n.* a flat cake made with flour, eggs, and milk and fried in a pan.

pancreas *n.* a gland close to your stomach that helps digestion.

panda

panda *n.* (*also* **giant panda**) a large black-and-white animal similar to a bear, found in China.

pane *n.* a sheet of glass in a window.

panel *n.* **1** a flat, rectangular piece of wood that is set into the surface of a door, wall, or ceiling. **2** a group of people chosen, especially to judge a contest or take part in a TV quiz.

panic *n.* a sudden feeling of great fear, especially one that spreads quickly from person to person. **panic** *v.*

panorama *n.* a wide view of an area. **panoramic** *adj.*

pansy *n.* a colorful garden flower.

pant *v.* to take short, quick breaths.

panther *n.* a type of leopard, especially the black leopard.

pantry *n.* a small room for storing food; larder.

pants *n. pl.* a piece of clothing for the lower part of the body, covering each leg; trousers.

paper *n.* **1** thin, flat sheets of material for writing or printing on, usually made from wood pulp. **2** a newspaper.

paperback *n.* a book with a paper cover.

papier mâché (*pay-per mah-shay*) *n.* a mixture of paper pulp and glue that hardens when it dries and that can be shaped into models, trays, or bowls.

papyrus (*pa-pye-rus*) *n.* (*pl.* papyri *or* papyruses) (*historical*) paperlike material made from a water reed and used in ancient Egypt.

parable *n.* a type of story that teaches a moral lesson.

parachute *n.* an umbrella-shaped device used for floating down from an aircraft. **parachute** *v.*, **parachutist** *n.*

parade *n.* **1** a line of people or vehicles moving along. *a carnival parade.* **2** soldiers gathered together for an inspection. **parade** *v.*

paradise *n.* **1** in some religions heaven, where good people go after they die. **2** any beautiful place.

paraffin *n.* oil used for burning in jet engines, heaters, and lamps.

paragliding *n.* the sport of gliding through the air using a type of parachute.

paragraph *n.* a section of a piece of writing. The first word of a paragraph starts on a new line.

parakeet *n.* a type of small parrot.

parallel *adj.* (of lines) going in the same direction and never meeting, always remaining the same distance apart. *Railroad tracks are parallel.*

parallelogram *n.* a four-sided shape with opposite sides that are parallel and equal in length.

paralyze *v.* to make a person or an animal lose all feeling or movement in a part of the body. **paralysis** *n.*

paramedic *n.* a person with some medical training who is not a doctor.

paraplegic (*pa-ra-plee-jik*) *n.* a person who is paralyzed in the legs and lower part of the body.

parasite *n.* an animal or plant that gets its food by living on or inside another living thing. **parasitic** *adj.*

parasol *n.* an umbrella that shades you from the sun.

parcel *n.* a package that has been wrapped up in paper, usually for sending things through the mail.

parch *v.* to make something very hot and dry. *The earth was parched by the Sun.*

parchment *n.* *(historical)* a material for writing on before paper was invented, made from dried skin of sheep or goats.

pardon *v.* to forgive or excuse somebody. **pardon** *n.*

parent *n.* a mother or father. **parental** *adj.*

parish *n.* an area that has its own church.

park¹ *n.* a public place with grass and trees.

park² *v.* to stop and leave a vehicle in a place for a time.

parking lot *n.* an area where people may leave their cars for a while.

parliament *n.* the group of people who make the laws of a country. **parliamentary** *adj.*

parole *n.* the release of a prisoner before the end of that person's prison sentence, on condition that he or she behaves well.

parrot *n.* a brightly colored tropical bird with a hooked beak.

parrot

parsley *n.* an herb used in cooking.

parsnip *n.* a pale yellow root vegetable.

part¹ *n.* **1** a piece of something; not the whole thing. **2** a character in a play. **take part** to be one of a group of people doing something. *I'm taking part in the school play this year.* **3** a line in your hair where it is combed in two directions.

part² *v.* to divide or separate. **part with** to give something away.

partial *adj.* **1** not complete. *a partial success.* **2** having a liking for a person or thing. *I'm partial to chocolate cake.* **partially** *adv.*

participate *v.* to take part. **participation** *n.*

particle *n.* a very small piece.

particular *adj.* **1** one rather than any other. *I want this particular color.* **2** difficult to please; fussy. *He's very particular about what he eats.*

particulars *n. pl.* details.

parting *n.* a leaving; a separation.

partition *n.* a structure that divides a room or space into two parts.

partly *adv.* not completely.

partner *n.* **1** one of a pair of people who do things together or share something. *Alice is my tennis partner.* **2** a husband, wife, or permanent lover. **partnership** *n.*

part of speech *n.* one of the grammatical groups into which words are divided, e.g. noun or verb.

partridge *n.* a game bird.

party *n.* **1** an occasion when a group of people meet to enjoy themselves, especially by eating, drinking, and dancing. **2** a group of people traveling together. **3** a group of people sharing the same political ideas.

pass¹ *v.* **1** to go by. *I pass the store on my way to school.* **2** to give from one person to another. *Please pass me the salt.* **3** to spend time. *A few hours passed quickly.* **4** to succeed in a test. *She passed her class.* **pass away** to die. **pass out** to faint.

pass² *n.* **1** a ticket or card that allows you to do something such as travel free or enter a building. **2** a road or way through or over mountains.

passage *n.* **1** the process of passing through somewhere. **2** a corridor or alley. **3** a short piece taken from a book or a musical work. **4** a journey by ship or plane.

passenger *n.* a person traveling in a vehicle who is not the driver or a member of the crew.

passion *n.* a very strong feeling, especially of love or anger. **passionate** *adj.*

Passover *n.* a Jewish religious festival at which the escape of the Israelites from Egypt is remembered.

passport *n.* a small book that travelers must show to prove who they are when going from one country to another.

password *n.* a secret word that allows you to enter a place or use a computer sytem.

past¹ *n.* **1** the time before now. **2** the form of a verb that shows that an action is in the past. *Won is the past of win.* **past** *adj.*

past² *prep., adv.* **1** up to and beyond. *You go past the school to get to the hospital.* **2** after. *ten minutes past.*

pasta *n.* a food made from flour and eggs, formed into different shapes.

paste¹ *n.* **1** a soft, wet mixture. *toothpaste.* **2** glue for sticking paper. *wallpaper paste.*

paste² *v.* to stick something with paste.

pastel¹ *n.* a soft crayon.

a
b
c
d
e
f
g
h
i
j
k
l
m
n
o
p
q
r
s
t
u
v
w
x
y
z

pastel[2] *adj.* pale. *pastel colors.*

pasteurize *v.* to treat milk by heating it, in order to kill harmful germs.

pastime *n.* something you do in your spare time; a hobby.

past participle *n.* a past form of a verb that you use with *have* or *had. Done* and *seen* are past participles.

pastry *n.* a mixture of flour, fat, and water, used in making pies.

pasture *n.* a field where animals graze.

pasty *(pay-stee) adj.* (of a person) pale.

pat *v.* (pats, patting, patted) to touch something lightly with an open hand. *She patted the dog.* **pat** *n.*

patch[1] *n.* **1** a part of something that is different from the rest, especially in color. *a black cat with a white patch on his back.* **2** a small piece of cloth put over a hole to mend it. **3** a small piece of ground.

patch[2] *v.* to put a patch over a hole to mend it.

patchwork *n.* small pieces of different fabrics sewn together.

patchy *adj.* (patchier, patchiest) having patches; uneven.

pâté *n.* a paste made from vegetables, meat, or fish that can be spread onto bread.

paternal *adj.* of or like a father.

path *n.* **1** a way across land for people to walk or ride on. **2** the line along which something is moving. *The island is in the path of the hurricane.*

pathetic *adj.* **1** making you feel pity. **2** *(informal)* useless; feeble.

patience *n.* the ability to be patient. *Patience is a virtue.*

patient[1] *adj.* able to wait a long time and put up with difficulties without complaining or getting angry.

patient[2] *n.* a person who is being treated by a doctor.

patio *n.* (*pl.* patios) a paved area by a house, where you can sit outside.

patriot *n.* a person who loves and is loyal to his or her country. *Winston Churchill is considered by most English people to have been a true patriot.* **patriotic** *adj.,* **patriotism** *n.*

patrol *v.* (patrols, patrolling, patrolled) to keep watch by moving regularly around an area. *His job is to patrol the factory at night.* **patrol** *n.*

patter *v.* to make quick, tapping sounds. *rain pattering on the roof.*

pattern *n.* **1** a repeated design on something. *My shirt has a pattern of circles and squares on it.* **2** a thing that is copied to make something else. *a dress pattern.* **patterned** *adj.*

pauper *n. (historical)* a very poor person.

pause *v.* to stop for a short time. *She paused before she spoke.* **pause** *n.*

pave *v.* to cover the ground with flat stones or concrete.

paw *n.* the foot of an animal.

pawn[1] *n.* the chess piece that has the lowest value.

pawn[2] *v.* to leave a valuable object at a place called a **pawnbroker's** in exchange for money. When the money is repaid, the object is returned.

pay[1] *v.* (paying, paid) **1** to give money in exchange for something. **2** to be useful or beneficial. *It pays to work hard for exams.* **3** to give. *Please pay attention.* **4** to suffer punishment. *She'll pay for her rudeness.*

pay[2] *n.* wages.

payment *n.* **1** the action of paying for somethng. **2** money paid.

PC *short for* personal computer.

PE *short for* physical education.

pea *n.* a small, round, green vegetable that grows in pods on a climbing plant.

peace *n.* **1** a time when there is no war. **2** a period of quiet and calm. **peaceful** *adj.,* **peacefully** *adv.*

peach *n.* a soft, juicy fruit with a hard pit and furry, orangey-pink skin.

peacock *n.* a large male bird with beautiful blue and green tail feathers.

peahen *n.* the female of the peacock.

peahen and peacock

peak *n.* **1** the top of a mountain. **2** the highest point of something. **3** the front part of a cap that is over your eyes.

peal *v.* (of bells) to ring loudly. **peal** *n.*

peanut *n.* a seed that grows in a pod under the ground.

pear *n.* a green fruit with white flesh that is round at the base and narrow at the top.

pearl *n.* a silver-white gem found in some oysters.

peasant *(historical)* *n.* a person who lived and worked on the land, especially in a poor area.

peat *n.* a soft, brown substance made of decayed plants, dug from the ground and used as a fuel and to improve the soil in gardening.

pebble *n.* a small, round stone.

peck *v.* (of birds) to use the beak to hit or pick up something.

peculiar *adj.* **1** strange; odd. **2** belonging to one particular place, person, or thing. *This is a custom that is peculiar to France.*

pedal¹ *n.* a part that you press with your foot to make something move or work.

pedal² *v.* (pedals, pedaling, pedaled) to use pedals to move or work something.

pedestrian *n.* a person walking in the street.

pedigree *adj.* (of an animal) from a line of ancestors of the same breed.

peel¹ *n.* the skin of a fruit or vegetable.

peel² *v.* **1** to remove the skin or covering from something. **2** to come off in thin pieces. *The paint on the walls had peeled.*

peep *v.* to look at something quickly or through a small opening. **peep** *n.*

peer¹ *v.* to look closely or hard, especially if you cannot see something well.

peer² *n.* a person of the same age and background as you.

peerage *n.* the nobility.

peg *n.* **1** a small piece of wood or other material, used for hanging things on. *Hang your coat on that peg.* **2** a clip for attaching clothes to a line. **3** a stake used for holding down a tent. **peg** *v.*

pelican *n.* a large water bird with a pouch under its beak for storing fish.

pellet *n.* a small, round piece of something.

pelt *v.* **1** to throw things at something. **2** to rain very hard.

pen *n.* **1** a tool for writing with ink. **2** an enclosed area for animals.

penalty *n.* **1** a punishment. **2** in games an advantage given to the other side when a player breaks a rule.

pencil *n.* a tool for writing and drawing containing a thin stick of a soft, black substance called graphite.

pendant *n.* an ornament that hangs from a necklace.

pendulum *n.* a swinging weight on a rod, used in some clocks.

penetrate *v.* to go into or through something.

penguin *n.* a large sea bird that cannot fly, found in the Antarctic.

penicillin *n.* a type of drug used for treating some infections.

peninsula *n.* a piece of land that sticks out into the sea.

penis *n.* the part of the body of a male human or animal used in sexual intercourse and for getting rid of urine.

penguin and chick

penknife *n.* (*pl.* penknives) a type of small, folding knife.

penny *n.* (*pl.* pennies) a small coin in the U.S. There are 100 pennies in one dollar.

pen pal *n.* a person who you befriend by writing and receiving letters, although you may never have met.

pension *n.* money paid regularly to somebody who has retired from work.

pentagon *n.* a five-sided shape. **pentagonal** *adj.*

pentathlon *n.* a sporting competition made up of five athletic events.

people *n. pl.* men, women, and children.

pepper *n.* **1** a hot-tasting powder used to flavor food. **2** a red, green, or yellow vegetable containing seeds; capsicum.

peppermint *n.* **1** a plant with strong-smelling leaves used as a flavoring. **2** a candy flavored with these leaves.

per *prep.* each; for each. *The dinner cost $25 per person.* **percent** out of every 100, often written as % with figures. *48 percent (48%) of children in our school arrive by car.*

percentage *n.* a number or amount in each 100.

perch¹ *n.* a resting place for a bird. **perch** *v.*

perch² *n.* a freshwater fish.

percussion instrument *n.* a musical instrument that is struck or shaken. Drums, tambourines, and triangles are percussion instruments.

perennial *adj.* lasting for many years. *perennial plants.*

a b c d e f g h i j k l m n o p q r s t u v w x y z

A
B
C
D
E
F
G
H
I
J
K
L
M
N
O
P
Q
R
S
T
U
V
W
X
Y
Z

perfect¹ *(pur-fikt) adj.* so good that it cannot be any better. **perfection** *n.*

perfect² *(pur-fekt) v.* to make something perfect. *He perfected his technique.*

perforate *v.* to make holes in something. **perforation** *n.*

perform *v.* **1** to carry out. *A surgeon performs operations.* **2** to give a show in front of an audience. *We performed our play in front of the entire school.* **performance** *n.,* **performer** *n.*

perfume *n.* **1** a pleasant smell. **2** a pleasant-smelling liquid that you put on your skin. **perfumed** *adj.*

perhaps *adv.* possibly; maybe.

peril *n.* a great danger. **perilous** *adj.*

perimeter *(pe-rim-uh-ter) n.* the outside edge of an area.

period *n.* **1** the punctuation mark (.) used at the end of a sentence. **2** a length of time. **2** the natural bleeding from a woman's womb that happens every month; menstruation.

periodical *n.* a magazine that is published regularly, often every month.

periscope *n.* a tube with mirrors that allows you to look over the top of something. Often used in submarines.

perish *v.* to die or be destroyed. *Many people perished in the earthquake.*

permanent *adj.* lasting a long time or forever. *permanent address.* **permanence** *n.*

permissible *adj.* allowed.

permission *n.* the allowing of somebody to do something. *The teacher gave us permission to go home early.*

permit¹ *(pur-mit) v.* (permits, permitting, permitted) to allow.

permit² *(pur-mit) n.* a document allowing somebody to do something.

perpendicular *adj.* standing exactly upright or at 90 degrees to another line.

perpetual *adj.* lasting forever. **perpetually** *adv.*

persecute *v.* to treat somebody cruelly, especially because of his or her religious or political beliefs. **persecution** *n.,* **persecutor** *n.*

persevere *v.* to keep trying to do something and not give up. **perseverance** *n.*

persist *v.* to keep doing something in spite of difficulty or opposition. **persistence** *n.,* **persistent** *adj.*

person *n.* any man, woman, or child.

personal *adj.* **1** of your own. *personal property.* **2** to do with a person's private business.

These letters are personal—please don't read them. **3** appearing yourself. *The mayor made an appearance on TV.*

personal computer *n.* a small computer used in homes and offices.

personality *n.* **1** the type of person you are. **2** a well-known person.

personal stereo *n.* a small, portable MP3, CD, or cassette player with headphones.

perspective *n.* **1** a way of drawing on a flat surface that makes objects that are farther away appear smaller, like they do in real life. **2** a point of view.

perspire *v.* to sweat. **perspiration** *n.*

persuade *v.* to try to make somebody do something by giving that person good reasons. **persuasion** *n.*

pessimist *n.* a person who tends to believe that things will turn out badly. **pessimism** *n.,* **pessimistic** *adj.*

pest *n.* **1** a creature that is harmful or that destroys things. **2** a person who keeps annoying you.

pester *v.* to keep annoying somebody, especially by asking the same thing many times.

pesticide *n.* a chemical used to kill pests, especially insects.

pet *n.* **1** a tame animal that you keep in your home. **2** a person who is treated as a favorite. *He is definitely the teacher's pet.*

petal *n.* one of the colored parts of a flower. See **flower.**

petition *n.* a written request signed by many people and sent to somebody in authority in order to try to get that person to do something.

petrify *v.* (petrifies, petrifying, petrified) **1** to make somebody very frightened. **2** to turn to stone.

petticoat *n.* *(old-fashioned)* a piece of clothing worn under a skirt or dress.

petty *adj.* not very important; trivial.

pew *n.* a bench in a church.

pewter *n.* a mixture of lead and tin.

PG *(short for* parental guidance*)* a certificate that is given to a movie, indicating that some scenes may not be suitable for children to watch.

pH *n.* a measure of how acidic or alkaline a substance is. A pH value of below 7 means that the substance is acidic, and above 7 means that it is alkaline.

phantom *n.* a ghost.

pharaoh *(fair-oh) n.* one of the kings

of ancient Egypt.

pharmacy *n.* a store where medicines are sold; drugstore. **pharmacist** *n.*

phase *n.* a stage in the development of something. *This is phase two of the building work.*

pheasant *n.* a long-tailed game bird.

phenomenon (*fee-**nom**-in-on*) *n.* (*pl.* phenomena) something very unusual or remarkable. **phenomenal** *adj.*

philosophical (*fil-o-**sof**-ik-ul*) *adj.* **1** to do with philosophy. **2** calm; accepting problems without getting easily upset.

pharaoh

philosophy (*fi-**loss**-o-fee*) *n.* **1** the study of the meaning of the universe and human life. **2** a person's beliefs and way of thinking. **philosopher** *n.*

phobia *n.* a strong fear of something.

phone *short for* telephone.

phony *adj.* (*informal*) fake; false. (*can also be spelled* phoney).

photo (*pl.* photos) *short for* photograph.

photocopier *n.* a machine that copies documents instantly.

photograph *n.* a picture taken with a camera and then printed on paper or stored on a computer or CD. **photograph** *v.*

photography *n.* the taking of pictures with a camera. **photographer** *n.*, **photographic** *adj.*

photosynthesis *n.* a process by which green plants absorb energy from sunlight to turn carbon dioxide and water into food.

phrase *n.* a group of words that has a meaning but does not make a complete sentence.

physical[1] *adj.* **1** to do with the body. *physical exercise.* **2** to do with things that can be seen and felt. *the physical world.* **physically** *adv.*

physical[2] *n.* an examination done by a doctor.

physics *n.* the science that includes the study of light, heat, sound, and

energy. **physicist** *n.*

pianist *n.* a person who plays the piano.

piano *n.* (*pl.* pianos) a large musical instrument with a keyboard.

piccolo *n.* (*pl.* piccolos) a small flute.

pick *v.* **1** to choose; to select. **2** to gather. *We picked some flowers.* **3** to remove small pieces of something from a surface, especially with your fingers. *Don't pick that scab!* **pick on** to be nasty to a particular person. *Stop picking on me!* **pick up 1** to lift. **2** to learn gradually. *She picked up a little Spanish on vacation.* **3** to collect. *I'll pick you up from your house at six.*

picket *n.* a person or group of people who stand outside a place of work to protest and to try to stop other workers from entering the building. **picket** *v.*

pickle *v.* to preserve food in vinegar or salt water. **pickle** *n.*

pickpocket *n.* a thief who steals from people's pockets or bags.

picnic[1] *n.* a meal eaten outside, away from home.

picnic[2] *v.* (picnics, picnicking, picnicked) to have a picnic.

picture[1] *n.* a drawing, painting, photograph, or other image.

picture[2] *v.* to imagine something.

picturesque (*pik-chur-esk*) *adj.* pretty.

pie *n.* a pastry case containing baked fruit.

piece *n.* **1** a part of something. *a piece of cake.* **2** a single object. *a piece of paper.* **3** an artistic work. *a piece of music.*

pier *n.* a long platform stretching from the shore into the sea.

pierce *v.* to make a hole in something.

piercing *adj.* loud and sharp. *a piercing cry.*

pig *n.* a farm animal kept for its meat.

pigeon *n.* a gray bird that is found in towns and cities.

piglet *n.* a young pig.

pigment *n.* **1** a substance that adds color to dyes or paints. **2** a natural coloring in your skin or hair.

pigsty *n.* a building where pigs are kept.

pigtail *n.* a braid of hair.

pike *n.* a freshwater fish.

pile *n.* a number of things lying on top of each other. *a pile of dirty laundry.* **pile** *v.*

pilgrim *n.* **1** a person who travels to visit a holy place. **2** a traveler, especially Pilgrim forefathers and foremothers who founded the first U.S. colonies, including Plymouth.

A
B
C
D
E
F
G
H
I
J
K
L
M
N
O
P
Q
R
S
T
U
V
W
X
Y
Z

pilgrimage *n.* a pilgrim's journey.

pill *n.* a small tablet of medicine.

pillar *n.* an upright post, often made of stone, for supporting a building.

pillow *n.* a large cushion on a bed, where you rest your head.

pillowcase *n.* a cover for a pillow.

pilot *n.* **1** a person who flies an aircraft. **2** a person who directs a ship in and out of a harbor. **pilot** *v.*

pimple *n.* a small spot on the skin; a zit.

pin *n.* a short, pointed piece of metal with a rounded head, used for holding things together. **pin** *v.*

pinafore *n.* **1** a sleeveless dress, similar to an apron. **2** an apron.

pincer *n.* the claw of a crab or lobster.

pinch² *v.* **1** to squeeze somebody's skin between your thumb and finger.

pinch² *n.* **1** an act of pinching something. **2** a small amount. *a pinch of salt.*

pine¹ *n.* **1** a tall evergreen tree that has cones and needlelike leaves **2** the wood from this tree.

pine² *v.* to feel very sad, especially because you miss somebody or something. *She pined for them.*

pineapple *n.* a large, juicy, tropical fruit with a prickly skin.

Ping-Pong *n.* table tennis.

pink *n.* a color between red and white. **pink** *adj.*

pint *n.* a measure for liquids, equal to 20 fluid ounces.

pioneer *n.* **1** a person who is among the first to explore a place and start living there. **2** a person who is among the first to do something. *pioneers of television.* **pioneer** *v.*

pious *adj.* following a religion very seriously. **piety** *n.*

pip *n.* the seed of a fruit.

pipe *n.* **1** a tube used for carrying water, gas, or other fluids. **2** a tube, usually wooden, used for smoking tobacco. **3** a musical instrument made of several tubes connected together, which you play by blowing.

pirate¹ *n.* **1** a person who robs ships at sea. **2** a person who illegally copies and sells computer programs, movies, or music. **piracy** *n.*

pirate² *v.* to copy computer programs, movies, or music illegally. **piracy** *n.*

pirouette *n.* in ballet a movement involving a rapid spin on one foot.

pistol *n.* a small gun that is held in one hand.

pit *n.* **1** a hole in the ground. **2** a coal mine.

pitch¹ *n.* **1** the highness or lowness of a musical note. **3** a sticky, black substance, like tar.

pirates

pitch² *v.* **1** to put up a tent. **2** to throw something. *He pitched the ball first.*

pitcher *n.* **1** a large jug. **2** the player who throws the ball in baseball.

pitchfork *n.* a long-handled fork, usually used for lifting hay.

pitfall *n.* a hidden difficulty or danger.

pity *n.* **1** a feeling of sadness caused by somebody else's troubles or suffering. **2** a cause of sadness or regret. *What a pity that Sarah isn't here.* **pity** *v.*

pixie *n.* in fairy tales a small, elflike or fairylike being. (*can also be spelled* pixy.)

pizza *n.* a flat piece of dough covered with tomatoes, cheese, and other foods, which is baked in a very hot oven.

placard *n.* a notice, especially one that is carried by somebody.

place¹ *n.* a particular area or position.

place² *v.* to put something somewhere.

placid (*plass*-id) *adj.* calm; not easily upset.

plague (*playg*) *n.* **1** a serious disease that spreads quickly to a lot of people. **2** something bad that comes in large quantities. *a plague of locusts.* **plague** *v.*

plaice *n.* an edible, flat sea fish.

plain¹ *adj.* **1** simple; ordinary; not decorated or fancy. *plain white walls.* **2** easy to understand, see, or hear. *It is plain to see that he is unhappy.*

plain² *n.* a large, flat area of country.

plainclothes *adj.* ordinary clothes; not a uniform. *They were plainclothes police officers.*

plan¹ *n.* **1** an idea of what you are going to do and how to do it. **2** a drawing of something to show what it will look like when it is built. **3** a map of a town or building as seen from above.

plan[2] *v.* (plans, planning, planned) to decide what you are going to do and how to do it.

plane *n.* 1 *short for* airplane. 2 a tool for making wood smooth. 3 a flat surface.

planet *n.* an object in space that moves around the Sun or around another star. *Mars, Earth, and Venus are planets.*

plank *n.* a long, flat piece of wood.

plankton *n.* tiny plants and animals living in water.

plant[1] *n.* 1 any living thing that grows in the ground. Plants usually have a stem, roots, and leaves. 2 a factory's buildings and machinery.

plant[2] *v.* 1 to put a plant or seed in the ground so that it will grow. 2 to hide something somewhere. *The terrorist planted a bomb on the plane.*

plaque *n.* 1 a flat piece of metal, china, or wood with words or pictures on it, attached to a wall; a sign. 2 a substance that forms on your teeth and can cause decay.

plaster[1] *n.* 1 a substance made of lime, water, and sand used for making a smooth surface on walls and ceilings. 2 a white powder mixed with water, which becomes hard when it dries, used for making models or holding broken bones in place.

plaster[2] *v.* 1 to cover a surface with plaster. 2 to cover something thickly with a substance.

plastic *n.* a strong, light, chemically produced substance, used to make many different things.

plastic surgery *n.* an operation to repair or improve the appearance of a person's skin or part of his or her body.

plate *n.* 1 a flat, round dish used for serving food. 2 a flat piece of metal or glass.

plateau (*pla-toe*) *n.* (*pl.* plateaus *or* plateaux) a flat area of land higher than the land around it.

platform *n.* 1 a raised sidewalk area beside the tracks at a railroad station. 2 a raised part of a floor where speakers or performers stand so that they can be seen by the audience.

platinum *n.* a valuable, silvery-white metal.

platypus *n.* an Australian mammal with fur, a beak, and webbed feet. Platypuses lay eggs, but they feed milk to their young.

play[1] *v.* 1 to do things for fun, not as work. 2 to take part in a game. 3 to act a part in a play. 4 to make music on an instrument. **player** *n.*

play[2] *n.* (*pl.* plays) a story that is acted out.

playful *adj.* 1 full of fun. 2 done for fun; not serious. *a playful argument.*

playground *n.* an area where children can play, sometimes with special equipment such as swings or a slide.

playing card *n.* one of a pack of cards used for playing card games.

playwright *n.* a person who writes plays.

plea *n.* 1 an urgent request. *a plea for cash.* 2 an accused person's answer to a charge in a law court.

plead *v.* 1 to beg somebody to do something. 2 to answer a charge in a law court. *He pleaded guilty to armed robbery.*

platypus

pleasant *adj.* enjoyable or friendly.

please[1] *v.* to give pleasure to somebody.

please[2] a word that you use to ask something politely.

pleasure *n.* a strong feeling of enjoyment or happiness.

pleat *n.* a fold in a piece of clothing that has been pressed or sewn into place. **pleated** *adj.*

plectrum *n.* a small piece of plastic or metal for plucking the strings of a guitar or similar instrument; a pick.

pledge *n.* a promise. **pledge** *v.*

plenty *n.* a large number or amount. **plentiful** *adj.*

pliable *adj.* easily bent.

plight *n.* a serious and difficult situation. *The TV show was about the plight of homeless people.*

plod *v.* (plods, plodding, plodded) to walk slowly and with heavy steps.

plot[1] *n.* 1 a secret plan to do something, usually bad. *a plot to assassinate the president.* 2 a small piece of ground. 3 the story of a book, movie, or play.

plot[2] *v.* (plots, plotting, plotted) 1 to plan something secretly. 2 to put information onto a chart or graph.

a b c d e f g h i j k l m n o p q r s t u v w x y z

A
B
C
D
E
F
G
H
I
J
K
L
M
N
O

P

Q
R
S
T
U
V
W
X
Y
Z

plow (*rhymes with* cow) *n.* a farm tool pulled by a tractor or animal, used to break up the ground to prepare it for planting. **plow** *v.*

pluck *v.* **1** to pull feathers off a bird. **2** to pull something sharply. *She plucked a gray hair from her head.* **3** to pick flowers or fruits. **4** to pull on the strings of a musical instrument.

plug¹ *n.* **1** an object that fits tightly into a hole to block it. *a sink plug.* **2** a device that connects electrical equipment to an electricity supply.

plug² *v.* (plugs, plugging, plugged) **1** to block a hole with a plug. **2** (*informal*) to advertise or promote something. **plug in** to put an electrical plug into an outlet.

plow

plum *n.* a soft red, purple, or yellow fruit with a pit inside.

plumage *n.* a bird's feathers.

plumber (*plumm-er*) *n.* a person who installs and repairs water pipes and tanks. *We've got a leak; it looks like we'll need to call a plumber.*

plumbing (*plumm-ing*) *n.* the system of water pipes and tanks in a building.

plump *adj.* slightly fat; rounded.

plunder *v.* to steal things, usually during a war. **plunder** *n.*

plunge *v.* **1** to jump or fall into water. *The man plunged into the river.* **2** to push something suddenly and firmly into something else. *Plunge the vegetables into boiling water.*

plural *n.* the form of a word that shows more than one. *Hands is the plural of hand, and mice is the plural of mouse.* **plural** *adj.*

plus *prep.* and; added to. *Four plus six equals ten (4 + 6 = 10).*

P.M. *short for* post meridiem (Latin for "after noon"). *1 P.M. is one o'clock in the afternoon.*

pneumatic (*new-mat-ik*) *adj.* **1** worked by air under pressure. *a pneumatic drill.* **2** filled with air.

pneumonia (*new-moan-ya*) *n.* a serious disease of the lungs.

poach *v.* **1** to cook something gently in liquid. **2** to catch fish or animals by hunting them illegally. **poacher** *n.*

pocket *n.* a small pouch sewn into clothes and bags, used for carrying things.

pod *n.* a long case that holds the seeds of many plants, such as peas.

podcast *n.* a digital recording of a radio show that you can download from the Internet and listen to later.

podiatrist (*po-di-a-trist*) *n.* a person who treats people's feet.

poem *n.* a piece of writing with a special rhythm. Poems are often written in short lines, sometimes with the last word of one line rhyming with the last word of a previous line.

poet *n.* a person who writes poems.

poetry *n.* poems.

point¹ *n.* **1** the sharp end of something such as a needle. **2** the main purpose of or reason for something. *What's the point of this game?* **3** a mark in a competition. **4** a dot. **5** a particular place or stage. *a meeting point.*

point² *v.* to stick out a finger or other thing in the direction of something. *He pointed a gun at her.*

poison *n.* a substance that causes illness or death if it is swallowed or breathed in. **poison** *v.*, **poisonous** *adj.*

poke *v.* to push something sharply with a stick or finger.

poker *n.* **1** a rod for stirring up a fire. **2** a card game in which players bet on the cards they are dealt.

polar *adj.* belonging to either the North or South poles.

polar bear *n.* a large, white bear that lives close to the North Pole.

pole *n.* **1** a tall, thin, rounded piece of wood, metal, or plastic. **2** one of the two points on Earth's surface (the North Pole and the South Pole) that are farthest from the equator. **3** one of the opposite ends of a magnet.

pole vault *n.* a sport in which you jump over a high bar using a flexible pole.

police *n.* the people whose job is to make sure that the law is obeyed.

policy *n.* a plan of action.

polish[1] *v.* to make something smooth and shiny by rubbing it.

polish[2] *n.* a substance used for polishing.

polite *adj.* having good manners. **politeness** *n.*

politician *n.* a person who is involved in politics.

politics *n. pl.* the art or study of government. **political** *adj.*, **politically** *adv.*

poll (*rhymes with* coal) *n.* a survey of people's opinions.

pollen *n.* the powder inside flowers that fertilizes other flowers.

pollinate *v.* to fertilize with pollen.

pollution *n.* harm to the environment caused by dirty or dangerous substances. **pollute** *v.*

polo *n.* a game similar to hockey, played by two teams on horseback.

poltergeist (*pole*-ter-gyste) *n.* a type of ghost believed to move furniture or throw objects around.

poly- *prefix* many. *A polygon is a flat shape with many sides.*

polyester *n.* an artificial material used to make clothing.

polyethylene *n.* a type of light plastic used to make bags.

pompous *adj.* behaving in a grand way because you think that you are very important.

pond *n.* a small area of water, smaller than a lake.

pony *n.* a small horse.

poodle *n.* a dog with thick, curly hair.

pool *n.* **1** a small area of water. **2** a swimming pool. **3** a game in which you use a stick, called a cue, to hit balls into pockets at the edge of a table.

poor *adj.* **1** having very little money. **2** not very good; bad. *poor test results.* **3** a word you use when you feel sorry for somebody. *Poor Samuel is sick again.*

pop[1] *n.* **1** a small bang. **2** (*informal*) a fizzy soft drink; soda. **3** modern, popular music.

pop[2] *v.* (pops, popping, popped) **1** to make a popping sound. **2** to move or put something somewhere quickly. *She popped her head around the door to say something.*

popcorn *n.* corn kernels that burst open when they are heated and eaten as a snack.

Pope *n.* the absolute head of the Roman Catholic Church.

poppadom *n.* in Indian cookery a round,

thin piece of bread made from lentils, which is fried in oil until it becomes crispy.

poppy *n.* a type of flower with large, usually red, petals.

popular *adj.* liked by a lot of people. **popularity** *n.*

populated *v.* with people living there.

population *n.* all the people living in a particular place. *The population of Paris is large.*

porcelain (*por*-sa-lin) *n.* fine china.

porch *n.* a covered entrance to a building.

porcupine *n.* a ratlike animal covered with pointed spikes.

pore[1] *n.* one of the tiny holes in your skin, through which you sweat.

pore[2] *v.* **pore over** to study or read carefully. *She loves to pore over fashion magazines.*

pork *n.* the meat from a pig.

porous *adj.* having lots of tiny holes that allow liquid or gas through.

porpoise *n.* (*pl.* porpoise) a sea animal of the dolphin and whale family.

porridge *n.* a breakfast food made from oats that have been boiled in milk or water.

port *n.* **1** a harbor, or a town with a harbor. **2** the left side of a ship or aircraft. **3** a strong, sweet, red wine.

portable *adj.* easy to carry around. *a portable television.*

portcullis *n.* (*historical*) a heavy framework of bars that is lowered to protect the entrance to a castle.

porter *n.* a person whose job is to carry luggage in a hotel or railroad station,

porcupine

to push hospital trolleys, or to act as a porter in an apartment building.

portfolio *n.* **1** a large, thin case for carrying documents, maps, or drawings. **2** a collection of documents or drawings that somebody has done.

porthole *n.* a round window in a ship.

portion *n.* a share, part, or helping of something.

portrait *n.* a picture of a person.

pose *v.* **1** to arrange yourself in a particular position. *We all posed for the photo.* **2** to pretend to be something that you are not. *She was posing as a nurse.* **3** to present a question or problem. *She posed a question to the ambassador.* **pose** *n.*

position[1] *n.* **1** the place where somebody or something is. **2** a way of standing or sitting. **3** a job.

position[2] *v.* to put something into position.

positive *adj.* **1** completely certain. *Are you positive that you saw her?* **2** meaning or saying "yes." *We got a positive answer.* **3** more than zero. *a positive number.*

possess *v.* to have or own something.

possession *n.* a thing that you own.

possessive *adj.* wanting to keep something all to yourself.

possible *adj.* able to happen or be done. **possibility** *n.*, **possibly** *adv.*

post *n.* **1** a tall piece of wood or metal standing in the ground. **2** a job; a position.

post- *prefix* after. *postwar.*

post card *n.* a card that you can write a message on and send in the mail without an envelope.

poster *n.* a large notice or picture that can be put up on a wall.

postmark *n.* a mark stamped on a letter to show where and when it was mailed.

postpone *v.* to put something off until later. **postponement** *n.*

pot *n.* a round container. *a plant pot.*

potato *n.* (*pl.* potatoes) a round root vegetable that grows underground.

potent *adj.* powerful; strong.

potential *n.* the ability to be successful in the future. **potential** *adj.*

potter *n.* a person who make pots and other objects out of clay.

pottery *n.* **1** pots and other things made out of baked clay. **2** a place where these things are made.

pouch *n.* **1** a small bag. **2** a pocket of skin on the front of kangaroos and other marsupials, where they carry their young.

poultry *n.* birds farmed for eggs and meat.

pounce *v.* to jump on something suddenly. *The cat pounced on the mouse.*

pound[1] *n.* **1** a measure of weight, equal to 16 ounces. **2** the main unit of money in the U.K.

pound[2] *v.* to hit something many times. *Ralph pounded on the door.*

pour *v.* **1** to let liquid flow from a jug or other container. **2** (of rain) to fall heavily.

poverty *n.* the state of being poor.

powder *n.* tiny grains of a substance.

power *n.* **1** strength or force. **2** the ability to do something. *This plant has magical powers.* **3** the ability or right to control people. *The police have the power to arrest people.* **4** energy. *nuclear power.* **powerful** *adj.*, **powerfully** *adv.*

power plant *n.* a building where electricity is produced.

practical *adj.* **1** concerned with doing things rather than with ideas. *The book is a practical guide to finding a job.* **2** useful and likely to work. *Your plan just isn't practical.* **3** good at doing or making things with your hands.

practical joke *n.* a trick played on somebody.

practically *adv.* **1** in a practical way. **2** almost; nearly. *I'm practically finished.*

practice[1] *n.* **1** the doing of something often so that you get better at it. **2** the doing of something. **3** the business of a doctor or lawyer.

practice[2] *v.* **1** to do something often so that you get better at it. **2** to do something regularly.

prairie *n.* a wide, grassy area of land in central North America.

praise *v.* to say good things about somebody. **praise** *n.*

prank *n.* a trick played on somebody.

power plant

prawn *n.* a small, edible shellfish, like a large shrimp.

pray *v.* to speak to God, especially to ask for something or to give thanks.

prayer *n.* the words that you use when you pray to God.

pre- *prefix* before. *Prehistoric means before history was written down.*

preach *v.* to give a talk about religious or moral matters.

precaution *n.* something that you do in order to prevent something bad from happening in the future.

precinct *n.* a district of a city or town, sometimes with its own police force.

precious *adj.* rare and very valuable.

precipice *(press-ip-iss) n.* the very steep side of a mountain or cliff.

precise *adj.* exact; accurate. **precision** *n.*

predator *n.* an animal that hunts other animals. **predatory** *adj.*

predecessor *n.* a person who had your job before you started doing it.

predict *v.* to say what is likely to happen in the future. **prediction** *n.*

preen *v.* (of birds) to clean and tidy feathers with the beak.

preface *(pref-iss) n.* an introduction to a book, which comes before the main text.

prefer *v.* (prefers, preferring, preferred) to like something better. **preferable** *adj.*, **preference** *n.*

prefix *n.* letters added to the beginning of a word to change its meaning. *Un-, pre-,* and *multi-* are all prefixes.

pregnant *adj.* having a baby growing inside the body. **pregnancy** *n.*

prehistoric *adj.* from the time before history was written down.

prejudice *n.* an unfair opinion that you have about somebody or something without knowing much about the person or thing.

premiere *(pre-meer) n.* the first performance of a movie or play.

premises *n. pl.* the building and land that a business uses.

premium *n.* money that you pay regularly for an insurance policy.

prepare *v.* to get ready. **preparation** *n.*

preposition *n.* a word used to show how the words before and after it are related. In the sentence *I walk to school everyday, to* is a preposition.

prescription *n.* a written instruction from a doctor to a pharmacist to provide medicine. **prescribe** *v.*

presence *n.* the state of being in a place.

present[1] *(prez-ent) adj.* in a place; there. *The entire class was present for the announcement.*

present[2] *(prez-ent) n.* **1** the time now. **2** a gift.

present[3] *(pri-zent) v.* **1** to give something in public. *The mayor presented the trophy to the winner.* **2** to show or offer something. *Please present your passport at the desk.* **3** to introduce something. *She is presenting a new show on TV.* **presentation** *n.*

presently *adv.* soon.

preserve *v.* to make something last or keep it in good condition. *The ancient Egyptians preserved their dead pharaohs as mummies.*

president *n.* **1** the leader of a republic. **2** the head of a company or organization. **presidential** *adj.*

press[1] *v.* **1** to push something. *Press the button.* **2** to iron clothes. **3** to persuade or force somebody strongly. *They pressed him for an answer.*

press[2] *n.* **1** a machine for printing. **2 the press** the newspapers.

pressing *adj.* urgent. *The pressing deadline was making her worry.*

pressure *n.* **1** the force with which one thing presses on another. *Apply pressure to the cut to stop it bleeding.* **2** strong persuasion or influence. *They put a lot of pressure on me to change my mind about taking the new job.*

presume *v.* to believe that something is true without being sure. *I presume that you want a dessert.* **presumption** *n.*

pretend *v.* to try to make somebody believe something that is not true. *He pretended that he was asleep.* **pretence** *n.*

pretext *n.* a false reason; an excuse.

pretty[1] *adj.* (prettier, prettiest) attractive; pleasant to look at. **prettily** *adv.*, **prettiness** *n.*

pretty[2] *adv. (informal)* fairly; relatively.

prevent *v.* to stop something from happening. **prevention** *n.*

preview *n.* a showing of a movie or play before it is seen by the public.

previous *adj.* former; coming before.

prey *(pray) n.* an animal that is hunted by another animal. **prey** *v.*

price *n.* the amount of money that something costs to buy.

priceless *adj.* too valuable to have a price. *priceless jewels.*

prick *v.* to make a small hole in something with a sharp point.

pricker, prickle *n.* a sharp point on a plant or animal. **prickly** *adj.*

pride *n.* the feeling of being proud.

priest *n.* a person who performs religious ceremonies, especially in some Christian churches.

prim *adj.* too formal and correct.

primary *adj.* first. **primarily** *adv.*

primary colors *n. pl.* in painting the colors red, yellow, and blue, which mix together to make all other colors.

primate *n.* a member of the group of mammals that includes monkeys, apes, and humans.

prime minister *n.* the leader of the government in some countries.

primitive *adj.* **1** belonging to the earliest times. *primitive societies.* **2** simple and rough. *They made a primitive boat out of pieces of wood.*

primrose *n.* a yellow spring flower.

prince *n.* a male member of a royal family, especially the son of a king or queen.

princess *n.* a female member of a royal family, especially the daughter of a king or a queen.

principal *adj.* **1** most important; main. **principally** *adv.* **2** the head in charge of a school.

principle *n.* a general rule or law.

print *v.* **1** to put words or pictures on to paper using a machine. **2** to write without using cursive writing. **print** *n.*, **printer** *n.*

printout *n.* a page or set of pages of printed information produced by a computer.

prior *adj.* earlier. *No prior knowledge of the subject is required.* **prior to** before.

priority *n.* **1** the right to be first. *Ambulances have priority over the other traffic.* **2** something that must be done first.

priory *n.* a building where a group of monks or nuns live and worship.

prism *n.* **1** in geometry a solid figure whose two ends are the same size and shape as each other and are parallel. **2** a transparent glass or plastic object with triangular ends, which splits light into the colors of the rainbow.

prison *n.* a building where people are kept as a punishment for committing crimes. **prisoner** *n.*

private *adj.* **1** for one person or a few people only; not public. *a private swimming pool.* **2** not to be shared with others; secret. *a private talk.* **3** not controlled by the government. *a private hospital.* **privacy** *n.*

privilege *n.* a special advantage that is only given to certain people. **privileged** *adj.*

prize[1] *n.* a reward for winning a competition or game.

prize[2] *v.* to value something highly.

pro- *prefix* for; in favor of. *pro-hunting.*

probable *adj.* likely to happen or be true. **probability** *n.*, **probably** *adv.*

probation *n.* **1** a trial period in a new job. **2** a period of time when someone who has committed a crime is not sent to prison but instead is supervised by a social worker called a **probation**

prism

officer. **probationary** *adj.*

probe *v.* to explore or examine closely. **probe** *n.*

problem *n.* **1** a difficulty to be overcome. **2** a question to be solved.

procedure *n.* a way of doing something.

proceed *v.* to move forward or continue with something.

proceeds *n. pl.* the money obtained from an event. *The proceeds from the concert are going to charity.*

process *n.* a series of actions for doing or making something. *The process of making paper is complicated.* **process** *v.*

procession *n.* a line of people or vehicles moving along. *a funeral procession.*

proclaim *v.* to announce something publicly; to declare officially. **proclamation** *n.*

prod *v.* (prods, prodding, prodded) to poke something. **prod** *n.*

produce[1] *(pro-dooss)* *v.* **1** to make something. **2** to bring something out to show it. *The magician produced a rabbit from his hat.* **3** to be in charge of putting on a movie or play. **producer** *n.*, **production** *n.*

produce[2] *(pro-dooss)* *n.* food grown or

produced on a farm or in a garden.

product *n.* **1** something that is produced. **2** the answer obtained when two numbers are multiplied. *18 is the product of 6 times 3.*

profession *n.* a job that needs special training, e.g. that of a doctor or teacher.

professional[1] *n.* **1** a person who works in a profession. **2** a person who is paid to do something, not an amateur.

professional[2] *adj.* **1** to do with a profession. **2** doing something for money; not as an amateur. **3** skillful; competent. **professionally** *adv.*

professor *n.* a teacher in a college or university.

proficiency *n.* skill. **proficient** *adj.*

profile *n.* **1** a side view of a face. **2** a short description of somebody's life or achievements.

profit *n.* the money gained by selling something for a higher price than it cost you to make or buy it. **profit** *v.*

profound *adj.* **1** intense; deep. **2** needing a lot of research or thought. *That's a very profound statement.*

program[1] *n.* a set of instructions for a computer. **program** *v.*, **programmer** *n.*

program[2] *n.* **1** a show broadcast on the TV or radio. **2** a list of planned events. **3** a booklet giving information about a play or concert.

progress *(pro-gress)* *v.* **1** to move forward. **2** to develop or improve. *The work on the new school building is progressing well.* **progress** *n.*, **progression** *n.*

prohibit *v.* to forbid something. *Smoking is prohibited.*

project[1] *(proj-ekt)* *n.* **1** a plan or scheme. **2** a piece of study or research. *We are doing a school project on the Romans.*

project[2] *(pro-jekt)* *v.* **1** to throw something forward. **2** to stick out. *The dock projects into the lake.* **3** to show a movie or image on a screen. **4** to forecast. *More job losses are projected for next year.* **projection** *n.*

projector *n.* a machine for showing pictures or movies on a screen.

prolong *v.* to make something last longer.

promenade *n.* a road or path beside the sea.

prominent *adj.* **1** standing out; easily seen. **2** famous or important. *a prominent businesswoman.* **prominence** *n.*

promise *v.* to say that you will definitely do something. **promise** *n.*

promising *adj.* likely to do or turn out well in the future. *He's a promising young musician.*

promote *v.* **1** to move somebody to a more important job than the one he or she already has. *He was promoted to the position of manager.* **2** to give a lot of publicity to something to try to sell it. *The author is promoting her new book.* **3** to help the progress of something. *A balanced diet promotes good health.* **promotion** *n.*

prompt[1] *adj.* immediate; without delay.

prompt[2] *v.* **1** to remind or encourage someone to do something. *The commercial prompted me to buy the product.* **2** to remind actors on stage of words they have forgotten.

prong *n.* one of the points of a fork.

pronoun *n.* a word used in place of a noun, such as *he, she, it,* and *this.*

pronounce *v.* to speak sounds or words in a particular way. **pronunciation** *n.*

proof *n.* evidence that shows that something is definitely true.

prop[1] *v.* (props, propping, propped) to support something. *Lee propped the ladder against the wall.*

prop[2] *n.* **1** a support. *The ceiling was held up with wooden props.* **2** an object used in a play or movie.

propaganda *n.* ideas, especially untrue ones, that are spread by a political group or an organization to influence people.

propel *v.* (propels, propelling, propelled) to drive or push something forward. **propulsion** *n.*

propeller *n.* a set of blades that spin around to drive a boat or aircraft.

proper *adj.* **1** right or correct. *Put your toys back in the proper place.* **2** respectable; behaving correctly. **properly** *adv.*

proper noun *n.* a name for a particular person, place, or thing, written with a capital letter. *Sam, New York,* and *Asia* are proper nouns.

property *n.* **1** the things that you own. **2** a building and the land around it. **3** a quality or characteristic. *the properties of acids.*

prophet *n.* **1** a person who predicts the future. **2** a religious teacher who tells what he or she believes is the will of God. **prophecy** *(prof-ess-ee)* *n.*, **prophesy** *(prof-ess-eye)* *v.*

a
b
c
d
e
f
g
h
i
j
k
l
m
n
o
p
q
r
s
t
u
v
w
x
y
z

proportion *n.* **1** a part of something. *A large proportion of Earth's surface is covered in water.* **2** one amount in relation to another. *The proportion of girls to boys here is two to one.*

propose *v.* **1** to suggest something; to put forward an idea. **2** to ask somebody to marry you. **proposal** *n.*

proprietor *n.* the owner of a business.

prosecute *v.* to accuse somebody in a court of law. **prosecution** *n.*

propeller

prospect *n.* an idea of what will happen in the future. *There is no prospect of the war ending soon.*

prosper *v.* to do well; to succeed. **prosperity** *n.*, **prosperous** *adj.*

protect *v.* to keep something safe from harm. **protection** *n.*, **protective** *adj.*

protein *(pro-teen) n.* a substance found in foods such as eggs, meat, and milk that is a necessary part of the diet of humans and animals.

protest *(proh-test) v.* to show that you are against something. *The demonstrators are protesting against the export of live animals.* **protest** *(proh-test) n.*

Protestant *n.* a member of a part of the Christian Church that separated from the Roman Catholic Church in the 1500s. **Protestant** *adj.*

proton *n.* one of the parts of the nucleus of an atom, carrying a positive electrical charge.

protractor *n.* an instrument used for measuring angles.

protrude *v.* to stick out. **protrusion** *n.*

proud *adj.* **1** pleased about your or somebody else's achievement. *She is proud of her son's success.* **2** thinking that you are more important or better than you really are.

prove *v.* to show that something is definitely true.

proverb *n.* a well-known saying that gives advice. *"A watched pot never boils" is a proverb.*

provide *v.* to give something that is needed. *Our teacher provided us with pens and pencils.* **provided that, providing** only if. *I'll go providing you come with me.*

province *n.* a region of a country.

provision *n.* **1** the providing of something. **2 provisions** a supply of food.

provisional *adj.* when something is used for the time being; temporary.

provoke *v.* to annoy somebody so that he or she reacts in an angry way. *The dog might bite if you provoke it.* **provocation** *n.*, **provocative** *adj.*

prowl *v.* to move around silently and carefully, like an animal waiting to attack.

prune[1] *n.* a dried plum.

prune[2] *v.* to cut off parts of a plant to control the way that it grows.

pry *v.* (pries, prying, pried) to look in a nosy way into other people's affairs.

P.S. written at the end of a letter when you want to add something. It is short for **postscript**. *Love from Susie. P.S. I hope to see you soon!*

psalm *(sahm) n.* a sacred song.

pseudonym *(soo-do-nim) n.* a false name, used by a writer.

psychiatrist *(sye-kye-a-trist) n.* a doctor who treats mental illness. **psychiatric** *(sye-kee-at-rik) adj.*, **psychiatry** *(sye-kye-a-tree) n.*

psychic *(sye-kik) adj.* able to read other people's minds or tell the future. **psychic** *n.*

psycho- *(sye-coh) prefix* to do with the mind.

psychologist *(sye-kol-o-jist) n.* an expert in psychology.

psychology *(sye-kol-o-jee) n.* the study of the mind and how it works. **psychological** *(sye-ko-loj-ik-ul) adj.*, **psychologically** *adv.*

pterodactyl *(te-ro-dak-til) n.* a prehistoric flying reptile.

p.t.o. *short for* please turn over. It is usually written at the bottom of a page.

puberty *(pyoo-ber-tee) n.* the time when a child's body develops into that of an adult.

public *adj.* to do with or belonging to everybody. *public transportation, a public meeting.* **the public** all people. *The park is open to the public.*

publication *n.* **1** the publishing of something. **2** a book, magazine, or newspaper.

publicity *n.* advertising.

public school *n.* an elementary or high school in the U.S. that is supported by public funding and provides free education for children.

publish *v.* to produce a book, newspaper, or magazine and make it available to the public. **publisher** *n.*

pudgy *adj.* (pudgier, pudgiest) (*informal*) slightly fat.

puddle *n.* a small pool of water or other liquid on the ground.

puff[1] *n.* a small blast of air, wind, or smoke.

puff[2] *v.* **1** to blow with short puffs. *Smoke was puffing out of the chimney.* **2** to breathe quickly. *She was puffing hard as she reached the top of the stairs.* **puff out, puff up** to swell up.

puffin *n.* a sea bird with a large beak.

pull *v.* to move something, especially toward yourself, using force. **pull a face** to make a strange expression with your face. **pull down** to demolish a building. **pull out** to withdraw from doing something. **pull up** to stop a vehicle. **pull yourself together** to control your feelings after being upset.

pulley *n.* (*pl.* pulleys) a wheel with a rope around it, used to lift or move heavy things.

pulp *n.* a soft, wet mass produced by crushing something such as fruit or wood.

pulpit *n.* a raised platform in a church where the priest or minister stands.

pulse *n.* **1** the beating of your heart that you can feel in your wrist. **2** a regular beat. **pulse** *v.*

puma *n.* a large wild cat found in North and South America.

pump[1] *n.* a machine or device for forcing a liquid or gas into or out of something.

pump[2] *v.* to force a liquid or gas with a pump. *Your heart pumps blood around your body.*

pumpkin *n.* a very large, round, orange-colored fruit that grows on the ground. Often carved at Halloween.

pun *n.* a joke based on words that sound the same but that have a different meaning. "*Two pears make a pair*" is a pun.

punch[1] *v.* **1** to hit somebody using your fist. **2** to make a hole in something with a punch.

punch[2] *n.* **1** a blow with the fist. **2** a tool for making holes in paper or leather. **3** a drink made from fruit juices and sometimes alcohol.

punctual *adj.* on time. **punctuality** *n.*, **punctually** *adv.*

punctuation *n.* marks used in writing such as periods, commas, and exclamation points. **punctuate** *v.*

puncture *n.* a small hole in something, such as a tire, made by a sharp object. **puncture** *v.*

pulley

punish *v.* to make somebody suffer because he or she has done something wrong. **punishment** *n.*

punt *n.* a long, flat-bottomed boat, moved with a pole.

puny *adj.* (punier, puniest) small and weak.

pupa (*pyoo-pa*) *n.* (*pl.* pupae *or* pupas) the stage in an insect's development between the larva and the adult.

pupil *n.* the round, dark part of your eye, through which light passes. See **eye**.

puppet *n.* a doll that you move by pulling strings or by putting your hand inside and moving your fingers.

puppy *n.* a young dog.

purchase[1] *v.* to buy something.

purchase[2] *n.* a thing you have bought.

pure *adj.* clean; not mixed with anything else. **purity** *n.*

purify *v.* (purifies, purifying, purified) to make something pure.

purple *n.* a reddish-blue color. **purple** *adj.*

purpose *n.* **1** a reason for doing something. **2** a reason why something exists. *a multipurpose tool.* **on purpose** deliberately.

purr *n.* the low sound made by a cat when it is pleased. **purr** *v.*

purse[1] *n.* a small container used for carrying money.

purse[2] *v.* to close your lips tightly.

pursue *v.* to follow or chase after somebody or something. **pursuit** *n.*

pus *n.* a thick, yellowish fluid produced from an infected wound.

push *v.* **1** to move something away from you with force. **2** to press on something. *Push the button.* **push** *n.*

a b c d e f g h i j k l m n o p q r s t u v w x y z

put *v.* (puts, putting, put) **1** to place somewhere. **2** to express in words. *You have a funny way of putting things!* **put off 1** to delay. **2** to stop somebody from liking something. **put up** to let somebody stay in your home overnight. **put up with** not to complain about something even though you do not like it.

putt *v.* in golf to hit the ball gently along the ground toward the hole.

putty *n.* a soft paste that hardens when it is dry and is used for holding glass in window frames or sealing cracks.

puzzle¹ *n.* **1** a game that makes you think a lot. *a crossword puzzle.* **2** something that is difficult to understand or explain.

puzzle² *v.* to do something that causes somebody to become confused.

pylon *n.* a tall metal tower supporting electric cables.

pyramid *n.* **1** a solid shape with sloping sides that come to a point at the top. **2 the Pyramids** structures of this shape that were used as tombs for pharaohs in ancient Egypt.

python *n.* a large snake that crushes its prey.

quack *v.* to make a noise like a duck. **quack** *n.*

quad *short for* quadruplet *or* quadrangle.

quadrangle *n.* a square courtyard with buildings around it.

quadrant *n.* a quarter of a circle.

quadrilateral *n.* a flat shape with four straight sides.

quadruped *n.* an animal with four feet.

quadruplet *n.* one of four babies born at the same time to the same mother.

quail *n.* a small bird similar to a partridge, sometimes shot as game.

quaint *adj.* attractively odd and old-fashioned. *a quaint little fishing village on the coast.* **quaintness** *n.*

quake *v.* to shake, especially with fear.

qualify *v.* (qualifies, qualifying, qualified) to reach the required standard so that you can do something, especially by passing tests or exams. *Sarah has qualified as a doctor.* **qualification** *n.*

quality *n.* **1** the standard of something; how good something is. *The camera was not good quality.* **2** a characteristic of somebody or something. *He has all the qualities of a good father.*

quantity *n.* an amount of something. *a large quantity of food.*

quarantine *n.* a time when an animal or person is kept away from others because it might have a disease.

quarrel *v.* (quarrels, quarreling, quarreled) to argue. **quarrel** *n.*, **quarrelsome** *adj.*

quarry *n.* a place where stone is taken from the ground. **2** an animal being hunted.

quarter *n.* **1** one of four equal parts of something; a fourth. **2** a part of a town. *the Latin quarter of Paris.* **3 quarters** a place to stay, especially for soldiers.

quarterfinal *n.* one of the games or matches of a contest to decide who will take part in the semifinals.

quartet *n.* a group of four singers or

musicians who play together.

quartz *n.* a hard mineral found in rocks in the form of crystals and used in electronic clocks and watches.

quaver[1] *v.* (of a voice) to tremble.

quartz

quaver[2] *n.* a note in music equal to half a crotchet in length.

quay *(kee) n.* (*pl.* quays) a landing place for boats to load and unload.

queasy *adj.* (queasier, queasiest) feeling slightly sick. **queasiness** *n.*

queen *n.* **1** the female ruler of a country or the wife of a king. **2** the playing card with a picture of a queen on it. **3** the most powerful chess piece.

queer *adj.* strange; odd.

quench *v.* **1** to take away your thirst by drinking enough. **2** to put out a fire.

query[1] *n.* a question.

query[2] *v.* (queries, querying, queried) to express doubt about something. *I would like to query this bill.*

quest *n.* a long search.

question[1] *n.* something that you ask when you need an answer.

question[2] *v.* **1** to ask somebody questions. **2** to doubt something. *He questioned the truth of the statement.*

question mark *n.* the punctuation mark (?) used at the end of a question.

questionnaire *n.* a list of questions to be answered by several people.

quiche *(keesh) n.* a pastry case filled with beaten egg, cheese, ham, or vegetables and baked.

quick *adj.* **1** done or happening in a short time. **2** moving at a fast speed. **quickness** *n.*

quicksand *n.* wet sand that sucks down anybody who stands on it.

quiet *adj.* **1** making little or no noise. **2** calm. *a quiet life.* **quietness** *n.*

quill *n.* *(historical)* a large feather, especially one used as a pen.

quilt *n.* a bed cover filled with feathers or other soft material.

quilted *adj.* made of two layers of material with padding in between. *a quilted jacket.*

quit *v.* (quits, quitting, quit *or* quitted) to stop doing something; to give something up. *He has quit smoking.*

quite *adv.* **1** fairly, relatively. *Tania can sing quite well.*

quiver[1] *v.* to tremble.

quiver[2] *n.* a long case for arrows.

quill

quiz *n.* (*pl.* quizzes) a competition in which somebody is asked questions to test his or her knowledge.

quota *n.* a set share of something.

quotation *n.* words that somebody has spoken or written, repeated by somebody else.

quotation marks *n. pl.* a pair of punctuation marks used to mark the beginning and end of a passage of speech.

quote *v.* to repeat words that were first spoken or written by somebody else.

Qur'an *n. alternative spelling of* Koran.

a
b
c
d
e
f
g
h
i
j
k
l
m
n
o
p
q
r
s
t
u
v
w
x
y
z

rabbi *(rab-eye)* *n.* *(pl.* rabbis) a Jewish
  religious leader.
rabbit *n.* a small mammal with long ears
  and a short tail that lives in fields and
  burrows in the wild.
rabble *n.* a noisy crowd of people.
rabies *n.* a very serious disease caught
  from the bite of an infected dog or
  other animal, causing mental illness
  and often death. **rabid** *adj.*

raccoon

raccoon *n.* a furry North American
  mammal with a long striped tail. *(can
  also be spelled* racoon).
race[1] *n.* **1** a competition to find out which
  person, animal, or vehicle is the fastest.
  a horse race. **2** a group of people who
  share the same ancestors and history and
  have similar physical characteristics.
race[2] *v.* **1** to participate in a race. **2** to run
  or move very fast.
racial *adj.* to do with race. *racial prejudice.*
  racially *adv.*
racist *adj.* thinking that some races of
  people are superior to others and
  treating people unfairly or badly
  because of this. **racism** *n,* **racist** *n.*
rack[1] *n.* **1** a frame or shelf made of bars,
  for holding things. *a coat rack.*
  2 *(historical)* an instrument used for
  torturing victims by stretching them.
rack[2] *v.* **rack your brains** to think hard
  about something.
racket *n.* **1** a bat with strings used in tennis,

badminton, and squash *(can also be
  spelled* racquet). **2** a loud, unpleasant
  noise. **3** *(informal)* an illegal way of
  making money. *a drug racket.*
racoon *another spelling of* raccoon.
racquet *another spelling of* racket.
radar *n.* a way of finding out where an
  object is by sending out radio waves
  that hit the object and bounce back.
radiant *adj.* **1** sending out rays of heat
  or light. **2** showing joy and happiness.
  radiance *n.*
radiate *v.* **1** to send out rays of heat or
  light. **2** to spread out from the center.
radiation *n.* the sending out of rays of
  heat or light or invisible emissions
  from a radioactive substance.
radiator *n.* **1** a metal container through
  which hot water is pumped, for heating a
  room. **2** a device in a car through which
  water is pumped to cool down the engine.
radio *n.* *(pl.* radios) an instrument that
  sends or receives electrical waves through
  the air and turns them into sounds that
  you can hear.
radioactive *adj.* giving off powerful and
  dangerous rays. **radioactivity** *n.*
radiography *n.* photography of the inside of
  the body using x-rays. **radiographer** *n.*
radish *n.* a plant with a hot-tasting red
  root, eaten raw in salads.
radius *n.* *(pl.* radii *or* radiuses) a straight
  line from the center to the edge of a
  circle. See *circle.*
raffle *n.* a way of raising money by
  selling numbered tickets, a few of
  which will win prizes. **raffle** *v.*
raft *n.* **1** a flat boat made from logs that
  are attached to each other. **2** a small,
  inflatable boat used in emergencies.
rafter *n.* one of the sloping beams of
  wood that supports a roof.
rag *n.* **1** an old or torn piece of cloth.
  2 rags old, torn clothes.
rage[1] *n.* great anger.
rage[2] *v.* **1** to show violent anger. **2** (of a
  storm or battle) to be violent.
raid *n.* **1** a surprise attack on a place.
  2 a surprise visit by the police to search for
  a criminal, stolen goods, or drugs. **raid** *v.*
rail *n.* **1** a stationary bar used as a fence
  or for hanging things on. *a towel rail.*
  2 the railroad. *to travel by rail.* **3 rails** the
  long metal bars that a train runs on.
railing *n.* a fence made of a rail.

railroad *n.* (*pl.* railroads) **1** a system of transportation using trains that run on tracks. **2** a track that trains run on.

rain *n.* drops of water falling from the sky. **rain** *v.*, **rainy** *adj.*

rain forest

rainbow *n.* an arch of many colors in the sky, caused by sunlight shining through rain or mist.

rain forest *n.* a tropical forest where a lot of rain falls.

raise *v.* **1** to lift something. *Raise your hand.* **2** to collect an amount of money. *We raised $300 for the charity.* **3** to grow crops or breed animals for food. **4** to take care of children as they grow up.

raisin *n.* a dried grape.

rake *n.* a tool like a comb on a long handle, used for making dirt smooth or for collecting leaves and grass. **rake** *v.*

rally *n.* **1** a large meeting of people for a special purpose. *a peace rally.* **2** a meeting of cars or motorcycles for a competition or race. **3** in tennis and other racket sports a long series of shots before a point is scored; a volley.

ram¹ *n.* a male sheep.

ram² *v.* (rams, ramming, rammed) **1** to run into something and cause damage to it. *The truck rammed into the front of the store.* **2** to hit or push with great force.

Ramadan *n.* the ninth month of the Islamic year, when Muslims fast between sunrise and sunset.

ramble *v.* **1** to walk around in the countryside. **2** to talk for a long time in a confused way.

ramp *n.* a sloping path leading from one level to another.

rampage *v.* to rush around angrily or violently.

The elephants rampaged through the jungle.

rampart *n.* a mound or wall built as a defense.

ramshackle *adj.* falling down; in a state of disrepair.

ran *past of* run.

ranch *n.* a large farm for cattle or horses, especially in North America.

random *adj.* done without any plan or purpose. *a random collection of objects.*

rang *past of* ring.

range¹ *n.* **1** a selection or variety. *The store sells a wide range of items.* **2** the distance that an object can be thrown or a sound can be heard. *What is the range of this missile?* **3** a line of mountains. **4** a piece of ground with targets for shooting or archery practice.

range² *v.* to vary between two limits. *They have five children ranging in age from two to 16.*

ranger *n.* a person who takes care of a forest or park.

rank *n.* **1** a title or position that shows how important somebody is. *General is a high rank in the army.* **2** a row or line. *ranks of soldiers.*

ransack *v.* to search a place in a chaotic way to try to find or steal something.

ransom *n.* money paid to a kidnapper for the release of someone.

rap *n.* **1** a quick knock. *a rap on the door.* **2** a type of music in which the words of a song are spoken in a rhythmical way. **rap** *v.*

rapid *adj.* quick; fast. **rapidity** *n.*

rapids *n. pl.* a place in a river where the water flows very fast over rocks.

rapier *n.* a light sword with a narrow, double-edged blade.

rappel *v.* to lower yourself down a steep rock face using ropes; abseil.

rare *adj.* **1** unusual; not often seen. **2** (of meat) cooked very lightly.

rarity *n.* something that is unusual and not seen often.

rascal *n.* a naughty person.

rash¹ *n.* a lot of spots on your skin.

rash² *adj.* acting too quickly, without thinking first; reckless. **rashness** *n.*

rasher *n.* a thin slice of bacon.

raspberry *n.* a small, red, soft fruit.

raspberries

A
B
C
D
E
F
G
H
I
J
K
L
M
N
O
P
Q
R
S
T
U
V
W
X
Y
Z

rat *n.* a rodent with a long tail that is similar to a mouse but larger.

rate¹ *n.* **1** the number of times that something happens within a given period. *The annual crime rate has risen.* **2** the speed at which something happens. *She works at a fast rate.* **3** a charge or payment. *interest rates.* **4** a quality or standard. *first-rate.*

rate² *v.* to value or estimate. *I don't rate this book very highly.*

rather *adv.* **1** fairly, relatively. **2** preferably. **3** more correctly.

ratio (*ray-sho* or *ray-shee-oh*) *n.* (*pl.* ratios) one size or amount in relation to another. *The ratio of men to women with the disease is eight to one.*

ration *n.* a set amount of something, often food, that each person is allowed when there is a shortage. **ration** *v.*

rational *adj.* sensible and reasonable. *There must be a rational explanation for the noises that you heard last night.* **rationally** *adv.*

rattle¹ *v.* to make repeated short, sharp sounds. *The coins rattled in the tin.*

rattle² *n.* a baby's toy that makes a rattling noise when you shake it.

rattlesnake *n.* a poisonous snake with bony joints on its tail that rattle when shaken.

rave¹ *v.* **1** to talk wildly or angrily. **2** to talk

rattlesnake

very enthusiastically about something. *Everyone is raving about her latest book.*

ravenous *adj.* very hungry.

ravine (*rav-een*) *n.* a deep, narrow valley.

ravioli *n.* small squares of pasta containing meat, vegetables, or cheese.

raw *adj.* **1** uncooked. *raw meat.* **2** in a natural state; not processed or manufactured. *raw materials.*

ray *n.* (*pl.* rays) **1** a narrow line of light or heat. **2** a flat sea fish with a long tail.

razor *n.* **1** an instrument with a sharp blade for shaving hair from the skin. **2** an electric instrument with blades, used for shaving.

re- *prefix* again; once more. *To redo is to do something again.*

reach *v.* **1** to arrive somewhere. **2** to stretch out your hand to touch or get hold of something. *I'm not tall enough to reach the top shelf.* **3** to be long enough or high enough to come to a certain point. *The curtains reach down to the floor.*

react *v.* **1** to behave in a certain way as a result of something. *How did your mom react when you told her the news?* **2** to change chemically when mixed with another substance. *Hydrogen reacts with oxygen to form water.* **reaction** *n.*

reactor *n.* a machine in which nuclear energy is produced.

read *v.* (reading, read) to look at writing and understand it, saying it out loud or to yourself.

readily *adv.* **1** willingly. **2** easily. *Fresh fruit is readily available all year round.*

ready *adv.* (readier, readiest) **1** prepared. **2** willing.

real *adj.* **1** actually existing; not imagined. **2** genuine; not fake.

realistic *adj.* showing or seeing things as they really are. *a realistic drawing.* **realistically** *adv.*

reality *n.* that which is real rather than just imaginary.

realize *v.* to become aware of something as a fact. *I suddenly realized that I was lost.* **realization** *n.*

really *adv.* **1** in fact; truly. **2** very.

realm (*relm*) *n.* a kingdom.

realtor *n.* a person whose job is selling houses and land for people.

reap *v.* to cut and collect a crop.

rear¹ *n.* the back part. **rear** *adj.*

rear² *v.* **1** to breed animals. **2** to raise children. **3** (of an animal) to stand up on its back legs.

reason *n.* the cause of or the explanation for something.

reasonable *adj.* **1** fair and sensible. **2** moderate; a fair amount. *I got a reasonable grade on the test.* **reasonably** *adv.*

reassure *v.* to take away somebody's doubts and fears. *The doctor reassured her that she would recover.* **reassurance** *n.*

rebel¹ (*reb-ul*) *n.* a person who fights against the people in power.

rebel² (*re-bel*) *v.* (rebels, rebelling, rebelled) to fight against authority. *She rebelled against her strict parents.*

rebellion *n.*, **rebellious** *adj.*

rebound *v.* **1** to bounce back. **2** in basketball to intercept the ball after it has been shot.

rebuke *v.* to tell somebody off. **rebuke** *n.*

recall *v.* **1** to remember something. **2** to order somebody to return. *The government recalled its ambassador.*

recede *v.* to move back.

receipt *(re-seet) n.* a piece of paper showing that money has been paid.

receive *v.* to get something that has been given or sent to you.

receiver *n.* **1** the part of a telephone that you speak into and hold to your ear. **2** an apparatus that receives television or radio broadcasts.

recent *adj.* happening, done, or made a short time ago. *a recent photo.*

reception *n.* **1** a formal party. *a wedding reception.* **2** the way in which people react to something. *The movie got an enthusiastic reception.* **3** the part of a hotel, hospital, or business where visitors enter and are dealt with. **4** the quality of radio or television signals. *The TV reception is very bad in this area.*

receptionist *n.* a person who works in an office, hotel, or business, answering the phone and greeting visitors as they arrive.

recession *n.* a time when a country's or city's trade is doing badly.

recipe *(ress-ip-ee) n.* instructions on how to prepare or cook a certain dish.

recital *n.* a performance of music or poetry by one person or by a small group.

recite *v.* to say something out loud that you have learned by heart.

reckless *adj.* done without thinking about the dangerous things that could happen; careless. *reckless driving.* **recklessness** *n.*

reckon *v.* to calculate something.

recline *v.* to lie back or lie down.

recognize *v.* to know somebody or something because you have seen or heard that person or thing before. **recognition** *n.*

recollect *v.* to remember something.

recommend *v.* to suggest something because you think that it is good or suitable. *My friend recommended this book.* **recommendation** *n.*

record¹ *(ri-kord) v.* **1** to put sounds or pictures on a tape or disk so that they can be listened to or watched again. **2** to write something down so that it

will be remembered.

record *(rek-ord) n.* **1** the best performance so far in a sport or competition. *He holds the world record for the long jump.* **2** a written report of facts or events. **3** a flat vinyl disk that makes sounds when it is played on a record player. Most people now listen to music recorded as digital files on a CD or an MP3 player.

recorder *n.* a musical instrument you play by blowing into one end and covering the holes with your fingers.

record player *n.* a machine designed for playing records.

recorder

recover *v.* **1** to get better after an illness, accident, or shock. **2** to get something back. *The police recovered the stolen jewelry.* **recovery** *n.*

recreation *n.* the sports or hobbies that people do in their spare time.

recruit¹ *n.* a person who has just joined an army, club, or other group.

recruit² *v.* to get people to join an army, club, or place of work. **recruitment** *n.*

rectangle *n.* a four-sided shape with opposite sides equal and four right angles. **rectangular** *adj.*

recuperate *v.* to get better after an illness; to recover. **recuperation** *n.*

recur *v.* (recurs, recurring, recurred) to happen again. *He did get better, but unfortunately his illness has recurred.* **recurrence** *n.*, **recurrent** *adj.*

recycle *v.* to treat things that have already been used so that they can be used again. *recycled paper.*

red *n.* the color of blood. **red** *adj.*

red herring *n.* a false clue that takes people's attention away from what is really happening.

red tape *n.* the existence of too many official forms and rules that delay people from doing business.

reduce *v.* to make something smaller or less. **reduction** *n.*

159

redundant *adj.* **1** exceeding what is necessary. "*The police officer was in the police*" *is a redundant statement.* **2** no longer needed. **redundancy** *n.*

reed *n.* **1** a tall, stiff stalk of grass that grows in or close to water. **2** the part of a wind instrument, made of cane or metal, that vibrates and makes a sound when you blow into it.

reef *n.* a line of rocks or coral close to the surface of the sea.

reek *v.* to smell strongly of something unpleasant.

reel[1] *n.* a cylinder on which thread, film, or fishing lines are wound.

reel[2] *v.* **1** to stagger. **2** to feel dizzy.

refectory *n.* a dining hall in a school, convent, or monastery.

refer *v.* (refers, referring, referred) **refer to 1** to mention. *The letter refers to your behavior at school.* **2** to look in a book for information. *What does this notice refer to?* **3** to be connected with something. *What does this notice refer to?* **4** to pass on to somebody else. *The case was referred to the federal court.*

referee *n.* a person who controls a sports game and makes sure that the players do not break the rules.

reference *n.* **1** a mention. *I saw references to our town in this book.* **2** a note about somebody's character or ability. *Did your boss give you a good reference?*

reference book *n.* a book, such as a dictionary or an encyclopedia, where you look up information.

referendum *n.* (*pl.* referendums *or* referenda) a vote by the people of a country about a single matter.

refine *v.* to make something purer than it already is. *refined sugar.*

refinery *n.* a place where something, such as sugar or oil, is refined.

reflect *v.* **1** to send back light, heat, or sound. *The white sand reflects the Sun's heat.* **2** to give an image of something. *She saw her face reflected in the mirror.* **3** to think carefully about something. **reflection** *n.*, **reflective** *adj.*

reflex *n.* an action that is automatic such as jerking your knee when somebody hits your kneecap.

reform (*ri-form*) *v.* to make something better by making changes to it. **reform** *n.*, **reformation** *n.*

refraction *n.* the bending of a ray of light when it passes from one substance to another. **refract** *v.*

refrain[1] *v.* to stop yourself from doing something. *Please refrain from eating in the store.*

refrain[2] *n.* a chorus coming at the end of each verse of a song.

refresh *v.* to make somebody or something look or feel cooler, less tired, or less thirsty. *The shower refreshed him.* **refreshing** *adj.*

refreshments *n. pl.* food and drink.

refrigerator *n.* see **fridge**.

refrigerate *v.* to keep things cool and fresh by putting them in a fridge. **refrigeration** *n.*

refuel *v.* (refuels, refueling, refueled) to be filled again with fresh fuel.

refuge *n.* a shelter from danger.

refugee *n.* a person who has been forced to leave his or her home or country, for example, because of war or famine.

refund (*ri-fund*) *v.* to pay back money. **refund** (*ree-fund*) *n.*

refuse[1] (*ri-fyooz*) *v.* to say that you will not do something. **refusal** *n.*

refuse[2] (*ref-yooss*) *n.* garbage; things that are thrown away.

regal *adj.* royal.

regard *v.* to consider somebody or something in a certain way. *He is regarded as one of the best novelists alive today.*

regarding *prep.* concerning; to do with.

regards *n. pl.* good wishes. *Please give my regards to your parents.*

reggae (*reg-ay*) *n.* a type of music with a very strong rhythm, originally from the West Indies.

regiment *n.* a large group of soldiers, commanded by a colonel.

region (*ree-jun*) *n.* an area or district. **regional** *adj.*

reflection

register[1] *n.* a book containing a written list or record. *a register of births, marriages, and deaths.*

register[2] *v.* **1** to enter a name or a vehicle on an official list. *He is registered as disabled.* **2** to show something. *The thermometer registered 70 degrees.* **registration** *n.*

regret *v.* (regrets, regretting, regretted) to be sorry about something. *I have no regrets about my decision.* **regret** *n.*, **regretful** *adj.*, **regretfully** *adv.*

regular *adj.* **1** happening again and again, with roughly the same amount of space or time in between. *The group meets at regular intervals.* **2** usual. *What are your regular hours?* **3** even. *His pulse is regular.* **regularity** *n.*

regulate *v.* to control something. *Traffic lights regulate the traffic.*

regulation *n.* a rule or instruction.

rehearse *v.* to practice something before performing it in front of an audience. **rehearsal** *n.*

reign *(rain) v.* to rule as a king or queen. **reign** *n.*

reindeer *n.* (*pl.* reindeer *or* reindeers) a large deer that lives in cold parts of the world.

reinforce *v.* to make something stronger. **reinforcement** *n.*

reindeer

reins *(rains) n. pl.* straps fastened to a bridle for guiding a horse or pony.

reject *v.* to refuse to accept something. **rejection** *n.*

rejoice *v.* to feel or show joy.

relate *v.* **1** to form a connection between things. **2** to tell a story. *He related the story of how he came to America.*

related *adj.* in the same family as somebody. *She's related to John; she's his cousin.*

relation *n.* **1** a member of your family. **2** a connection between things.

relationship *n.* **1** the way in which people get along. *She has a good relationship with her parents.* **2** the way in which things or people are connected. *Is there a relationship between violence on TV and violent crime in real life?*

relative[1] *n.* a member of your family.

relative[2] *adj.* compared with something else. *She used to be rich but now lives in relative poverty.*

relax *v.* **1** to rest and become less worried or tense. *You need to relax after a hard day's work.* **2** to become less tight or stiff. *Allow your muscles to relax.* **3** to make something less strict. *The government has relaxed some of the rules.* **relaxation** *n.*

relay[1] *(ree-lay) n.* (*pl.* relays) a race in which each member of a team goes part of the distance, starting from where the previous person finished.

relay[2] *(ree-lay* or *ree-lay) v.* to receive and pass on a message.

release *v.* **1** to set a person or an animal free. *The kidnappers have released their hostages.* **2** to make something available to the public. *The movie was released here first.* **release** *n.*

relevant *adj.* to do with the subject being discussed. **relevance** *n.*

reliable *adj.* able to be trusted and depended on. **reliability** *n.*

relic *n.* something that is left from a past time. *relics of an ancient civilization.*

relief *n.* **1** the stopping or lessening of pain or worry. *It was a relief to find that the children were safe.* **2** help given to people who need it. *famine relief.*

relief map *n.* a map that shows high and low areas of land.

relieve *v.* to stop or lessen pain or worry. *She was given pills to relieve the pain.*

religion *n.* a belief in, or the worship of, a god or gods. **religious** *adj.*

relish[1] *v.* to enjoy something very much.

relish[2] *n.* **1** a type of sauce. **2** a strong appreciation.

reluctant *adj.* not willing to do something. *Peter was reluctant to admit that he was wrong.* **reluctance** *n.*

rely *v.* (relies, relying, relied) to need or have trust in somebody or something. *I am relying on you to help me.* **reliability** *n.*, **reliable** *adj.*

remain *v.* to be left. *Nothing remained of the house after the fire.*

A
B
C
D
E
F
G
H
I
J
K
L
M
N
O
P
Q
R
S
T
U
V
W
X
Y
Z

remainder *n.* **1** the things or people that are left over. **2** in math the number that is left over in division.

remains *n. pl.* **1** what is left after other parts have gone or been taken away. **2** someone's dead body.

remark *v.* to make a comment about something. **remark** *n.*

remarkable *adj.* worth noticing; extraordinary. **remarkably** *adv.*

remedy *n.* a cure for an illness or for something bad. **remedy** *v.*

remember *v.* to keep something in your mind or bring it back into your mind.

remind *v.* to make somebody remember something. **reminder** *n.*

remnant *n.* a small piece or amount that is left over. *a remnant of cloth.*

remorse *n.* deep regret for something bad that you have done.

remote *adj.* faraway; isolated.

remote control *n.* a device that controls something, such as a television, from a distance.

remove *v.* to take something away. **removal** *n.*

rendezvous (*ron-day-voo*) *n.* (*pl.* rendezvous) an arrangement to meet at an agreed time and place.

renew *v.* **1** to begin an activity again. **2** to make something valid for a further period. *I need to renew my train pass.* **3** to replace something that is old or broken with something new. **renewal** *n.*

renovate *v.* to make something as good as new again. *The old house has been renovated.* **renovation** *n.*

renowned *adj.* famous.

rent *n.* money paid for using an apartment, house, or store that is owned by somebody else. **rent** *v.*

rental *n.* **1** money paid as rent. **2** the action of renting something.

repair *v.* to make something that is broken whole again or to make something work again. **repair** *n.*

repay *v.* (repays, repaying, repaid) to pay back. **repayment** *n.*

repeat *v.* to say or do a thing again. **repeat** *n.*

repeatedly *adv.* many times.

repel *v.* (repels, repelling, repelled) **1** to force somebody or something to move away. *She was able to repel her attackers.* **2** to cause a feeling of disgust in somebody.

repent *v.* to be very sorry about the bad things that you have done. **repentance** *n.*,

repentant *adj.*

repetition *n.* the action of repeating something. *He repeated the words.*

repetitive *adj.* doing or saying the same thing over and over again.

replace *v.* **1** to put something new in place of something old. *You should replace the mug that you broke.* **2** to take somebody's place or role. **3** to put something back where it came from. **replacement** *n.*

replica *n.* an exact copy of something.

reply *v.* (replies, replying, replied) to answer. **reply** *n.*

report¹ *v.* **1** to tell or write about something. *All the newspapers reported the speech.* **2** to make a complaint about somebody to a person in authority. *He reported his neighbor to the police for selling stolen goods.* **3** to announce that you are present and available to do something.

report² *n.* a description of what has been done. *a school report.*

report card *n.* a report of a student's progress at school.

reporter *n.* a person who reports on the news for a newspaper or for a radio or TV show.

represent *v.* **1** to act or speak for other people. *Your senator represents you in Congress.* **2** to stand for something. *The dots on the map represent hotels.* **representation** *n.*

representative *n.* **1** a person who acts or speaks for other people. *Each country has sent a representative to the conference.* **2** a traveling salesperson for a company.

reprieve *v.* to pardon a criminal or postpone a punishment, especially the death penalty. **reprieve** *n.*

reprimand *v.* to tell somebody off. **reprimand** *n.*

reproach *v.* to blame or criticize somebody for a mistake or fault.

reproduce *v.* **1** to make a copy of something. **2** to produce young. **reproduction** *n.*

reptile *n.* a cold-blooded animal that lays eggs. *Crocodiles, snakes, and tortoises are all reptiles.*

republic *n.* a country that has a president as its head of state instead of a king or queen. **republican** *adj.*

Republican Party *n.* one of the two main political parties in the U.S. **Republican** *n.*

repulsive *adj.* disgusting.

reputation *n.* the opinion that people have of somebody or something. *This restaurant* *has a reputation for good food and service.*

request *v.* to ask for something politely. **request** *n.*

require *v.* **1** to need something. *Do you require any help?* **2** to order somebody to do something. *The law requires all motorcyclists to wear helmets.* **requirement** *n.*

rescue *v.* to save somebody or something from danger. **rescue** *n.*

research *n.* careful study of a subject to find out new information. *scientific research.* **research** *v.*

resemble *v.* to be or look like somebody or something. **resemblance** *n.*

resent *v.* to feel angry about something because you think that it is insulting or unfair. **resentment** *n.*

reservation *n.* **1** something that is kept back or withheld. *a table reservation.* **2** land set aside by the government for a special purpose, especially the use of Native American people.

reserve[1] *v.* to ask for something to be kept so that you can use it later.

reserve[2] *n.* **1** a piece of land set aside for the protection of animals or plants. *a nature reserve.* **2** something kept for later use. *reserves of food.* **3** an extra player in a team who will play if another player is injured. **reserved** *adj.* shy.

reservoir *n.* an artificial lake where water is stored.

residence *n.* a house, especially one that is big and impressive. *the governor's residence.*

resident *n.* a person who lives in a particular place.

residential *adj.* consisting of houses rather than offices or stores. *a residential area of the city.*

resign *(re-zine)* *v.* **1** to give up a job. **2** to accept something, even though you are not happy about it. *She had resigned herself to losing the game.* **resignation** *n.*

resin *n.* a sticky substance produced by certain trees such as pines and firs.

resist *v.* **1** to fight against something. **2** to stop yourself from doing something that you want to do. *I couldn't resist telling her my secret.* **resistance** *n.*

resolute *adj.* with your mind firmly made up; determined.

resolution *n.* a firm decision to do something.

resolve *v.* **1** to make a firm decision to do something. **2** to solve a problem. **resolve** *n.*

resort[1] *n.* a place where a lot of people go on vacation. *a beach resort.*

resort[2] *v.* **resort to** to do or make use of something because there is no other way to get what you want. *She had to resort to standing on a ladder because she couldn't reach the shelf.*

resources *n. pl.* supplies of things that a country or person has and can use. *The country is rich in natural resources such as oil, coal, and gas.*

respect[1] *v.* **1** to have a high opinion of someone. *I respect you for telling the truth.* **2** to treat somebody or something with consideration.

respect[2] *n.* **1** a high opinion of someone. **2** consideration. *She has no respect for her parents.* **3** a particular detail or part of something. *In some respects, I think the book was much better than the movie.*

respectable *adj.* **1** behaving in a decent, correct way. **2** good enough.

respiration *n.* the action of breathing. **respiratory** *adj.*

human respiratory system

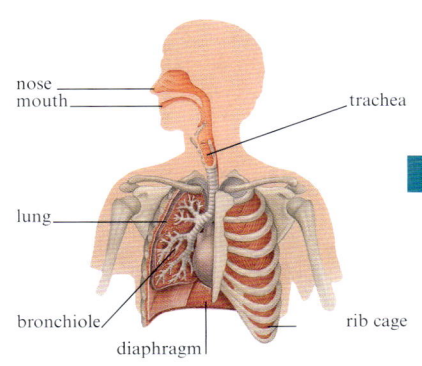

nose
mouth
trachea
lung
bronchiole
rib cage
diaphragm

respond *v.* **1** to give an answer. *I sent her a letter explaining my actions, but it seemed unlikely that she would respond.* **2** to do something as a reaction to something else. *Simon responded to the question I asked by laughing out loud.*

a b c d e f g h i j k l m n o p q **r** s t u v w x y z

A
B
C
D
E
F
G
H
I
J
K
L
M
N
O
P
Q
R
S
T
U
V
W
X
Y
Z

response *n.* a reply or reaction to something. *He gave no response to my question.*

responsible *adj.* **1** having a duty to make sure that something is done. *I am responsible for checking the equipment.* **2** being the cause of something. *Who was responsible for the accident?* **3** sensible and able to be trusted. **responsibility** *n.*

rest[1] *n.* a time of sleeping or relaxing after work or some other activity.

rest[2] *v.* **1** to stop work or another activity for a while. **2** to lean against something. *Her arm rested on the table.* **3** to stay fixed. *Her gaze rested on the money.* **4** to depend. *Our hopes rest on him.*

rest[3] *n.* **1** what is left after a part has gone. **2** all the other people or things.

restaurant *n.* a place where you can buy and eat meals.

restless *adj.* not able to stay still or calm. **restlessness** *n.*

restore *v.* **1** to repair something so that it looks as it was before. **2** to bring or give something back. *The police were called in to restore law and order in the city.* **restoration** *n.*

restrain *v.* to hold somebody back. *He had to be restrained from hitting the man.* **restraint** *n.*

restrict *v.* to limit. **restriction** *n.*

result *n.* **1** something that happens because of something that took place before. **2** a final score or mark in a game, contest, or examination.

resume *v.* to begin again.

resurrection *n.* coming back to life after death. **resurrect** *v.*

retail *v.* to sell items to the public. **retail** *n.*, **retailer** *n.*

retain *v.* to keep something. *Please retain your receipt.* **retention** *n.*

retaliate *v.* to do something bad to somebody in return for something bad that he or she has done to you. **retaliation** *n.*

retina *n.* (*pl.* retinas *or* retinae) the part at the back of your eye that sends a message of what is seen to the brain. See **eye**.

retire *v.* **1** to stop working when you reach a certain age. *Jack retired at the age of 65.* **2** to go away to somewhere quiet or private. *She retired to her room to read the newspaper.* **3** to stop in the middle of a sports game or race because of an injury. **retirement** *n.*

retreat *v.* to move back. **retreat** *n.*

retrieve *v.* to get back something that was lost. **retrieval** *n.*

return *v.* **1** to come or go back. **2** to give, put, or send something back. **return** *n.*

reunion *n.* a meeting of people who have not met for a long time.

rev[1] *n.* the unit for measuring the speed of an engine. It is an abbreviation of *revolutions per minute.*

rev[2] *v.* (revs, revving, revved) to make the engine of a motor vehicle run quickly, e.g. when starting it.

reveal *v.* to uncover or to make something known.

revel *v.* **revel in** to enjoy or get pleasure from something.

revelation *n.* the revealing or realization of something that was previously secret or hidden. *an amazing revelation.*

revenge *n.* harm done to somebody in return for something bad that he or she has done.

revenue *n.* **1** the money that a government receives from taxes. **2** the money that a company or organization receives.

reverse[1] *v.* **1** to go backward in a vehicle. *Mom reversed the car into the garage.* **2** to change something to the complete opposite of what it was. *reverse a decision.* **reversal** *n.*

reverse[2] *n.* **1** the opposite. **2** a gear in a vehicle that makes it go backward. **3** the back of a coin, medal, painting, or other object.

review *v.* **1** to write a report about a book or movie, giving your opinion of it. **2** to consider something again. *Let's review our decision.* **review** *n.*

revise *v.* **1** to go back over work that you have already done; to prepare for a test. **2** to make corrections or improvements to something. **revision** *n.*

revive *v.* **1** to bring back to consciousness, strength, or health. *He fainted, but the fresh air soon revived him.* **2** to bring back into use. *The theater group revived a play from the 1500s.* **revival** *n.*

revolt *v.* **1** to rebel against somebody or something. *The army revolted against the king.* **2** to make somebody feel horror or disgust. *When I look at him, it revolts me.* **revolt** *n.*

revolting *adj.* horrible and disgusting.

revolution *n.* **1** a violent attempt by the people of a country to change the way they are governed. **2** a great change in ideas or ways of doing things. *The Industrial Revolution changed the British landscape forever.* **3** a movement in a circle around a central point. **revolutionary** *adj.*

revolutionize *v.* to change something completely. *Computers have revolutionized the way we work.*

revolve *v.* to turn around in a circle. *The Earth revolves around the Sun.*

revolver *n.* a small gun.

reward *n.* a present that you receive in return for something good that you have done. **reward** *v.*

rheumatism (*room-u-tiz-um*) *n.* a medical condition that causes stiffness and pain in the joints.

rhinoceros *n.* (*pl.* rhinoceros *or* rhinoceroses) a large, thick-skinned animal with one or two horns on its

rhinoceros

nose, found in Africa and Asia. Often shortened to **rhino**.

rhombus *n.* (*pl.* rhombuses *or* rhombi) a flat shape like a diamond, with four equal sides but no right angles.

rhubarb *n.* a plant with long, red-skinned stalks that you can eat when cooked.

rhyme[1] (*rime*) *v.* (of two words) to end with the same sound. *"Pale" rhymes with "mail."*

rhyme[2] *n.* a short poem.

rhythm (*rith-um*) *n.* a regular, repeated pattern of sounds in music or poetry. **rhythmic** *adj.*, **rhythmical** *adj.*, **rhythmically** *adv.*

rib *n.* one of the curved bones of your chest, which protect your lungs.

ribbon *n.* **1** a long, thin piece of material used for decorating presents or tying back hair. **2** a thread of ink in a typewriter.

rice *n.* the edible seeds or grains of a type of grass grown on wet land in warm, tropical countries.

rich *adj.* **1** having a lot of money or valuable possessions. **2** having a lot of something. *Oranges are rich in vitamin C.* **3** (of food) containing a lot of butter, eggs, oil, or sugar. **4** very beautiful and expensive. *rich fabrics.*

riches *n. pl.* wealth.

rickety *adj.* unsteady; likely to collapse. *a rickety old chair.*

ricksha, rickshaw *n.* a small, two-wheeled carriage pulled by a person, commonly used in some Asian countries.

ricochet (*rik-o-shay*) *v.* to hit something and bounce off it at an angle.

rid *v.* (rids, ridding, rid) to free somebody or something from a harmful or annoying thing. *He rid the house of rats.* **get rid of** to remove or free yourself of something.

riddle *n.* a puzzling question that has a funny or clever answer.

ride[1] *v.* (riding, rode, ridden) to travel on a horse or bicycle. **rider** *n.*

ride[2] *n.* **1** a journey on a horse or bicycle. **2** a journey in a car or other vehicle.

ridge *n.* a raised line along the top of something, e.g. a narrow strip of land along the top of a mountain.

ridicule *v.* to make fun of something.

ridiculous *adj.* silly or outrageous enough to be laughed at.

rifle *n.* a long gun that you hold up to your shoulder when you fire it.

rift *n.* **1** a split or crack. **2** a serious disagreement between people that stops them from being friends.

rig[1] *n.* an oil rig.

rig[2] *v.* (rigs, rigging, rigged) to fit a ship or boat with ropes and sails. **rigging** *n.*

right[1] *adj.* **1** of, on, or toward the side of you that is toward the east when you are facing north. *I write with my right hand.* **2** correct. **3** morally correct and fair. **right** *adv.*

A
B
C
D
E
F
G
H
I
J
K
L
M
N
O
P
Q
R
S
T
U
V
W
X
Y
Z

right² *n.* **1** something you are allowed to do, especially by law. *Everyone has the right to a fair trial in court.* **2** that which is morally correct and fair. *the difference between right and wrong.* **3** the right side or direction. *Turn to the right.*

right³ *adv.* **1** exactly. *He stood right behind me.* **2** immediately. *I'll go right now.* **3** completely; all the way. *Go right to the end of the road.*

right angle *n.* an angle of 90 degrees, like any of the angles in a square. See **triangle**.

right away *adv.* immediately.

right-handed *adj.* using your right hand more easily than your left.

right-wing *adj.* in politics having traditional, conservative views.

rigid *adj.* **1** completely stiff. **2** very strict. **rigidity** *n.*

rim *n.* an edge of something rounded. *the rim of a cup.*

rind *n.* the hard outer layer of cheese or bacon or the peel of some fruits.

ring¹ *n.* **1** a band of metal worn on your finger. **2** a circle. **3** an enclosed space for boxing or wrestling matches or circus performances.

ring² *v.* (ringing, rang, rung) **1** to make the sound of a bell. **2** to press or shake a bell so that it makes a sound.

ringleader *n.* a person who leads others, especially into doing something wrong.

ringlet *n.* a long curl of hair.

rink *n.* **1** an area of ice for skating. **2** a smooth floor for roller skating.

rinse *v.* to wash in clean water.

riot *n.* a noisy, violent protest by a crowd of people. **riot** *v.*, **riotous** *adj.*

rip *v.* (rips, ripping, ripped) to tear roughly. **rip off** *(informal)* to cheat somebody.

ripe *adj.* ready to be picked or eaten. *ripe bananas.* **ripen** *v.*, **ripeness** *n.*

ripple *n.* a small wave on the surface of water. **ripple** *v.*

rise¹ *v.* (rising, rose, risen) **1** to move upward. **2** to increase. **3** to get up. *Melissa rose early to catch the train.*

rise² *n.* an increase. *price rises.*

risk *v.* **1** to take a chance that something bad might happen. **2** to put something in danger. *She risked her own life to save the old lady who had fallen into the river.* **risk** *n.*, **risky** *adj.*

ritual *n.* a set of actions that are always done in the same way in a particular situation, for example, as part of a religious ceremony.

rival *n.* a person or group of people that you are competing against. **rival** *v.*, **rivalry** *n.*

river *n.* a large stream of water that flows into a lake or into the sea.

road *n.* a wide path with a hard, level surface for vehicles, people, or animals to travel on.

roam *v.* to wander around.

roar *v.* to make a loud, deep sound like the noise that a lion makes. **roar** *n.*

roast *v.* to cook food in a hot oven.

rob *v.* (robs, robbing, robbed) to steal something from a person or place. **robber** *n.*, **robbery** *n.*

robe *n.* a long, loose piece of clothing.

robin *n.* a small bird with a red breast.

robot *n.* a machine that can perform some of the actions of a human being. **robotic** *adj.*

robust *adj.* strong and healthy.

rock¹ *n.* **1** the very hard material that forms part of the surface of Earth. **2** a large stone. **3** a type of music with a heavy beat and a simple tune.

rocket

rock² *v.* to sway gently backward and forward or from side to side.

rocket *n.* **1** a tube containing explosive material used for launching missiles and spacecraft. **2** a firework that shoots into the air and explodes.

rod *n.* a long, thin stick or bar.

rode *past of* ride.

rodent *n.* a mammal with large front teeth for gnawing, for example a rat, beaver, or squirrel.

rodeo *n.* (*pl.* rodeos) a contest in which cowboys show their skills at catching cattle and riding horses.

rogue *(rohg)* *n.* a person who is dishonest or mischievous.

role *n.* **1** the part played

by an actor. **2** the job done by somebody.

roll¹ *v.* **1** to move along by turning over and over like a ball or a wheel. *The coin rolled under the table.* **2** to turn something over and over to make a tube or ball. *We rolled up the carpet.* **3** to flatten something by moving a heavy object over it.

roll² *n.* **1** a tube made by turning something over and over on itself many times. *a roll of carpet.* **2** a small, round piece of bread made for one person. **3** a long, deep sound. *a roll of thunder.*

Rollerblades *(trademark) n. pl.* roller skates with the wheels in a single line.

roller coaster *n.* a ride in an amusement park consisting of a raised railway with steep slopes and sharp curves, which you ride on in small, open carriages.

roller skates *n. pl.* boots with wheels for skating on smooth, hard surfaces. **roller-skate** *v.*, **roller skating** *n.*

rolling pin *n.* a long tube used to roll out dough or pastry to flatten it.

$$\underset{1}{\text{I}} \quad \underset{2}{\text{II}} \quad \underset{3}{\text{III}} \quad \underset{4}{\text{IV}} \quad \underset{5}{\text{V}}$$

$$\underset{6}{\text{VI}} \quad \underset{7}{\text{VII}} \quad \underset{8}{\text{VIII}} \quad \underset{9}{\text{IX}} \quad \underset{10}{\text{X}}$$

$$\underset{50}{\text{L}} \quad \underset{60}{\text{LX}} \quad \underset{100}{\text{C}} \quad \underset{500}{\text{D}} \quad \underset{1,000}{\text{M}}$$

Roman numerals

ROM (*short for* read-only memory) a computer memory storing information that you can read but not change.

Roman Catholic *n.* a member of the part of the Christian Church that has the Pope as its leader. **Roman Catholic** *adj.*

romance *n.* **1** a relationship between people who are in love. **2** a story about love. **3** a feeling of excitement and adventure. **romantic** *adj.*

Roman numerals *n. pl.* the letters that are sometimes written to represent numbers, first used in ancient Rome.

roof *n.* a covering on top of a building or car.

rook *n.* **1** a large, black bird similar to a crow. **2** a chess piece, also called a castle.

room *n.* **1** a part of a building with its

rose

own walls, floor, and ceiling. **2** space.

roost *n.* a perch where a bird settles to sleep. **roost** *v.*

root *n.* **1** the part of a plant that grows under the ground. **2** the part of a hair or tooth that attaches it to the rest of the body. **3** the cause of something. *I think I've discovered the root of the problem.*

rope *n.* thick, strong cord, made by twisting strands together.

rose¹ *past of* rise.

rose² *n.* **1** a pleasant-smelling garden flower that grows on a bush with thorns. **2** a deep pink color.

rosemary *n.* a strong-smelling evergreen shrub that is used in cooking.

Rosh Hashana *n.* the Jewish New Year.

rosy *adj.* (rosier, rosiest) **1** pink. *rosy cheeks.* **2** bright; hopeful. *The future looks rosy.*

rot *v.* (rots, rotting, rotted) to go off; to decay. **rot** *n.*

rota *n.* (*pl.* rotas) a list showing when duties are to be done and the people to do them.

rotary *adj.* turning round like a wheel.

rotate *v.* **1** to turn like a wheel. **2** to go through a repeating series of changes. **rotation** *n.*

rotor *n.* a blade that spins around fast on the top of a helicopter. See **helicopter**.

rotten *adj.* **1** decayed or having gone bad. *rotten eggs.* **2** *(informal)* very bad, unpleasant. *rotten luck.*

A
B
C
D
E
F
G
H
I
J
K
L
M
N
O
P
Q
R
S
T
U
V
W
X
Y
Z

rough (*rhymes with* cuff) *adj.* **1** bumpy; not smooth or even. *rough ground.* **2** stormy; not gentle or calm. *rough seas.* **3** approximate; not meant to be exact. *It wasn't meant to be accurate; it was only a rough estimate.*

round[1] *adj.* shaped like a circle or a ball.

round[2] *n.* **1** one stage of a contest. *Our team was knocked out in the first round of the soccer tournament.* **2** a series of calls or deliveries. *a mailman's round.* **3** a burst of cheering or shooting. *a round of applause.* **4** a song for two or more singers in which each singer begins at a different time.

roundabout *n.* a moving circular platform with toy horses, animals, or cars for children to ride on at a fair.

rounded *adj.* curved.

rounders *n.* a game for two teams played with a bat and ball.

rouse *v.* **1** to wake somebody up. **2** to stir up or excite something. *Ruby's interest was roused by the colorful cover of the travel magazine.*

route *(root* or *rowt)* *n.* the road or path that you follow in order to get somewhere.

routine *(roo-**teen**)* *n.* a regular, set way of doing things. *It was his routine to go for a jog before work.*

row[1] (*rhymes with* go) *n.* a line. *a row of houses.*

row[2] (*rhymes with* go) *v.* to use oars to make a boat move through water.

rowdy *adj.* (rowdier, rowdiest) noisy and rough. *a rowdy party.*

royal *adj.* to do with a king or queen. **royalty** *n.*

rub *v.* (rubs, rubbing, rubbed) to move one thing backward and forward against another thing while pressing. *The neighbor's cat rubbed its head rhythmically against my leg.* **rub out** to remove pencil or chalk marks with an eraser.

rubber *n.* **1** a strong, elastic, waterproof material that is made from the sap of a tropical plant from chemicals, used for making tires and other things. **rubbery** *adj.*

rubber

rubbish *n.* **1** things that you throw away because you do not want them anymore; garbage; trash. **2** nonsense. *Stop talking rubbish!*

rubble *n.* broken bricks and stones from ruined or demolished buildings.

ruby *n.* a red precious stone. **ruby** *adj.*

rucksack *n.* a type of bag that you carry on your back by means of straps over the shoulders; backpack; knapsack.

rudder *n.* a flat, upright piece of wood, metal, or fiberglass at the back of a boat or aircraft that is used for steering.

ruddy *adj.* **1** having a healthy, glowing complexion. **2** reddish.

rude *adj.* bad-mannered; not polite. **rudeness** *n.*

ruffle *v.* **1** to make hair or feathers untidy. *The wind ruffled her hair.* **2** (of a bird) to erect its feathers, usually in anger or as a display.

rug *n.* a piece of thick, woolen material that covers part of a floor.

rugby *n.* a game played with an oval ball that can be kicked, carried, or passed from hand to hand.

rugged *(**rug**-id)* *adj.* **1** rough and rocky. *The Alps are a rugged range of mountains.* **2** strong and tough. *the movie's rugged hero.* **3** having features that are strongly marked and furrowed. *My grandfather has a very rugged face.*

ruin[1] *v.* **1** to spoil something completely. **2** to make somebody lose all of his or her money.

ruin[2] *n.* **1** the complete loss of all your money. *The company is facing ruin.* **2** **ruins** what is left of a building after it has been destroyed.

rule[1] *n.* **1** a statement of what you must or must not do. *It is against the rules to smoke in the building.* **2** government. *This city was once under foreign rule.* **as a rule** usually.

rule[2] *v.* **1** to govern a country. *William the Conqueror ruled England after 1066.* **2** to decide something. *The judge ruled that the new evidence should be heard in court.*

ruler *n.* **1** a long, straight piece of plastic, wood, or metal that is used for drawing straight lines or for measuring things. **2** a person who rules or governs a country.

ruling *n.* an official decision.

rum *n.* an alcoholic drink made from sugar cane.

rumble *v.* to make a deep sound like thunder. **rumble** *n.*

rummage *v.* to turn things over while searching for something. *She rummaged through the drawers in search of her passport.*

rumor *n.* a story that is passed around but that may not be true. *I heard a rumor that the government was preparing to remove our funding.*

rump *n.* the back part of an animal.

run[1] *v.* (runs, running, ran, run) **1** to move fast on your legs. **2** to travel. *This bus runs every day of the week except for Sunday.* **3** to organize or manage something. *Jane runs the local women's soccer team.* **4** to flow. *Tears ran down his cheeks.* **5** to work or function. *Trains run on tracks.* **6** to continue; to go on. *The movie runs for more than two and a half hours.* **run out of** to have no more of something. *We ran out of milk.* **run over** to knock down or drive over a person or an animal in a vehicle.

run[2] *n.* **1** an act of running. **2** a point scored in baseball or cricket. **3** an enclosed area in which animals or birds are kept. *a chicken run.*

rung[1] *past of* ring.

rung[2] *n.* a step of a ladder.

runner *n.* a person who runs.

runner-up *n.* (*pl.* runners-up) the person or team that comes second in a competition or race.

runny *adj.* (runnier, runniest) liquid or watery. *The eggs looked undercooked and runny.*

runway *n.* (*pl.* runways) a strip of land where an aircraft takes off and lands.

rural *adj.* to do with the countryside.

rush[1] *v.* to move quickly; to hurry. **rush** *n.*

rush[2] *n.* a tall grass that grows close to water.

runway

rust *n.* the reddish-brown coating that forms on iron and some other metals when they get wet. **rust** *v.*, **rusty** *adj.*

rustle *v.* to make a soft, whispering or crackling sound, like the sound of dry leaves. **2** to steal cattle or horses. **rustle** *n.*

rut *n.* **1** a deep track made by a wheel. **2** a set and boring way of life.

ruthless *adj.* cruel; without pity.

rye *n.* a cereal that produces a grain used for making bread and whiskey.

a b c d e f g h i j k l m n o p q **r** s t u v w x y z

Sabbath *n.* the day of the week that is set aside for religious worship and rest.

saber *(say-ber) n.* a sword with a curved blade.

sabotage *(sab-o-tahj) v.* to damage something on purpose. **sabotage** *n.*

sachet *(sash-ay) n.* a small, sealed packet containing a powder or liquid. *a sachet of shampoo.*

sack¹ *n.* a large bag made out of strong cloth, paper, or plastic.

sacred *(say-krid) adj.* holy.

sacrifice *v.* **1** to offer something precious to a god, especially an animal or person that has been killed for this purpose. **2** to give something up for the benefit of another person or to gain something more important. *He sacrificed his job for the sake of his son.* **sacrifice** *n.*, **sacrificial** *adj.*

sad *adj.* (sadder, saddest) unhappy. **sadden** *v.*, **sadness** *n.*

saddle¹ *n.* a seat for the rider of a horse or a bicycle.

saddle² *v.* to put a saddle on a horse.

safari *(sa-far-ee) n.* an expedition, usually in a hot country, at one time for hunting wild animals but today for watching and photographing them. *The Johnsons' dream was to go on safari in Africa to see the elephants.*

safari

safe¹ *adj.* **1** protected from danger. **2** offering protection; not dangerous. **safety** *n.*

safe² *n.* a strong box where money and valuables can be locked away safely.

safeguard *v.* to protect something.

safety pin *n.* a curved pin with a part that covers its point when it is closed.

sag *v.* (sags, sagging, sagged) to droop or hang down. *The bed sags in the middle.*

sage *n.* an herb used in cooking.

said *past of* say.

sail¹ *n.* **1** a sheet of cloth against which wind blows to drive a ship or boat through water. **2** the arm of a windmill.

sail² *v.* **1** to travel in a ship or boat. **2** (of a ship) to start a voyage. *The ferry sails at 3:00 P.M.* **sailing** *n.*

sailor *n.* a member of a ship's crew.

saint *n.* **1** a title given by the Christian Church to a very good or holy person after his or her death. **2** a very good, kind person. **saintly** *adj.*

sake *n.* **for the sake of 1** in order to help somebody or something. *They stayed together for the sake of their children.* **2** in order to get something. *For the sake of peace, he agreed.*

salad *n.* a mixture of cold, raw vegetables, e.g. tomatoes and lettuce.

salamander *n.* a small amphibian similar to a lizard.

salami *n.* a type of spicy sausage, eaten cold.

salary *n.* a regular payment, usually made once a month, to somebody for the work that he or she does.

sale *n.* **1** the selling of something. **2** a time when a store sells items cheaper than usual.

saliva *(sa-lie-va) n.* the liquid in your mouth.

salmon *(sam-un) n.* (*pl.* salmon or salmons) a large, edible fish with pink flesh.

salt *n.* **1** a white substance found under the ground and in sea water, used for flavoring food. **2** any chemical compound formed from a metal and an acid. **salty** *adj.*

salute *v.* to raise your hand to your forehead as a sign of respect, as soldiers do. **salute** *n.*

salvage *v.* to save something from loss or destruction. *He salvaged some of his possessions from the fire.*

salvation *n.* the saving of somebody or something.

same *adj.* exactly alike; not different.

sample[1] *n.* a part taken from something to show what the rest of it is like. *The doctor took a blood sample.*

sample[2] *v.* to try something to see if you like it. *He sampled the food.*

samurai (*sam-uh-rye*) *n.* (*pl.* samurai or samurais) (*historical*) a traditional Japanese warrior.

samurai warrior

sanction[1] *v.* to allow or authorize something, often someone's behavior.

sanction[2] *n.* **1** permission or approval. **2 sanctions** measures taken by a country to prevent trade with another country that is not obeying international law.

sanctuary *n.* **1** a sacred place. **2** a place where somebody is safe from people who want to attack or arrest him or her. **3** place where wild birds or animals are protected.

sand *n.* tiny grains of crushed rock or shells found on beaches and in deserts. **sandy** *adj.*

sandal *n.* a type of open shoe with straps to attach it to your foot.

sandwich *n.* two slices of bread with food in between them.

sane *adj.* having a healthy mind. **sanity** *n.*

sang *past of* sing.

sanitation *n.* systems for protecting people's health such as providing clean water and sewage disposal.

sank *past of* sink.

sap[1] *n.* the juice in the stems of plants.

sap[2] *v.* (saps, sapping, sapped) to weaken something gradually. *The long walk sapped our strength.*

sapling *n.* a young tree.

sapphire *n.* a blue precious stone.

sarcasm *n.* remarks that mean the opposite of what they seem to mean, often used to criticize somebody or hurt that person's feelings. **sarcastic** *adj.*, **sarcastically** *adv.*

sardine *n.* a small edible fish like a herring, often sold in tins.

sari (*sah-ree*) *n.* a long piece of ornate material, often worn by Indian women.

sash *n.* a wide band of material worn around the waist or over one shoulder.

sat *past of* sit.

satchel *n.* a bag for carrying school books, hung from a strap over your shoulder.

satellite *n.* **1** a moon or other natural object orbiting a planet. **2** a manufactured object fired into space to orbit Earth.

satellite dish *n.* a dish-shaped object that receives television broadcasts sent by satellite (**satellite television**).

satire *n.* a form of comedy that makes fun of people, groups, or ideas to show how stupid or bad they are. **satirical** *adj.*

satisfactory *adj.* good enough. **satisfactorily** *adv.*

satisfy *v.* (satisfies, satisfying, satisfied) to give somebody what they need or want so that person is pleased. **satisfaction** *n.*

saturate *v.* to make something so wet that no more liquid can be absorbed. **saturation** *n.*

Saturday *n.* the seventh day of the week.

sauce *n.* a thick liquid served with food.

saucepan *n.* a deep, metal cooking pot with a handle and sometimes a lid.

saucer *n.* a small, curved plate on which a cup stands.

sauna (*saw-na*) *n.* a room filled with steam, where you sit and sweat.

saunter *v.* to stroll.

sausage *n.* a food made of ground meat stuffed into a tube of edible skin.

savage[1] *adj.* **1** wild and fierce. *a savage beast.* **2** extremely violent.

savage[2] *v.* to attack somebody violently. *The child was savaged by a large dog.*

savanna *n.* a grassy plain with only a few trees in hot countries. (*can also be spelled* savannah.)

save *v.* **1** to rescue from danger. **2** to keep money to use in the future. **3** not to waste something. *We should all save electricity.* **4** in soccer to stop a goal from the opposing team. **save** *n.*

a
b
c
d
e
f
g
h
i
j
k
l
m
n
o
p
q
r
s
t
u
v
w
x
y
z

171

A B C D E F G H I J K L M N O P Q R S T U V W X Y Z

savings *n. pl.* money that you have saved. *I used my savings to pay for a vacation for my family.*

savory *adj.* salty and spicy; not sweet.

saw[1] *past of* see.

saw[2] *n.* a tool with sharp teeth used for cutting wood.

saw[3] *v.* (sawing, sawed, sawn) to cut something with a saw.

sawdust *n.* the dust that you get when you saw wood.

saxophone *n.* a curved metal musical instrument of the woodwind group, played by blowing, often used to play jazz. **saxophonist** *n.*

say *v.* (saying, said)
1 to speak words.
2 to give information. *The clock says that it's 2:30.*

saying *n.* a well-known phrase or proverb.

scab *n.* a hard, dry covering that forms over a wound as it heals.

saxophone

scaffolding *n.* a structure of poles and planks used when a building is being put up or repaired.

scald *v.* to burn with hot liquid or steam.

scale[1] *n.* **1** one of the thin, hard pieces of skin that cover the bodies of fish and reptiles. **2** a series of numbers or amounts for measuring something. *The company salary scale starts at $20,000.* **3** a group of musical notes going up or down in order. **4** the measurements on a map compared with the real size of the area shown. **5** an instrument for weighing people or things.

scale[2] *v.* to climb up something. *He scaled the wall quickly.*

scalene *n.* a triangle with three sides of different lengths. See **triangle**.

scalp *n.* the skin and hair on your head.

scalpel *n.* a small knife used by surgeons.

scamper *v.* to run around playfully.

scampi *n. pl.* shrimp that have been boiled or sautéed and served with garlic and butter sauce.

scan *v.* (scans, scanning, scanned)
1 to examine something carefully. *We scanned the horizon for any sign of a ship.*
2 to look at something quickly but not in detail. *He scanned the newspaper for news of the accident.* **3** to pass a beam of light or x-rays over something in order to examine it. **4** to convert text or an image into digital form so that it can be read by a computer. **scan** *n.*, **scanner** *n.*

scandal *n.* something that a lot of people think is very shocking or disgraceful. **scandalous** *adj.*

scapegoat *n.* a person who gets all the blame for the mistakes of others.

scar *n.* the mark left on skin by a wound after it has healed. **scar** *v.*

scarce *adj.* in short supply; not enough. *Water is scarce because of the drought.* **scarcity** *n.*

scarcely *adv.* only just; almost not. *There's scarcely any hot water left.*

scare *v.* to frighten. **scare** *n.*, **scary** *adj.*

scarecrow *n.* a figure of a person, dressed in old clothes, used to frighten birds away from crops.

scarf *n.* (*pl.* scarves *or* scarfs) a strip or square of material that you wear around your neck or head.

scarlet *n.* bright red. **scarlet** *adj.*

scatter *v.* **1** to throw something so that it is spread over a wide area. *Anthony scattered crumbs on the bird table.* **2** to go off in different directions.

scavenge *v.* to search among garbage, collecting food or other things for your own use. **scavenger** *n.*

scene *(seen)* n. **1** the place where an event happens. *the scene of the crime.* **2** one part of a play or movie that is set in one place. **3** a view or painting. *She paints scenes of life in the country.* **4** a public show of anger. *Please don't make such a scene!*

scenery *(seen-er-ree)* n. **1** the natural features of a place such as hills, fields, and trees. **2** the painted background of a theater stage.

scenic *(see-nic)* adj. surrounded by beautiful scenery.

scent *(sent)* n. **1** a pleasant smell. **2** the trail of a smell, used to track an animal. *The dog picked up the rabbit's scent.* **3** a pleasant-smelling liquid that you put on your skin; perfume.

scent

schedule *(sked-jool)* *n.* the time set for doing something.

scheme[1] *(skeem)* *n.* a plan.

scheme[2] *v.* to plan something secretly; to plot.

scholar *n.* **1** a person who has studied a subject in depth. **2** a person who has won a scholarship. **scholarly** *adj.*

scholarship *n.* money given to a student who has done well, to enable him or her to go to a school or college.

school *n.* **1** a place where children go to be taught. **2** a place where you can be taught a particular skill. *a riding school.* **3** a group of fish or other sea creatures swimming together; a shoal.

schooner *n.* a fast sailing ship.

science *n.* knowledge gained by studying, observing, and experimenting. *Biology, chemistry, and physics are all branches of science.* **scientific** *adj.,* **scientifically** *adv.*

science fiction *n.* stories about future life on Earth or space travel.

scientist *n.* a person who studies science.

scissors *n. pl.* a cutting tool with two blades that are connected.

scoff *v.* to mock something. *John scoffed at my idea.*

scold *v.* to tell somebody off.

scone *(skone)* *n.* a flat, round cake, usually eaten with butter.

scoop[1] *n.* **1** a tool like a large spoon, used for serving food. **2** an important news story that one newspaper reports before its rivals.

scoop[2] *v.* to lift something with a scoop or with your hands. *I scooped the ice cream.*

scooter *n.* **1** a child's toy made of a board with two wheels and a handlebar, which is moved by pushing one foot against the ground. **2** a small motorcycle.

scope *n.* **1** the opportunity or room to do something. *There is scope in your work for improvement.* **2** a range; how far something extends. *Foreign words are beyond the scope of this dictionary.*

scorch *v.* to burn something slightly.

score[1] *n.* **1** the number of points or goals gained in a game. **2** a written piece of music. **3** *(old-fashioned)* twenty.

score[2] *v.* **1** to gain points or goals in a game. **2** to make a cut or scratch on a surface.

scorn *n.* a very low opinion of somebody or something; contempt. *She dismissed my suggestion with scorn.* **scorn** *v.,* **scornful** *adj.,* **scornfully** *adv.*

scorpion *n.* an animal of the spider family, with a poisonous sting in its curved tail.

scour *v.* **1** to clean something by rubbing it hard. **2** to search a place thoroughly for something.

scorpion

scout *n.* a person who is sent ahead to find out about the enemy.

scowl *n.* to give an angry look. **scowl** *n.*

scramble *v.* **1** to climb or crawl up something using your hands as well as your feet. *We scrambled to the top of the hill.* **2** to struggle to get hold of something. *They all scrambled for the ball.* **3** to jumble up a message.

scrambled eggs *n. pl.* eggs mixed with milk and cooked in butter.

scrap[1] *n.* **1** a small piece of something. *She wrote a note on a scrap of paper.* **2** old cars or other metal objects that have been thrown away. **3** *(informal)* a fight.

scrap[2] *v.* (scraps, scrapping, scrapped) to get rid of something.

scrapbook *n.* a blank book where you stick pictures, post cards, or other things that interest you.

scrape *v.* **1** to rub against something sharp or rough. *Dad scraped his car on the wall.* **2** to clean or peel by rubbing with something sharp. *We scraped the paint off the door.* **scrape through** to only just manage to succeed. *I scraped through the exam.*

scratch[1] *v.* **1** to mark or hurt by moving something sharp across a surface. **2** to rub your skin with your fingernails to stop it from itching.

scratch[2] *n.* a mark made by scratching. **up to scratch** to be good enough. **start from scratch** to start from the very beginning.

scrawl *v.* to write or draw untidily or quickly. **scrawl** *n.*

scream *v.* to shout or cry out in a loud, high-pitched voice. **scream** *n.*

screech *v.* to make a harsh, high-pitched sound. **screech** *n.*

screen[1] *n.* **1** the part of a television or computer on which pictures or data appear. **2** a flat, covered framework used especially to hide or protect something. *She undressed behind a screen so that no one would see her.* **3** a flat, white surface on which movies are shown.

screen[2] *v.* **1** to protect or shelter something with a screen. **2** to test somebody to find out if he or she has a disease. **3** to show a movie on a screen.

screw[1] *n.* a nail with a spiral groove, called the thread, which is driven into something by a twisting motion.

screw[2] *v.* **1** to fasten something with a screw. **2** to fix a lid in place with a twisting action. **screw up** to twist paper or cloth into a tight ball.

screwdriver *n.* a tool for putting screws into surfaces.

scribble *v.* **1** to make untidy or meaningless marks with a pen or pencil. **2** to write something quickly and carelessly. **scribble** *n.*

script *n.* **1** the written version of a play, movie, or broadcast. **2** a system of writing; an alphabet.

scripture *n.* religious writing.

scroll[1] *n.* a roll of paper with writing or pictures on it.

scroll[2] *v.* to move text on a computer screen up or down to see different parts of it.

scroll

scrounge *v.* *(informal)* to get what you want by begging for it from somebody.

scrub[1] *v.* (scrubs, scrubbing, scrubbed) to clean something by rubbing it hard, especially with a wet brush.

scrub[2] *n.* a stunted tree or bush.

scruff *n.* the back of the neck.

scruffy *adj.* (scruffier, scruffiest) untidy. **scruffily** *adv.*

scuba diving *n.* diving using special breathing apparatus. **scuba diver** *n.*

scuffle *n.* a small fight. **scuffle** *v.*

scuba diver

air tank
wetsuit
respirator
underwater camera
coral reef

sculptor *n.* a person who is skilled in making statues or carvings.

sculpture *n.* **1** the art of modeling or carving figures or shapes. **2** a figure or shape carved or modeled out of wood, stone, or clay. **sculpt** *v.*

scum *n.* dirty foam found on the surface of a liquid.

scurry *v.* (scurries, scurrying, scurried) to run with short, quick steps. *The mouse scurried into its hole.*

scythe *(sythe) n.* a large tool with a curved blade for cutting grass or grain.

sea *n.* a large area of salt water.

sea anemone *n.* a small, plantlike sea creature usually found living on rocks and seaweed.

seagull *n.* a large gray or white sea bird.

seahorse *n.* a small fish with a head shaped like a horse's head.

seal[1] *n.* a furry animal, with flippers for swimming, that lives on land and sea.

seal² *n.* **1** a piece of wax with a design stamped into it, attached to a document to show that it is legal. **2** something that joins tightly or closes up completely. *There is a rubber seal running around the lid of the jar.*

seal³ *v.* to close something completely.

sea lion *n.* a large type of seal, found mostly in the Pacific Ocean.

seam *n.* **1** the line where two pieces of material are sewn together. **2** a layer of coal or other mineral, found underground.

search *v.* to look carefully in order to find something. **search** *n.*

seashell *n.* the hard outer covering of some sea creatures.

seashore *n.* the beach.

seaside *n.* a place beside the sea.

season¹ *n.* **1** one of the four divisions of the year. *The four seasons are spring, summer, fall, and winter.* **2** the usual time when something takes place. *the mating season.* **seasonal** *adj.*

season² *v.* to add salt, pepper, herbs, or spices to food. **seasoning** *n.*

season ticket *n.* a ticket that can be used as many times as you like for a certain period of time.

seat¹ *n.* something that you can sit on.

seat² *v.* **1** to give somebody a seat. **2** to have seats for a certain number of people. *This table seats eight.*

seat belt *n.* a belt that is attached to a seat in a car to prevent the passenger from being thrown out in an accident.

sea urchin *n.* a small sea creature with spines on its shell.

seaweed *n.* a plant that grows in the sea.

secluded *adj.* quiet and private. *a secluded cottage on the cliff top.* **seclusion** *n.*

second¹ *adj., adv.* next after the first. **second** *n.,* **secondly** *adv.*

second² *n.* one sixtieth of a minute.

second³ *v.* to support somebody's idea or proposal at a meeting.

secondary *adj.* less important.

secondhand *adj.* already used by somebody else; not new.

secret¹ *(see-krit) adj.* not known by many people. **secrecy** *n.*

secret² *n.* a piece of information that is, or must be, kept hidden.

secret agent *n.* a spy.

secretary *n.* **1** a person whose job is to type letters, keep records, and make business arrangements for other people.

secrete *(si-kreet) v.* to produce a liquid. *Your skin secretes sweat when you feel hot.* **secretion** *n.*

secretive *adj.* liking to keep things secret.

sect *n.* a group of people with strong, especially religious, beliefs that have separated from a larger group.

section *n.* a part of something.

secure¹ *adj.* **1** safe; free from danger. **2** firmly attached. **security** *n.*

secure² *v.* **1** to make something safe. **2** to fasten something.

see *v.* (seeing, saw, seen) **1** to notice or look at something with your eyes. **2** to understand. *I see what you mean.* **3** to find out. *I'll see what's going on.* **4** to make sure. *See that he eats his lunch.* **see through** not to be deceived by a trick or a lie. **see to** to deal with, to take care of something.

seed *n.* the part of a plant or tree from which a new plant may grow.

seedling *n.* a young plant that has just begun to grow from a seed.

seek *v.* (seeking, sought) to try to find something or someone.

seem *v.* to appear to be. *She seemed nice.*

seep *v.* to flow slowly. *Blood seeped through his bandage.*

seesaw *n.* a plank balanced on a central support; when a person sits on one end, it goes down as the other end goes up.

seethe *v.* **1** (of a liquid) to boil or bubble. **2** to be very angry.

segment *n.* a part of something. *Divide the orange into segments.*

segregate *v.* to keep one group of people away from other groups. **segregation** *n.*

seize *(seeze) v.* to take something suddenly or by force. **seize up** to become stuck. **seizure** *n.*

circle divided into eight equal segments

a
b
c
d
e
f
g
h
i
j
k
l
m
n
o
p
q
r
s
t
u
v
w
x
y
z

seldom *adv.* not often; rarely.

select *v.* to choose from a number of things. **selection** *n.*

selective *adj.* choosing carefully.

self *n.* (*pl.* selves) your own personality and nature.

self-confident *adj.* believing in your own abilities. **self-confidence** *n.*

self-conscious *adj.* embarrassed or worried about what other people think of you.

self-defense *n.* the act of protecting yourself against attacks.

selfish *adj.* only caring about yourself, rather than about other people. **selfishness** *n.*

self-service *adj.* referring to a place where customers serve themselves. *a self-service restaurant.*

self-sufficient *adj.* needing no help or support from anybody else.

sell *v.* (selling, sold) to give something in exchange for money. **sell out** to sell all of something.

selves *plural of* self.

semaphore *n.* a way of signaling using your arms or flags to form different positions for each letter.

semi- *prefix* half. *semicircle.*

semicircle *n.* half of a circle.

semicolon *n.* a punctuation mark (;) that shows a pause within a sentence.

semifinal *n.* one of the two games or matches of a contest to decide who will participate in the final.

send *v.* (sending, sent) to make somebody or something go somewhere. *Send me a post card.* **send for** to ask somebody to come.

senile *adj.* having the mental weaknesses and diseases associated with old age. **senility** *n.*

senior *adj.* **1** older. **2** higher in rank. **3** a person in the final year of high school or college. **seniority** *n.*

sensation *n.* **1** a feeling. *I've got a tingling sensation in my toes.* **2** a state of great excitement. *The news of the scandal caused a great sensation.*

sensational *adj.* causing great excitement or interest.

sense[1] *n.* **1** one of the ways that your body has of telling you what is going on around you. The senses are sight, hearing, touch, smell, and taste. **2** meaning. *The word "bat" has more*

than one sense. **3** the ability to feel or understand something. *She has no sense of direction.* **4** the ability to think carefully about something and do the right thing. *I'm glad you had the sense to go to the doctor.*

sense[2] *v.* to feel something. *He sensed that she was angry with him.*

senseless *adj.* **1** stupid and pointless. *a senseless act.* **2** unconscious.

sensible *adj.* **1** able to behave in an intelligent way and not do stupid things. **2** practical. *sensible shoes.* **sensibly** *adv.*

sensitive *adj.* **1** easily affected by something or easily damaged. *sensitive*

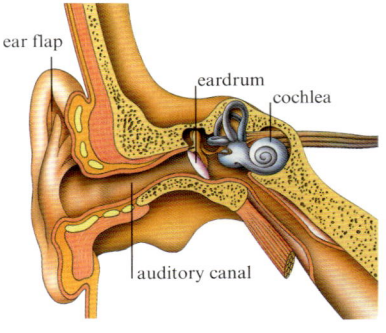

hearing, one of the five senses

ear flap

eardrum

cochlea

auditory canal

skin. **2** reacting to something. *Photographic film is sensitive to light.* **3** easily feeling hurt or offended. **sensitivity** *n.*

sensor *n.* a device that detects and measures light, heat, or pressure.

sent *past of* send.

sentence[1] *n.* **1** a group of words that together make a complete statement. **2** a punishment that is given to a criminal by a law court.

sentence[2] *v.* to announce in a law court the punishment that a criminal will receive.

sentimental *adj.* **1** to do with the emotions. *This ring has sentimental value.* **2** showing or causing too much emotion. *I didn't like the movie— I thought it was sentimental.* **sentimentality** *n.,* **sentimentally** *adv.*

sentry *n.* a soldier who stands outside a building in order to guard it.

separate[1] (*sep-er-ut*) *adj.* divided; not

separate² *(sep-er-ate)* *v.* **1** to set or keep apart. *Separate the clean clothes from the dirty ones.* **2** to go in different directions. *We separated at the intersection.* **3** to live apart by choice. *His parents separated.* **separation** *n.*

September *n.* the ninth month of the year.

septic *adj.* when a wound becomes infected with germs.

sequel *n.* a story that is a continuation of an earlier story.

sequence *n.* a series of things coming after each other in a particular order.

serene *adj.* calm; peaceful. **serenity** *n.*

serf *n.* *(historical)* a medieval slave who was bought and sold with the land on which he or she worked. **serfdom** *n.*

sergeant *(sar-junt)* *n.* an officer in the armed forces or in the police force.

serial *n.* a story told in parts instead of all at once. *a television serial.*

serial number *n.* a number identifying one in a series of things that were produced.

series *n.* *(pl.* series*)* **1** a number of similar things coming one after the other. *a series of accidents.* **2** a set of television or radio programs.

serious *adj.* **1** solemn and thoughtful; not laughing or joking. **2** important. **3** very bad or worrying.

sermon *n.* a serious talk given during a religious service.

serpent *n.* a snake.

serrated *adj.* having notches or teeth along one edge, like a saw.

servant *n.* a person who works in somebody else's home, doing cooking, cleaning, and other jobs.

serve *v.* **1** to bring food to somebody at the table. **2** to help a customer in a store. **3** to be able to be used as something. *The cave served as a shelter.* **4** to work for somebody. *He*

medieval servant and master

served in the army for ten years. **5** in tennis and other games to throw the ball up and hit it with the racket to start a game.

service *n.* **1** the process of serving customers in a restaurant or store. **2** help or work that you do for somebody. **3** a business or organization that provides something for the public. *the ambulance service.* **4** a religious ceremony. **5 services** the armed forces.

session *n.* **1** a time spent doing a particular activity. *an aerobics session.* **2** a meeting of a court or council.

set¹ *n.* **1** a group of things that belong together. *a set of tools.* **2** the scenery for a play or movie. **3** a group of six or more games that form part of a match in tennis.

set² *v.* (sets, setting, set) **1** to put. *He set the tray down on the table.* **2** to give somebody a task to do. *Our teacher has set us some difficult questions for homework.* **3** to become firm and solid. *Has the jelly set yet?* **4** to adjust. *I'll set my alarm for 6:30.* **5** to arrange or fix. *Please set the table for lunch.* **6** (of the Sun) to go down below the horizon. **set off, set out** to start a journey.

settee *n.* a long, wooden bench.

setting *n.* a place where something takes place. *The castle is the perfect setting for a ghost story.*

settle *v.* **1** to go to live somewhere. *My uncle settled in Canada.* **2** to make yourself comfortable. *I settled in the armchair.* **3** to decide or sort something out. *settle an argument.* **4** to come to rest. *Dust had settled on the books.* **5** to pay a bill. **settle in** to become used to new surroundings. **settler** *n.*

settlement *n.* **1** an agreement. *a pay settlement.* **2** a small community.

sever *v.* to cut or break something off.

several *adj.* more than a few, but not many. **several** *pron.*

severe *adj.* **1** very bad; serious. *a severe drought.* **2** strict or harsh. *a severe punishment.* **severity** *n.*

sew *v.* (sewing, sewed, sewn) to use a needle and thread to connect pieces of cloth together or attach something to cloth.

sewage *(soo-wij)* *n.* dirty water and waste matter that is carried away in sewers.

sewer (*soo-wer*) *n.* an underground pipe for carrying away dirty water and waste matter from drains.

sex *n.* **1** the fact of being male or female. **2** sexual intercourse. **sexual** *adj.*, **sexually** *adv.*

sexist *n.* discriminating against one sex, usually women. **sexism** *n.*

sexual intercourse *n.* the physical act between a man and a woman in which the man's penis is inserted into the woman's vagina.

shabby *adj.* (shabbier, shabbiest) old and worn out. *shabby clothes.* **shabbily** *adv.*, **shabbiness** *n.*

shack *n.* a roughly built hut.

shade¹ *n.* **1** a darker area caused by blocking light. *The dog sat in the cool shade.* **2** something that protects against light or heat. *a lampshade.* **3** a color, especially how dark or light it is. *a darker shade of green.* **shady** *adj.*

shade² *v.* **1** to shelter from the Sun or light. **2** to make a part of a drawing darker by filling it in. **shading** *n.*

shadow¹ *n.* a dark shape caused by a person or thing blocking the light.

shadow² *v.* to follow somebody closely.

shaft *n.* **1** the long, straight part or handle of a tool or weapon. **2** a revolving rod that turns a machine or an engine. **3** a deep, narrow hole leading to a mine. **4** a ray of light.

shaggy *adj.* (shaggier, shaggiest) covered with thick, rough hair or fur.

shake *v.* (shaking, shook, shaken) to move vigorously from side to side or up and down. *I was shaking with fear. Shake the bottle.* **shake** *n.*, **shaky** *adj.*

shallow *adj.* going down a short way; not deep. *The river is shallow here.*

shame *n.* **1** a feeling of sadness, guilt, and regret at something bad or stupid that you have done. **2** a pity. *What a shame you can't come to our party.*

shampoo *n.* liquid soap for washing your hair. **shampoo** *v.*

shamrock *n.* a green plant like a clover with three leaves on each stem, used as the national symbol of Ireland.

shanty *n.* a roughly built hut.

shape¹ *n.* **1** the form or outline of something. **2** condition. *He's in good shape because he exercises every day.*

shape² *v.* **1** to give a certain shape to

something. **2** to develop. *Our plans are shaping up well.*

share¹ *v.* to divide something among two or more people.

share² *n.* **1** one part of something that is divided among several people. **2** one of the parts into which ownership of a company can be divided and which people can buy.

shark *n.* a sea fish with a skeleton made from cartilage and a pointed fin on its back. Sharks vary greatly in size and come in a wide range, including hammerhead, great white, and nurse.

sharp¹ *adj.* **1** having an edge or point that cuts things easily. **2** sudden; quick. *a sharp bend in the road.* **3** clear and easy to see. *These photos are very sharp.* **4** sour. **5** angry; severe. *a sharp voice.* **6** able to see, hear, or learn well. *He has a sharp mind.*

great white shark

sharp² *adv.* punctually. *one o'clock sharp.*

sharp³ *n.* a sign (#) in music that indicates that note should be played higher by half a tone.

sharpen *v.* to make something sharper.

shatter *v.* to break into many small pieces. *The glass shattered.*

shave *v.* to cut away hair with a razor.

shawl *n.* a large piece of material worn around the shoulders.

sheaf *n.* (*pl.* sheaves) a bundle, especially of corn or of papers.

shear *v.* (shearing, sheared, shorn) to cut the wool from a sheep.

shears *n. pl.* a tool like large scissors.

sheath *n.* a cover for a sword or dagger.

shed¹ *n.* a small hut, used for storing things such as garden tools.

A B C D E F G H I J K L M N O P Q R **S** T U V W X Y Z

shed² v. (sheds, shedding, shed) to let something fall or drop off. *Some trees shed their leaves in the fall.*

sheen n. brightness; shine.

sheep n. (*pl.* sheep) a farm animal kept for its wool and meat.

sheer adj. **1** very steep. *a sheer drop to the sea.* **2** complete. *sheer nonsense.* **3** (of material) very thin; almost transparent.

sheet n. **1** a thin, rectangular piece of material used on a bed. **2** a thin, flat piece of paper, metal, glass, or ice.

sheik *(shake)* n. an Arab chief. (*can also be spelled* sheikh.)

shelf n. (*pl.* shelves) a board attached to a wall or inside a cupboard, where things are kept.

shell n. **1** the hard outer covering of a shellfish, tortoise, egg, or nut. **2** a metal case filled with explosives.

shellfish n. (*pl.* shellfish) a soft-bodied water creature covered with a shell. *Mussels and oysters are shellfish.*

shelter n. **1** a place where you are protected from bad weather or kept safe from harm. **2** the state of being protected or kept safe. **shelter** v.

shepherd n. a person who takes care of sheep.

sheriff n. **1** in the U.S. the chief law officer of a county. **2** in Scotland a judge.

sherry n. a type of strong wine.

shield¹ n. **1** a wide piece of metal, wood, or strong plastic, used to protect the person carrying it from attacks. **2** something that protects. *a heat shield.*

shield² v. to cover or protect something.

shift¹ v. to move something.

shift² n. a period of time that a group of people are working, ending when another group takes their place.

shimmer v. to shine with an unsteady light. *The moonlight shimmered on the lake.* **shimmer** n.

shin n. the front part of your leg, right below the knee.

shine v. (shining, shone) to give out or reflect light; to be bright. **shiny** adj.

shingle n. small pebbles.

shingles n. pl. a disease related to chickenpox that causes a painful rash around the middle of the body.

ship¹ n. a large boat, usually for traveling on the sea.

ship² v. (ships, shipping, shipped) to transport something by ship. *Most of the oil in the world is shipped on vast oil tankers.*

shipwreck n. **1** an accident in which a ship is sunk or badly damaged at sea. **2** a wrecked or badly damaged ship. **shipwreck** v.

shipyard n. a place where ships are built or sent to be repaired.

shirk v. to avoid doing something that you should do, especially work.

shirt n. a piece of clothing worn on the top half of the body. A formal shirt usually has a collar, sleeves, and buttons down the front.

shiver v. to shake with cold or fear. **shiver** n., **shivery** adj.

shoal n. a group of fish swimming together; a school.

shock¹ n. **1** a sudden, unpleasant surprise. **2** the effect on your body of an electric current passing through it. *I got a slight shock when I touched the wire.* **3** a violent shaking. *earthquake shocks.* **4** an unhealthy condition of the body caused by a bad shock or a physical injury. *She was suffering from shock.* **shocking** adj.

shock² v. to upset or horrify somebody. *Everyone was shocked by her death.*

shoddy adj. (shoddier, shoddiest) when something is of poor quality.

shoe n. an outer covering for your foot.

shoelace n. a string for tying up a shoe.

shone past of shine.

shook past of shake.

shoot¹ v. (shooting, shot) **1** to fire a bullet from a gun or an arrow from a bow. **2** to move quickly. *She shot out of the room.* **3** to kick or hit a ball at a goal. **4** to photograph, film, or video. **5** (of a plant) to grow new buds.

shoot² n. a new growth on a plant.

Greek soldier
with a shield and spear

shooting star

shooting star *n.* a meteor.

shop² *v.* (shops, shopping, shopped) to go to stores and buy things. **shopper** *n.*

shopkeeper *n.* a person who owns or manages a store.

shoplifter *n.* a person who steals from a store. **shoplifting** *n.*

shore *n.* the land running along the edge of a sea or lake.

shorn *past participle of* shear.

short *adj.* **1** measuring a small distance from one end to the other; not long. **2** small in height; not tall. **3** taking a small amount of time. **4** not enough; less than it should be. *When I checked my change, I found that it was ten cents short.* **short of** not having enough of something. *We're short of bread today; some people won't be able to have any with their lunch.* **short** *adv.*, **shortness** *n.*

shortage *n.* a lack of something.

shortbread *n.* a crumbly cookie made from flour, butter, and sugar.

shortcoming *n.* a fault.

shortcut *n.* a short way of getting somewhere or doing something. *We took a shortcut across the field.*

shorten *v.* to make or become shorter.

shorthand *n.* a way of writing quickly using strokes and dots to show sounds, often used by secretaries.

shortly *adv.* soon; before long.

shorts *n. pl.* short pants that end just above the knees.

short-tempered *adj.* easily made angry.

shot¹ *past of* shoot.

shot² *n.* **1** the firing of a gun. *We heard a shot in the distance.* **2** a throw, hit, kick, or turn in a game or competition. *a shot at goal.* **3** a photograph. **4** lead bullets used in cartridges. **5** an attempt to do something. **6** an injection.

shotput *n.* a sports event in which the competitors throw a heavy metal ball as far as possible with one hand.

should *v.* **1** used to say or ask what is the right thing to do. *You should phone her.* **2** used to say what is likely. *They left a long time ago so they should be home by now.*

shoulder *n.* the part of your body between your neck and the top of your arm.

shoulder blade *n.* the wide, flat bone at the top of your back near your shoulder; scapula.

shout *v.* to call out or speak loudly. **shout** *n.*

shove *v.* to push somebody or something roughly. **shove** *n.*

shovel *n.* a tool like a large spade with curved sides, for moving sand, coal, or snow. **shovel** *v.*

show¹ *v.* (showing, showed, shown) **1** to let something be seen. *Show me what you have written.* **2** to demonstrate how to do something. *Can you show me how to print from this computer?* **3** to be visible. *Anger showed in her face.* **show off 1** to display something. **2** to try to impress people. **show up** to arrive. *Jill showed up just before dinner.*

show² *n.* **1** a play or other entertainment. **2** a type of public display or exhibition. *a dog show.*

shower *n.* **1** a short fall of light rain. **2** a device that sprays water on you from above, used for washing yourself. **3** a lot of things falling or coming at one time. *a shower of bullets.* **shower** *v.*

shrank *past of* shrink.

shrapnel *n.* small pieces of metal from an exploding bomb.

shred *n.* a narrow piece torn off something. *My coat was torn to shreds.* **shred** *v.*

shrew *n.* an animal similar to a small mouse with a long nose.

shrewd *adj.* cunning; sharp.

shriek *v.* to make a high-pitched scream or laugh. **shriek** *n.*

shrew

shrill *adj.* (of a sound) very high-pitched and piercing.

shrimp *n.* a small, edible shellfish with a long tail.

shrine *n.* a sacred place.

shrink *v.* (shrinking, shrank, shrunk) **1** to become smaller. *Wool often shrinks in hot water.* **2** to move back because you are afraid or disgusted. *He shrank back in horror.*

shrivel *v.* (shrivels, shriveling, shriveled) to dry up or wither. *The plants shriveled up in the heat.*

shrub *n.* a small bush.

shrug *v.* (shrugs, shrugging, shrugged) to raise your shoulders to show doubt or lack of interest. **shrug** *n.*

shrunk *past participle of* shrink.

shudder *v.* to shake suddenly with cold or fear. **shudder** *n.*

shuffle *v.* **1** to mix playing cards before a game. **2** to move your feet slowly along the ground without lifting them. **shuffle** *n.*

shun *v.* (shuns, shunning, shunned) to avoid or keep away from somebody.

shut *v.* (shuts, shutting, shut) to close something. *Please shut that door!*

shutter *n.* **1** a wooden or metal cover for a window. **2** the moving cover over the lens of a camera, which opens when a photograph is taken.

shuttle *n.* **1** a bus, plane, or other vehicle that travels regularly between two places. **2** a device used in weaving for carrying a thread backward and forward across the other threads.

shuttlecock *n.* a cork ball with feathers or a light plastic frame attached to it, used in badminton.

shy¹ *adj.* nervous about talking to people that you do not know. **shyness** *n.*

shy² *v.* (shies, shying, shied) to turn away in sudden fear.

sick *adj.* **1** not well; ill. **2** needing to vomit. *I feel sick.* **3** tired of something. *I'm sick of telling you to clean your room.* **4** vomiting. **sickness** *n.*

sicken *v.* to disgust somebody.

sickle *n.* a tool with a curved blade for cutting grass or grain.

sickly *adj.* (sicklier, sickliest) unhealthy. *a sickly child.*

side *n.* **1** an edge or surface of something. *An octagon has eight sides.* **2** one of the two parts of something that are not the top, bottom, front, or back. *the side of the house.* **3** the right or left part of the body. **4** a team or group that is opposing another, usually in sports.

side effect *n.* an additional, often bad, effect of taking a drug.

sidetrack *v.* to distract somebody from what he or she was going to do or say.

sidewalk *n.* a path at the side of a road.

sideways *adv.* to or toward one side. *Crabs move sideways.*

siding *n.* **1** the material used for the outside surface of some buildings. *aluminum siding.* **2** a short track beside a railroad line where trains can stand when they are not being used.

sieve

siege *(seej)* *n.* the surrounding of a building or town by an army until the people inside surrender.

siesta *(see-ess-ta)* *n.* a short nap taken in the afternoon.

sieve (*rhymes with* give) *n.* a container made of wire or plastic netting attached to a ring, used to separate liquids from solids, or small pieces from large pieces. **sieve** *v.*

sift *v.* to put something through a sieve.

sigh (*rhymes with* die) *v.* to breathe out loudly, showing tiredness, boredom, or relief. **sigh** *n.*

sight *n.* **1** the ability to see. **2** something that you see. **3 sights** the interesting places worth visiting in a town or city.

sightseeing *n.* the activity of visiting the famous and interesting places and buildings in a town or city. **sightseer** *n.*

sign¹ (rhymes with *pine*) *n.* **1** a board with words or pictures giving information. **2** a symbol that stands for something. + *is the sign meaning "plus."* **3** a movement to show a meaning. *She made a sign to be quiet.* **4** a clue that shows something. *There was no sign of a break-in.*

sign² *v.* to write your name in your own way on something.

a
b
c
d
e
f
g
h
i
j
k
l
m
n
o
p
q
r
s
t
u
v
w
x
y
z

A B C D E F G H I J K L M N O P Q R S T U V W X Y Z

signal *n.* **1** a sign, for example, a hand movement or a light or sound giving a command or warning. *Car drivers have to signal before they turn.* **2** the wave of sound received or sent out by a radio or television. **signal** *v.*

signature *n.* a person's name written in their own writing.

significant *n.* important; meaning a lot. **significance** *n.*

signify *v.* (signifies, signifying, signified) to mean something; to be a sign of

Sikhs in traditional headdress

something. *A nod signifies agreement.*

signpost *n.* a post with a sign on it, showing the direction and distance of places.

Sikh *(seek) n.* a member of an Indian religion, called **Sikhism**, based on a belief in a single god. **Sikh** *adj.*

silent *adj.* without any sound. **silence** *n.*

silhouette *(sil-o-et* or *sil-oo-et) n.* the dark outline of something seen against the light.

silicon *n.* a chemical element found in sand and rocks and used in making electronic equipment.

silk *n.* very fine, smooth cloth made from fibers produced by caterpillars called **silkworms**. **silky** *adj.*

sill *n.* the ledge running along the bottom of a window.

silly *adj.* (sillier, silliest) foolish; not sensible. **silliness** *n.*

silt *n.* fine sand and mud left behind by flowing water.

silver *n.* **1** a precious, shiny, gray metal, used for making jewelry and coins. **2** money made of silver or of a metal that looks like silver. **3** cutlery or other objects made of silver; silverware. **4** the color of silver. **silver** *adj.*

similar *adj.* alike; almost the same. **similarity** *n.*

simile *n.* a phrase where a person or thing is described as being similar to something else. *As busy as a bee is a simile.*

simmer *v.* to boil very gently.

simple *adj.* **1** not difficult; easy. **2** plain; not complicated. *a simple design.* **simplicity** *n.,* **simply** *adv.*

simplify *v.* (simplifies, simplifying, simplified) to make something simpler. **simplification** *n.*

simulate *v.* **1** to pretend. *She already knew, but she simulated surprise at the news.* **2** to recreate a real situation, especially by using computers and moving machines. *The equipment simulates the experience of flying an airplane.* **simulation** *n.,* **simulator** *n.*

simultaneous *adj.* when something is happening at the same time as something else.

sin *n.* a wicked act, especially one that breaks a religious or moral law. **sin** *v.,* **sinful** *adj.,* **sinner** *n.*

since *conj.* **1** from the time that. *I haven't seen her since she moved.* **2** because. *Since Tony is away, I'll do it myself.* **since** *prep.*

sincere *adj.* meaning what you say; honest. **sincerely** *adv.,* **sincerity** *n.*

sing *v.* (singing, sang, sung) to make musical sounds with your voice. **singer** *n.*

singe *v.* (singeing, singed) to burn something slightly.

single *adj.* **1** one only. *a single-story house.* **2** for one person only. *a single bed.* **3** not married. *a single man.*

singular *adj.* the form of a word that shows only one. *Foot is the singular of feet.* **singular** *adj.*

sinister *adj.* seeming or suggesting evil. *a sinister disappearance.*

sink¹ *v.* (sinking, sank, sunk) **1** to go down under the surface of a liquid. *The stone sank to the bottom of the pool.* **2** to make a ship sink. **3** to go down slowly. *The Sun sank slowly behind the hills.*

sink² *n.* a basin with a drain and water supply connected to it.

sinus *n.* a hollow spaces in the bones of your head, found at the top of your nose.

sip *v.* (sips, sipping, sipped) to drink in very small mouthfuls. **sip** *n.*

siphon (*sigh-fon*) *n.* a tube used to flow liquid from one place to another. **siphon** *v.* (*can also be spelled* syphon.)

sir *n.* **1** a formal way of speaking or writing to a man, without using his name. **2 Sir** the title placed in front of the name of a knight.

siren *n.* a device that makes a loud wailing noise as a warning or signal.

sister *n.* **1** a girl or woman who has the same parents as you. **2** a nun.

sit *v.* (sits, sitting, sat) to rest on your bottom.

site *n.* a place where a building or town is, was, or will be built. *That field is the site for the new houses.*

sitting room *n.* a room in a house where people normally sit to relax, read, or watch television; a living room.

situated *v.* **be situated** to be in a particular place. *The library is situated right downtown.*

situation *n.* a set of circumstances at a certain time. *I found myself in an embarrassing situation.*

size *n.* the dimensions of something; how large something is.

sizzle *v.* to make a hissing sound when cooking. *meat sizzling in a frying pan.*

human skeleton

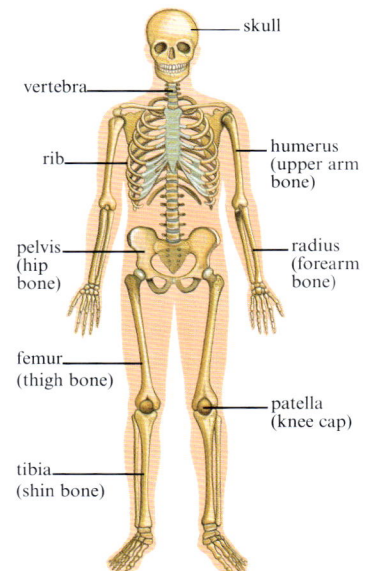

- skull
- vertebra
- rib
- humerus (upper arm bone)
- pelvis (hip bone)
- radius (forearm bone)
- femur (thigh bone)
- patella (knee cap)
- tibia (shin bone)

skate *n.* an ice skate or roller skate. **skate** *v.*

skateboard *n.* a narrow board on four wheels that you stand and ride on.

skeleton *n.* the framework of bones in the body of an animal or human.

skier

skeptic (*skep-tik*) *n.* a person who doubts the truth of what has been told. **skeptical** *adj.*

sketch[1] *n.* **1** a rough drawing. **2** a short, funny play.

sketch[2] *v.* to draw roughly and quickly.

ski[1] *n.* (*pl.* skis) one of a pair of long, narrow strips of fiberglass that are attached to boots for moving on snow.

ski[2] *v.* (skis, skiing, skied) to move on skis. **skier** *n.*

skid *v.* (skids, skidding, skidded) to slide sideways on a slippery surface.

skill *n.* the ability to do something well. **skillful** *adj.* **skillfully** *adv.*

skim *v.* (skims, skimming, skimmed) **1** to remove something from the surface of a liquid. *Skim the fat off the gravy.* **2** to move lightly and quickly over a surface.

skin *n.* **1** the natural outer layer of an animal or person. **2** the outer layer of a fruit.

skinny *adj.* (skinnier, skinniest) very thin.

skip *v.* (skips, skipping, skipped) **1** to move along with a little hop on each foot in turn. **2** to jump over a rope that is turning under your feet and over your head. **3** to miss something out. *I skipped the second chapter.*

skipper *n.* (*informal*) the captain of a boat or of a sports team.

skirt *n.* a piece of clothing, usually worn by women and girls, that hangs down from the waist.

skull *n.* the bony part of your head.

skunk *n.* a small, North American mammal that defends itself by letting off a bad smell.

a b c d e f g h i j k l m n o p q r **s** t u v w x y z

sky *n.* the space above Earth, where the Sun, Moon, and stars can be seen.

skyscraper *n.* a very tall building with many floors.

slab *n.* a thick, flat slice.

slack *adj.* **1** loose; not pulled tight. **2** lazy and careless. **3** quiet; not busy. *Business was slack; there were very few customers.*

slain *past participle of* slay.

slam *v.* (slams, slamming, slammed) to shut or put something down with force, making a loud noise. **slam** *n.*

slang *n.* words and phrases that you use in conversation, especially with people of your own age, but not when you are writing or being polite.

slant *v.* to slope. *His handwriting slants to the left.* **slant** *n.*

slap *v.* (slaps, slapping, slapped) to hit something with the palm of your hand. **slap** *n.*

slapstick *n.* a type of comedy that uses actions, not words, to make you laugh.

slash *v.* to make long cuts in something. **slash** *n.*

slate *n.* **1** a blue-gray stone that can be split into thin, flat sheets. **2** a piece of this, used as a roof tile.

slaughter *v.* **1** to kill animals for food. **2** to kill large numbers of people brutally. **slaughter** *n.*

slave *n.* a person who is owned by somebody and forced to work for him or her without pay. **slave** *v.*, **slavery** *n.*

slay *v.* (slays, slaying, slew, slain) *(old- fashioned* or *literary)* to kill somebody.

sled *n.* **1** a small vehicle with rods underneath instead of wheels, used for traveling on snow or ice. **2** a plastic variation of such a vehicle.

sleek *adj.* smooth and shiny. *sleek fur.*

sleep *v.* (sleeping, slept) to rest with your eyes closed in a state of natural unconsciousness. **sleep** *n.*

sleepless *adj.* unable to sleep; without sleep. *a sleepless night.*

sleepy *adj.* (sleepier, sleepiest) tired and feeling ready to sleep. **sleepily** *adv.*, **sleepiness** *n.*

sleet *n.* rain mixed with snow.

sleeve *n.* the part of a piece of clothing that covers your arm.

sleigh *(rhymes with* ray*) n.* a large sled, usually pulled by animals.

slender *adj.* thin or narrow.

slept *past of* sleep.

slew *past of* slay.

slice *n.* a thin piece cut from something. *a slice of bread.* **slice** *v.*

slick *n.* a patch of oil floating on water, usually at sea as a result of oil being spilled into the water.

slide¹ *v.* (sliding, slid) to move smoothly over a surface.

slide² *n.* **1** a structure in a playground with a smooth, sloping surface for children to slide down. **2** a small, transparent photograph for projecting onto a screen. **3** a piece of glass on which you put things to examine under a microscope.

slight *adj.* small or unimportant.

slim *adj.* (slimmer, slimmest) **1** thin. **2** very small. *a slim chance.*

slime *n.* unpleasantly wet, slippery stuff. **slimy** *adj.*

sling¹ *n.* **1** a piece of cloth used to support an injured arm. **2** a strap with a string attached to either end that is used for throwing stones.

sling² *v.* (slinging, slung) *(informal)* to throw something.

slip¹ *v.* (slips, slipping, slipped) **1** to slide accidentally and lose your balance. **2** to move quietly and easily. *She slipped out of the room.* **3** to do something with a quick, light movement. *I slipped off my shoes.*

slip² *n.* **1** a small mistake. **2** a small piece of paper. **3** an item of women's underwear, worn under a skirt or dress.

slipper *n.* a soft shoe worn indoors.

slippery *adj.* so smooth or wet that it causes slipping.

slit *v.* (slits, slitting, slit) to make a long, narrow cut in something. **slit** *n.*

slither *v.* to slide or slip.

slog *v.* (slogs, slogging, slogged) to work hard. **slog** *n.*

slogan *n.* an easily remembered phrase used in advertising.

slope *n.* a surface that has one end higher than the other, such as the

sloth

side of a hill. **slope** *v.*

sloppy *adj.* (sloppier, sloppiest) **1** careless. *sloppy work.* **2** half-liquid. *sloppy food.*

slot *n.* a small, narrow opening to push something into. *He inserted a coin into the slot.* **slot** *v.*

slug

sloth *(slawth) n.* **1** a slow-moving South American mammal that hangs upside down from the branches of trees. **2** extreme laziness. **slothful** *adj.*

slouch *v.* to stand or sit with your shoulders forward and your head hanging down.

slow *adj.* **1** moving at a low speed; not fast. **2** showing a time earlier than the right time. *That clock is slow.* **slow** *v.*, **slowness** *n.*

slug *n.* a creature like a snail with no shell.

sluggish *adj.* moving slowly.

slum *n.* an area with old, overcrowded houses in poor condition.

slump *v.* to fall suddenly or heavily.

slung *past of* sling.

sly *adj.* cunning and secretly deceitful. **slyness** *n.*

smack *v.* to hit somebody with the palm of your hand. **smack** *n.*

small *adj.* little; not big or much.

smart[1] *adj.* **1** intelligent **2** well-dressed; neat. **smartness** *n.*

smart[2] *v.* to have a sharp, stinging feeling. *The smoke made his eyes smart.*

smash *v.* to break something into pieces.

smear *v.* to spread something sticky or oily over a surface. **smear** *n.*

smell[1] *v.* (smelling, smelled) **1** to notice something through your nose. *I can smell smoke.* **2** to give out a smell. *My hands smell of onions.*

smell[2] *n.* **1** the ability to smell things. **2** something that you notice through your nose. **smelly** *adj.*

smile *v.* to turn up the corners of your mouth with pleasure. **smile** *n.*

smog *n.* smoke mixed with fog.

smoke[1] *n.* the cloudlike gases and particles of soot that are given off by something that is burning. **smoky** *adj.*

smoke[2] *v.* **1** to give off smoke. **2** to have

a cigarette or pipe in your mouth and breathe the smoke in and out. **3** to preserve food by hanging it in smoke.

smooth *adj.* **1** having an even surface; not rough or lumpy. **2** without problems or difficulties. *a smooth journey.* **smooth** *v.*, **smoothness** *n.*

smother *(rhymes with* mother*) v.* **1** to kill somebody by covering that person's face so that he or she is unable to breathe. **2** to cover something thickly. *She smothered the toast with butter.*

coral snake

smoulder *v.* to burn very slowly, without bursting into flame.

smudge *n.* a dirty mark. **smudge** *v.*

smug *adj.* (smugger, smuggest) too pleased with yourself.

smuggle *v.* to take goods into or out of a country illegally. **smuggler** *n.*

snack *n.* a small, quick meal.

snag *n.* a small difficulty.

snail *n.* a small creature with a soft body and a hard, protective shell.

snake *n.* a long, thin reptile without legs.

snap[1] *v.* (snaps, snapping, snapped) **1** to break suddenly with a sharp noise. **2** to bite at somebody suddenly. **3** to speak in a sharp, angry way.

snap[2] *n.* **1** the noise that is made by snapping. **2** a photograph. **3** a card game.

snare *n.* a trap for animals. **snare** *v.*

snarl *v.* to growl angrily, showing the teeth. **snarl** *n.*

snatch *v.* to seize something quickly. *She snatched my bag and ran away.*

sneak[1] *v.* to go somewhere quietly and secretly. *He sneaked out of the room.*

A
B
C
D
E
F
G
H
I
J
K
L
M
N
O
P
Q
R
S
T
U
V
W
X
Y
Z

sneak[2] *n. (informal)* a person who tells lies. **sneaky** *adj.*

sneer *v.* to curl your upper lip at one side in a type of smile that shows scorn. **sneer** *n.*

sneeze *v.* to blow out air suddenly and noisily through your nose and mouth in an involuntary action. **sneeze** *n.*

sniff *v.* to draw in air quickly and noisily through your nose. **sniff** *n.*

snip *v.* (snips, snipping, snipped) to cut something sharply and quickly.

sniper *n.* a person who shoots at people from a hidden position.

snippet *n.* a small piece or portion.

snob *n.* a person who looks down on people of a lower social class. **snobbery** *n.*, **snobbish** *adj.*

snoop *v. (informal)* to look around a place secretly to try to find out something.

snooze *v. (informal)* to take a brief nap. **snooze** *n.*

snore *v.* to make a snorting noise through your nose or mouth while you sleep. **snore** *n.*

snowboarder

snorkel *n.* a tube used for breathing when you are underwater. **snorkel** *v.*

snort *v.* to make a noise by forcing air through your nostrils. **snort** *n.*

snout *n.* the nose and mouth of an animal such as a pig.

snow *n.* white flakes of frozen water that fall from the sky in cold weather. **snow** *v.*, **snowy** *adj.*

snowball *n.* snow pressed into a ball.

snowboard *n.* a single board used as a ski

on snow. **snowboard** *v.* **snowboarder** *v.*

snowdrop *n.* a small, white flower, seen in the early spring.

snowplow *n.* a vehicle for clearing snow from roads or railroad tracks.

snug *adj.* (snugger, snuggest) warm and comfortable.

snuggle *v.* to get close to somebody for warmth or love.

soak *v.* **1** to put something in a liquid and leave it there. **2** to make something very wet. **soak up** to take in liquid; to absorb.

soap *n.* a substance used with water for washing. **soapy** *adj.*

soap opera *n.* a type of television series about the daily lives of a group of characters.

soar *v.* **1** to fly high in the sky. **2** to rise high and quickly. *Prices have soared.*

sob *v.* (sobs, sobbing, sobbed) to cry noisily. **sob** *n.*

sober *adj.* **1** not drunk. **2** serious and sensible. **3** (of colors) not bright. *a sober gray dress.*

soccer *n.* a game played by two teams who try to score goals by kicking a round ball.

social *adj.* **1** to do with people in communities and how they live. *social problems.* **2** living in communities. *Ants are social insects.* **3** to do with meeting and being friendly with other people. *a social club.* **socially** *adv.*

socialism *n.* a political system where the country's wealth is shared equally by all of the people and where the government controls all business and industry. **socialist** *adj., n.*

social security *n.* money paid by the government to people who are unemployed, disabled, or elderly.

social worker *n.* a person whose job is to help people in the community who have special needs.

society *n.* **1** all of the people who live in a group or country and the way that they live and interact. **2** a club.

sock *n.* a piece of clothing that you wear on your foot, inside your shoe.

socket *n.* a hole or set of holes into which something fits; plug; outlet.

soda *n.* **1** carbonated water. **2** a carbonated beverage with flavoring; pop. **2** any of several substances formed from sodium, e.g. baking soda (sodium bicarbonate).

sodium *n.* a metallic chemical element found in many substances, including salt.

sofa *n.* a long, soft seat with arms and a back for two or more people; couch.

Sun

solar system

soft *adj.* **1** not hard or firm. *a soft pillow.* **2** smooth and pleasant to touch. *soft fur.* **3** (of a sound) not loud. *a soft voice.* **4** (of a color) pale; not bright. **5** very easygoing; not strict. *Her dad is too soft on her.*

soft drink *n.* a cold drink that does not contain alcohol.

soften *v.* to make or become softer.

software *n.* computer programs.

soggy *adj.* (soggier, soggiest) wet and soft.

soil¹ *n.* the earth in which plants grow.

soil² *v.* to make something dirty.

solar *adj.* **1** to do with the Sun. **2** powered by energy from the Sun's rays.

solar system *n.* the Sun and the planets that revolve around it.

sold *past of* sell.

soldier *n.* a member of an army.

sole¹ *n.* **1** the underneath part of your foot or your shoe. **2** a flat, edible sea fish.

sole² *adj.* only. *She was the sole survivor of the crash.*

solemn *adj.* very serious. **solemnity** *n.*

solid¹ *adj.* **1** hard; not like a liquid or a gas. **2** not hollow. **solidity** *n.*

solid² *n.* a substance that is solid; not a liquid or a gas.

solidify *v.* (solidifies, solidifying, solidified) to become solid.

solitary *adj.* alone.

solo *n.* (*pl.* solos) a performance by a single person, especially of a musical piece. **soloist** *n.*

soluble *adj.* capable of dissolving.

solution *n.* **1** the answer to a problem or puzzle. **2** a liquid with something dissolved in it.

solve *v.* to find the answer to a problem or a puzzle.

somber (*som*-ber) *adj.* gloomy.

somebody, someone *pron.* a person.

somehow *adv.* in some way. *I'll get there somehow.*

somersault *n.* a rolling movement in which your heels go over your head. **somersault** *v.*

something *pron.* a thing.

sometime *adv.* at an unknown time in the past or future. *Let's meet sometime soon.*

sometimes *adv.* occasionally; not often.

somewhere *adv.* in or to some place.

son *n.* somebody's male child.

sonar *n.* a system that uses sounds and their echoes to find objects in deep water.

sonata *n.* a piece of music, often with three movements, for one or two instruments.

song *n.* **1** a piece of music with words that you sing. **2** singing.

sonnet *n.* a poem of 14 lines with a set pattern of rhymes.

soon *adv.* in a short time.

soot *n.* the black powder left by something that has been burned. **sooty** *adj.*

soothe *v.* **1** to calm or comfort somebody. **2** to make something less painful. **soothing** *adj.*

sophisticated *adj.* **1** knowing a lot about the world and about what is fashionable to do or wear. **2** able to do difficult and complicated things. *sophisticated machinery.* **sophistication** *n.*

sorcerer (*sor*-ser-er) *n.* in stories a person who casts magic spells. **sorcery** *n.*

sore¹ *adj.* painful. **soreness** *n.*

sore² *n.* a place that is painful or infected on your skin.

sorrow *adj.* sadness. **sorrowful** *adj.*

sorry *adj.* feeling sadness, regret, or sympathy. *I'm so sorry for your loss.*

sort¹ *n.* a type or kind.

sort² *v.* to arrange things into groups. *He sorted the laundry into two piles.* **sort out** to put something in order; to deal with something.

SOS *n.* a signaling call for urgent help or rescue. The letters SOS were chosen because they are quick to send and very easy to recognize when in Morse code.

a b c d e f g h i j k l m n o p q r **s** t u v w x y z

187

A
B
C
D
E
F
G
H
I
J
K
L
M
N
O
P
Q
R
S
T
U
V
W
X
Y
Z

soup

sought *past of* seek.

soul *n.* **1** the unseen part of a person that is often thought to continue after he or she dies. **2** a person. *a poor old soul.*

sound[1] *n.* something that you hear.

sound[2] *v.* **1** to give a certain impression. *You sound excited.* **2** to resemble something in sound. *That sounded like a train.* **3** to make a noise with something. *She sounded her horn.*

sound[3] *adj.* **1** strong; in good condition. *sound teeth.* **2** reliable and sensible. *sound advice.* **3** deep. *a sound sleep.* **4** thorough. *He has a sound knowledge of the surrounding area.*

soup *n.* a liquid food made from meat or vegetables cooked in water.

sour *adj.* sharp-tasting, like lemons. **sourness** *n.*

source *n.* **1** the place, person, or thing from which something comes. **2** the place where a river starts.

south *n.* one of the points of the compass. When you face the rising Sun, south is on your right. **south** *adj, adv.*

southern *adj.* in or of the south part of a place. *southern Africa.*

souvenir *(soo-ve-neer) n.* an object that you keep to remind you of a place, person, or event.

sovereign *(sov-rin) n.* a king or queen.

sow[1] *(rhymes with* how) *n.* a female pig.

sow[2] *(rhymes with* so) *v.* (sowing, sowed, sown) to put seeds in the ground so that they grow.

soybean *n.* a bean containing a lot of protein, used instead of animal products in some foods.

space *n.* **1** an empty area. **2** the area beyond Earth's atmosphere, where all of the stars and planets are.

spacecraft *n.* (*pl.* spacecraft) a vehicle for traveling in space.

spacious *adj.* having plenty of room.

spade *n.* **1** a tool for digging into the ground. **2 spades** one of the four suits in a pack of cards, with the symbol ♠ on them.

spaghetti *n.* long, thin strands of pasta.

span[1] *v.* (spans, spanning, spanned) to extend from one side of something to the other. *A bridge spans the river.*

span[2] *n.* **1** the distance between the tip of your little finger and your thumb when your hand is spread out. **2** the length of something. **3** the time for which something lasts.

spaniel *n.* a dog with large, droopy ears.

spank *v.* to hit somebody, especially on the buttocks, with the palm of your hand.

spare[1] *adj.* extra; not in use. *Do you have a spare tire?*

spare[2] *v.* **1** to have something available. *I can't spare any time today.* **2** to treat somebody with mercy. *They begged the king to spare them.*

spark *n.* a tiny, red-hot piece thrown off by something burning.

sparkle *v.* to shine with a lot of tiny, bright flashes of light. **sparkle** *n.*

sparrow *n.* a small, brown bird.

sparse *adj.* very thinly scattered; small in amount.

spat *past of* spit.

spawn *n.* the eggs of fish or frogs. **spawn** *v.*

speak *v.* (speaking, spoke, spoken) to talk; to say words.

speaker *n.* **1** a person who speaks. **2** a part of a radio or stereo system that turns electrical waves into sound.

spear *n.* a weapon that is thrown, consisting of a sharp point on the end of a long pole.

special *adj.* **1** different from usual; not ordinary. *a special occasion.* **2** for a particular purpose. *a special tool.* **specially** *adv.*

specialist *n.* a person who knows a lot about a particular subject.

specialize *v.* to work or study in a particular field. *a doctor specializing in eye surgery.*

specialty *n.* something that you make or do especially well.

species *n.* (*pl.* species) a group of animals or plants that are alike in some way. *Mice are a species of rodent.*

specific *adj.* **1** particular. **2** clear and detailed. **specifically** *adv.*

specify *v.* (specifies, specifying,

specified) to name or state something in a clear and detailed way. *She specified what color she wanted.* **specification** *n.*

specimen *n.* a sample.

speck *n.* a tiny piece of something, like dust.

speckled *adj.* covered with small spots. *a speckled hen.*

spectacle *n.* an impressive show or display.

spectacles *n. pl.* lenses set into a frame that you wear to improve your eyesight; eyeglasses.

spectacular *adj.* impressive; amazing.

spectator *n.* a person who watches an event.

spectrum *n.* (*pl.* spectra) all of the different colors that are produced when light goes through a prism or a drop of water.

speculate *v.* to guess. **speculation** *n.*

speech *n.* **1** the ability to speak. **2** a talk given to a group of people.

speed[1] *n.* **1** the rate at which something moves. **2** movement at a fast rate. *The traffic was traveling at high speed.*

statue of the Sphinx

speed[2] *v.* (speeding, sped) to travel very fast or faster than is allowed by law.

speedometer *n.* an instrument in a vehicle that shows how fast you are traveling.

spell[1] *v.* (spelling, spelled) to write or say the letters of a word in the correct order. **spelling** *n.*

spell[2] *n.* **1** magic words that are supposed to make something happen. **2** a period of time. *a spell of fine weather.*

spend *v.* (spending, spent) **1** to use money to buy things. **2** to pass time.

sperm *n.* one of the cells produced by males that can fertilize a female egg.

sphere *(sfeer)* *n.* a round object like a ball. **spherical** *adj.*

Sphinx *(sfinks)* *n.* in Greek mythology a monster with a lion's body and a woman's head.

spice *n.* a substance obtained from part of a plant, used to flavor food. *The picture shows a selection of spices.* **spicy** *adj.*

spider *n.* a small creature with eight legs that spins webs.

spike *n.* a sharp point. **spiky** *adj.*

spill *v.* (spilling, spilled *or* spilt) to pour out accidentally. *I spilled some milk.*

spin *v.* (spinning, spun) **1** to turn around quickly in one spot. **2** to make thread by twisting fibers together.

spinach *n.* a plant with dark green leaves that is eaten as a vegetable.

spinal *adj.* to do with the spine.

spine *n.* **1** the line of bones down the middle of your back. **2** a prickle on an animal. **3** the narrow part of a book, where the pages are connected together.

spiral *adj.* winding around and around, like a telephone cord. **spiral** *n.*

spire *n.* a tall pointed part on the top of a church tower.

spirit *n.* **1** a person's soul. **2** a ghost. **3** a strong, alcoholic drink such as whiskey or gin. **4** liveliness or courage. *She showed a lot of spirit in overcoming her illness.* **5** spirits a person's feelings. *He's in high spirits today.*

spiritual *adj.* to do with the soul or religion. **spirituality** *n.,* **spiritually** *adv.*

spit[1] *v.* (spitting, spat) to send out saliva from your mouth. **spit** *n.*

spit[2] *n.* a long metal rod that is pushed through a piece of meat and that then turns around over a flame until the meat is cooked.

spite *n.* the wish to hurt or upset somebody. **spiteful** *adj.,* **spitefully** *adv.* **in spite of** taking no notice of something. *They set off in spite of the bad weather.*

splash *v.* to make something wet with drops of liquid. **splash** *n.*

sponge

splendid *adj.* very good or very impressive. *a splendid palace.*

splint *n.* a piece of wood and plastic, used to keep a broken bone in a set position while it heals.

a
b
c
d
e
f
g
h
i
j
k
l
m
n
o
p
q
r
s
t
u
v
w
x
y
z

A
B
C
D
E
F
G
H
I
J
K
L
M
N
O
P
Q
R
S
T
U
V
W
X
Y
Z

splinter *n.* a thin, sharp, broken piece of wood or something similar. **splinter** *v.*

split *v.* (splits, splitting, split) to break or divide into parts. **split** *n.*

spoil *v.* (spoiling, spoiled *or* spoilt) **1** to make something less good than before. **2** to let someone always have what he or she wants so that that person becomes selfish.

spoke[1] *n.* one of the rods connecting the center to the rim of a wheel.

spoke[2] *past of* speak.

spoken *past participle of* speak.

sponge *n.* **1** a sea creature with a light, soft skeleton that is full of holes and soaks up water. **2** a piece of a sponge or a similar material used for washing or cleaning. **3** a type of light cake, often with two layers and a sweet center of whipped cream or jelly. **spongy** *adj.*

sponsor *n.* **1** a person or company that pays for an event as a form of advertising. **2** a person who promises to pay money if another person completes a task, e.g. a walk for a charity. **sponsor** *v.*, **sponsorship** *n.*

spontaneous *adj.* done on the spur of the moment; not planned beforehand. *a spontaneous act of kindness.* **spontaneity** *n.*

spoon *n.* an implement with a handle and a small, shallow bowl, often used for eating soup or cereal.

sports *n. pl.* games or competitions involving physical activity.

spot[1] *n.* **1** a small, round mark. **2** a place. *a nice spot for a picnic.* **3** a small, red mark on your skin.

spot[2] *v.* (spots, spotting, spotted) to notice something. *Can you spot the mistake in this picture?*

spotless *adj.* very clean.

spotlight *n.* a strong beam of light that is used to light up a small area.

spouse *n.* a husband or wife.

spout *n.* the part of a pitcher or teapot where the liquid is poured out.

sprain *v.* to twist a joint, for example, your ankle, and injure it. **sprain** *n.*

sprang *past of* spring.

sprawl *v.* **1** to sit or lie with your arms and legs spread out widely. **2** to spread out in a disorganized way. *The suburbs have sprawled into the countryside.*

spray *n.* (*pl.* sprays) a mist of small, flying drops of liquid. **spray** *v.*

spread *v.* (spreading, spread) **1** to cover a surface with something. *I spread the bread with butter.* **2** to open out. *Spread the map out on the table.* **3** to reach a wider area or a larger number of people. *The disease is spreading.* **4** to distribute over a wider area or to a larger number of people. *Spread the news!* **spread** *n.*

spreadsheet *n.* a computer program that can do mathematical calculations.

sprig *adj.* a small piece of a plant.

spring[1] *v.* (springing, sprang, sprung) to jump or move suddenly.

spring[2] *n.* **1** the warmer season of the year when plants begin to grow again after the cold winter. **2** a wire coil that returns to its original shape after being pressed down. **3** a small stream of water flowing out of the ground.

sprinkle *v.* to scatter in small drops or pieces. *He sprinkled salt on his food.*

sprint *v.* to run very fast. **sprinter** *n.*

sprout[1] *v.* to start to grow.

sprout[2] *n.* a small, round, green vegetable, also called a Brussels sprout.

spun *past of* spin.

spur[1] *n.* a sharp point on a rider's boot, used to dig into the horse's side to make it go faster. **on the spur of the moment** without planning it.

spur[2] *v.* (spurring, spurred) to encourage somebody to do something. *The thought of the prize spurred her into action.*

spurt *v.* to burst out in a sudden stream. *Water spurted from the pipe.* **spurt** *n.*

spy[1] *n.* a person who tries to get secret information, e.g. about the military operations of another country.

spy[2] *v.* (spies, spying, spied) **1** to be a spy. **2** to notice something.

squabble *v.* to quarrel about something unimportant. **squabble** *n.*

squad *n.* a small group of soldiers or other people working together.

squalid *adj.* filthy. **squalor** *n. The family was relieved to move out of the squalid apartment.*

squander *v.* to waste something. *She squanders all of her money on gambling.*

square[1] *n.* **1** a shape with four equal sides and four right angles. **2** an open space with buildings on all sides. **square** *adj.*

square[2] *v.* to multiply a number by itself. *Three squared is nine.*

square root *n.* the number that, when multiplied by itself, gives a certain other number. *Four is the square root of 16.*

squid

squash¹ *v.* to press or crush something so that it becomes flat.

squash² *n.* **1** a game for two players in a walled court using rackets and a rubber ball. **2** the state of being crowded in a small space.

squat *v.* (squatting, squatted) **1** to sit on your heels. **2** to occupy a building without permission. **squat** *n.*

squawk *n.* a loud, harsh cry. **squawk** *v.*

squeak *v.* to make a short, high-pitched sound like a mouse. **squeak** *n.*

squeal *v.* to make a long, high-pitched sound. **squeal** *n.*

squeeze *v.* **1** to press something tightly. **2** to force somebody or something into a small space. **squeeze** *n.*

squid *n.* a sea creature with tentacles.

squint¹ *v.* to look at something with your eyes half closed, especially in bright light.

squint² *n.* to have eyes that look in two directions at the same time.

squirrel *n.* a small gray or red mammal with a bushy tail.

squirt *v.* to shoot out a narrow jet of liquid. **squirt** *n.*

St. 1 a short way of writing saint. *St. Patrick.* **2** a short way of writing street. *Main St.*

stab *v.* (stabbing, stabbed) to push a knife or pointed object into somebody. **stab** *n.,* **stabbing** *n.*

stable¹ *n.* a building in which horses and other animals are kept.

stable² *adj.* **1** firm and steady. *This chair is not stable.* **2** firmly established; not changing. *stable government.* **3** sensible;

not easily upset. *a stable personality.*

stack *n.* a large pile. **stack** *v.*

stadium *n.* (*pl.* stadiums *or* stadia) a large sports arena with seats for spectators.

staff *n.* **1** all the people employed by an organization. **2** a thick stick.

stag *n.* an adult male deer.

stage¹ *n.* **1** a raised platform in a theater on which people perform plays. **2** a point in the development of something.

stage² *v.* to organize an event. *The residents are staging a protest about the plans to knock down the apartment building.*

stagecoach *n.* *(historical)* a horse-drawn vehicle carrying passengers and mail on regular routes.

stagger *v.* **1** to walk unsteadily. **2** to shock somebody deeply. *I was staggered by his rudeness.* **3** to arrange events so that they do not begin or end at the same time. *The employees were asked to stagger their vacations.*

staggering *adj.* astonishing.

stagnant *adj.* (of water) standing still instead of flowing and therefore not pure. **stagnate** *v.*

stalagmite / stalactite

stain *n.* a mark that is difficult to remove. **stain** *v.*

stained glass *n.* colored glass cut into shapes and then attached in a pattern using lead; usually seen in church windows.

stairs *n. pl.* a set of steps in a building.

stake *n.* **1** a strong stick, pointed at one end, used, for example, as part of a fence. **2** a sum of money that you risk or gamble. **3** an investment in a company. **at stake** at risk. **stake** *v.*

stalactite *n.* an icicle-shaped rock formation hanging from the roof of a cave, caused by water dripping.

stalagmite *n.* an icicle-shaped rock formation rising up from the floor of a cave, caused by water dripping.

stale *adj.* no longer fresh.

A
B
C
D
E
F
G
H
I
J
K
L
M
N
O
P
Q
R
S
T
U
V
W
X
Y
Z

stalemate *n.* a point in an argument or a game of chess when neither side can win.

stalk[1] *adj.* the main stem of a plant or one of the stems of a plant that holds a leaf, flower, or fruit.

stalk[2] *v.* **1** to follow an animal or person closely and secretly. **2** to walk stiffly and proudly. *She stalked out of the room in a fury.*

stall[1] *n.* **1** a stand or booth with items for sale. **2** a part of a barn or stable for one animal. **3** a small compartment.

stall[2] *v.* **1** to stop a car engine by mistake. *He stalled at the lights.* **2** to delay doing something. *stall for time.*

stallion *n.* an adult male horse.

stamen *n.* one of the threadlike parts in the center of a flower that produces the pollen. See **flower**.

stamina *n.* strength to go on exercising or working for a long time.

stammer *v.* to have difficulty saying the first letter of words when you are speaking. **stammer** *n.*

stamp[1] *n.* **1** a small piece of printed paper that you stick to a letter or package to show that you have paid to mail it. **2** a small object that you use to print a design or mark on paper. *a date stamp.*

stamp[2] *v.* **1** to bring your foot down with force. **2** to print on something with a stamp. **3** to put a postage stamp on something. **stamp out** to stop or put an end to something.

stampede *n.* a sudden rush by a large group of animals or people in a panic. **stampede** *v.*

stand[1] *v.* (standing, stood) **1** to be upright. *Helen stood at the top of the stairs.* **2** to get up on your feet. *I stood up when Dinesh came into the room.* **3** to be situated somewhere. *The hotel stands on a cliff top.* **4** to remain unchanged. *My decision still stands.* **5** to put up with something; to bear. *I can't stand rudeness!* **stand for** to represent. *"UN" stands for "United Nations."* **stand in** to take somebody's place. **stand out** to be easily noticed. **stand up for** to support or defend somebody. **stand up to** to defend yourself against somebody.

stand[2] *n.* **1** an object for holding or supporting something. *a coat stand.* **2** a booth where items are displayed. **3** a structure at a sports arena with seats for spectators.

standard[1] *n.* **1** a level against which things can be judged or measured. *His work does not reach the required standard.* **2** a flag.

standard[2] *adj.* usual or ordinary. *This is a standard-sized box of cereal.*

stank *past of* stink.

staple[1] *n.* a small piece of wire that is forced through pieces of paper to attach them together. **staple** *v.*, **stapler** *n.*

staple[2] *adj.* chief; main. *Rice is the staple food in many countries.*

star[1] *n.* **1** any of the bodies in the sky that appear at night as small, bright lights. **2** a shape with a number of points, usually five or six. **3** a famous actor or performer.

starfish

star[2] *v.* (starring, starred) to have the main part in a play or movie.

starboard *n.* the right side of a ship or aircraft if you are facing the front.

starch *n.* **1** a substance found in foods such as potatoes and rice. **2** a substance used for making clothes stiff. **starch** *v.*, **starchy** *adj.*

stare *v.* to look hard at something for a long time. *Everyone stared at her green hair.* **stare** *n.*

starfish *n.* (*pl.* starfish *or* starfishes) a small sea creature with five points or arms.

starling *n.* a common bird with dark, glossy feathers.

starry *adj.* full of stars. *a starry sky.*

start *v.* **1** to begin. **2** to make a machine go. **3** to jump in surprise or fright. **start** *n.*

startle *v.* to suddenly give somebody a shock or fright.

starve *v.* to suffer or die from hunger. **starvation** *n.*

state[1] *n.* **1** the condition of somebody or something. *The house is in a messy state.* **2** a country or part of a country with its own government and laws.

state[2] *v.* to say something very clearly and definitely.

statement *n.* **1** something that is stated. **2** a record of all of the money paid into and out of an account.

static *adj.* not moving or changing.

static electricity *n.* electric sparks caused by friction.

station *n.* **1** a place where trains or buses stop so that passengers can get on and off. **2** a headquarters or center. *a fire station, a police station.*

stationary *adj.* standing still, not moving.

stationery *n.* all types of writing materials.

statistics *n. pl.* figures that give information about something. **statistical** *adj.*, **statistically** *adv.*

statue *n.* a model of a person or animal that has been made from stone, metal, clay, or another material.

status *n.* a position or ranking.

stay *v.* **1** to continue to be. **2** to live for a time somewhere. **stay** *n.*

steady[1] *adj.* (steadier, steadiest) **1** firm; not shaking or moving. *Hold the camera steady.* **2** regular, even, or not changing. *a steady pace.* **steadily** *adv.*

steady[2] *v.* (steadies, steadying, steadied) to make something steady.

steak *n.* a thickly-sliced piece of meat or fish.

steal *v.* (stealing, stole, stolen) **1** to take something that does not belong to you, without permission. **2** to move secretly and quietly. *He stole out of the room.*

steam[1] *n.* the hot gas that water turns into when it boils. **steamy** *adj.*

steam[2] *v.* **1** to give off steam. **2** to cook something by steam.

steam engine *n.* an engine, especially a train engine, powered by steam.

steamroller *n.* a steam-driven vehicle with wide, heavy wheels, used for flattening road surfaces.

steel *n.* a strong, very hard metal made from iron and carbon.

steep *adj.* sloping sharply. **steepness** *n.*

steeple *n.* a church tower with a spire.

steer *v.* to control the direction of a vehicle, usually using a steering wheel or rudder.

stem *n.* the part of a plant from which the leaves and flowers grow.

stench *n.* a strong, unpleasant smell.

stencil *n.* a sheet of cardboard, plastic, or metal with a pattern cut out of it. The pattern is applied to a surface by painting over the stencil. **stencil** *v.*

step[1] *n.* **1** the movement of lifting your foot and putting it down again when walking or dancing. **2** one of the places to put your feet when going up or down a flight of stairs or a ladder. **3** one stage in doing something.

step[2] *v.* (steps, stepping, stepped) to take a step; to walk.

step- *prefix* related through one parent. *stepfather, stepsister.*

stereo *n.* (*pl.* stereos) a system for playing recorded music in which different instruments or voices are transmitted through different speakers.

stereotype *n.* a set idea about a type of person or thing. **stereotypical** *adj.*

sterile *adj.* **1** completely clean and free from germs. **2** unable to produce young. **sterility** *n.,* **sterilize** *v.*

stern[1] *adj.* serious and severe.

stern[2] *n.* the back part of a ship.

stethoscope *n.* an instrument used by a doctor to listen to a patient's breathing or heartbeat.

stethoscope

stew[1] *n.* meat or vegetables cooked in liquid for a long time.

stew[2] *v.* to cook by boiling slowly.

steward *n.* **1** a person who attends to passengers on an airplane or ship. **2** a person who helps organize a race, concert, or other large public event.

stewardess *n.* a female steward on a ship or airplane; cabin crew member.

stick[1] *n.* **1** a long, thin piece of wood. **2** a long, thin piece of something. *a stick of dynamite.*

stick[2] *v.* (sticking, stuck) **1** to push something that is pointed into something else. **2** to attach something to something else using glue. **3** to become fixed in place. *My boot got stuck in the mud.* **stick out 1** to be farther out than something else. *His front teeth stick out.* **2** to be very noticeable. **stick up for** to support or defend somebody.

sticker *n.* a sticky label with a picture or words on it.

sticky *adj.* (stickier, stickiest) capable of sticking to things.

stiff *adj.* **1** firm, not easy to bend. **2** moving with difficulty or pain. *a stiff neck.* **3** severe; harsh. *a stiff punishment.* **4** too formal in behavior. **stiffen** *v.*

A B C D E F G H I J K L M N O P Q R S T U V W X Y Z

stifle *v.* **1** to suffocate. **2** to stop something from happening. *She stifled a giggle.*

still¹ *adj.* **1** staying in one position, not moving. **2** (of a drink) not carbonated.

still² *adv.* **1** continuing until now. *Is it still snowing?* **2** even so. *Alice was sick, but she still went out.* **3** even. *We drove for hours, but we had still further to go.*

stilts *n. pl.* **1** long poles with parts where you put your feet to walk high up above the ground. **2** tall poles on which a house is sometimes built.

stimulate *v.* to make a person or thing more active or interested. **stimulation** *n.*

sting¹ *n.* **1** the part of some creatures, such as bees, that can prick your skin; stinger. **2** the wound or pain caused by this.

sting² *v.* (stinging, stung) **1** to wound with a sting. **2** to feel or cause a sharp or tingling pain. *The soap in my eyes made them sting.*

stingy (*stin-jee*) *adj.* (stingier, stingiest) not generous. **stinginess** *n.*

stink *v.* (stinking, stank, stunk) to smell very unpleasant. **stink** *n.*

stir¹ *v.* (stirring, stirred) **1** to move liquid or solid materials around with a spoon or a stick. **2** to move slightly. *She stirred in her sleep.* **3** to rouse somebody.

stir² *n.* a disturbance or fuss.

stirrup *n.* a metal loop hung from a horse's or pony's saddle to support a rider's foot.

stitch¹ *n.* **1** the loop made in wool or thread by a needle when knitting or sewing. **2** a sudden pain in your side; cramp.

stitch² *v.* to sew something.

stock¹ *n.* **1** the goods in a store or warehouse. **2** a liquid in which meat or vegetables have been boiled, used to make soups or sauces. **3** a share in the value of a company. **4 stocks** *(historical)* a wooden structure with holes for the feet, where criminals used to be put as a punishment.

stock² *v.* to keep a supply of items for sale. *The supermarket stocks the best wine in town.*

stocking *n.* an extremely tight-fitting piece of women's clothing that covers the foot and leg.

stocky *adj.* (stockier, stockiest) short and stout.

stodgy *adj.* (stodgier, stodgiest) (of food) heavy and not easily digested.

stirrup

stole *past of* steal.

stolen *past participle of* steal.

stomach *n.* the organ of your body where food is digested.

stone *n.* **1** a hard, solid substance found in the ground. **2** a small piece of this.

stony *adj.* (stonier, stoniest) full of or covered with stones.

stood *past of* stand.

stool *n.* a seat without a back.

stoop *v.* to bend your body forward and down at the same time.

stop *v.* (stopping, stopped) **1** to finish moving or happening. **2** to finish doing something. **3** to prevent. **4** to fill a hole or gap. **stop** *n.*

stopwatch *n.* a watch that you can stop and start, used for timing races.

store¹ *v.* to keep things until they are needed. **storage** *n.*

store² *n.* **1** a place where merchandise is sold. **2** a supply of something that you keep for future use. **3** a place where things are kept.

stork *n.* a large, white-and-black bird with a long beak, neck, and legs.

stork

storm¹ *n.* very bad weather, with strong winds, heavy rain, and often thunder and lightning.

storm² *v.* **1** to move somewhere in an angry and noisy way. *Dad stormed out of the room.* **2** to attack a place suddenly. *They stormed the castle.*

story *n.* **1** an account of people and events that are real or imaginary. **2** one level of a building; a floor.

stout *adj.* **1** sturdy; solid. **2** strong. *stout boots.*

stove *n.* an apparatus for cooking or for heating a room.

stowaway *n.* (*pl.* stowaways) a person who hides in a ship or aircraft in order to travel in secret or without having to pay.

liver · · · · · · stomach

large intestine · · · · · · small intestine

stomach and digestive system

straight[1] *adj.* **1** not bent or curved. *a straight line.* **2** level. *That picture isn't straight.* **3** honest. *a straight answer.* **4** neat and organized. *It took hours to get the room straight.* **straighten** *v.*

straight[2] *adv.* **1** in a straight line. **2** directly.

straightforward *adj.* **1** simple; without difficulty. *a straightforward task.* **2** honest and open. *He is a fairly straightforward person.*

strain[1] *v.* **1** to try very hard to do something. *He had to strain his ears to hear her.* **2** to injure a part of your body by using it too much or by stretching the muscles. **3** to separate matter from liquid by using a sieve or a similar implement.

strain[2] *n.* **1** a force that pulls or stretches something. **2** the bad effect of too much work or worrying.

strait *n.* a narrow strip of sea between two pieces of land.

strand *n.* a length of something, especially hair or thread.

stranded *adj.* left helpless somewhere.

strange *adj.* **1** odd; unusual. **2** unfamiliar; not known or seen before.

stranger *n.* **1** a person you do not know. **2** a person who is in a place for the first time. *I'm a stranger in this town.*

strangle *v.* to kill somebody by squeezing his or her throat hard. **strangulation** *n.*

strap[1] *n.* a strip of leather or cloth used to fasten, hold, or carry things.

strap[2] *v.* (strapping, strapped) to fasten something with straps.

strategy *n.* a plan for achieving something. **strategic** *adj.*, **strategically** *adv.*

straw *n.* **1** dry stalks of hay. **2** a thin tube for drinking through.

strawberry *n.* a small, red, soft fruit.

stray[1] *v.* to wander away.

stray[2] *adj.* **1** wandering; lost. *a stray cat.* **2** scattered. *stray crumbs.*

streak[1] *n.* a long mark or stripe.

streak[2] *v.* to run fast.

stream[1] *n.* **1** a small river. **2** a flow of anything. *We had a stream of customers.*

stream[2] *v.* to move or flow fast.

streamer *n.* a long strip of colored paper, used for decorating a place.

streamline *v.* **1** to shape a vehicle so that it can cut through air or water easily. **2** to make a process or system faster or more efficient.

street *n.* a road, usually with sidewalks.

strength *n.* the state of being strong. **strengthen** *v.*

strenuous *adj.* needing a lot of effort. *a strenuous climb.*

stress[1] *n.* the effect of too much worry or work on a person.

stress[2] *v.* to give special emphasis or importance to something.

stretch[1] *v.* **1** to make or become longer or bigger, especially by pulling. **2** to reach or extend.

stretch[2] *n.* **1** an act of stretching. **2** a length of time or distance. *this stretch of coast.*

stretcher *n.* a light, folding bed for carrying sick or injured people.

injured woman on a stretcher

strict *adj.* **1** not allowing people to break rules or behave badly. **2** exact. *strict rules.* **strictness** *n.*

stride *v.* (striding, strode, stridden) to walk with long steps. **stride** *n.*

strife *n.* trouble or fighting.

strike *v.* (striking, struck) **1** to hit hard. **2** to stop work as a protest. **3** to make a ringing sound. *The clock struck two.* **4** to impress. *I was struck by her beauty.* **5** to make a flame by rubbing. *He struck a match.* **strike** *n.*

striker *n.* an attacking player in soccer.

striker

striking *adj.* noticeable; impressive.

string *n.* **1** thin cord or rope. **2** a piece of thin wire or nylon on a musical instrument. **3 the strings** the group of musical instruments in an orchestra that have strings.

strip¹ *n.* a long, narrow piece of something.

strip² *v.* (stripping, stripped) **1** to take off all your clothes. **2** to tear off. *Dad stripped off all the paint.*

stripe *n.* a band of color. **striped** *adj.*, **stripy** (*or* **stripey**) *adj.*

strive *v.* (striving, strove, striven *or* strived) to try hard; to struggle.

strode *past* of stride.

stroke¹ *v.* to move your hand gently over something, often with affection.

stroke² *n.* **1** an act of stroking something. **2** a hit. *a stroke of the ax.* **3** a sudden occurrence of something. *a stroke of luck.* **4** a sudden illness that can paralyze part of a person's body or leave the person unable to speak well. **5** one movement of a pen or paintbrush. **6** a particular type or style of movement used in swimming.

stroll *v.* to walk along slowly, for pleasure. **stroll** *n.*

stroller *n.* a small carriage for a baby, pushed along by a person on foot.

strong *adj.* **1** powerful; not weak. **2** not easily broken or damaged. **3** very noticeable; intense. *a strong smell.*

strove *past* of strive.

struck *past* of strike.

structure *n.* **1** something that has been built. **2** the way that the parts of something are arranged.

struggle *v.* **1** to try hard to do something difficult. *Lauren is struggling with her homework.* **2** to fight with somebody while trying to escape. **struggle** *n.*

strut¹ *v.* (strutting, strutted) to walk along in a stiff, proud way.

strut² *n.* a wooden or metal bar that supports something.

stub¹ *n.* the short, blunt end piece, for example, of a cigarette or pencil.

stub² *v.* (stubbing, stubbed) to hit your toe against something.

stubborn *adj.* not willing to change or to do what other people want. **stubbornness** *n.*

stuck *past* of stick.

student *n.* a person who is studying at school.

studio *n.* (*pl.* studios) **1** a room where an artist or photographer works. **2** a place where movies, CDs, or radio and television shows are made.

studious *adj.* spending a lot of time studying.

study¹ *v.* (studies, studying, studied) **1** to spend time learning about something. **2** to look carefully at something. *We studied the map.*

study² *n.* a room where somebody reads, writes, or studies.

stuff¹ *n.* any material or substance.

stuff² *v.* to pack or fill something tightly. *The pillow is stuffed with feathers.* **stuffing** *n.*

stuffy *adj.* (stuffier, stuffiest) **1** full of stale air. *a stuffy room.* **2** too formal and old-fashioned.

stumble *v.* **1** to trip and almost fall. **2** to make mistakes or hesitate when speaking. *She stumbled over the lines.*

stump *n.* the part of something that is left when the rest has been cut or broken off. *a tree stump.*

stun *v.* (stuns, stunning, stunned) **1** to make a person or an animal unconscious by applying a blow to the head. **2** to shock somebody.

stung *past* of sting.

stunk *past participle* of stink.

stunning *adj.* when something is very attractive or impressive.

stunt¹ *n.* something daring or spectacular, done to attract attention.

stunt² *v.* to stop something growing or developing properly.

stupid *adj.* silly or lacking common sense. **stupidity** *n.*

sturdy *adj.* (sturdier, sturdiest) strong; well built.

stutter *v.* to stammer. **stutter** *n.*

sty *n.* **1** a painful, red swelling on your eyelid. (*can also be spelled* stye.) **2** a pen in which pigs are kept; pigsty.

style *n.* **1** the way something is done or made. *different styles of architecture.* **2** elegance in dress or behavior. *He has style.* **stylish** *adj.*

Styrofoam *n.* a light, artificial substance used to make packaging material and disposable cups.

sub- *prefix* under; below. *substandard.*

subdue *v.* to bring somebody or something under control.

subdued *adj.* quiet or lacking strength. *Kareem is very subdued today.*

subject[1] (**sub**-jekt) *n.* **1** a thing or person that is being talked or written about. **2** an area of study at school. **3** a citizen. *a British subject.*

subject[2] (*sub*-**jekt**) *v.* to make somebody suffer something. *They subjected him to cruel treatment.*

submarine *n.* a type of boat that has been designed to travel under water.

submarine

submerge *v.* to put something under water.

submit *v.* (submitting, submitted) **1** to give in to somebody stronger. **2** to hand in a piece of written work. **submission** *n.*

subscribe *v.* to pay for a magazine or newspaper to be sent to you regularly. **subscription** *n.*

subside *v.* **1** to sink lower. *The flood gradually subsided.* **2** to become quieter. *The applause subsided.*

subsidy *n.* money paid by a government or other organization to keep the price of something artificially low. **subsidize** *v.*

substance *n.* anything that can be seen or touched; a material.

substantial *adj.* **1** large. *a substantial meal.* **2** solid; strong.

substitute *v.* to put something in the place of something else. *Substitute margarine for butter in this recipe.* **substitute** *n.*

subtle (*sut*-ul) *adj.* not very noticeable or obvious. *a subtle difference.* **subtlety** *n.*, **subtly** *adv.*

subtract *v.* to take one number or quantity away from another. **subtraction** *n.*

suburb *n.* an area on the edge of a town or city where people live. **suburban** *adj.*

subway *n.* (*pl.* subways) **1** an underground train system. **2** an underground tunnel for pedestrians.

succeed *v.* **1** to manage to achieve something that you were trying to do. **2** to follow after someone and take that person's place. *Who will succeed John Fraser as the manager of the*

club? **success** *n.*, **successful** *adj.*

suck *v.* **1** to draw liquid or air into your mouth. **2** to hold something in your mouth, licking it without biting it, for example, a lollipop. **3** to draw something in. *Vacuum cleaners suck up dust.* **suction** *n.*

sudden *adj.* happening quickly and unexpectedly. **suddenness** *n.*

sue *v.* to start a legal case, usually in order to get money from somebody.

suede (*swade*) *n.* a type of leather with a soft surface, like velvet.

suffer *v.* to experience pain or unhappiness. **suffering** *n.*

sufficient *adj.* enough.

suffix *n.* a letter or letters added to the end of the word to make another word such as *-ness* added to *good* to make *goodness.*

suffocate *v.* **1** to die because you cannot breathe. **2** to kill somebody by stopping that person's breathing. **suffocation** *n.*

sugar *n.* a sweet substance obtained from plants such as sugar cane and sugar beets. **sugary** *adj.*

suggest *v.* to put forward an idea. **suggestion** *n.*

sugar

refined sugar

sugar beet

sugar cane

suicide *n.* the act of killing yourself deliberately. **suicidal** *adj.*

suit[1] *n.* **1** a jacket with pants or a skirt, made to be worn together. **2** one of the four sets of playing cards (hearts, clubs, diamonds, spades). **3** a case in a law court.

suit[2] *v.* **1** to look good on somebody. *That color really suits you.* **2** to be convenient or suitable. *Would Friday suit you for a meeting?*

suitable *adj.* right or convenient for somebody or something. **suitability** *n.*

suitcase *n.* a case with flat sides for carrying your clothes in when you are traveling from one place to another.

a
b
c
d
e
f
g
h
i
j
k
l
m
n
o
p
q
r
s
t
u
v
w
x
y
z

suite *(sweet)* *n.* **1** a set of related items that are used together. *a bedroom suite.* **2** a set of rooms in a hotel. *The honeymoon suite.*

sulfur, sulphur *n.* a yellow chemical element with a strong, unpleasant smell, used to make matches and gunpowder.

sulk *v.* to show anger by being silent. *Carol sulked at the dinner table.* **sulky** *adj.,* **sulkily** *adv.*

sullen *adj.* bad-tempered and silent.

sultan *n.* a Muslim ruler.

sultana *n.* **1** the wife, daughter, or sister of a sultan. **2** a dried, seedless grape.

sum¹ *n.* **1** the total made by adding two or more numbers together. **2** an amount of money. **3** a problem in arithmetic.

sum² *v.* (summing, summed) **sum up** to give the main points of something.

summary *n.* a short description of the main points. *The newspaper printed a summary of her speech.* **summarize** *v.*

summer *n.* the warmest season of the year, between spring and fall.

summit *n.* **1** the top of a mountain. **2** an important meeting of world leaders.

summon *v.* to order somebody to come.

sumo *n.* a Japanese form of wrestling.

sun *n.* **1 Sun** the star that shines during the day and gives us heat and light. **2** light and heat from the Sun. **sunny** *adj.*

sunbathe *v.* to lie or sit in the sun in order to get a suntan.

sunburn *n.* red, sore skin caused by spending too long in the sun.

Sunday *n.* the first day of the week.

sundial *n.* an instrument for telling the time using the shadow of a rod cast on its surface by the sunlight.

sunflower *n.* a variety of tall, large, yellow flower.

sung *past participle of* sing.

sunglasses *n. pl.* glasses with dark lenses to protect your eyes in bright sunlight.

sunk *past participle of* sink.

sunrise *n.* the rising of the Sun over the horizon in the morning.

sunset *n.* the going down of the Sun below the horizon in the evening.

sunshine *n.* bright light from the Sun.

suntan *n.* a brown color of the skin caused by spending time in the sun.

super *adj.* extremely good; wonderful.

super- *prefix* above; over; more than. *superpower.*

superb *adj.* when something is excellent or magnificent.

superficial *adj.* on the surface only. *The cut is only superficial—it will soon heal.* **superficially** *adv.*

superior *adj.* **1** better. **2** higher in ranking. **3** thinking that you are better than others. **superiority** *n.*

supermarket *n.* a large, self-service store selling food and other items.

supernatural *adj.* not capable of being explained by the laws of nature. *a supernatural being.*

supersonic *adj.* able to travel faster than the speed of sound.

superstition *n.* a belief in powers that cannot be explained, especially a belief that certain things bring good or bad luck. **superstitious** *adj.*

supervise *v.* to be in charge of work and make sure that it is done correctly. **supervision** *n.,* **supervisor** *n.*

supper *n.* an evening meal or snack; dinner.

supple *adj.* able to bend and stretch easily. *Exercise will keep your body supple.* **suppleness** *n.*

supplement *n.* something that is added to something else. **supplement** *v.,* **supplementary** *adj.*

supply *v.* (supplies, supplying, supplied) to give or provide something. **supplier** *n.,* **supply** *n.*

support *v.* **1** to carry the weight of something. *That bridge won't support heavy trucks.* **2** to give somebody money, help, or encouragement. *Her family supported her in her decision.* **support** *n.,* **supporter** *n.*

suppose *v.* to think that something is true, but not be sure.

suppress *v.* **1** to stop something by using force. *The army suppressed the rebellion.* **2** to prevent a feeling from being seen. *During the boring movie, she managed to suppress a yawn.*

supreme *adj.* greatest; most important; best. **supremacy** *n.*

sure *adj.* having no doubt; certain.

surf¹ *n.* the foam that is produced as waves break on the shore.

surf² *v.* **1** to ride on the surf, using a long, narrow board called a **surfboard**. **2** to look at different Web sites on the

a
b
c
d
e
f
g
h
i
j
k
l
m
n
o
p
q
r
s
t
u
v
w
x
y
z

Internet. **surfer** *n.*

surface *n.* the outside or top layer of something. *the surface of the Moon.*

surgeon *(ser-jun) n.* a doctor who performs medical operations.

surgery *n.* the treatment of a disease or injury by operating. **surgical** *adj.*, **surgically** *adv.*

surly *adj.* (surlier, surliest) rude and unfriendly. **surliness** *n.*

surplus *n.* the amount that is left over.

surprise *n.* **1** the feeling that you have when something unexpected happens. **2** an unexpected event. **surprise** *v.*

surrender *v.* to give up; to admit that you are defeated. **surrender** *n.*

surround *v.* to be all around something.

surroundings *n. pl.* everything that is around somebody or something.

survey¹ *(ser-vay) v.* **1** to look at something carefully. *She surveyed the garden from her window.* **2** to measure and make a map of an area of land. **surveyor** *n.*

survey² *(ser-vay) n.* (*pl.* surveys) **1** an act of surveying a building. **2** a study of something or of people's opinions.

survive *v.* to continue to live or exist. **survival** *n.*, **survivor** *n.*

suspect¹ *(suss-pekt) v.* **1** to believe that something could be true. *I suspect that she's unhappy.* **2** to believe that a person is guilty of something.

suspect² *(suss-pekt) n.* a person who is thought to be guilty of a crime.

suspend *v* .**1** to hang something up. **2** to stop something for a while. **3** to stop somebody from doing his or her job or from going to school for a while, as a punishment. **suspension** *n.*

suspense *n.* a state of uncertainty or worry.

suspicion *n.* the feeling of suspecting somebody or something.

suspicious *adj.* **1** feeling or showing suspicion or mistrust. **2** causing suspicion.

sustain *v.* **1** to support physically or mentally. **2** to allow something to continue for a time. **3** to suffer an injury or other bad experience. **sustainable** *adj.*

swallow¹ *v.* to make foods or drinks go down your throat.

swallow² *n.* a small bird with long, slim wings and a forked tail.

swam *past of* swim.

swamp *n.* wet, marshy ground.

swan with her cygnets

swan *n.* a type of large, white, long-necked water bird.

swap *v.* (swapping, swapped) to exchange one thing for another. *We swapped phone numbers.* **swap** *n.*

swarm *n.* a large group of bees or other insects moving together. **swarm** *v.*

swat *v.* (swatting, swatted) to kill an insect by hitting it with something flat.

sway *v.* to move from side to side.

swear *v.* (swearing, swore, sworn) **1** to make a solemn promise. **2** to use curse words. *Please don't swear like that here.*

sweat *n.* the liquid that comes out of your skin when you are hot or nervous. **sweat** *v.*, **sweaty** *adj.*

sweater *n.* a jacket or pullover, especially one that is knitted.

sweatshirt *n.* a thick, cotton, long-sleeved shirt.

sweep *v.* (sweeping, swept) **1** to clean by removing dirt or dust with a bedroom. **2** to move quickly and with force. *The giant waves swept the boat out to sea.*

sweet¹ *adj.* **1** tasting like sugar; not salty or sour. **2** pleasant; lovely. *a sweet smell.* **sweetness** *n.*

sweet² *n.* **1** a small piece of sweet food.

swell *v.* (swelling, swelled, swollen) to become bigger or fatter. *The insect bite made her finger swell up.* **swelling** *n.*

sweltering *adj.* very hot.

swept *past of* sweep.

swerve *v.* to change direction suddenly. *The driver swerved to avoid hitting the dog.*

A
B
C
D
E
F
G
H
I
J
K
L
M
N
O
P
Q
R
S
T
U
V
W
X
Y
Z

swift[1] *adj.* quick. **swiftness** *n.*

swift[2] *n.* a bird similar to a swallow.

swim *v.* (swimming, swam, swum) to use your arms and legs to move yourself through water. **swim** *n.*, **swimmer** *n.*

swindle *v.* to cheat somebody out of money.

swing[1] *v.* (swinging, swung) to move, while suspended, backward and forward or from side to side.

swing[2] *n.* a seat for swinging, hung on ropes or chains from a support.

swipe *v.* **1** to try to hit something by making a swinging movement. **2** to put a credit or other card through an electronic machine. **3** *(informal)* to steal something. **swipe** *n.*

swirl *v.* to move around and around. *The falling leaf swirled through the air.*

switch *n.* **1** a device for turning a light or other electrical appliance on and off. **2** a sudden change. **switch** *v.*

switchboard *n.* a type of console, in an office or hotel, where telephone calls are connected.

swivel *v.* (swiveling, swiveled) to turn on a central point.

swollen *past participle of* swell.

swoop *v.* to rush or fly downward. *The eagle swooped on its prey.* **swoop** *n.*

sword *(sord) n.* a weapon with a handle and a long blade.

swore *past of* swear.

sworn *past participle of* swear.

swum *past participle of* swim.

swung *past of* swing.

syllable *n.* a word or part of a word spoken with one breath. *Ambulance has three syllables: am-bu-lance.*

syllabus *n.* (*pl.* syllabuses *or* syllabi) a list of subjects to be studied.

symbol *n.* a thing that stands for or represents something. *The dove is a symbol of peace.* **symbolic** *adj.*, **symbolize** *v.*

symmetrical *adj.* having the same shape and size on both sides of a central line. **symmetry** *n.*

sympathy *n.* an understanding of other people's feelings and problems. **sympathetic** *adj.*, **sympathetically** *adv.*, **sympathize** *v.*

symphony *(sim-fa-nee) n.* a long piece of music for a large orchestra.

symptom *n.* a sign that you have an illness. *Sneezing, a fever, and a headache are the symptoms of flu.*

synagogue *(sin-a-gog) n.* a Jewish place of worship.

synonym *n.* a word that has the same meaning, or almost the same meaning, as another word. *Reply* is a synonym of *answer.*

synthesizer *n.* an electronic keyboard instrument that can make many different sounds.

synthetic *adj.* created artificially.

syphon *another spelling of* siphon.

syringe *n.* an instrument with a tube and a needle, used to take blood from a patient or to inject medication.

syrup *n.* a sticky, sweet liquid, made mostly from sugar.

system *n.* **1** an arrangement of several parts that work together. *the subway system.* **2** a way of organizing something. *a system of education.*

symmetrical shape

Tt

tab *n.* a small piece of metal, paper, or cloth attached to something so that it can be pulled or identified.

tabby *n.* a gray or brown striped cat.

table *n.* **1** a piece of furniture with a flat top on legs. **2** a list of facts or figures arranged in columns.

tablespoon *n.* a large spoon used for serving or measuring food.

tablet *n.* a flat block of stone with words cut into it.

table tennis *n.* a game played on a table with small bats and a light ball, often indoors; Ping-Pong.

tabloid *n.* a small-sized newspaper.

taboo *n.* anything forbidden for religious reasons or by social custom.

tack¹ *n.* a small, flat-headed nail.

tack² *v.* **1** to attach something with tacks. *They tacked down the carpet.* **2** to sew with long, loose stitches. **3** to sail a boat on a zigzag course into the wind.

tackle¹ *v.* **1** to deal with a difficulty. *We still have several problems to tackle.* **2** to try to take the ball from another player in a game such as football.

tackle² *n.* equipment for a sport or another activity, especially in fishing.

tact *n.* skill in dealing with people so that you do not upset them. **tactless** *adj.*, **tactful** *adj.*

tactics *n. pl.* plans or methods used to win a game, contest, or battle. **tactical** *adj.*

tadpole

tadpole *n.* a young frog or toad at the stage between the egg and adult.

taffy *n.* a sticky, chewy candy made from boiled sugar and butter.

tag *n.* **1** a small label. **2** a chasing game.

tail *n.* **1** the part of a creature that sticks out behind the rest of its body. **2** the end part. *the tail of a plane.*

tailor *n.* a person whose job is making suits, coats, and other clothes, especially for men.

take *v.* (taking, took, taken) **1** to reach out for something and grasp or hold it. *Take this money.* **2** to carry or lead to another place. *I took the books back to the library.* **3** to accept. *Do you take credit cards?* **4** to need or require. *It takes a long time to learn to play the piano.* **5** to travel by bus, train, or other vehicle. *We're taking the next bus to Chicago.* **6** to do an action. *They decided to take a walk.* **take after** to be or look like somebody in your family. *Doesn't Ella take after her mom?* **take off** **1** to remove clothes. **2** (of a plane) to leave the ground. **3** to copy the way somebody talks or behaves. **take over** to take control of something. *Miriam took over the business when her father retired.*

takeout *n.* food prepared and bought in a restaurant and eaten at home.

talcum powder *n.* a fine powder used for rubbing on your body after a bath.

tale *n.* **1** a story. **2** a lie. *Don't tell tales.*

talent *n.* a special ability or skill. *He has a talent for music.* **talented** *adj.*

talk¹ *v.* to say things; to speak.

talk² *n.* **1** a conversation or discussion. **2** a short lecture.

talkative *adj.* talking a lot.

tall *adj.* high or higher than average.

Talmud *n.* a very old book of Jewish laws and traditions.

talon *n.* a sharp claw.

tambourine *n.* a musical instrument shaped like a shallow drum, with jingling metal disks around it.

tambourine

tame *adj.* (of an animal) used to living with people; not wild or dangerous. **tame** *v.*

tamper *v.* to interfere with or touch something when you should not. *Someone has tampered with this lock.*

tan¹ *n.* **1** light brown. **2** a suntan.

tan² *v.* (tans, tanning, tanned) **1** to turn brown in the sun. **2** to turn animal skin into leather by treating it with chemicals.

tandem *n.* **1** a bicycle for two people. **2** a two-wheeled carriage pulled by horses harnessed in single file.

a b c d e f g h i j k l m n o p q r s **t** u v w x y z

A B C D E F G H I J K L M N O P Q R S **T** U V W X Y Z

tang *n.* a sharp taste or smell. **tangy** *adj.*

tangent *n.* a straight line that touches a circle or curve without crossing it.

tangerine *n.* a small, loose-skinned orange.

tangle *n.* a messy, twisted mass of threads or hair. **tangle** *v.*

tank *n.* **1** a large container for liquids. **2** a heavy, steel-covered military vehicle armed with guns.

tanker *n.* a ship, plane, or truck used for

tanker

carrying liquids, especially oil.

tantrum *n.* a sudden fit of bad temper.

tap[1] *n.* a device for controlling the flow of a liquid or gas; faucet.

tap[2] *v.* (tapping, tapped) **1** to knock lightly. *I tapped on the door.* **2** to attach a listening device secretly to a telephone.

tap dance *n.* a dance done with special shoes that make a tapping sound.

tape[1] *n.* **1** a strip of magnetic material used for recording sound or pictures, contained in a plastic box. **2** a strip of cloth, metal, paper, or plastic.

tape[2] *v.* **1** to record something on tape. **2** to fasten something with tape.

tape measure *n.* a narrow strip of paper or plastic used for measuring the length of something.

taper *v.* to become thinner at one end.

tape recorder *n.* an instrument for recording sound on tape and playing it back again.

tapestry *n.* a cloth with pictures or designs woven into it.

tar *n.* a thick, black, sticky liquid that comes from oil, used for covering the surface of roads.

tarantula *n.* a large, poisonous spider.

target *n.* **1** something that you aim at when shooting or attacking. **2** a result that you are trying to achieve.

tarmac *n.* a mixture of tar and small stones used for making the surface of roads, especially airport runways.

tarpaulin *n.* strong, waterproof cloth; tarp.

tart[1] *n.* an open pie, usually filled with

something sweet such as fruit or jelly.

tart[2] *adj.* sharp; sour. **tartness** *n.*

tartan *n.* a traditional Scottish woolen cloth with squares of different colors.

task *n.* a job; a piece of work.

tassel *n.* a bunch of hanging threads used to decorate clothing or furniture.

taste[1] *n.* **1** the ability to recognize the flavor of foods and drinks. **2** the flavor that a food or drink gives in your mouth. *This cheese has a salty taste.* **3** the ability to know what is good, fine, or beautiful. *He has good taste in clothes.* **4** something you like. *We have the same taste in music.*

taste[2] *v.* **1** to recognize the flavor of something. *Can you taste ginger in this cake?* **2** to try a little of a food or a drink. *Taste this and tell me if it's too salty.* **3** to have a particular flavor. *Honey tastes sweet.*

tattoo *n.* a colored design on a person's skin, made by pricking with needles and putting in dyes.

tatty *adj.* (tattier, tattiest) shabby; in bad condition.

taught *past of* teach.

taunt *v.* to tease somebody in a cruel way. **taunt** *n.*

taut *(tawt) adj.* stretched tight.

tavern *n. (historical)* an inn for travelers.

tawny *adj.* yellowish-brown in color.

tax *n.* money that is paid to the government by people and businesses to help pay for public services. **tax** *v.*, **taxation** *n.*

taxi *v.* (taxies, taxiing, taxied) (of an airplane) to travel on the runway before or after takeoff.

taxicab *n.* a car with a driver that can be hired for short journeys.

tea *n.* a drink made from the dried leaves of a plant grown in Asia and Africa.

teach *v.* (teaching, taught) to give somebody knowledge or a skill. **teacher** *n.*

teak *n.* a tree that grows in Asia or its very hard wood.

team *n.* **1** a group of people who play a sport or game together on the same side. **2** a group of people who work together.

teapot *n.* a type of china or metal pot with a spout for making and pouring out tea.

teapots

tear[1] (*rhymes with* where) *v.* (tearing, tore, torn) **1** to pull something apart or make a hole in something with a sudden pulling action. *She tore the photo to pieces.* **2** to rush. *He tore down the road on his bike.* **tear** *n.*

tear[2] (*rhymes with* here) *n.* a drop of liquid from your eye.

tease *v.* to annoy or laugh at somebody playfully and often unkindly.

teaspoon *n.* a spoon used to stir hot drinks.

teat *n.* an animal's nipple, through which it feeds milk to its young.

technical *adj.* **1** to do with a science or a practical skill. *They have the technical knowledge to build permanent space stations.* **2** to do with a particular subject. *There are a lot of technical words connected with computing.* **technically** *adv.*

technique *n.* the way in which something is done; a method.

technology *n.* the practical use of science. **technological** *adj.*

teddy bear *n.* a stuffed toy bear.

tedious *adj.* long and boring.

teem *v.* to be full of moving people or things. *The river was teeming with fish.*

teenager *n.* a person between the ages of 13 and 19. **teenage** *adj.*

teens *n. pl.* the years of your life between the ages of 13 and 19.

tee shirt *another spelling of* T-shirt.

teeth *plural of* tooth.

teethe *v.* to grow your first teeth.

teetotal *adj.* never drinking alcohol.

tele- *prefix* at or over a distance. *telephone, telescope.*

telecommunications *n. pl.* the sending of information by telephone, radio, television, or satellite.

telegram *n.* a message sent by telegraph or radio.

telegraph *n.* a system of sending messages using an electrical current along wires.

telephone *n.* an instrument used for talking to people over long distances by using an electrical current traveling along wires or radio waves. **telephone** *v.*

telescope *n.* a tube-shaped instrument that makes distant things appear larger and nearer.

televise *v.* to broadcast on television.

television *n.* **1** an apparatus with a screen that shows moving pictures with sound. **2** the sending of pictures and sounds for people to watch on their televisions.

tell *v.* (telling, told) **1** to give information to somebody. **2** to order somebody to do something. **3** to know or see something. *I can't tell the difference between the kittens in the litter.* **tell off** *(informal)* to speak angrily to somebody because he or she has done something wrong.

temper *n.* a tendency to get angry easily. *She has a terrible temper.* **lose your temper** to show that you are angry.

temperament *n.* the way you feel and behave. *an easygoing temperament.*

temperamental *adj.* easily getting upset or excited; moody.

temperate *adj.* (of climate) neither very hot nor very cold.

temperature *n.* **1** a measurement of how hot or cold something is. **2** a fever.

tempest *n.* *(literary)* a violent storm.

template *n.* a pattern that you trace around and use as a guide for cutting paper, cloth, or metal.

temple *n.* **1** a building used for worship. **2** the small, flat area on each side of your forehead.

tempo *n.* (*pl.* tempos *or* tempi) the speed at which a piece of music is played.

temple

temporary *adj.* lasting only for a limited time; not permanent. **temporarily** *adv.*

tempt *v.* to make somebody want to do something, especially something that he or she should not do. **temptation** *n.*

tenant *n.* a person who rents a house or an apartment.

tend *v.* **1** to be likely to behave in a certain way. **2** to care for something.

tendency *n.* how a person or thing usually behaves. *She has a tendency to get angry.*

a b c d e f g h i j k l m n o p q r s **t** u v w x y z

A
B
C
D
E
F
G
H
I
J
K
L
M
N
O
P
Q
R
S
T
U
V
W
X
Y
Z

tender *adj.* **1** soft; not hard or tough. *This meat is very tender.* **2** sensitive or sore. *My leg still feels tender where I banged it.* **3** loving and gentle. *tender looks.* **tenderness** *n.*

tendon *n.* a tough cord joining a muscle to a bone.

tennis *n.* a game for two or four players using rackets to hit a ball to each other over a net in a specially marked area (a **tennis court**).

tenor *n.* **1** a high male singing voice. **2** a male singer with a high voice.

tense¹ *adj.* **1** nervous or worried. **2** tightly stretched. *tense muscles.* **tense** *v.,* **tension** *n.*

tense² *n.* the form of a verb that shows when an action happened, such as the past tense and the present tense.

tent *n.* a shelter made of canvas or nylon, stretched over a frame of poles and held up with ropes.

tentacle *n.* a long, thin part of an animal that it uses to feel or grasp. *An octopus has tentacles.*

tepid *adj.* slightly warm.

tentacle

term *n.* **1** period when school or court is in session. **2** a limited length of time. **3** a word or phrase. **4 terms** the conditions of an agreement.

terminal¹ *n.* **1** a building where passengers arrive and depart by plane, bus, or other vehicle. **2** a computer monitor connected to a network.

terminal² *adj.* (of an illness) not able to be cured; fatal.

terminate *v.* to end or stop. *The train terminates here.*

terrace *n.* **1** a level area cut into the side of a slope. **2** an open, paved area next to a restaurant or house where people can sit.

terra-cotta *n.* a brownish-red clay used for making pots, tiles, and other objects.

terrapin *n.* a small type of turtle.

terrestrial *adj.* to do with Earth.

terrible *adj.* very bad; horrible.

terribly *adv.* **1** very badly. **2** very. *I'm terribly sorry.*

terrier *n.* a breed of small dog.

terrific *adj.* **1** marvelous; wonderful. *terrific news.* **2** very great or powerful. *a terrific storm.* **terrifically** *adv.*

terrify *v.* (terrifies, terrifying, terrified) to make somebody very frightened.

territory *n.* **1** an area of land. **2** an area of land controlled by one country or ruler. **territorial** *adj.*

terror *n.* very great fear.

terrorist *n.* a person who tries to frighten people or governments into doing what he or she wants by using violence or threats. *The bomb was planted by terrorists.* **terrorism** *n.*

terrorize *v.* to frighten people very much.

test¹ *v.* **1** to try out or examine something to see what it is like. S*hould drugs be tested on animals?* **2** to ask somebody questions or set them exercises to find out what they know or what they can do.

test² *n.* **1** a set of questions or exercises to find out what you know or what you can do. **2** a medical examination. *an eye test.* **3** a procedure for trying out or examining something to see what it is like.

testicles *n. pl.* two glands in a man's body that produce sperm.

testify *v.* (testifies, testifying, testified) to give evidence in a law court.

test tube *n.* a glass tube that is closed at one end, used in chemical tests.

tether *n.* a rope or chain for tying an animal to a post. **tether** *v.*

text *n.* the part of a book or newspaper that is written.

textbook *n.* a book used for teaching a subject in a school or college.

textile *n.* a woven cloth or fabric.

texture *n.* the way that something feels when you touch it.

thank *v.* to tell somebody that you are grateful to him or her. **thanks** *n.*

thankful *adj.* pleased and grateful. **thankfully** *adv.*

thatch *n.* a roof covering made from straw or reeds. **thatched** *adj.*

thaw *v.* to make or become soft or liquid

again after freezing. *Take the meat out of the freezer to thaw.*

theater *n.* a place where plays are performed.

theatrical *adj.* to do with the theater.

theft *n.* the action of stealing.

their *adj.* belonging to them. *This is their house.* **theirs** *pron.*

theme *n.* the main subject.

theme park *n.* a park with many different amusements, all based on a single idea.

theater

then *adv.* **1** at that time. **2** after that; next. **3** in that case.

theology *n.* the study of religion. **theological** *adj.*

theory *n.* **1** an explanation that has not been proved. *There are many theories about the origin of life.* **2** the main ideas about a subject, rather than its practice. **theoretical** *adj.*

therapy *n.* a treatment of a mental or physical illness. **therapeutic** *adj.*, **therapist** *n.*

there *adv.* in, at, or to that place.

therefore *adv.* for that reason. *Lucy is sick and therefore can't come.*

thermal *adj.* **1** to do with heat. *thermal currents.* **2** keeping something warm by stopping heat from escaping. *thermal underwear.*

thermometer *n.* an instrument for measuring temperature.

thermostat *n.* a device for automatically controlling temperature in a room.

thesaurus *n.* (*pl.* thesauri *or* thesauruses) a book that has lists of words with similar meanings grouped together.

thick *adj.* **1** having a long

distance from one side to the other; not thin. *thick walls.* **2** having a certain distance between the opposite sides. *The glass is two inches thick.* **3** having a lot of things close together; dense. *a thick forest.* **4** (of a liquid) not flowing easily. *thick soup.* **5** *(informal)* stupid. **thicken** *v.*, **thickness** *n.*

thicket *n.* a group of small trees or bushes growing close together.

thief *n.* (*pl.* thieves) a person who steals. **thieve** *v.*

thigh (*rhymes with* my) *n.* the top part of your leg between your hip and knee.

thimble *n.* a small metal or plastic object worn on the end of your finger to avoid pricking it when sewing.

thin *adj.* (thinner, thinnest) **1** not very wide between its two sides; not thick. *thin paper.* **2** slim; not fat. **3** sparse; not dense. *His hair is getting thin.* **4** (of a liquid) watery. *thin soup.* **thin** *v.*, **thinness** *n.*

thing *n.* **1** any object that is not living. **2 things** belongings.

think *v.* (thinking, thought) **1** to use your brain. **2** to believe; to have an opinion.

third[1] *adj.* next after second. **third** *adv.*, *n.*

third[2] *n.* one of three equal parts of something. *One third of 60 is 20.*

thirst *n.* **1** the dry feeling that you have in your mouth and throat when you need to drink. **2** a strong desire for something. *the thirst for knowledge.* **thirsty** *adj.*

thistle *n.* a prickly wild plant with purple flowers.

thorax *n.* **1** the chest of a person or an animal. **2** the middle section of an insect's body. See **insect.**

thorn *n.* a sharp point sticking out from the stem of a plant such as a rose.

thorough *adj.* careful; attending to every detail. *Nadim gave his room a thorough clean.* **thoroughness** *n.*

thoroughfare *n.* a main road or highway.

thoroughly *adv.* **1** in a careful way; attending to every detail. **2** completely. *I'm thoroughly bored.*

though[1] *conj.* although. *Though it's sunny, it's a little cold.*

though[2] *adv.* however. *I bought it. It was expensive, though.*

thought[1] *past of* think.

thought[2] *n.* **1** an idea. **2** the process of thinking.

thermometer

thoughtful *adj.* **1** thinking carefully.
2 thinking about other people;
considerate. **thoughtfully** *adv.*

thoughtless *adj.* not thinking about
other people; inconsiderate.
thoughtlessness *n.*

thrash *v.* **1** to hit many times with a stick
or whip. **2** to defeat easily. **3** to move
about violently. *She was thrashing her
arms around in the water.*

thread[1] *n.* **1** a long, thin piece of cotton or
silk, used for sewing. **2** the spiral ridge
around a screw. **threads** *(informal)* clothes.

thread[2] *v.* to put a thread through a hole
such as the eye of a needle.

threadbare *adj.* worn thin. *His clothes
were old and threadbare.*

threat *n.* **1** a warning that you are going
to hurt or punish somebody. **2** a sign of
something dangerous or unpleasant in
the future. *the threat of war.* **3** something
that is likely to cause harm. *Nuclear
weapons are a threat to our future.*

threaten *v.* **1** to make a threat. **2** to be
about to come. *A storm is threatening.*

three-dimensional, 3-D *adj.* having
length, width, and height; not flat.
A cube is a three-dimensional shape.

thresh *v.* to beat stalks of corn in order
to separate the grains.

threshold *n.* **1** a piece of wood or stone
under the door of a building. **2** a
beginning. *She is on the threshold of
an amazing career.*

threw *past of* throw.

thrifty *adj.* (thriftier, thriftiest) careful
about how you spend your money.

thrill *n.* a sudden, strong feeling of
excitement or pleasure. **thrill** *v.*

thriller *n.* a book, movie, or play with an
exciting plot, usually about a crime.

thrive *v.* to grow strong and healthy.
The business is thriving.

throat *n.* the front of your neck and the
tubes inside that take food and air into
your body.

throb *v.* (throbs, throbbing, throbbed)
to beat strongly and regularly. *Her toe
throbbed with pain.*

throne *n.* a special chair for a king,
queen, emperor, or other ruler.

throng *n.* a large crowd. **throng** *v.*

throttle[1] *v.* to strangle somebody.

throttle[2] *n.* a device that controls the
flow of fuel into a vehicle's engine.

through *prep.* **1** from one side or end to the
other. *The train went through the tunnel.*
2 from the beginning to the end. *They
are traveling through the night.* **3** because
of; by way of. *The accident was caused by
carelessness.* **through** *adv.*

throughout *prep.* **1** in all parts of. *The
band is known throughout the U.S.*
2 from the start to the finish of
something. *He interrupted me
throughout my talk.*

throw *v.* (throwing, threw, thrown) **1** to
send something through the air with
force. *Throw the ball to me.* **2** to puzzle
or confuse somebody. *The question
really threw me.* **throw up** *(informal)*
to vomit. **throw** *n.*

thrush *n.* a
songbird with a
speckled brown
breast.

thrust *v.* (thrusting,
thrust) to push
something with
force. *They thrust
their way through
the crowd.* **thrust** *n.*

thud *n.* the dull sound
made by a heavy
object falling to the
ground. **thud** *v.*

thrush

thug *n.* a violent, brutal person.

thumb[1] *n.* the short, thick finger located
on each hand.

thumb[2] *v.* to turn over the pages of
a book with your thumb and fingers.

thumbtack *n.* a pin with a large, flat
head for attaching paper to a surface

thunder[1] *n.* the deep, rumbling sound that
you hear after a flash of lightning.

thunder[2] *v.* to make the sound of, or a
sound like, thunder.

thunderstorm *n.* a storm with thunder
and lightning.

Thursday *n.* the fifth day of the week.

thus *conj.* in this or that way; therefore.

thyme *(time) n.* an herb used in cooking.

tiara *n.* a small crown or band decorated
with jewels.

tick[1] *n.* **1** the short, light,
regular sound made by a
clock or watch. **2** a small
mark, like this ✔, used
to show that something
is correct. **3** a tiny,

blood-sucking insect.

tick² *v.* **1** to make short, light, regular sounds like a clock or watch. **2** to mark something with a tick.

ticket *n.* a piece of printed cardboard or paper that shows that you have paid to travel on a train or bus or to gain entrance to a movie or museum.

tickle *v.* to touch somebody's skin lightly. *I tickled the baby's feet and made her laugh.* **tickle** *n.*

tide *n.* the regular rise and fall of the ocean. **tidal** *adj.*

tidings *n. pl. (old-fashioned)* news.

tidy *adj.* (tidier, tidiest) in good order; neat. **tidily** *adv.*, **tidiness** *n.*, **tidy** *v.*

tie¹ *v.* (ties, tying, tied) **1** to fasten with string, rope, or similar cord. **2** to score the same number of points in a game or contest. *Two people tied for first place.*

tie² *n.* **1** a thin piece of cloth worn knotted around the neck of a shirt. **2** an equal score or result in a game or competition.

tigers

tier (*rhymes with* ear) *n.* one of a number of rows or levels set one above the other. *The wedding cake had four tiers.* **tiered** *adj.*

tiger *n.* a large wild cat with a striped coat, found in Asia.

tight *adj.* **1** fitting very closely. *My pants are too tight.* **2** firmly fastened or attached; hard to move or undo. *This knot is too tight.* **3** firmly stretched. *Make sure the rope is tight.* **tight** *adv.*, **tighten** *v.*

tightrope *n.* a tightly stretched rope or wire on which acrobats balance high up above the ground.

tights *n. pl.* a tight-fitting piece of clothing that covers your feet, legs, and body up to your waist.

tigress *n.* a female tiger.

tile *n.* one of the flat pieces of baked clay or other material used to cover floors, walls, or roofs. **tile** *v.*

till¹ *v.* to plow.

till² *conj., prep.* until.

tiller *n.* the handle that turns a boat's rudder from side to side.

tilt *v.* to lean to one side.

timber *n.* cut wood used for constructing things or buildings.

time¹ *n.* **1** the passing of minutes, days, hours, and years. **2** a particular hour, shown on a clock. *What time is it?* **3** a particular point or period connected with an event. *breakfast time.* **4** an amount of minutes or hours. *I don't have time to help you now.* **5** an occasion. *She won four times.*

time² *v.* **1** to measure how long something takes. *She timed the drive to school.* **2** to choose the right time to do something. *He timed his entrance perfectly.*

times *prep.* multiplied by.

timetable *n.* a list of the times of trains, classes at school, or when other things will happen.

timid *adj.* easily frightened; shy.

tin *n.* **1** a silvery metal. **2** a container made of tin.

tingle *v.* to have a slight prickling feeling. *My fingers were tingling with cold.* **tingle** *n.*

tinkle *v.* to make a sound of, or like, the ringing of small bells.

tinsel *n.* strings of glittering, sparkling material used for decoration.

tint *n.* a shade of a color. **tinted** *adj.*

tiny *adj.* (tinier, tiniest) very small.

tip¹ *n.* **1** the top or point of something. **2** a piece of useful information. **3** a small gift of money to a waiter, hairdresser, or someone who has done a service for you.

tip² *v.* (tips, tipping, tipped) **1** to fall or lean over. **2** to empty something from a container. *I tipped the water down the drain.* **3** to give a small gift of money to a waiter, hairdresser, or someone who has performed a service for you.

tipsy *adj.* slightly drunk.

tiptoe *v.* to walk quietly on your toes.

tire¹ *n.* an air-filled rubber ring around the wheel of a car, bicycle, or other vehicle.

tire² *v.* **1** to become tired. **2** to make somebody tired.

tired *adj.* **1** feeling that you need to rest or sleep. **2** **tired of** bored with.

A
B
C
D
E
F
G
H
I
J
K
L
M
N
O
P
Q
R
S
T
U
V
W
X
Y
Z

tiresome *adj.* annoying or boring.

tissue *n.* **1** thin, soft paper. **2** a paper handkerchief. **3** the mass of cells that make up an animal or plant.

title *n.* **1** the name of a book, play, movie, etc. **2** a word, such as Mr., Ms., Sir., Lady, or Dr., put in front of a name to show the person's rank or occupation.

toadstools

toad *n.* an amphibian similar to a frog, with a rough skin.

toadstool *n.* a type of fungus similar to a mushroom that is often poisonous.

toast[1] *n.* grilled bread. **toast** *v.*

toast[2] *v.* to hold up your glass and wish somebody good luck, happiness, or good health before you drink. **toast** *n.*

tobacco *n.* a plant whose dried leaves are smoked in cigarettes, cigars, and pipes.

toboggan *n.* a type of long, light sled. **toboggan** *v.*

today *n.* **1** (on) this day. **2** (at) the present time.

toddler *n.* a child who has just learned to walk.

toe *n.* one of the five fingerlike parts of your foot.

toga *n.* *(historical)* a loose robe worn by men in ancient Rome.

together *adv.* with each other; with another person or thing.

toil *v.* to work very hard and for a long time. **toil** *n.*

toilet *n.* a type of bowl into which you get rid of urine and feces, with a water supply for washing this into a drain.

toiletries *n. pl.* soap, toothpaste, and other things that you use when you are washing yourself or styling your hair.

token *n.* **1** a sign or symbol. *Please accept this gift as a token of my thanks.* **2** a piece of printed paper, plastic, or metal used in place of money. *a book token.*

told *past of* tell.

tolerate *v.* to put up with or endure something. *I really couldn't tolerate his rudeness any longer.* **tolerance** *n.*, **tolerant** *adj.*

toll[1] *n.* a tax charged for crossing a bridge or using a certain road. **take its toll** to cause damage or loss.

toll[2] *v.* to ring slowly and solemnly. *The bell tolled for the dead soldiers.*

tomatoes

tomato *n.* (*pl.* tomatoes) a round, red, juicy fruit often eaten in salads.

tomb *(toom) n.* a grave.

tombstone *n.* a block of stone placed over a grave that shows who is buried there.

tomorrow *n.* **1** (on) the day after today. **2** (in) the future.

ton *n.* **1** a measure of weight, equal to around 2,000 pounds. **2 tons** *(informal)* a lot.

tone *n.* **1** the quality of a sound. *He spoke in a gentle tone.* **2** a shade of a color. *various tones of green.*

tongs *n. pl.* a tool with two parts connected at one end, used for picking things up.

tongue *n.* the flap of muscle inside your mouth that you use for tasting, swallowing, and speaking.

tongue twister *n.* a phrase that is not easy to say quickly such as *She sells seashells on the seashore.*

tonight *n.* (on) the evening or night of this day.

tonsillitis *n.* an infection of the tonsils that makes them red and painful.

tonsils *n. pl.* a pair of soft, fleshy lumps at the back of your throat.

too *adv.* **1** as well; also. *Can I come too?* **2** more than is required or wanted. *This coat is too small for me now.*

tool *n.* a piece of equipment that you use to do a particular job.

tooth *n.* (*pl.* teeth) **1** one of the hard, bony parts in your mouth, used for chewing food. **2** one of the pointed parts on a saw or comb.

tooth

crown — enamel
gum — pulp cavity (blood vessels and nerves)
dentine (bonelike substance)
root
jawbone

toothache *n.* pain in a tooth.

toothpaste *n.* a creamy substance used to clean your teeth.

top *n.* **1** the highest point of something. **2** the upper surface of something. **3** a lid. **4** a piece of clothing that you wear on the top part of your body. **5** a spinning toy. **top** *adj.*

topic *n.* a subject that you speak or write about. *I chose dinosaurs as the topic for my essay.*

topical *adj.* interesting and important at the present time.

topple *v.* to make or to become unsteady and fall.

Torah *n.* the holy Jewish scriptures.

torch *n.* a flaming piece of wood or rope, often carried as an ornamental light in processions.

tore *past of* tear.

torment *v.* **1** to make somebody suffer very much. *He was tormented by worry.* **2** to annoy somebody on purpose. **torment** *n.*

torn *past participle of* tear.

tornado *n.* (*pl.* tornadoes or tornados) a violent, whirling storm that has the power to cause great damage.

torpedo *n.* (*pl.* torpedoes) a tube-shaped bomb that is fired underwater, usually

tornado

by submarines. **torpedo** *v.*

torrent *n.* **1** a rushing stream. **2** a heavy flow of something. **torrential** *adj.*

torso *n.* (*pl.* torsos) the main part of your body, not including your head or limbs.

tortoise *n.* a slow-moving land reptile with a hard shell.

torture *v.* to treat somebody cruelly as a punishment or in order to force him or her to confess something. **torture** *n.*

toss *v.* **1** to throw something carelessly. **2** to turn restlessly from side to side. *She couldn't stop tossing and turning*

all night. **3** to decide something by throwing a coin up into the air to see which side faces upward when it falls.

total[1] *adj.* counting everything; complete.

total[2] *n.* the number or amount that you get when you add all numbers or amounts together. **total** *v.*

totem pole *n.* a pole carved with characters from traditional Native American stories. A **totem** is a spiritual symbol or emblem.

toucan *n.* a colorful bird with a large beak, found in South America.

touch *v.* **1** to feel something with your hand. **2** to come into contact with something. **3** to affect the feelings of somebody. *I was touched by her incredible kindness toward my family.* **touch** *n.*, **touching** *adj.*

touchdown *n.* the act of bringing the ball across the opponent's goal line in football.

touchy *adj.* easily upset or offended.

tough *(tuff) adj.* **1** strong; not easily broken or damaged. **2** able to bear hardship, pain, or illness. **3** difficult to chew. *This meat is tough!* **4** difficult. *a tough decision.* **toughen** *v.*

tour *n.* a journey on which you visit a number of different places. **tour** *v.*

tourist *n.* a person who travels for pleasure, visiting places of interest. **tourism** *n.*

tournament *n.* a large contest in which many players or teams come together to compete against each other.

tow *v.* to pull a vehicle along by a rope or a chain.

toward *prep.* in the direction of. *The car was coming toward us.*

towel *n.* a piece of thick cloth or paper used for drying things.

tower *n.* **1** a tall, narrow building. **2** a tall, narrow part of a building.

town *n.* a place with many houses, stores, and other buildings that is larger than a village but smaller than a city.

toxic *adj.* poisonous.

toy[1] *n.* (*pl.* toys) an object for a child to play with.

toy[2] *v.* to play with something carelessly. *He wasn't hungry and just sat toying with his food.*

trace *v.* **1** to find out where somebody or something is by following clues or a trail. **2** to copy a picture by covering it with very thin paper and drawing around the outline.

trace² *n.* **1** a small sign or mark left by something. *She vanished without a trace.* **2** a small amount. *Traces of poison were found in the cup.*

trachea *n.* the tube leading from your throat to your lungs.

track¹ *n.* **1** tracks a series of marks left behind by a person, animal, or vehicle. **2** a path or rough road. **3** a racecourse for athletes, horses, racecars, or other vehicles. **4** a railroad line. **5** one song or piece of music on an MP3 player, CD, or tape.

track² *v.* to follow something by looking for the signs or tracks that it has left behind.

tracksuit *n.* a pair of loose pants and a top that you wear for sports.

tractor *n.* a strong vehicle used to pull farm machinery.

trade¹ *n.* **1** the buying and selling of goods. **2** a person's job.

trade² *v.* **1** to buy and sell. **2** to exchange. *I traded my bike for skates.*

trademark *n.* a special name or sign used to show who made something and to prevent illegal copying.

trade union *n.* an organization of workers who bargain with employers for fair wages or better working conditions.

tradition *n.* a belief or custom handed down from one generation to another. **traditional** *adj.*, **traditionally** *adv.*

traffic¹ *n.* vehicles, such as cars, ships, or aircraft, that move along a particular route.

traffic² *v.* (traffics, trafficking, trafficked) to buy and sell something illegally. *They were arrested for trafficking in drugs.*

tragedy *n.* **1** a play about unhappy events, with a sad ending. **2** a very sad event. **tragic** *adj.*, **tragically** *adv.*

trail¹ *n.* **1** a series of marks left by somebody or something as they pass. *He left a trail of footprints behind him.* **2** a path through the countryside.

trail² *v.* **1** to drag or be dragged along. *Your scarf is trailing on the ground.* **2** to walk slowly and wearily. **3** to follow the trail of somebody or something. **4** (of a plant) to grow over a surface.

trailer *n.* **1** a vehicle used for carrying things, towed by a car or truck. **2** a series of short pieces taken from a movie, used to advertise it.

train¹ *n.* **1** a railroad engine with connected cars or trucks. **2** a part of a long dress that trails behind the wearer. *The bride wore a dress with a train.* **3** a series of connected thoughts or events.

train² *v.* **1** to learn how to do something. *She's training to be a doctor.* **2** to teach a person or an animal how to do something. *They train guide dogs for blind people.* **3** to prepare for a sports event by practicing or exercising.

train

trainer *n.* a person who trains people or animals.

traitor *n.* a person who betrays his or her country or friends.

tram *n.* a kind of bus that runs on tracks like a train, powered by electricity.

tramp *v.* to walk with heavy footsteps. **2** to go for a long walk.

trample *v.* to step heavily on something.

trampoline *n.* a piece of equipment used for gymnasts to bounce on, made out of a sheet of strong material attached to a framework by springs.

tranquil (*tran-kwil*) *adj.* calm and peaceful. **tranquillity** *n.*

trans- *prefix* across; through. *transatlantic.*

transaction *n.* a business deal.

transfer¹ (*trans-fur*) *v.* (transferring, transferred) to move something from one place to another.

transfer² (*trans-fur*) *n.* **1** an act of transferring somebody or something. **2** a design or picture that can be transferred from one surface to another.

transform *v.* to change completely. *A witch had transformed him into a frog.* **transformation** *n.*

transfusion *n.* the injection of blood into somebody who is very sick or who has lost a lot of blood in an accident.

transistor *n.* **1** a small device that controls the flow of an electrical current. **2** a portable radio.

translate *v.* to put something into

another language. **translation** *n.*, **translator** *n.*

transmit *v.* (transmits, transmitting, transmitted) **1** to pass something on. *Some insects transmit diseases.* **2** to send out television or radio signals. **transmission** *n.*

transparent *adj.* able to be seen through, like glass. **transparency** *n.*

transplant *v.* **1** to remove a plant from where it is growing and plant it somewhere else. **2** to remove a part of somebody's body, such as the heart or a kidney, and put it into the body of a person who is very sick. **transplant** *n.*

transport *(trans-port) v.* to carry people, animals, or goods from one place to another, usually in a vehicle.

transportation *n.* **1** the process of transporting people, animals, or goods. **2** a vehicle or a way of traveling.

trap¹ *n.* **1** a device for catching animals. **2** something that tricks you.

trap² *v.* (trapping, trapped) to catch in a trap or by a trick.

trapdoor *n.* a door in a floor or ceiling.

trapeze *n.* a bar hung on ropes high up above the ground on which acrobats and gymnasts perform.

trapezoid *n.* (*pl.* trapezoids) a four-sided shape with two of its sides parallel.

trash *n.* worthless, discarded items; garbage.

trash can *n.* a container for garbage that you keep outside your house.

travel *v.* (traveling, traveled) to go from one place to another. **travel** *n.*, **traveler** *n.*

trawler *n.* a fishing boat that drags a wide, bag-shaped net along the bottom of the sea. **trawl** *v.*

tray *n.* (*pl.* trays) a flat piece of plastic, metal, or wood used for carrying food and drinks.

trawler

treacherous *(trech-er-us) adj.*
1 betraying people who trust you.
2 dangerous. *The road conditions were treacherous.* **treachery** *n.*

tread¹ *v.* (treading, trod, trodden) to put your foot down on something.

tread² *n.* the raised pattern on the outside of a tire.

treason *n.* betrayal of your country, especially by giving away important information to an enemy.

treasure¹ *n.* a store of valuable things such as gold and jewels.

treasure² *v.* to value something highly.

treasury *n.* **1** Treasury the government department that controls a country's money. **2** a place where a treasure is stored.

treat¹ *v.* **1** to deal with somebody or something in a certain way. *The Smiths treat Julius like their own son.* **2** to try to make a sick or injured person well again. **3** to put something through a process, especially to protect or preserve it. *The wood is treated with chemicals to stop it from rotting.* **4** to buy a meal, present, or something special for somebody. **treatment** *n.*

treat² *n.* something that gives you special pleasure. *Mom took us to the movies as a special treat.*

treaty *n.* a written agreement made between countries.

treble *adj.* high in pitch. *He plays a treble recorder.*

tree *n.* the tallest type of plant, with a thick, wooden trunk.

trek¹ *n.* a long and difficult journey.

trek² *v.* (trekking, trekked) to make a long and difficult journey.

tremble *v.* to shake with fear, cold, or excitement.

tremendous *adj.* **1** very great or large. **2** *(informal)* very good; excellent.

trench *n.* a long, narrow ditch.

trend *n.* **1** a general direction or course. **2** a fashion.

trendy *adj.* (trendier, trendiest) fashionable.

trespass *v.* to go illegally on somebody else's land. **trespasser** *n.*

tri- *prefix* three. *tricycle.*

trial *n.* **1** the examination of an accused person in a law court. **2** a test. *Trials of the new drug will begin shortly.*

A
B
C
D
E
F
G
H
I
J
K
L
M
N
O
P
Q
R
S
T
U
V
W
X
Y
Z

triangle *n.* **1** a flat shape with three sides. **2** a triangular, metal musical instrument. **triangular** *adj.*

tribe *n.* a group of people who share the same ancestors, customs, and language. **tribal** *adj.*, **tribesman** *n.*, **tribeswoman** *n.*, **tribespeople** *n.*

tributary *n.* a stream that flows into

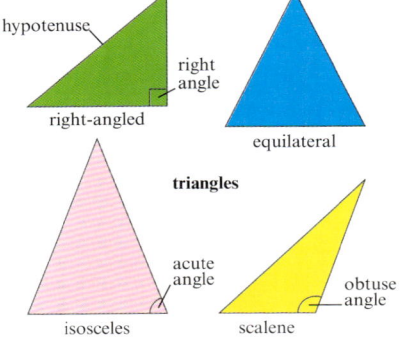

hypotenuse

right angle

right-angled

equilateral

triangles

acute angle

obtuse angle

isosceles

scalene

a river or another stream.

tribute *n.* something you say or do that shows your respect or admiration for somebody. *We paid tribute to her skills as a musician.*

trick *n.* **1** something done to cheat or deceive somebody **2** a clever or skillful action done to amuse people. *a magic trick.* **trick** *v.*

trickle *v.* to flow in a thin stream.

tricky *adj.* (trickier, trickiest) when something is difficult or awkward.

tricycle *n.* a three-wheeled cycle.

trifle *n.* **1** something that is not important. **2** a dessert usually made from cake soaked in rum or sherry, custard, fruit, jam, and whipped cream.

trifling *adj.* not very important.

trigger *n.* the lever on a gun that you pull to fire it.

trim *v.* (trims, trimming, trimmed) to cut the edges or ends off something. **trim** *n.*

trimming *n.* something added as a decoration. *She wore a lovely dress with lace trimming.*

trinket *n.* a small ornament or piece of jewelry of little value.

trip[1] *v.* (trips, tripping, tripped) to catch your foot on something and fall or almost fall.

trip[2] *n.* a journey. *Have a good trip.*

triple *adj.* **1** three times as much or as many. **2** made of three parts. **triple** *v.*

triplet *n.* one of three babies born to the same mother at the same time.

tripod *n.* a three-legged stand, especially for a camera.

triumph *n.* a great success or victory. **triumph** *v.*, **triumphant** *adj.*

trivial *adj.* minor; of very little importance.

troll *n.* in stories an ugly, bad-tempered dwarf or giant that lives in a cave.

trolley *n.* (*pl.* trolleys) **1** a streetcar. **2** a wheeled carriage that travels on an overhead track.

trombone *n.* a brass musical instrument with a sliding tube.

troops *n. pl.* soldiers.

trombone

trophy *(troh-fee) n.* a prize, such as a plaque, won in a competition.

tropic *n.* **1** one of the two imaginary circles running around Earth at around 23 degrees north and south of the equator. **2 tropics** the hot regions between these circles. **tropical** *adj.*

trot *v.* (trotting, trotted) to run with short steps like a horse's or pony's slow run. **trot** *n.*

trouble[1] *n.* difficulty, problems, or worry.

trouble[2] *v.* **1** to cause somebody worry or problems. *This problem has been troubling me for a while.* **2** to bother somebody. *Sorry to trouble you, but do you have the time?*

trough *(troff) n.* a long, narrow container for animals' food or water.

trout *n.* (*pl.* trout or trouts) an edible freshwater fish.

trowel *n.* **1** a garden tool like a small spade. **2** a tool with a flat blade for spreading mortar or plaster.

truant *n.* a student who is absent from school when he or she is supposed to be there. **truancy** *n.*

truce *n.* a rest from fighting or

quarreling, agreed by both sides.

truck *n.* a type of vehicle that is used to carry or pull loads.

trudge *v.* to walk with slow, heavy steps. *They trudged through the snow.*

true *adj.* **1** based on fact or reality; not imagined or made up. *a true story.* **2** correct; not invented or wrong. 0 *It's true that Earth is round.* **3** real; genuine. *true love.* **truly** *adv.*

truffle *n.* **1** an edible fungus that grows underground. **2** a soft candy made out of a chocolate mixture.

trumpet *n.* a brass musical instrument, played by pressing valves.

truncheon *n.* a short, thick stick carried by police officers as a weapon.

trunk *n.* **1** the main stem of a tree. **2** the main part of your body, not including your head or limbs. **3** a large box for storing or carrying clothes and other things. **4** the long nose of an elephant. **5** a large storage compartment in a car, usually at the rear. **6 trunks** shorts worn by men and boys for swimming.

trust *v.* to believe that somebody is honest or reliable. *Can I trust you to behave while I'm out?* **trust** *n.*

trustworthy *adj.* able to be trusted.

truth *n.* the true facts. *I'm telling you the truth.* **truthful** *adj.,* **truthfully** *adv.*

try[1] *v.* (tries, trying, tried) **1** to make an effort to do something. *I tried to open the window, but I couldn't.* **2** to test something by using it. *Have you tried this new shampoo?* **3** to judge somebody in a law court.

try[2] *n.* **1** an effort or attempt. **2** in rugby a way of scoring by placing the ball over the other team's goal line with your hand.

trying *adj.* making you annoyed or impatient. *He is a very trying person!*

T-shirt *n.* a cotton shirt that you pull on over your head, usually with short sleeves and no collar or buttons. (*can also be spelled* tee shirt.)

tub *n.* **1** a plastic container for food. *a tub of margarine.* **2** a wide, open container. *I planted some flowers in tubs on the patio.* **3** short for *bathtub.*

tuba *n.* a large brass musical instrument that makes low notes.

tubby *adj.* (*informal*) short and fat.

tube *n.* **1** a hollow cylinder. **2** the

underground railroad system in London, England. **tubular** *adj.*

tuber *n.* a swelling on the underground stem of a plant such as a potato.

tuck *v.* to fold or push something into or under a place. *She tucked her shirt into her pants.* **tuck in 1** to push bedclothes tightly around somebody in bed.

Tuesday *n.* the third day of the week.

tuft *n.* a bunch or clump of grass or hair.

tug *v.* (tugs, tugging, tugged) to pull something hard. **tug** *n.*

tugboat *n.* a small boat that tows large ships in and out of a port.

tuition (*tyoo-***ish***-un*) *n.* teaching or instruction.

tulip *n.* a plant with brightly colored, cup-shaped flowers that grows from a bulb.

tumble *v.* to fall down suddenly.

tumbler *n.* a tall drinking glass with straight sides.

tummy *n.* (*informal*) the stomach; belly.

tumor *n.* a lump or swelling in the body made up of abnormal cells.

tuna *n.* (*pl.* tuna *or* tunas) a large sea fish eaten as food.

tuna

tundra *n.* a level, treeless plain found in Arctic regions.

tune[1] *n.* a pattern of musical notes. **in tune** singing or playing the right notes.

tune[2] *v.* **1** to adjust a musical instrument to the correct pitch. **2** to adjust a radio or television to a particular station.

tunic *n.* **1** a loose-fitting garment that extends to the knees.

tunnel[1] *n.* an underground passage.

tunnel[2] *v.* (tunneling, tunneled) to dig under the ground.

turban *n.* a long piece of cloth wound around the head, worn especially by Muslim and Sikh men.

A
B
C
D
E
F
G
H
I
J
K
L
M
N
O
P
Q
R
S
T
U
V
W
X
Y
Z

turbine *n.* an engine with curved blades, powered by the action of water,

turbine

steam, gas, or hot air.

turf *n.* grass and the soil below it.

turkey *n.* (*pl.* turkeys) a large bird that is either wild or kept on farms for its meat.

turmoil *n.* a state of wild confusion.

turn¹ *v.* **1** to go around; to revolve. *Turn the wheel.* **2** to change direction. *I turned to face her.* **3** to change. *Water turns into ice when it freezes.* **4** to become. *Her hair turned white.* **5** to find a certain page in a book. *Turn to page 23.* **6** to adjust the switch on a television, heater, or other appliance. *I'll just turn the radio off.* **turn down** to refuse. *She turned down the offer.*

turn² *n.* your chance or duty to do something. *It's your turn to clean up.*

turnip *n.* a round root vegetable with white or yellowish flesh.

turnstile *n.* a gate that turns, allowing only one person to pass through at a time.

turquoise *n.* **1** a greenish-blue precious stone. **2** the color of this stone.

turret *n.* a small tower on a castle or other building.

turtle *n.* a sea reptile with a round shell and flippers for swimming.

tusk *n.* a long, curved tooth sticking out from the mouth of some animals, including the elephant and the walrus.

tutor *n.* a teacher who instructs individual students or small groups.

tutu *n.* a ballet dancer's short skirt, made of layers of stiff material that stick out.

TV *short for* television.

twice *adv.* two times.

twig *n.* a small, thin branch.

twilight *n.* the dim light between sunset and night.

twin *n.* one of two children born to the same mother at the same time.

twinkle *v.* to shine with little flashes of light. **twinkle** *n.*

twirl *v.* to turn or spin around and around. **twirl** *n.*

twist *v.* **1** to turn or bend. *The path twists and turns through the forest.* **2** to wind around or together. *He twisted the pieces of string to make a rope.* **twist** *n.,* **twisted** *adj.*

twitch *v.* to make slight jerking movements.

tycoon *n.* a rich, powerful person who works in business or industry.

type¹ *n.* a kind or sort.

type² *v.* to use a typewriter or computer keyboard to write something.

type³ *n.* the letters used to print words.

typewriter *n.* a machine with keys that you press to print letters onto paper.

typhoon *(tie-foon) n.* a very violent tropical storm.

typical *adj.* having the usual characteristics. *a typical teenager.* **typically** *adv.*

tyrant *n.* a cruel and unfair ruler. **tyrannical** *adj.,* **tyranny** *n.*

udder *n.* the baglike part of a female mammal, such as a cow, from which milk comes.

UFO *n.* (*short for* unidentified flying object) a flying object that cannot be identified and that is therefore thought to come from outer space.

ugly *adj.* (uglier, ugliest) unpleasant to look at; not attractive. *an ugly, modern building.* ugliness *n.*

ulcer *n.* a sore area on your skin or inside your body. *a stomach ulcer.*

ultimate *adj.* 1 last; final. *Our ultimate goal is to win the championship.* 2 the greatest. *the ultimate achievement.*

ultimatum *n.* a final warning hat if somebody does not do as you ask, you will take action against him or her.

ultra- *prefix* extremely. *ultralight, ultramodern.*

ultraviolet light *n.* a type of light that cannot be seen by the human eye, but that causes your skin to tan.

umbilical cord *n.* a cord connecting an unborn mammal to its mother before it is born.

umbrella *n.* a folding, covered framework on a stick with a handle, used to keep you dry in the rain.

umpire *n.* a person who watches a game of tennis, baseball, or cricket to make sure that it is played according to the rules.

umbrella

un- *prefix* 1 not. *unequal, unhappy, unlucky.* 2 used to show the opposite of an action. *unfasten, undo.*

unanimous *(yoo-nan-im-us) adj.* agreed by everybody. *a unanimous decision.*

uncanny *adj.* strange; mysterious. uncannily *adv.*

uncle *n.* the brother of your mother or father or the husband of your aunt.

uncouth *adj.* rough and rude.

uncover *v.* 1 to take the cover off something. 2 to discover something.

under *prep.* 1 lower than or below. 2 less than. *prices under $10.* 3 controlled or ruled by. *The hotel has recently come under new management.* 4 having or using. *under a false name.* under *adv.*

under- *prefix* 1 below. *underground.* 2 not enough; too little. *underweight.*

undercarriage *n.* 1 the supporting structure of a vehicle. 2 an airplane's landing gear.

undercover *adj.* acting or done in secret. *an undercover agent.*

underdog *n.* a person or team that is expected to lose a contest, fight, or game.

underestimate *v.* 1 to think that somebody or something is not as strong as that person or thing really is. 2 to guess that the amount of something is less than it really is.

undergo *v.* (undergoes, undergoing, underwent, undergone) to suffer or experience something.

underground *adj., adv.* below the surface of the ground.

undergrowth *n.* bushes and plants growing among trees.

underline *v.* 1 to draw a line under a word or words. 2 to stress something to show that it is especially important.

undermine *v.* to make something weaker.

underneath *adv., prep.* under or below.

underpants *n. pl.* underwear worn over the buttocks.

underpass *n.* a road that passes under another road.

underprivileged *adj.* having a worse standard of living or fewer rights than most people. *a charity for underprivileged children.*

understand *v.* (understanding, understood) 1 to see the meaning of something. 2 to know the reasons for something. *I don't understand why you're so angry.* 3 to know somebody or something well. 4 to believe that something is true. *I understand you're moving soon.* understanding *adj., n.*

understudy *n.* an actor who learns the part of another actor and is able to take his or her place if necessary.

undertake *v.* (undertaking, undertook, undertaken) to agree to do something. *I undertook to be in charge of the funeral arrangements.* undertaking *n.*

A
B
C
D
E
F
G
H
I
J
K
L
M
N
O
P
Q
R
S
T
U
V
W
X
Y
Z

undertaker *n.* a person who arranges funerals as a profession.

underwater *adj., adv.* under the surface of the water.

underwear *n. pl.* clothes worn next to your skin underneath your outer clothes.

undo *v.* (undoes, undoing, undid, undone) **1** to open something that was wrapped or tied. *Can you undo this knot?* **2** to reverse or remove the effects of something.

undress *v.* to take off your clothes.

undue *adj.* too great; more than is actually necessary.

unearth *v.* to dig up or discover something after searching.

uneasy *adj.* anxious; worried. **uneasily** *adv.*, **uneasiness** *n.*

unemployed *adj.* without a paid job. **unemployment** *n.*

unfold *v.* **1** to open and spread out. **2** (of a story) to gradually become known. *Please unfold the map.*

unfounded *adj.* not based on fact; not true. *Your doubts are unfounded.*

uni- *prefix* one. *unicycle.*

unicorn *n.* in stories a magical animal like a horse with a single horn in the middle of its forehead.

uniform[1] *n.* a set of clothes worn by all of the members of a group of people such as students or soldiers.

uniform[2] *adj.* all the same; not changing or varying. *The sky was a uniform gray.*

unicorn

unify *v.* (unifies, unifying, unified) to join several things together to form a single whole.

union *n.* **1** the joining together of things or people. **2** a trade union.

unique (*yoo-neek*) *adj.* being the only one of its kind.

unisex *adj.* for both men and women. *unisex clothing.*

unison *n.* **in unison** together. *They answered in unison.*

unit *n.* **1** a single thing that is complete in itself. *The building is divided into ten units.* **2** a quantity that is used as a standard. *A foot is a unit of length.*

unite *v.* to join together. **unity** *n.*

universal *adj.* to do with or affecting everybody or everything.

universe *n.* everything that exists, including all the stars and planets.

university *n.* a place where people study for degrees and do research.

unkempt *adj.* messy.

unleaded *adj.* (of gasoline) without lead in it.

unless *conj.* if not. *I'm not going unless you come too.*

unload *v.* to remove things from a ship, truck, or other vehicle.

unravel *v.* (unraveling, unraveled) to undo threads that are tangled, woven, or knitted.

unruly *adj.* badly behaved; not obeying laws or rules. **unruliness** *n.*

unscathed *adj.* not harmed.

unscrupulous *adj.* having no moral principles; not honest or fair.

unsightly *adj.* ugly.

untie *v.* (unties, untying, untied) to undo something that was tied.

until *prep.* up to a particular time. *We stayed until one o'clock.*

unusual *adj.* strange or remarkable; not usual. **unusually** *adv.*

unwieldy *adj.* difficult to move or handle.

unwind *v.* (unwinding, unwound) **1** to undo something that was wound in a ball or around something. **2** to relax.

unwrap *v.* (unwraps, unwrapping, unwrapped) to reveal something by taking off the wrapping.

up *adv., prep.* **1** from a lower to a higher level or amount. **2** from a lying position to sitting or standing. *What time did you get up today?* **3** completely so that it is finished. *Who used up all the milk?* **4** as far as. *He came up to me and shook my hand.* **5** along. *I was walking up the road.* **6** into pieces. *He tore up the letter.*

upbringing *n.* the way that a child is raised.

update *v.* to bring up to date by including all of the latest information. *This dictionary is updated regularly to include new words.* **update** *n.*

upheaval *n.* a great change or disturbance.

uphill *adv.* up a hill or slope.

upholstery *n.* the padding and covering of chairs and sofas.

upkeep *n.* the keeping of something in good condition, or the cost of this. *The museum charges an entrance fee to pay for the upkeep of the building.*

upon *prep.* on.

upper *adj.* higher; farther up.

upright *adj.* **1** standing straight up; vertical. *a row of upright posts.* **2** honest and decent. *an upright citizen.* **upright** *adv.*

uprising *n.* a fight against the people in power; a revolt.

uproar *n.* a lot of shouting or protest, especially because people are angry. *The president's speech caused uproar in the senate.*

upset¹ *v.* (upsetting, upset) **1** to make somebody unhappy or worried. **2** to knock something over.

upset² *adj.* unhappy or worried.

upside down *adv.* with the top part underneath. **upside-down** *adj.*

uptight *adj.* *(informal)* nervous; tense.

up-to-date *adj.* **1** modern. **2** having the latest information.

uranium *n.* a radioactive metal.

urban *adj.* to do with a town or city.

urge¹ *v.* to encourage somebody strongly. *We urged him to go home.*

urge² *n.* a strong, sudden impulse or desire to do something.

urgent *adj.* so important that it needs immediate action. **urgency** *n.*

urine *(yur-in)* *n.* waste liquid that people and animals get rid of from their bodies.

urn *n.* **1** a vase, especially one for holding the ashes of a dead person. **2** a large, metal container with a spigot, for pouring hot drinks.

usage *n.* **1** the way that something is used. **2** the way in which the words of a language are used.

use¹ *(yooz)* *v.* **1** to do a job with something. *May I use your pen?* **2** to take something. *I've used your mug.* **3** to treat somebody badly in order to get what you want. **use up** to finish something. *He used up all the paint.*

use² *(yooss)* *n.* **1** the action of using something. **2** the way that something is used. *Plastics have many different uses.*

used *(yoozd)* *adj.* secondhand; not new. *used cars.*

used to *(yooss too)* *v.* words that refer to something that happened often or that was true in the past. *We used to go there every year.* **be used to** to know something well. *She's used to children because she has two young nephews.*

useful *adj.* helpful; serving a purpose. **usefully** *adv.*, **usefulness** *n.*

useless *adj.* **1** not useful. **2** *(informal)* very bad. *I'm useless at chess.* **uselessness** *n.*

user *n.* a person who uses something.

user-friendly *adj.* easy to understand and use.

usher, usherette *n.* a person who shows other people to their seats in a theater.

usual *adj.* happening or used most often. **usually** *adv.*

utensil *n.* a tool or container, especially one used in cooking.

utter¹ *v.* to say something or make a sound. *She uttered a sigh of relief.*

utter² *adj.* complete; total. *I heard nothing but utter silence.*

U-turn *n.* a turn in the shape of a U, made by a vehicle in order to go back the way that it has come.

urn

A
B
C
D
E
F
G
H
I
J
K
L
M
N
O
P
Q
R
S
T
U
V
W
X
Y
Z

vacant *adj.* **1** empty; not occupied. *Does the hotel have any rooms vacant?* **2** (of a person's expression) showing no intelligence or interest.

vacate *v.* to leave a place empty.

vacation *n.* a time when you are staying away from home for relaxation, often on a trip.

vaccinate *(vak-sin-ate)* *v.* to protect somebody from a disease, usually by giving him or her a shot. **vaccination** *n.*

vacuum¹ *n.* a space from which all air or other gas has been removed.

vacuum² *v.* to clean with a vacuum cleaner.

vacuum bottle *n.* a container with double walls enclosing a vacuum, for keeping liquids hot or cold.

vacuum cleaner *n.* a machine that cleans carpets by sucking up dirt.

vagina *(va-jye-na)* *n.* the passage in a woman's body leading to her womb.

vague *adj.* not clear; not definite. *Through the fog we saw the vague outline of a ship.* **vagueness** *n.*

vain *adj.* **1** too proud of what you look like or what you can do. **2** unsuccessful. *They made a vain attempt to find the dog.*

valentine *n.* **1** a card sent to people you love on Valentine's Day, February 14. **2** the person that you send a valentine to.

valiant *adj.* brave.

valid *adj.* **1** legally acceptable. *My visa is only valid for one year.* **2** reasonable and acceptable. *I hope you have a valid excuse for being so late.* **validity** *n.*

valley *n.* (*pl.* valleys) an area of low land between hills or mountains, often with a river running through it.

valuable *adj.* of great value.

valuables *n. pl.* belongings that are worth a lot of money.

value¹ *n.* **1** the usefulness or importance of something. *His experience is of great value to the company.* **2** the amount of money that something is worth. *The*

painting has a value of $200.

value² *v.* **1** to decide how much something is worth. *The painting has been valued at $200.* **2** to think of something as good or important. *She values her freedom.*

valve *n.* a device that controls the flow of liquid, air, or gas, allowing it to move in one direction only.

van

vampire *n.* in stories a dead person who rises from the grave at night to suck the blood of living people.

van *n.* a covered vehicle for carrying people or goods.

vandal *n.* a person who deliberately destroys or damages things. **vandalism** *n.,* **vandalize** *v.*

vanilla *n.* a sweet-smelling substance produced from the pods of a type of orchid, usually used for flavoring ice cream or cake.

vanish *v.* to disappear suddenly.

vanity *n.* too much pride in what you look like or what you can do.

vanquish *(van-kwish)* *v.* to defeat.

vapor *n.* the gaslike form into which a substance can be changed by heating. *Steam is water vapor.*

variable *adj.* changing a lot; not staying the same.

varied *adj.* full of variety.

variety *n.* **1** a number of different types of things. *The store sells a huge variety of toys.* **2** a type. *a variety of apple.*

various *adj.* several different. *The shirt is available in various colors.*

varnish *n.* a clear liquid that is painted onto wood or other surfaces to give them a glossy surface. **varnish** *v.*

vary *v.* (varies, varying, varied) **1** to make or become different; to change. **2** to be different from each other. *These cards vary in price from 99¢ to $2.99.* **variation** *n.*

vase *(vayse* or *vahz)* *n.* a jar of pottery

or glass, used as an ornament to hold cut flowers.

vast *adj.* very large. **vastness** *n.*

vat *n.* a large container used for storing liquids.

vault¹ *v.* to jump over or onto something, using your hands or a pole for support.

vault² *n.* **1** an underground room, often used to store valuable things. **2** a room beneath a church, used for burials. **3** an arched roof.

VCR *short for* video cassette recorder.

VDT (*short for* visual display terminal) a screen on which information from a computer is displayed.

veal *n.* the meat from a calf.

veer *v.* to change direction suddenly. *The car veered across the road.*

vegan (*vee-gan*) *n.* a person who does not eat or use any animal products. **vegan** *adj.,* **veganism** *n.*

vegetable *n.* a part of a plant grown as food.

vegetarian *n.* a person who does not eat meat or fish. **vegetarian** *adj.,* **vegetarianism** *n.*

vegetation *n.* all of the plants growing in a certain place.

vehicle (*vee-i-kul*) *n.* something, especially a machine with an engine, that transports people or goods.

veil (*vale*) *n.* a piece of thin cloth worn over a woman's face.

vein (*vane*) *n.* **1** one of the tubes that carries blood back to the heart. **2** a line on a leaf.

velvet *n.* cloth with a thick, soft surface on one side.

vendetta *n.* a long-lasting, bitter quarrel between people or groups.

vending machine *n.* a machine selling candy, drinks, or other things, operated by putting coins in a slot.

veneer *n.* a thin layer of good-quality wood covering a cheaper material.

vengeance *n.* harm done to somebody in return for something bad that he or she has done; revenge.

venison *n.* the meat from a deer.

venom *n.* the poison of some snakes and spiders. **venomous** *adj.*

vent *n.* a hole to allow air, smoke, or gas to pass in or out.

ventilate *v.* to allow fresh air to pass through a room or building. **ventilation** *n.*

ventriloquist *n.* a person who can speak without seeming to move his or her lips so that it seems like a voice is coming from a mannequin or a puppet. **ventriloquism** *n.*

venture¹ *v.* to dare to go somewhere or do something.

venture² *n.* a project that involves risk. *a business venture.*

venue (*ven-yoo*) *n.* the place where an event, such as a concert or game, takes place.

veranda *n.* a covered platform running around the side of a house. (*can also be spelled* verandah.)

verb *n.* a word or words showing what somebody or something does in a sentence. In the sentence *I saw her, saw* is the verb.

verbal *adj.* **1** spoken; not written. **2** to do with words. **verbally** *adv.*

verdict *n.* **1** the decision of a judge or jury at the end of a trial in a court of law. **2** somebody's opinion or judgment about something.

verify *v.* to make sure that something is true or correct. **verifiable** *adj.,* **verification** *n.*

verge *n.* a border or boundary. **on the verge of** about to do something. *He was on the verge of laughing.*

versatile *adj.* **1** having many different uses. *a versatile tool.* **2** having many different skills. *a versatile entertainer.*

verse *n.* **1** one section of a song or poem, made up of several lines. **2** poetry.

version *n.* **1** a thing that is based on something else but that is different in some way. *I haven't read the* Harry Potter *books, but I have seen the movie versions.* **2** one person's description of an event. *Her version of what happened was different from mine.*

versus *prep.* against. *the Celtics versus Knicks game.*

vertebra *n.* (*pl.* vertebrae or vertebras) one of the bones of your spine.

vertebrate *n.* one member of a group of animals that has a backbone.

vertical *adj.* straight up and down; upright. **vertically** *adv.*

vessel *n.* **1** a ship or boat. **2** a container for carrying liquids.

vest *n.* a sleeveless piece of clothing, usually with buttons, worn over a shirt or top or as part of a suit.

veteran *n.* **1** a person who has served in the armed forces, especially during a war. **2** a person who is experienced in something.

veterinarian *n.* a doctor for animals (*vet* for short).

veto *n.* (*pl.* vetoes) the power to forbid something. *The president used his veto to prevent the changes.* **veto** *v.*

vex *v.* (vexes, vexing, vexed) to annoy or irritate somebody.

via (**vy**-*a* or **vee**-*a*) *prep.* by way of. *We drove from New York to Boston via Providence.*

viable *adj.* capable of succeeding. *I don't think that your plan is viable.*

viaduct *n.* a long bridge that carries a railroad or road over a valley.

vibrate *v.* to shake very quickly. *a washing machine vibrates.* **vibration** *n.*

vice *n.* **1** evil or immoral actions. **2** a bad habit or serious moral fault. *Lying and greed are vices.* **3** a tool that holds an object in one place while you are working on it.

vice- *prefix* next in rank to. *vicepresident, vicecaptain.*

vice versa *adv.* the other way around. *I needed his help and vice versa.*

vicinity *n.* the area surrounding a particular place. *They live in the vicinity of the park.*

vicious *adj.* violent and spiteful. *a vicious attack.* **viciousness** *n.*

victim *n.* a person who is harmed or killed by somebody or something.

victor *n.* the winner of a contest or battle.

victory *n.* success in a battle or contest. **victorious** *adj.*

video *n.* (*pl.* videos) **1** the visual portion of a TV show. **2** a videotape containing a visual or musical performance.

videotape *n.* magnetic tape for recording and playing back sound and pictures in a video cassette recorder.

vie *v.* (vies, vying, vied) to compete with somebody. *I vied with him for first place.*

view¹ *n.* **1** the scene that you can see from a certain place. *a wonderful view of the sea.* **2** an opinion. *What are your views on capital punishment?*

view² *v.* to look at something. **viewer** *n.*

vigilant *adj.* watching carefully. **vigilance** *n.*

vigorous *adj.* strong and energetic. *vigorous exercise.* **vigor** *n.*

vile *adj.* horrible; disgusting.

villa *n.* a large country house of a wealthy person.

village *n.* a group of houses and other buildings that is smaller than a town.

villain *n.* a wicked person. **villainy** *n.*

villein *n.* (*historical*) in the Middle Ages a slave who was bought and sold with the land on which he or she worked.

vindictive *adj.* spiteful; wanting revenge.

vine *n.* **1** a climbing plant that grapes grow on. **2** any climbing or trailing plant.

vinegar *n.* a sour-tasting liquid made from wine or cider, used for flavoring and preserving food.

vineyard (**vin**-yard) *n.* a piece of land where grapes are grown.

vintage *n.* the wine that was made in a particular year, especially when it is of high quality.

vintage car *n.* an old car, built between 1919 and 1930.

vinyl *n.* a type of strong plastic.

viola *n.* a stringed musical instrument that is larger than a violin.

violent *adj.* **1** using physical force, often to hurt or kill somebody. *a violent man.* **2** very strong; uncontrolled. *a violent storm.* **violence** *adj.*

violet *n.* **1** a small, purple flower with a pleasant smell. **2** a bluish-purple color. **violet** *adj.*

violin *n.* a stringed musical instrument played with a bow. **violinist** *n.*

VIP *short for* very important person.

viper *n.* a poisonous snake, an adder.

virgin *n.* a person who has never had sexual intercourse. **virginity** *n.*

virtually *adj.* almost. *I've virtually finished this book.*

virtual reality *n.* the creation on computer of an environment that gives the user the impression that it is real.

virtue *n.* **1** goodness of character. **2** a good quality. *Honesty and generosity are virtues.* **virtuous** *adj.*

virus *n.* **1** a tiny living thing, smaller than a bacterium, that can cause disease. **2** hidden instructions written into a computer program that are intended to destroy data. **viral** *adj.*

visa (**vee**-za) *n.* a stamp in a passport allowing a person to enter a country.

viscount (**vie**-count) *n.* a nobleman.

visible *adj.* able to be seen. *The ship was visible on the horizon.* **visibility** *n.*

vision *n.* **1** the power to see; sight.

violin

2 something that you see in your imagination. **3** the ability to see or plan into the future.

visit *v.* to go to see a person or place. **visit** *n.*, **visitor** *n.*

visor *(vye-zor) n.* **1** a part of a helmet that you pull down to cover your eyes. **2** a shade that protects your eyes from the sun.

visual *adj.* to do with eyesight and seeing. **visually** *adv.*

visualize *v.* to form a clear picture of something in your mind. *I attempted to visualize what the room would look like without furniture.*

vital *adj.* very important or necessary. **vitally** *adv.*

vitality *n.* liveliness and energy.

vitamin *n.* a substance found in food that we need in order to stay healthy.

vivid *adj.* **1** bright. *vivid colors.* **2** producing a clear picture in your mind. *vivid memories.*

vivisection *n.* the use of live animals in scientific experiments.

vixen *n.* a female fox.

vocabulary *n.* **1** all of the words used in a particular language. **2** all the words used by a particular person or group.

vocal *adj.* to do with the voice.

vocalist *n.* a singer.

vocation *n.* **1** a strong wish to do a particular job such as medical work, teaching, or caring for people in some way. **2** an occupation or profession of this type. **vocational** *adj.*

vodka *n.* a strong, colorless, alcoholic drink made from grains.

vogue *n.* the fashion at a particular time.

voice *n.* the sounds that come from your mouth when you speak or sing.

void *n.* an empty space.

volcano *n.* (*pl.* volcanoes *or* volcanos) a mountain with an opening, called a crater, at the top from which molten rock, gas, and ashes may erupt or have erupted in the past. **volcanic** *adj.*

vole *n.* a small burrowing rodent.

volley *n.* (*pl.* volleys) **1** in tennis or soccer the hitting or kicking of a ball before it has bounced. **2** a number of shots fired or missiles thrown at the same time. **volley** *v.*

volcano

volleyball *n.* a game in which two teams try to hit a ball over a high net using their hands.

volt *n.* a unit used for measuring the force of electricity.

voltage *n.* an electrical force that is measured in volts.

volume *n.* **1** the amount of space that something takes up or contains. *What is the volume of the gas tank?* **2** a large book, especially one of a set. **3** loudness.

voluntary *adj.* **1** done by choice, not by accident and not because you are asked or forced. *a voluntary agreement.* **2** done or working without payment. *Tara does voluntary work at the local hospital.* **voluntarily** *adv.*

volunteer *v.* to offer to do something without being asked or forced. **volunteer** *n.*, **volunteer** *adj.*

vomit *v.* to bring food up from your stomach through your mouth. **vomit** *n.*

vote *v.* to make a choice in an election or debate by raising your hand or writing on a piece of paper. **vote** *n.*

voucher *n.* a written record of spending.

vow *v.* to make a serious promise. **vow** *n.*

vowel *n.* any of the letters *a, e, i, o,* and *u.*

voyage *n.* a long journey, especially by sea or in space.

vulgar *adj.* having bad manners; rude. **vulgarity** *n.*

vulnerable *adj.* unprotected against attacks and easily hurt or damaged.

vulture *n.* a large bird that feeds on the bodies of dead animals.

vultures

a
b
c
d
e
f
g
h
i
j
k
l
m
n
o
p
q
r
s
t
u
v
w
x
y
z

waddle *v.* to walk with short, unsteady steps, moving from side to side like a duck does.

wade *v.* to walk through water.

waders *n. pl.* high, waterproof boots worn while fishing.

wading bird *n.* a long-legged bird that wades through shallow water in search of food.

wafer *n.* a thin, light type of cookie.

waffle¹ *n.* a type of crisp, square pancake.

waffle² *v.* *(informal)* to talk or write for a long time without saying anything important.

wag *v.* (wagging, wagged) to move from side to side or up and down. *The dog wagged its tail.*

wage¹ *v.* to take part in something. *They waged war for five years.*

wage² *n.* the money that you get for working, usually paid weekly.

waggle *v.* to move from side to side.

wagon *n.* **1** an open cart with four wheels. **2** a horse-drawn vehicle, used for transporting goods.

wail *v.* to let out a long, loud cry of sorrow. **wail** *n.*

waist *n.* the narrower part of your body between your chest and your hips.

wait *v.* to stay where you are, expecting something to happen. **wait on** to serve food and drinks to somebody. **wait** *n.*

waiter *n.* a man who serves food and drinks in a restaurant.

waitress *n.* a woman who serves food and drinks in a restaurant.

wake¹ *v.* (waking, woke, woken) **1** to stop sleeping. **2** to stop somebody from sleeping.

wake² *n.* **1** the track left in water by a ship. **2** a watch over a dead body before burial. Also called *viewing.*

walk *v.* to move along on your feet. **walk** *n.*, **walker** *n.*

walkover *n.* an easy victory.

wall *n.* **1** a structure made of brick or stone, used to enclose an area of land. **2** a side of a building or room. **walled** *adj.*

wallaby *n.* a small type of kangaroo.

wallet *n.* a small, folding case for holding money and credit cards.

wallow *v.* **1** to roll around with enjoyment in mud or water. **2** to enjoy something greatly. *He wallowed in self-pity.*

walnut *n.* **1** a tree whose wood is used for making furniture. **2** the edible nut produced by this tree. See **nut**.

walrus *n.* (*pl.* walrus *or* walruses) a large sea animal found in the Arctic, similar

walrus

to a seal but with two long tusks.

waltz *n.* a type of ballroom dance. **waltz** *v.*

wand *n.* a long, thin rod used by a magician or fairy.

wander *v.* to go from place to place with no definite plan or purpose.

wane *v.* to become smaller or less. *The Moon is waning.*

wangle *v.* *(informal)* get something by being intelligent or cunning. *Kim has wangled a free ticket to the concert.*

want *v.* **1** to wish to have or do something. **2** to need something. *Your cat wants to be washed!* **want** *n.*

wanted *adj.* being searched for, especially by the police.

war *n.* armed fighting between countries or groups of people.

ward¹ *n.* **1** a room with beds for patients in a hospital. **2** one of the parts into which a town is divided for voting in elections. **3** a child who is under the legal control and care of a person who is not his or her parent or of a law court.

ward² *v.* **ward off** to defend yourself against something.

warden *n.* a person who is in charge of a prison.

warder *n.* a guard of a gate or tower.

wardrobe *n.* a type of cabinet where you hang clothes.

warehouse *n.* a large building where goods are stored.

warm *adj.* **1** fairly hot. **2** keeping you warm. a *warm coat.* **3** friendly and kind. **warm** *v.*, **warmth** *n.*

warn *v.* to tell somebody about a danger or about something bad that may happen. **warning** *n.*

warp *v.* to become twisted or bent because of heat or dampness.

warrant *n.* a document that gives somebody the right to do something. *a search warrant.*

warren *n.* a group of rabbit burrows.

warrior *n.* a fighter.

wart *n.* a small, hard lump on your skin.

Native American warrior

wary *adj.* (warier, wariest) cautious about something or somebody. **warily** *adv.*

was *past of* be.

wash *v.* **1** to clean something with soap and water. **2** to flow over or against something. *I let the waves wash over my feet.* **wash** *n.*

washer *n.* a flat ring used to make a joint tight, such as on a faucet.

wasp *n.* a flying insect with yellow-and-black stripes and a stinger.

waste[1] *v.* to use more than you need of something, or not use something in a useful way.

waste[2] *n.* **1** an act of wasting something. **2** unwanted material that you throw away or get rid of. **waste** *adj.*, **wasteful** *adj.*

watch[1] *v.* **1** to look carefully at somebody or something. **2** to be careful about something. *You should watch your diet.* **3** to guard or take care of somebody or something.

watch[2] *n.* a small clock that you wear on your wrist.

water[1] *n.* clear liquid that falls as rain.

water[2] *v.* **1** to give water to plants. **2** (of the eyes or mouth) to produce tears or saliva.

watercolor *n.* **1** a paint that you mix with water. **2** a painting done with this paint.

watch

waterfall *n.* a natural fall of water from a height such as from a rock or a cliff.

waterlogged *adj.* completely soaked or flooded with water.

watermark *n.* a faint design on paper that can be seen when it is held up to the light.

watermelon *n.* a large melon with red, juicy flesh and green skin.

water polo *n.* a ball game played in a pool between teams of swimmers.

waterproof *adj.* not allowing water to pass through. *a waterproof jacket.*

water-skiing *n.* the sport of skiing on water, towed by a motorboat.

watertight *adj.* so closely fitted that water cannot pass through. *a watertight seal.*

waterwheel *n.* a wheel that uses the force of falling water to run machines.

watt *n.* a unit of electrical power.

wattage *n.* the electrical power of something measured in watts.

wattle and daub *n. (historical)* twigs woven and held together with mud or clay, often used in earlier times for building houses.

wave[1] *n.* **1** a moving ridge on the surface of water, especially the ocean. **2** a curve or curl in your hair. **3** a vibration traveling through the air carrying heat, light, or sound. **4** a waving movement of your hand. **5** a sudden, strong increase. *a wave of emotion.*

wave[2] *v.* **1** to move your hand from side to side in the air, usually to say hello or goodbye. **2** to move something from side to side in the air. *They were waving flags.*

wavelength *n.* **1** the distance between two sound or radio waves. **2** the length of the radio wave used by a radio station for broadcasting its shows.

waver *v.* to be uncertain; to hesitate.

wavy *adj.* having curves. *a wavy line.*

wax[1] *n.* **1** a substance made from fat or oil that is used to produce candles, furniture polish, and other things. **2** the yellow substance found in your ears.

wax[2] *v. (formal)* to grow or increase. *The Moon is waxing.*

way *n.* (*pl.* ways) **1** a road or path that you follow to get somewhere. *Do you know your way home?* **2** a direction. *Which way is north?* **3** a method of doing something. *What's the best way to cook rice?* **4** a distance. *Australia is a long way from the U.S.* **5 ways** habits.

a
b
c
d
e
f
g
h
i
j
k
l
m
n
o
p
q
r
s
t
u
v
w
x
y
z

A
B
C
D
E
F
G
H
I
J
K
L
M
N
O
P
Q
R
S
T
U
V
W
X
Y
Z

weak *adj.* lacking strength or power. **weakness** *n.*

weaken *v.* to make or become weak.

weakling *n.* a weak person or animal.

wealth *n.* **1** riches. **2** a large quantity. *a wealth of information.*

wealthy *adj.* (wealthier, wealthiest) rich.

wean *v.* to gradually make a child or young animal used to food other than its mother's milk.

weapon *n.* an object, such as a gun or sword, used for fighting.

wear *v.* (wearing, wore, worn) **1** to be dressed in or have something on your body. **2** to become thin or damaged through use. *The carpet in the hall is beginning to wear.* **wear off** to gradually become less. **wear out 1** to make or become so damaged or thin that it cannot be used anymore. **2** to make somebody very tired. **wear** *n.*

weary *adj.* (wearier, weariest) tired. **wearily** *adv.*, **weariness** *n.*

weasel *n.* a small wild animal with a long, slender body that feeds on mice, rabbits, and other small animals.

weather *n.* the conditions in the atmosphere, like heat, rain, or cloudiness.

weathervane *n.* a flat piece of metal that swings in the wind to show the way that it is blowing.

weave[1] *v.* (weaving, wove, woven) **1** to pass threads over and under each other to make cloth on a loom. **2** to pass strips of a material over and under each other to make baskets.

weave[2] *v.* (weaving, weaved) to move in and out between things or people.

web *n.* **1** a net made by a spider. **2 the Web** the Internet.

webbed *adj.* (of feet) with skin between the toes. *Ducks have webbed feet.*

webcam *n.* a digital camera that transmits images on the Internet.

weblog *see* blog.

Web site, website *n.* a group of pages on the Internet, often about a similar subject.

wedding *n.* a marriage ceremony.

wedge[1] *n.* a piece of wood, rubber, or other material with one end that is thicker than the other.

wedge[2] *v.* **1** to keep something in place using a wedge. **2** to push something firmly into a small space.

Wednesday *n.* the fourth day of the week.

weed[1] *n.* a wild plant that grows where it is not wanted.

weed[2] *v.* to pull up weeds.

week *n.* **1** a period of seven days, especially from Sunday to Saturday. **2** the working days of the week, not Saturday and Sunday. **weekly** *adj.*, *adv.*

weekend *n.* Saturday and Sunday.

weep *v.* (weeping, wept) to have tears falling from your eyes; to cry.

weigh *v.* **1** to measure how heavy something is on scales. **2** to have a certain weight. *This box weighs two pounds.*

weight *n.* **1** the heaviness of someone or something. **2** a piece of metal weighing a certain amount.

weir *n.* a shallow dam constructed across a river to control its flow.

weird *adj.* very odd; strange.

welcome[1] *v.* to show that you are happy to see somebody or have something. *She welcomed us at the door.* **welcome** *n.*, **welcoming** *adj.*

welcome[2] *adj.* received with pleasure. *The extra money was very welcome.* **welcome to** allowed to do something. *You're very welcome to help yourself to tea or coffee.*

weld *v.* to join pieces of metal or plastic, by first heating the edges to soften them and then letting them harden together.

welfare *n.* the health, comfort, happiness, and general well-being of a person.

well[1] *adj.* healthy; not sick.

well[2] *adv.* **1** in a good or right way. *Amy can swim very well.* **2** thoroughly. *I don't know him very well.*

well[3] *n.* a deep hole in the earth from which you can get water, oil, or gas.

Wellington boot *n.* high, rubber boots that you wear to keep your legs dry if you are walking over wet ground.

well-known *adj.* famous; known by many people.

well-off *adj.* rich.

went *past of* go.

wept *past of* weep.

were *past of* be.

we're *conj.* we are.

werewolf *n.* in stories a person who can change into a wolf at the full moon.

west *n.* **1** one of the points of the compass; the direction that you face to see the sun set. **2 the West** Europe and North America. **west** *adj.*, *adv.*

western[1] *adj.* in or of the west of a place.

western² *n.* a movie or book about cowboys in the west of the U.S. in the 1800s and early 1900s.

wet¹ *adj.* (wetter, wettest) **1** soaked or covered in water or another liquid. **2** rainy. *wet weather.*

wet² *v.* (wetting, wet, wetted) to make something wet.

whack *v.* *(informal)* to hit somebody or something very hard. **whack** *n.*

whale *n.* a large sea mammal that breathes air through an opening on the head.

whaling *n.* the hunting of whales.

wharf *n.* (*pl.* wharves *or* wharfs) a place where ships are loaded and unloaded.

humpback whales

what *adj., pron.* **1** used in questions. *What time is it?* **2** the thing that. *Tell me what you want.* **3** used to show surprise or to express something strongly. *What a stupid thing to say!*

whatever *adj., pron.* **1** anything that. *Show me whatever you have.* **2** no matter what. *Whatever he may say, I still don't believe him.*

wheat *n.* the grain from which most flour is made.

wheel¹ *n.* a circular object that turns around an axle in its center.

wheel² *v.* to push something or someone along on wheels.

wheelbarrow *n.* a cart with one wheel at the front, pushed along by two handles.

wheelchair *n.* a chair on wheels for a person who is not able to walk.

wheeze *v.* to breathe with difficulty, making a whistling sound. **wheezy** *adj.*

when *adv., conj.* **1** at what time? **2** at the time that. *Call me when you get in.*

whenever *adv., conj.* **1** at any time. *You can come whenever you want.* **2** every time that. *Whenever I hear this song,* *I feel happy.*

where *adv., conj.* **1** in or to what place. *Where have you been?* **2** at or to the place that. *Sit where she tells you to.*

whereas *conj.* but. *Polly is blonde, whereas I have dark hair.*

wherever *adv., conj.* at or to any place.

whether *conj.* if. *I don't mind whether you come or not.*

which *adj., pron.* **1** what person or thing. *Which flavor do you want?* **2** used to refer to a particular person or thing. *the subject on which she wrote.*

whichever *adj., pron.* no matter which.

while¹ *n.* a period of time. *She'll be back in a while.*

while² *conj.* **1** during the time that. *Did anyone call while I was out?* **2** although. *While I sympathize, I can't do much to help.*

while³ *v.* to pass time. *We whiled away the hours playing card games.*

whim *n.* a sudden idea or change of mind.

whimper *v.* to make soft crying sounds. **whimper** *n.*

whine *v.* **1** to make a long, high-pitched, unpleasant sound. **2** to complain in an annoying way.

whip¹ *n.* a long rope or strip of leather joined to a handle, often used for hitting animals to control them.

whip² *v.* (whipping, whipped) **1** to hit with a whip. **2** to beat cream or an egg until it is thick. **3** to move quickly and suddenly. *She whipped out a gun from her bag.*

whirl *v.* to turn around fast in circles. **whirl** *n.*

whirlpool *n.* a place in a river or ocean where the current moves in a circle.

whirlwind *n.* a very strong wind that blows in circles.

whisk¹ *n.* a kitchen tool made of wire, used for beating eggs or cream.

whisk² *v.* **1** to beat eggs or cream with a fork or whisk. **2** to move quickly and suddenly. *The waiter whisked our plates away as soon as we had finished.*

whisker *n.* **1** one of the long, stiff hairs that grows close to the mouth of animals such as cats and mice. **whiskers** hair on the sides of a man's face.

whiskey, whisky *n.* a strong, alcoholic drink made from grain.

whisper *v.* to speak very quietly and softly. **whisper** *n.*

whist *n.* a card game for four players.

A B C D E F G H I J K L M N O P Q R S T U V **W** X Y Z

whistle¹ *v.* to make a high-pitched sound by blowing through your tightened lips.

whistle² *n.* an instrument that you blow through to make a whistling sound.

white¹ *n.* the color of pure snow.

white² *adj.* **1** having the color of pure snow. **2** light-colored. *white wine.*

white³ *n.* the liquid around an egg yolk.

whizz *v.* (whizzing, whizzed) to move very quickly, often making a buzzing sound.

who *pron.* **1** what person or people? *Who did that?* **2** used to refer to a certain person. *I know who he is.*

whoever, whomever *pron.* **1** any person or people. *Invite whoever you want to the party.* **2** any person that. *Whoever calls, tell him or her I'm out.*

whole *adj.* complete; with nothing missing. *Tell me the whole story.* **whole** *n.*, **wholly** *adv.*

whole note *n.* in music a whole note is equal to four crotchets in length.

wholesale *n.* the buying and selling of goods in large quantities.

wholesome *adj.* healthy; good for you.

whom *pron.* who.

whooping cough (*hoo-ping koff*) *n.* an infectious disease that makes you cough and make a loud noise as you breathe in.

who's *conj.* who is; who has.

whose *adj., pron.* **1** belonging to whom. *Whose book is this?* **2** of whom. *She's the girl whose mom is a model.*

why *adv.* for what reason?

wick *n.* the thread running through a candle, which you light.

wicked *adj.* **1** evil. **2** (*informal*) very good. **wickedness** *n.*

wicket *n.* in cricket a set of three stumps at which the ball is bowled.

wide *adj.* **1** far from one side to the other. *a wide road.* **2** measuring a certain amount from side to side. *five feet wide.* **3** great; large. *a wide range of choices.* **widen** *v.*

widespread *adj.* found or happening in many places.

widow *n.* a woman whose husband is dead and who has not married again.

widower *n.* a man whose wife is dead and who has not married again.

width *n.* the distance from one side to the other of something.

wife *n.* (*pl.* wives) the woman that a man is married to.

wig *n.* an artificial covering of hair, made to fit the head.

wiggle *v.* to move from side to side.

windmill

wigwam *n.* a dome-shaped hut or tent made by Native Americans.

wild *adj.* **1** natural; not tamed or cultivated by humans. **2** uncontrolled, especially because of anger or excitement. *The spectators went wild.*

wilderness *n.* an area of wild land where nobody lives.

wildlife *n.* wild animals and plants

will¹ *v.* (would) used to talk about future actions and events.

will² *n.* **1** determination. *She has the will to succeed.* **2** a desire; what you want. *They did it against my will.* **3** a document that says what will happen to somebody's property when he or she dies. *My father left me money in his will.*

willing *adj.* ready and happy to do what is wanted or needed.

willow *n.* a tree with long, thin branches.

wilt *v.* (of a plant) to start to droop.

wily (*wye-lee*) *adj.* (wilier, wiliest) cunning; sly.

win *v.* (wins, winning, won) **1** to come first in a contest or game. **2** to get a prize. **3** to get something by working or trying hard. *She finally won the respect of the other students in the class.* **win** *n.*, **winner** *n.*

winch *n.* a machine for lifting things, worked by winding a rope around a revolving cylinder. **winch** *v.*

wind¹ (*rhymes with* kind) *v.* (winding, wound) **1** to wrap something around and around another thing. **2** to turn a key or handle around to make something work. *Wind up the clock.* **3** to twist and turn. *The river winds through a valley.* **wind down** (*informal*) to diminish slowly.

wind² (*rhymes with* grinned) *n.* moving air. **windy** *adj.*

wind instrument *n.* a musical instrument played by blowing into it.

windmill *n.* a mill powered by wind blowing against its blades.

window *n.* an opening, usually covered by glass, to let in light and air.

windshield *n.* the front window of a car.

windsurfing *n.* the sport of moving across water on a long board with a sail attached to it. **windsurfer** *n.*

wine *n.* an alcoholic drink, usually made from grapes.

wing *n.* **1** one of the parts of a bird or insect used for flying. **2** one of the large, flat parts on the side of an aircraft that it uses to fly. **3** a part of a building that sticks out to the side. **4** a section of a building for a specific purpose.

windsurfing

wink *v.* to open and close one eye quickly.

winter *n.* the coldest season of the year, between the fall and the spring. **wintry** (*or* **wintery**) *adj.*

wipe *v.* to rub something to make it clean or dry. **wipe out** to destroy completely. *Disease has wiped out the entire village.*

wire *n.* a long, very thin piece of metal that can be bent and twisted.

wisdom *n.* knowledge, experience, and good sense.

wisdom tooth *n.* one of the four back teeth that grow after childhood.

wise *adj.* possessing knowledge and experience and being able to use it well.

wish *v.* **1** to want or desire something. *I wish we could go to the beach.* **2** to say that you hope somebody will have something. *I wished Ben a happy birthday.* **wish** *n.*

wit *n.* **1** the ability to say intelligent and funny things. **2 wits** intelligence; common sense. *Use your wits.*

witch *n.* a person, usually a woman, who is supposed to have magic powers.

witchcraft *n.* the use of magic powers.

with *prep.* **1** accompanying. *I walk to school with my sister.* **2** using. *Cut it with a knife.* **3** having something. *the boy with red hair.* **4** because of. *He was shaking with fear.*

withdraw *v.* (withdrawing, withdrew, withdrawn) **1** to move back or away. *The general has withdrawn his troops.* **2** to decide not to take part in something. *John has withdrawn from the race.* **3** to remove something; to take something out or away. *I withdrew the $50 needed to buy the gift from my bank account.* **withdrawal** *n.*

withdrawn *adj.* quiet; not liking to talk to people.

wither *v.* to dry up and die. *The plant withered in the hot sun.*

withhold *v.* (withholding, withheld) to refuse to give something. *She withheld her permission.*

within *adv., prep.* **1** inside. **2** before the end of a period of time. *You'll get the results within three weeks.*

without *prep.* not having something.

witness *n.* a person who sees something happen and who can describe it later, especially in a law court. **witness** *v.*

witty *adj.* (wittier, wittiest) funny in an intelligent way. *a witty remark.* **wittily** *adv.*

wizard *n.* **1** a man who is supposed to have magic powers. **2** (*informal*) a very skilled person at something. *She's a computer wizard.*

wobble *v.* to move unsteadily from side to side. **wobbly** *adj.*

woe *n.* great sadness. **woeful** *adj.*

wok *n.* a deep, bowl-shaped frying pan, used especially in Chinese cookery.

woke *past of* wake.

woken *past participle of* wake.

wolf *n.* (*pl.* wolves) a wild animal similar to a dog that hunts in a pack.

woman *n.* (*pl.* women) a fully grown female human.

wolf

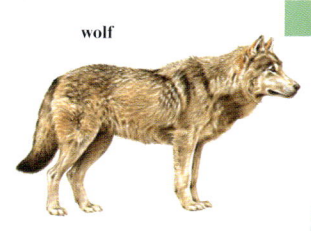

a b c d e f g h i j k l m n o p q r s t u v **w** x y z

womb *n.* the part of the body of a female mammal where her young develop before they are born.

wombat

wombat *n.* a small Australian marsupial that lives in burrows.

won *past of* win.

wonder[1] *v.* **1** to ask yourself something. **2** to be amazed at something.

wonder[2] *n.* **1** a feeling of amazement and admiration. **2** something that gives you this feeling.

wonderful *adj.* excellent; marvelous.

won't *conj.* will not.

wood *n.* **1** a number of trees growing together in one place. **2** the substance that forms the trunk and branches of trees. **wooden** *adj.*

woodpecker *n.* a bird that pecks holes in the bark of trees in search of insects.

woodwind *n.* musical instruments, made of wood or metal, that you play by blowing through a mouthpiece and into a hollow tube. *Flutes and clarinets are woodwind.*

woodwork *n.* **1** the act of making things out of wood. **2** the parts of a building that are made from wood.

wool *n.* **1** the natural covering found on sheep. **2** thread made from this covering. **woolen** *adj.*

word *n.* **1** a sound, spoken or written, that has a meaning. **2** a short conversation. **3** news. **4** a promise.

word processing *n.* using a computer to write or edit letters and reports.

wore *past of* wear.

work[1] *n.* **1** the effort made to achieve or make something. **2** employment. **3** a painting, book, or play. **4** anything that you have made or done by working. **5** the place where you work. **6 works** structures such as bridges and dams.

work[2] *v.* **1** to put effort into doing something. **2** to do a job. **3** to function

correctly. **work out 1** to solve something. **2** to have the result you hoped for. **3** to do physical exercises, especially in a gym, to stay in shape. **workout** *n.*

workshop *n.* a place where things are made or fixed.

world *n.* **1** Earth and everything on it. **2** a particular area of activity. *the world of fashion.*

worm *n.* a small, creeping creature with no backbone.

worn *past participle of* wear.

worm

worry *v.* (worries, worrying, worried) to be anxious about something. **worry** *n.*, **worrier** *n.*

worse *adj., adv.* less good or well.

worsen *v.* to make or become worse.

worship *v.* (worshiping, worshiped *or* worshipped, worshipping) **1** to praise God or a god. **2** to love or admire somebody greatly. **worship** *n.*

worst *adj., adv.* least good or well.

worth *adj.* **1** having a value of. *This ring is worth thousands of dollars.* **2** interesting or good enough for something. *The museum is worth a visit.* **worth** *n.*

worthless *adj.* having no value.

would *v.* **1** past of will. **2** used to talk about things that are possible. *It would be nice to see you.* **3** used to make a polite request. *Would you mind moving your car, please?*

wound[1] (*rhymes with* spooned) *n.* an injury or cut. **wound** *v.*

wound[2] (*rhymes with* round) *past of* wind.

wove *past of* weave.

woven *past participle of* weave.

wrap *v.* (wraps, wrapping, wrapped) to fold or roll something around somebody or something.

wrapper *n.* a plastic or paper cover in which something is wrapped.

wrath (*rath*) *n.* (*formal*) great anger.

wreath *n.* a ring of flowers or leaves.

wreck *v.* to damage something so badly that it cannot be used again. **wreck** *n.*

wreckage *n.* the remains of something that has been wrecked.

wren *n.* a small, brown bird.

wrench[1] *v.* to pull or twist something with force. *He wrenched the steering wheel from her hand.*

wrench[2] *n.* a strong tool for turning nuts and bolts.

wrestle *v.* **1** to fight by getting hold of your opponent and trying to throw him or her to the ground. **2** to struggle.

wrestling *n.* the sport in which two people try to throw each other to the ground. **wrestler** *n.*

wretched *adv.* very unhappy; miserable.

wring *v.* (wringing, wrung) to twist and squeeze wet cloth to remove the water.

wrinkle *n.* a small crease in your skin or in paper or cloth. **wrinkle** *v.*

wrist *n.* the joint that connects your arm and your hand.

write *v.* (writing, wrote, written) **1** to form letters, especially with a pen or pencil on paper. **2** to compose a book, piece of music, or other work. **writer** *n.*, **writing** *n.*

writhe *v.* to twist backward and forward, especially in pain. *He was writhing around in agony.*

wrong *adj.* **1** not correct; not right. **2** bad or evil. **3** not suitable. *I wore the wrong clothes to the interview.* **wrong** *adv.*

wrote *past of* write.

wrung *past of* wring.

Xmas *a short way of writing* Christmas.

x-ray *n.* **1** a ray of energy that can pass through solid things. **2** a photograph produced by x-rays on film, used for showing the inside of something, especially a part of the body or suitcases at airport security. **x-ray** *v.*

x-ray

xylophone *(zy-lo-fone)* *n.* a musical instrument made up of a row of bars that the player strikes with small hammers.

a
b
c
d
e
f
g
h
i
j
k
l
m
n
o
p
q
r
s
t
u
v
w
x
y
z

Yy

yacht *(yat)* *n.* **1** a light sailing boat. **2** a large, motor-driven boat used for cruising. **yachting** *n.*

yacht

yak *n.* a long-haired ox found in Tibet.

yam *n.* the edible root of a tropical plant similar to the potato.

yank *v.* to pull something suddenly and with force. **yank** *n.*

yap *v.* (yapping, yapped) to give a high-pitched bark, like small dogs do. **yap** *n.*

yard *n.* **1** a measurement of length, equal to three feet (36 inches). **2** an enclosed piece of ground beside a building. **3** the garden at the back or front of a house.

yarn *n.* **1** wool or cotton spun into thread. **2** a long, exaggerated story.

yashmak *n.* a type of veil covering the lower part of the face, worn by some Muslim women. (can also be spelled *yashmac*.)

yawn *v.* to open your mouth wide and take a deep breath when you are tired or bored. **yawn** *n.*

year *n.* **1** the amount of time that it takes Earth to travel around the Sun, just over 365 days. **2** the period from January 1 to December 31. **3** any period of twelve months.

yearn *(yurn)* *v.* to long for something. *She yearned to see her children again.* **yearning** *n.*

yeast *n.* a type of fungus used for making bread rise and for making beer.

yell *v.* to shout loudly. **yell** *n.*

yellow *n.* the color of lemons and egg yolks. **yellow** *adj.*

yelp *n.* a sudden, sharp cry. **yelp** *v.*

yesterday *n.* (on) the day before today.

yet[1] *adv.* **1** up till now; so far. *I haven't met her new boyfriend yet.* **2** even. *He asked for yet more money.*

yet[2] *conj.* but; nevertheless.

yield *v.* **1** to give in; to surrender. **2** to produce something. *How much milk does that herd of cows yield?* **yield** *n.*

yodel *v.* (yodeling, yodeled) to sing in a voice that constantly changes between an ordinary and a very high-pitched sound. **yodel** *n.*

yoga *n.* a system of physical exercises designed to relax the body and mind, based on an ancient Hindu system of philosophy and meditation.

yogurt *n.* a sour-tasting, semiliquid food made by adding bacteria to milk.

yoke *n.* a wooden frame placed over the necks of oxen to keep them together when they are pulling a cart or plow.

yolk *(rhymes with oak)* *n.* the yellow part inside an egg.

Yom Kippur *n.* a Jewish holy day of fasting and prayer.

young[1] *adj.* having lived for a short time; not old.

young[2] *n. pl.* young animals.

youngster *n.* a young person.

your *adj.* belonging to you.

you're *conj.* you are.

youth *n.* **1** the time when you are young. **2** a young person, especially a teenage boy.

youthful *adj.* seeming or looking young.

yo-yo *n.* a toy consisting of a reel that winds and unwinds from a string.

A B C D E F G H I J K L M N O P Q R S T U V W X **Y** Z

Zz

zany *(zay-nee) adj.* funny in an absurd or unusual way. **zanily** *adv.*

zap *v.* (zaps, zapping, zapped) *(informal)* **1** to strike or shoot something suddenly. **2** to change television channels using a remote control.

zeal *(zeel) n.* enthusiasm; eagerness. **zealous** *(zel-us) adj.*

zebra *n.* an African animal like a horse with black-and-white stripes.

zebras

zero *n.* (*pl.* zeros) nothing; the figure 0.

zest *n.* **1** enthusiasm; lively enjoyment. **2** the outer skin of an orange or lemon.

zigzag *n.* a line with sharp bends or angles. **zigzag** *adj., v.*

zinc *n.* a bluish-white metal.

zip code *n.* a series of numbers added to the end of an address so that mail can be sorted by machine.

zipper *n.* a fastener with two sets of teeth that fit together when a sliding tab is pulled between them. **zip** *v.*

zodiac *n.* in astrology an imaginary strip across the sky divided into 12 equal parts called the signs of the zodiac. Each sign takes its name from a group of stars.

zombie *n.* a dead body that is said to be brought back to life by witchcraft.

zone *n.* an area made separate from the rest of a building or town for a specific purpose. *This side of the street is a no-parking zone.*

zoo *n.* a place where wild animals are kept for people to look at them.

zoology *(zoo-ol-o-jee) n.* the scientific study of animals. **zoological** *adj.*, **zoologist** *n.*

zoom *v.* to move fast with a low, humming or buzzing noise.

zoom lens *n.* a lens on a camera that you adjust to make a distant object gradually appear closer.

zucchini *(zoo-kee-nee) n.* a long, green squash.

a
b
c
d
e
f
g
h
i
j
k
l
m
n
o
p
q
r
s
t
u
v
w
x
y
z